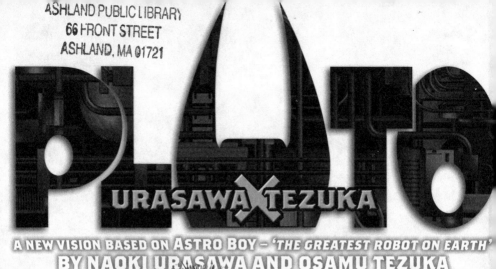

# PLUTO

## URASAWA X TEZUKA

**A NEW VISION BASED ON ASTRO BOY – '*THE GREATEST ROBOT ON EARTH*'**
**BY NAOKI URASAWA AND OSAMU TEZUKA**

WITH **TAKASHI NAGASAKI**
VISED BY **MACOTO TEZKA**
PERATION OF TEZUKA PRODUCTIONS

# Act 32 THE SCARS OF MEMORY

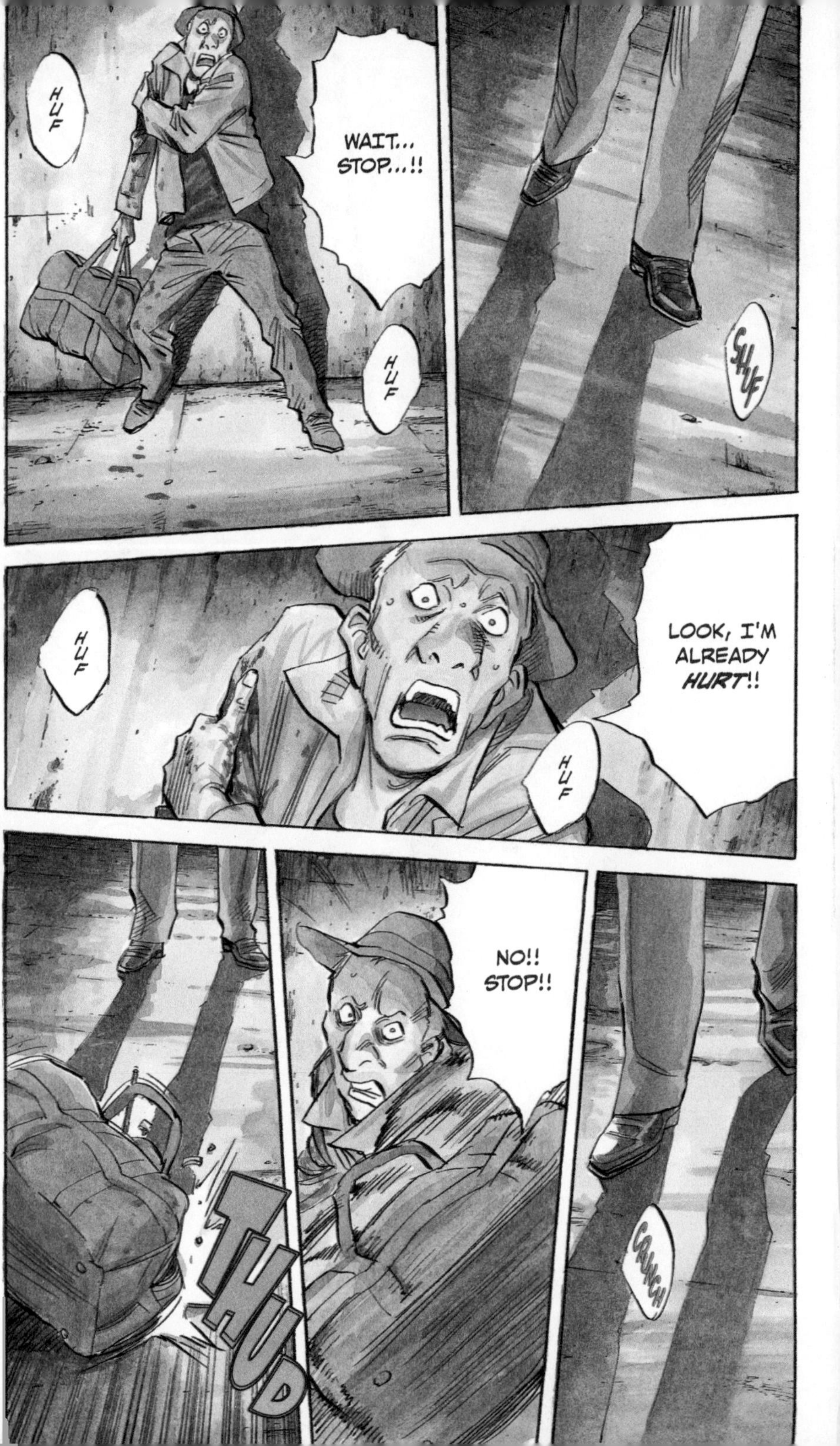
SHUF
WAIT... STOP...!!
HUF
HUF
LOOK, I'M ALREADY HURT!!
HUF
HUF
CRUNCH
NO!! STOP!!
THUD

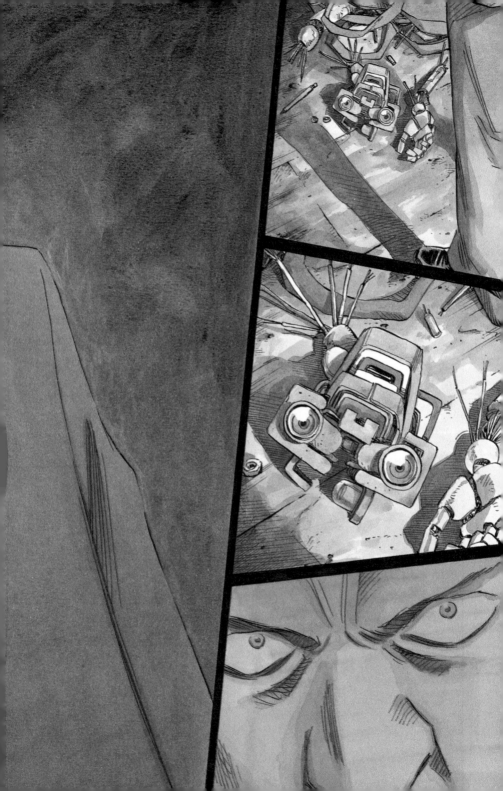

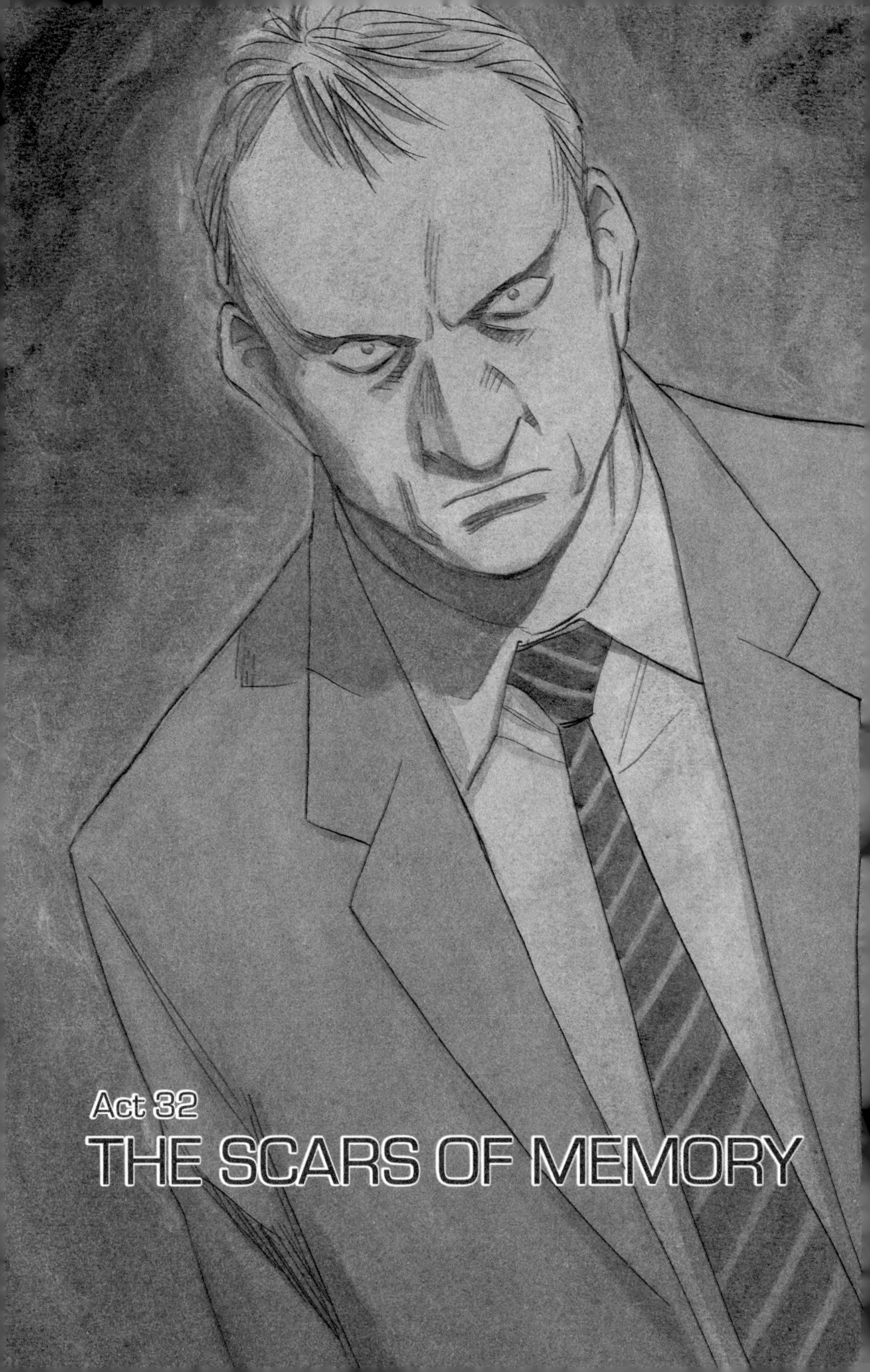
Act 32
THE SCARS OF MEMORY

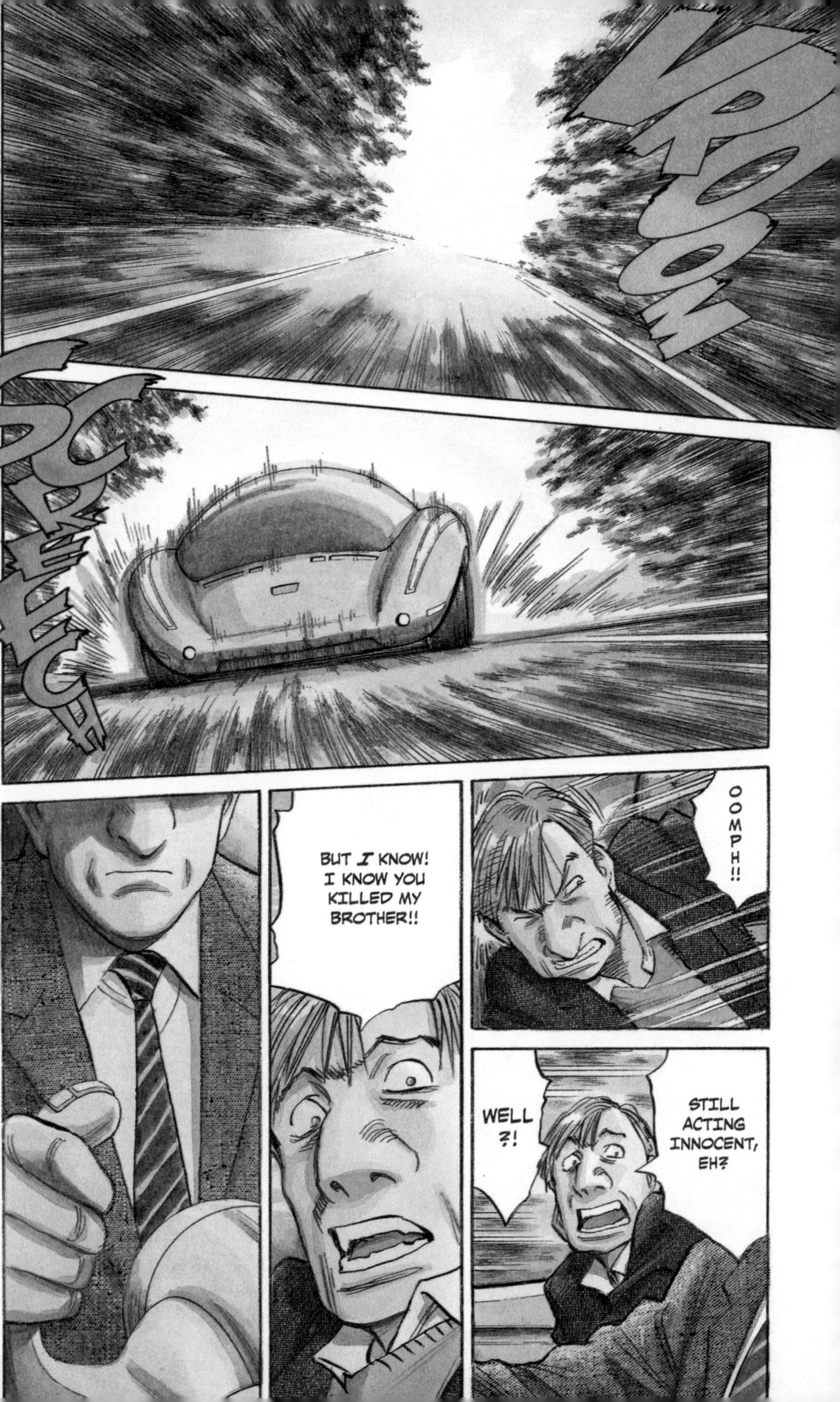
VROOM
SCREECH
OOMPH!!
STILL ACTING INNOCENT, EH?
WELL?!
BUT *I* KNOW! I KNOW YOU KILLED MY BROTHER!!

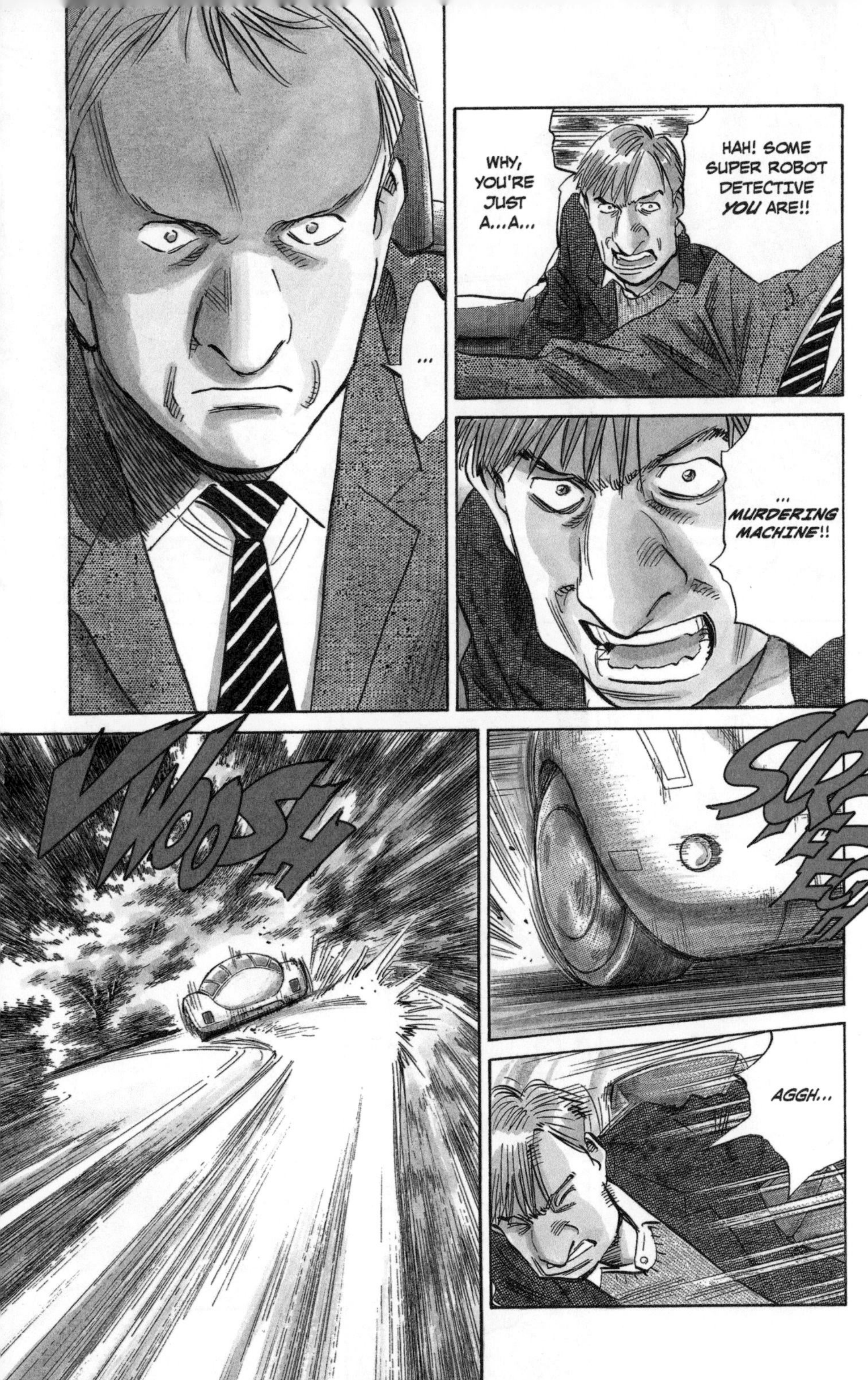
HAH! SOME SUPER ROBOT DETECTIVE *YOU* ARE!!
WHY, YOU'RE JUST A...A...
... *MURDERING MACHINE*!!
...
SCREECH
AGGH...
WHOOSH

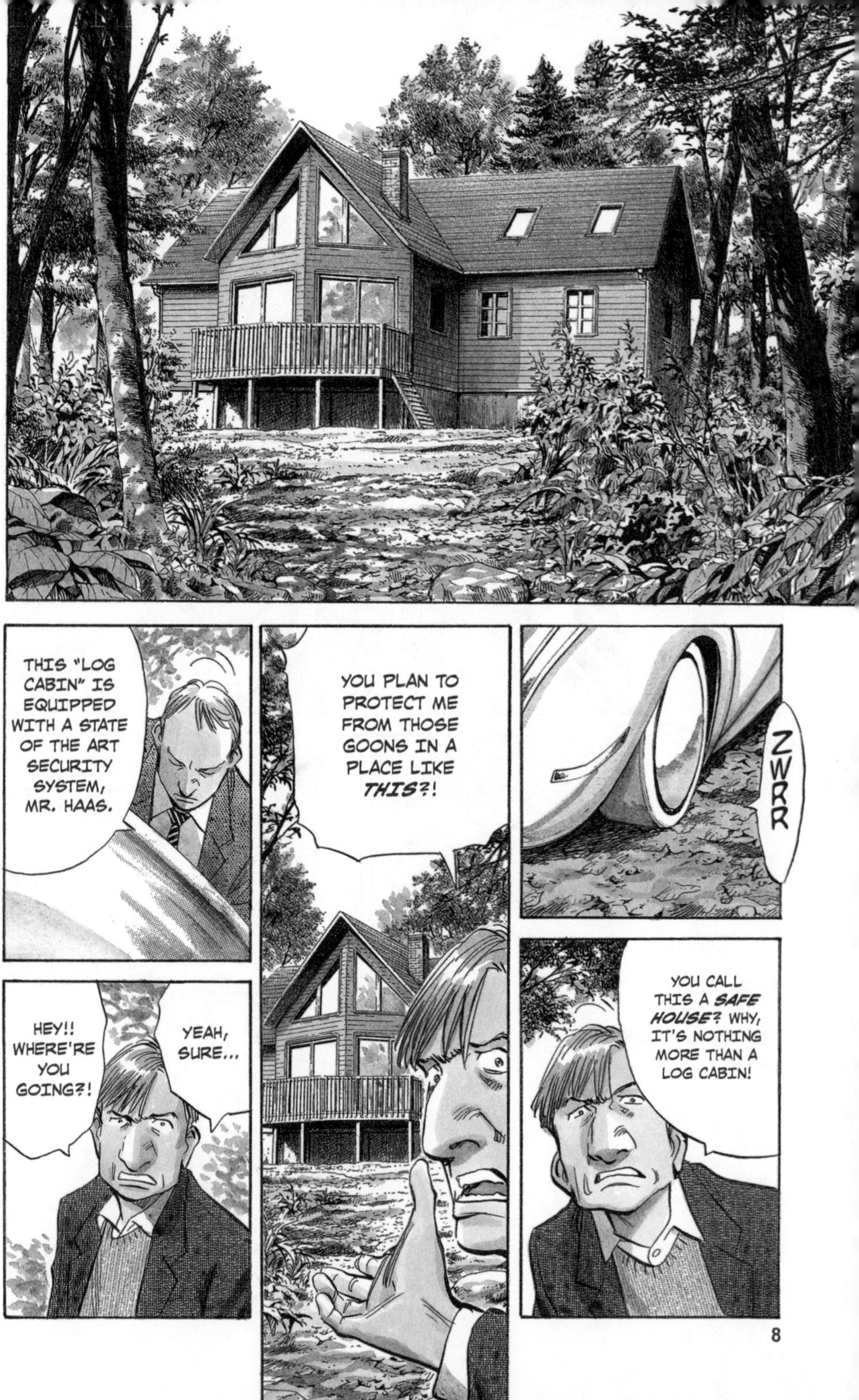
ZWRR
YOU CALL THIS A SAFE HOUSE? WHY, IT'S NOTHING MORE THAN A LOG CABIN!
YOU PLAN TO PROTECT ME FROM THOSE GOONS IN A PLACE LIKE THIS?!
THIS "LOG CABIN" IS EQUIPPED WITH A STATE OF THE ART SECURITY SYSTEM, MR. HAAS.
YEAH, SURE...
HEY!! WHERE'RE YOU GOING?!

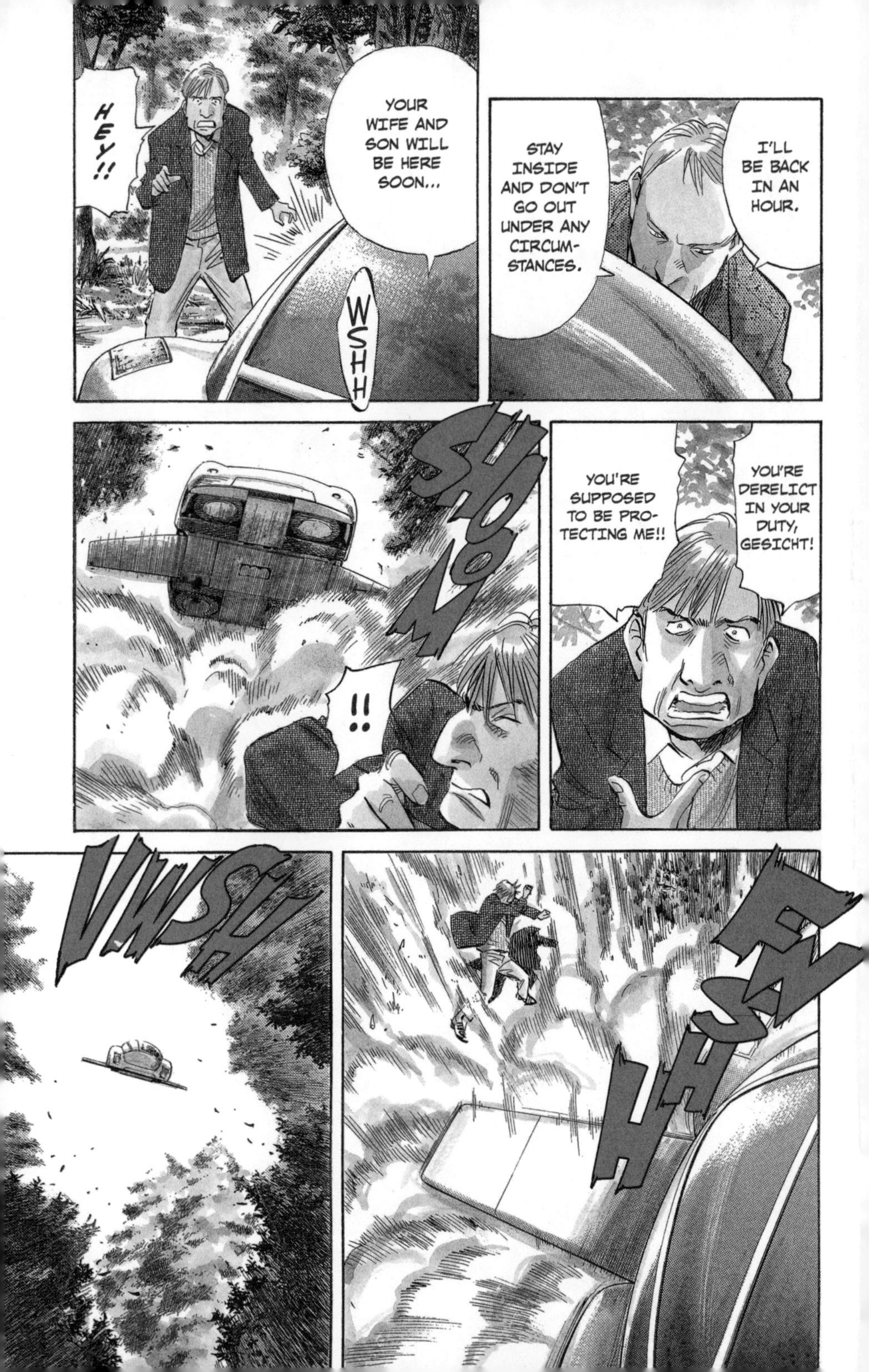
I'LL BE BACK IN AN HOUR.
STAY INSIDE AND DON'T GO OUT UNDER ANY CIRCUM-STANCES.
YOUR WIFE AND SON WILL BE HERE SOON...
WSHH
HEY!!
YOU'RE DERELICT IN YOUR DUTY, GESICHT!
YOU'RE SUPPOSED TO BE PRO-TECTING ME!!
SHOOOM
!!
FWSHH
VWSH

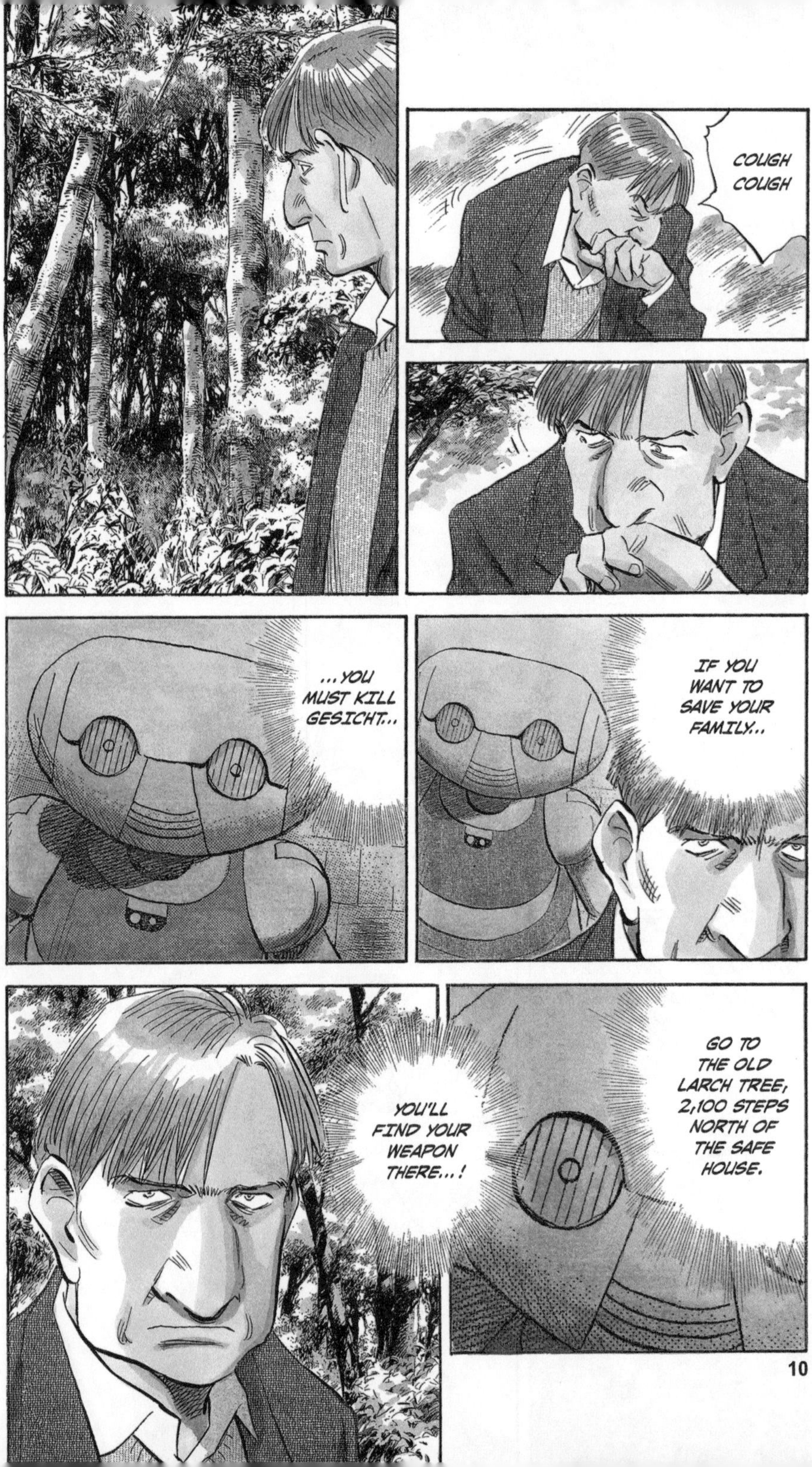
COUGH
COUGH
IF YOU WANT TO SAVE YOUR FAMILY...
...YOU MUST KILL GESICHT...
GO TO THE OLD LARCH TREE, 2,100 STEPS NORTH OF THE SAFE HOUSE.
YOU'LL FIND YOUR WEAPON THERE...!

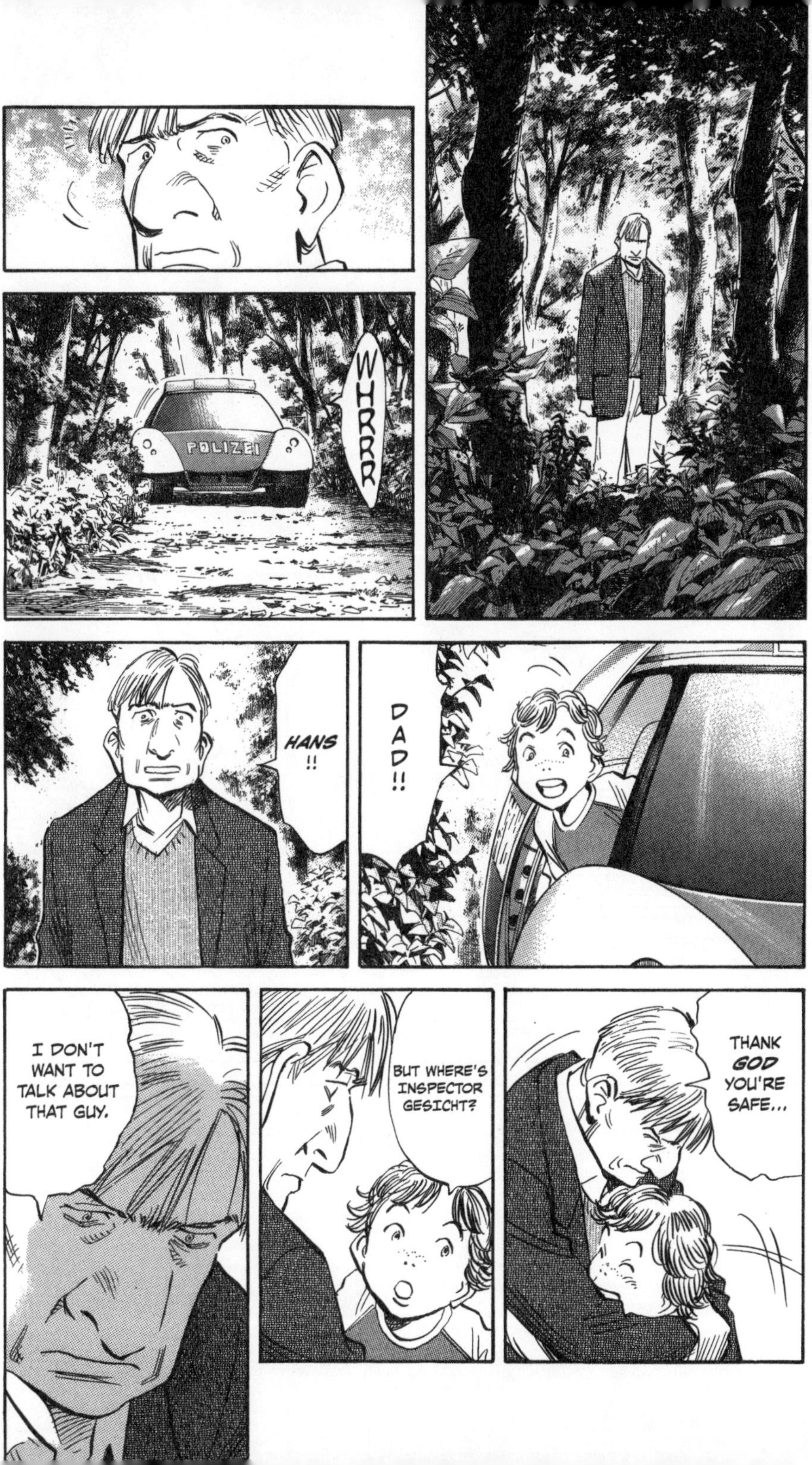
WHRRR
POLIZEI
DAD!!
HANS !!
THANK GOD YOU'RE SAFE...
BUT WHERE'S INSPECTOR GESICHT?
I DON'T WANT TO TALK ABOUT THAT GUY.

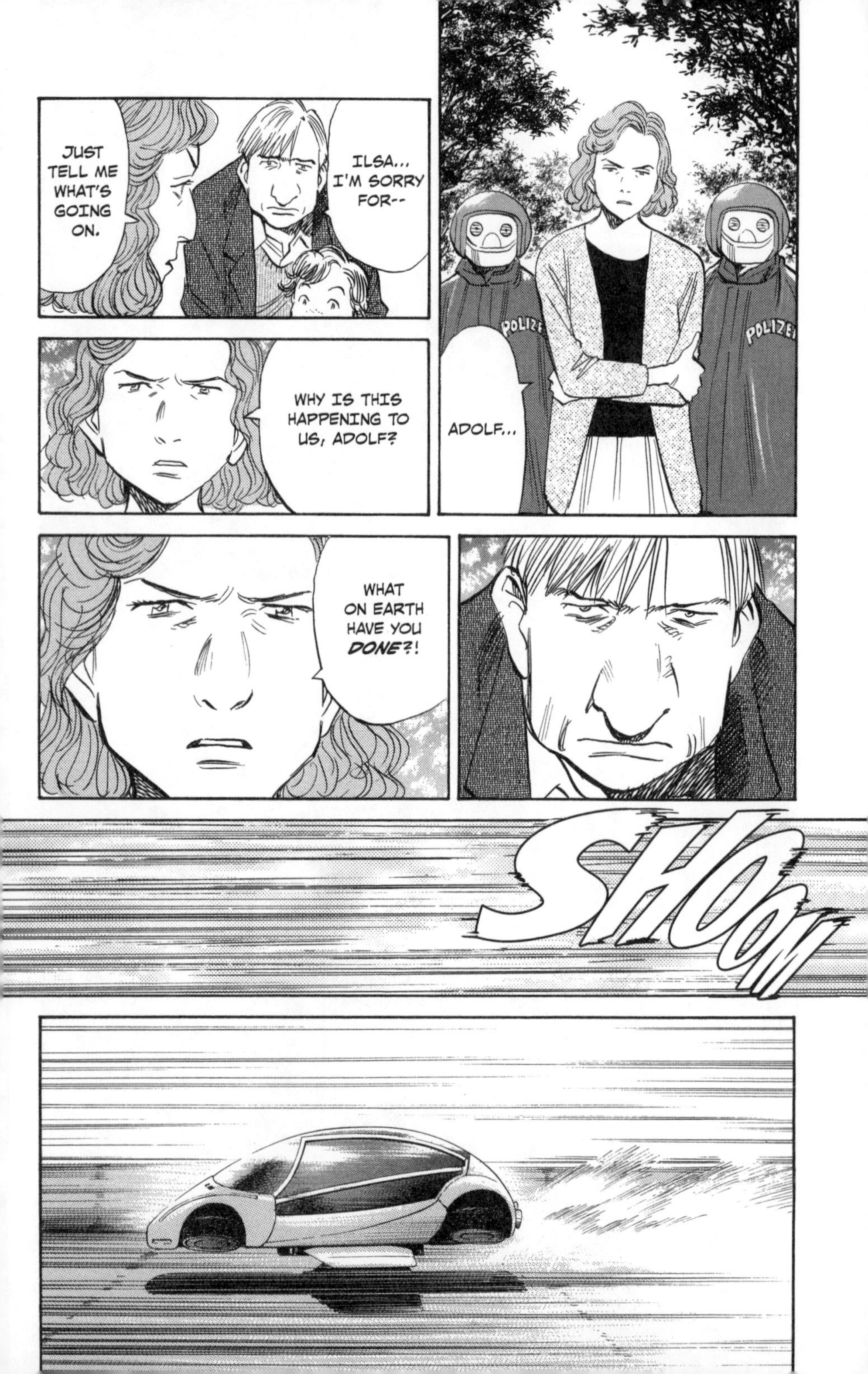
ADOLF...
ILSA... I'M SORRY FOR--
JUST TELL ME WHAT'S GOING ON.
WHY IS THIS HAPPENING TO US, ADOLF?
WHAT ON EARTH HAVE YOU *DONE*?!
SHOOM

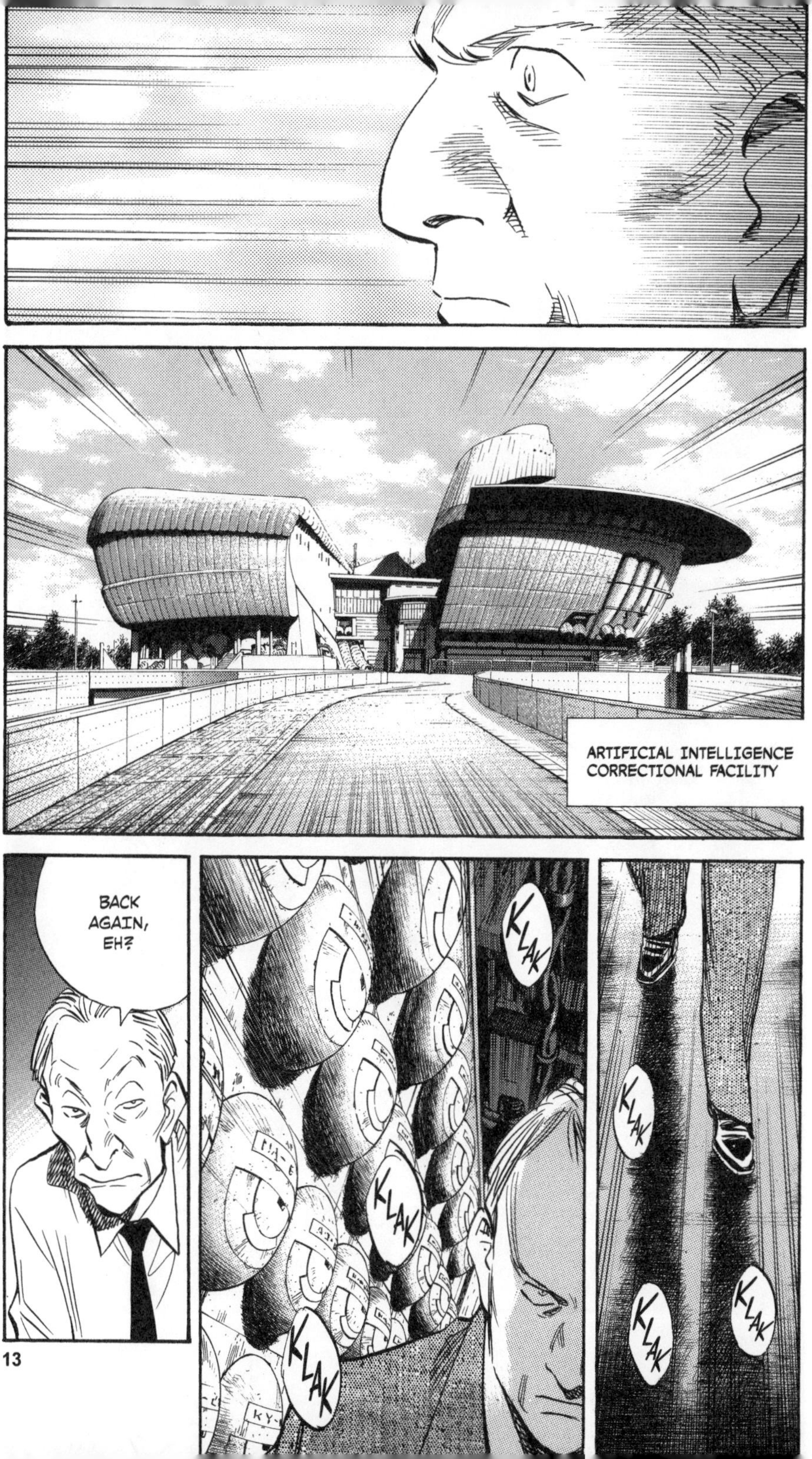
ARTIFICIAL INTELLIGENCE CORRECTIONAL FACILITY
KLAK
KLAK
KLAK
KLAK
KLAK
KLAK
BACK AGAIN, EH?

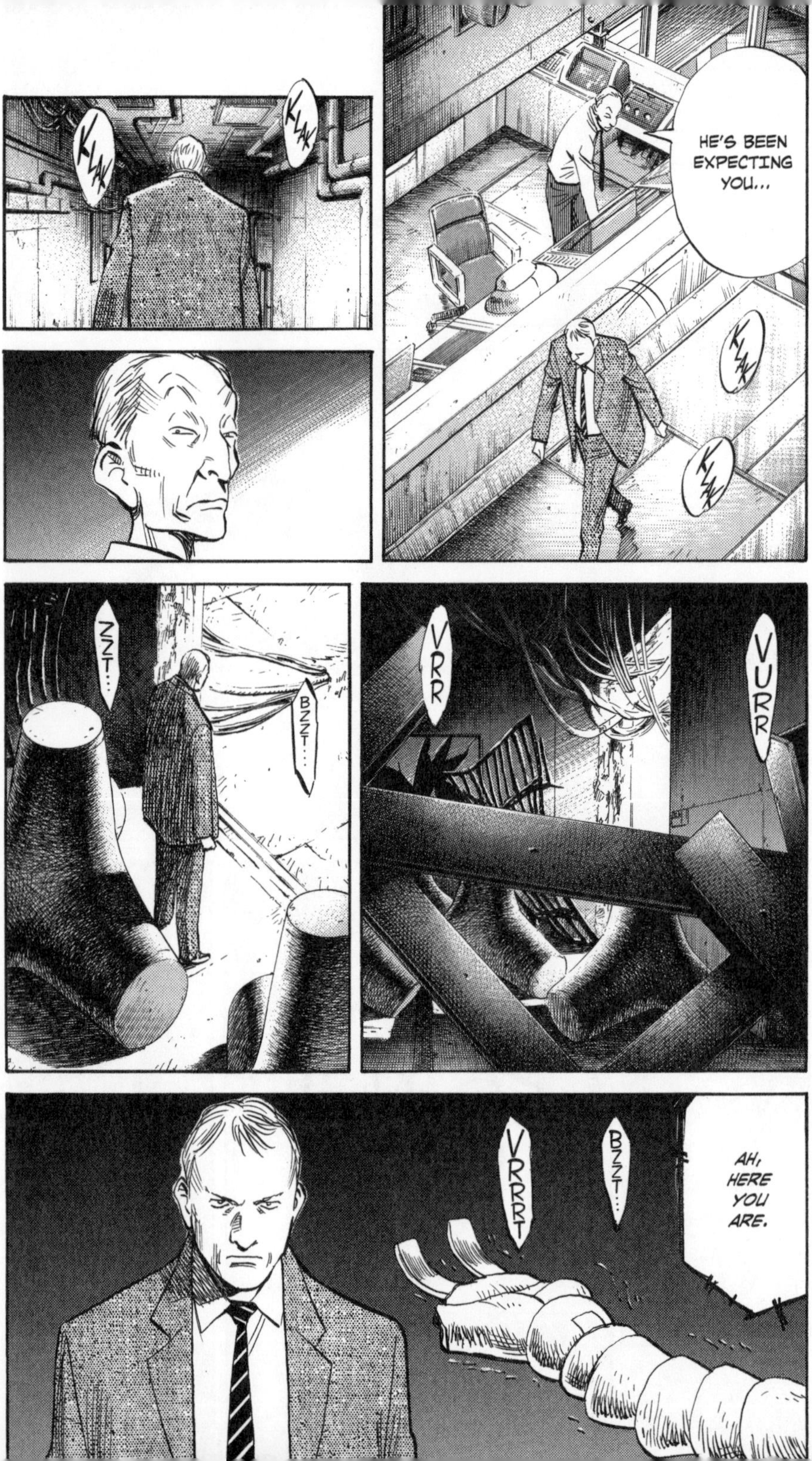
HE'S BEEN EXPECTING YOU...
KLAK
KLAK
KLAK
KLAK
VURR
VRR
BZZT...
ZZT...
AH, HERE YOU ARE.
BZZT...
VRRRT

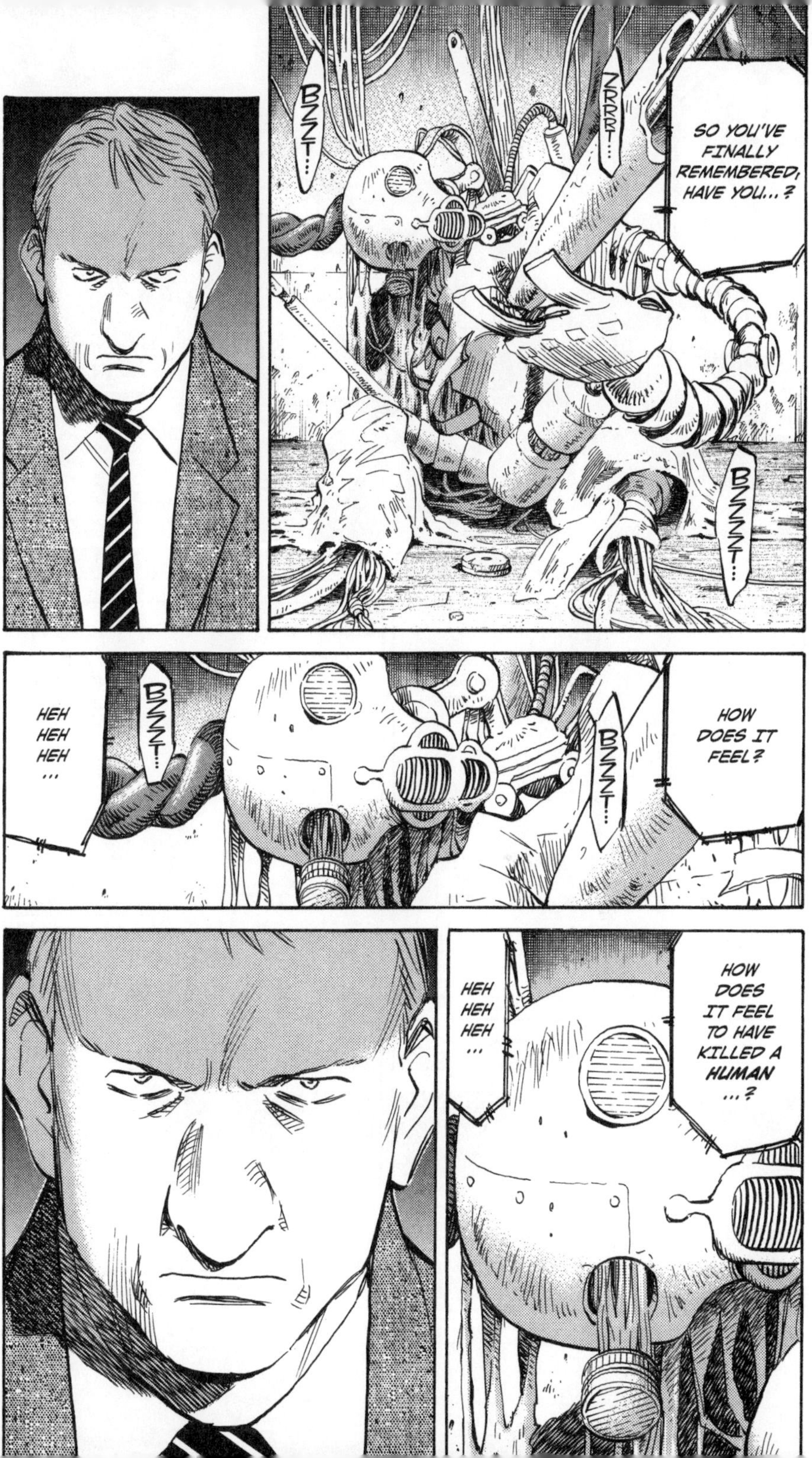
ZRRRT...
SO YOU'VE FINALLY REMEMBERED, HAVE YOU...?
BZZT...
BZZZZT...
HOW DOES IT FEEL?
BZZZT...
BZZZT...
HEH HEH HEH ...
HOW DOES IT FEEL TO HAVE KILLED A *HUMAN* ...?
HEH HEH HEH ...

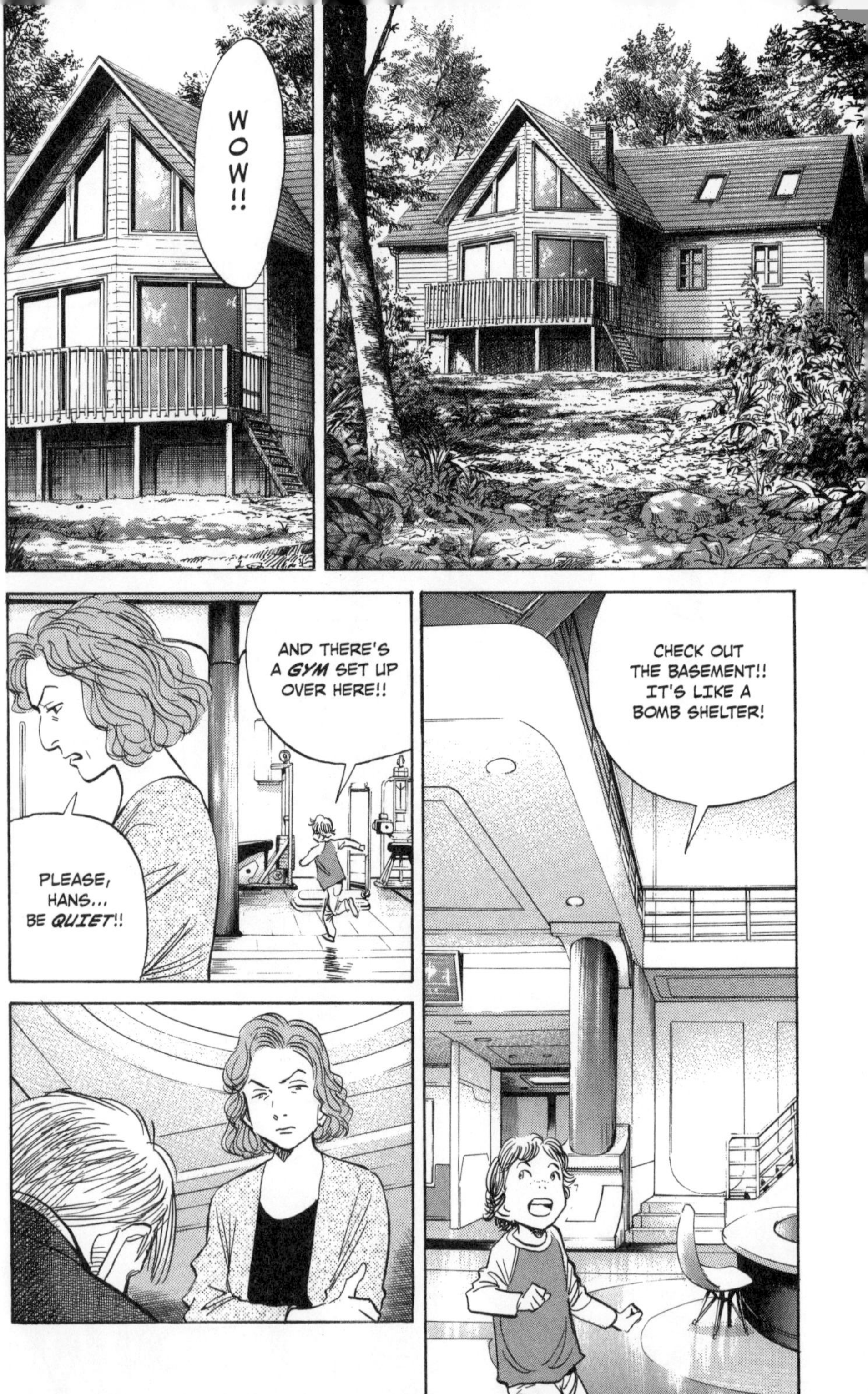
WOW!!
CHECK OUT THE BASEMENT!! IT'S LIKE A BOMB SHELTER!
AND THERE'S A *GYM* SET UP OVER HERE!!
PLEASE, HANS... BE *QUIET*!!

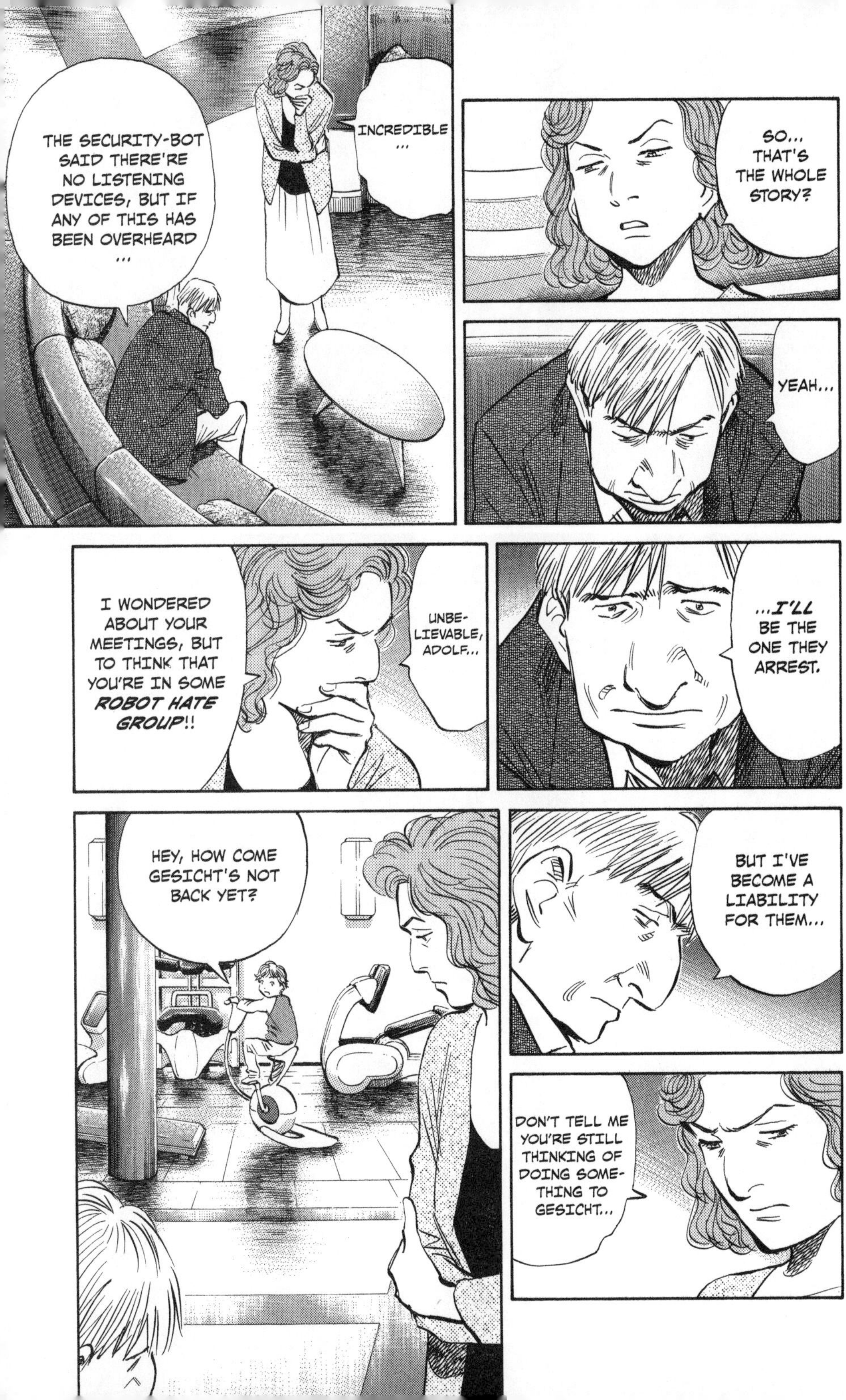
SO... THAT'S THE WHOLE STORY?
YEAH...
INCREDIBLE...
THE SECURITY-BOT SAID THERE'RE NO LISTENING DEVICES, BUT IF ANY OF THIS HAS BEEN OVERHEARD...
...I'LL BE THE ONE THEY ARREST.
UNBE-LIEVABLE, ADOLF...
I WONDERED ABOUT YOUR MEETINGS, BUT TO THINK THAT YOU'RE IN SOME ROBOT HATE GROUP!!
BUT I'VE BECOME A LIABILITY FOR THEM...
DON'T TELL ME YOU'RE STILL THINKING OF DOING SOME-THING TO GESICHT...
HEY, HOW COME GESICHT'S NOT BACK YET?

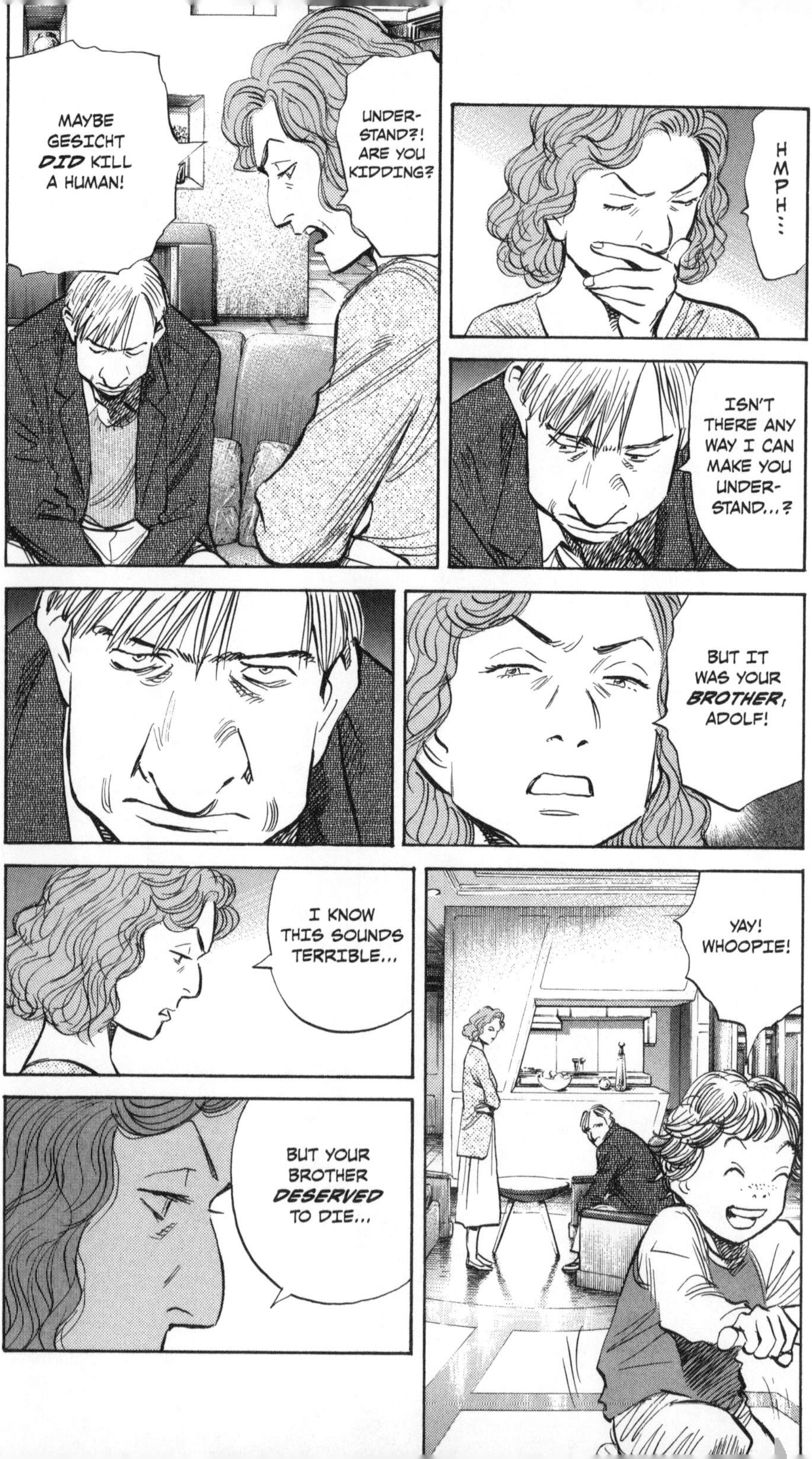
HMPH...
ISN'T THERE ANY WAY I CAN MAKE YOU UNDER-STAND...?
UNDER-STAND?! ARE YOU KIDDING?
MAYBE GESICHT *DID* KILL A HUMAN!
BUT IT WAS YOUR *BROTHER*, ADOLF!
YAY! WHOOPIE!
I KNOW THIS SOUNDS TERRIBLE...
BUT YOUR BROTHER *DESERVED* TO DIE...

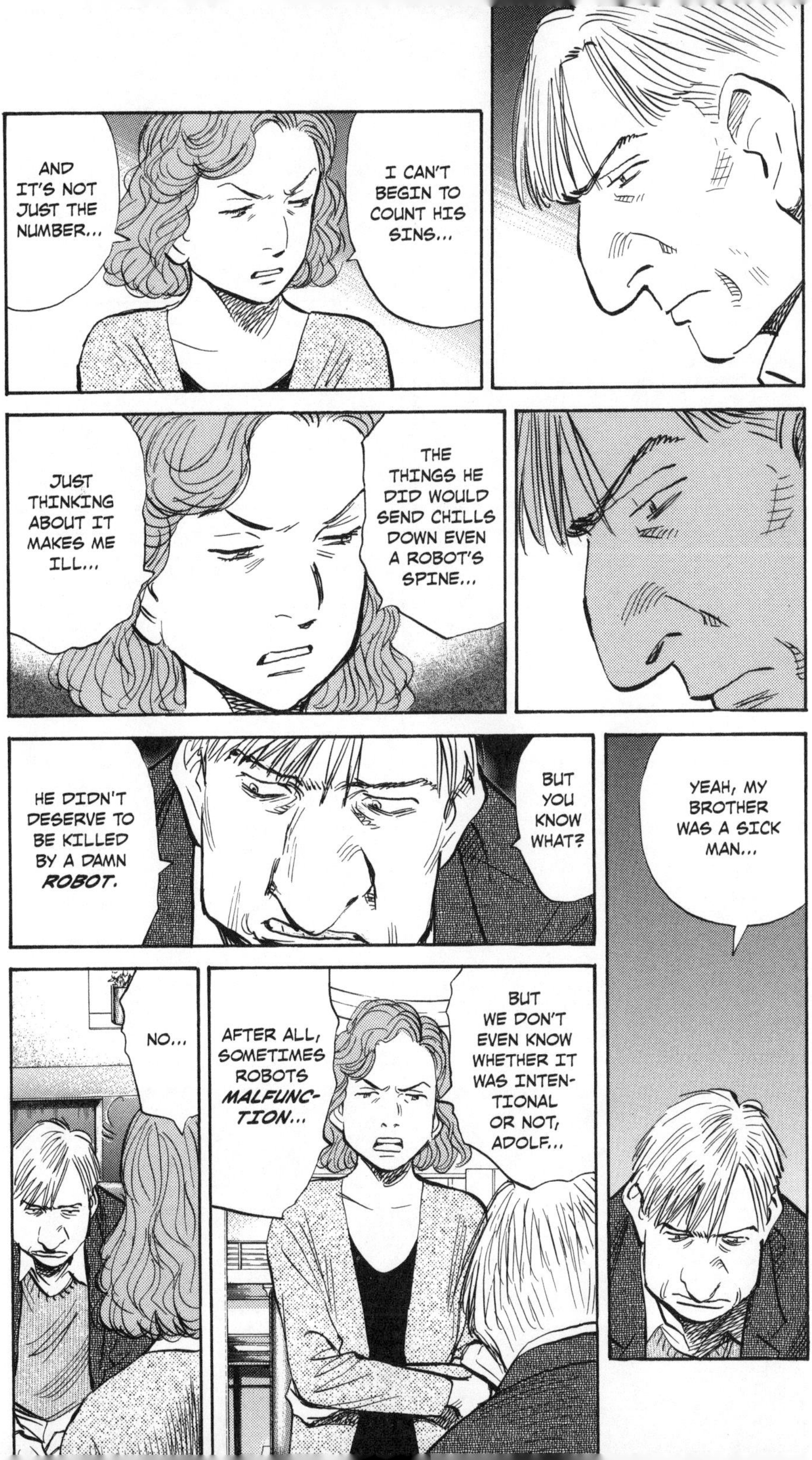
I CAN'T BEGIN TO COUNT HIS SINS...
AND IT'S NOT JUST THE NUMBER...
THE THINGS HE DID WOULD SEND CHILLS DOWN EVEN A ROBOT'S SPINE...
JUST THINKING ABOUT IT MAKES ME ILL...
YEAH, MY BROTHER WAS A SICK MAN...
BUT YOU KNOW WHAT?
HE DIDN'T DESERVE TO BE KILLED BY A DAMN *ROBOT*.
BUT WE DON'T EVEN KNOW WHETHER IT WAS INTEN-TIONAL OR NOT, ADOLF...
AFTER ALL, SOMETIMES ROBOTS *MALFUNC-TION*...
NO...

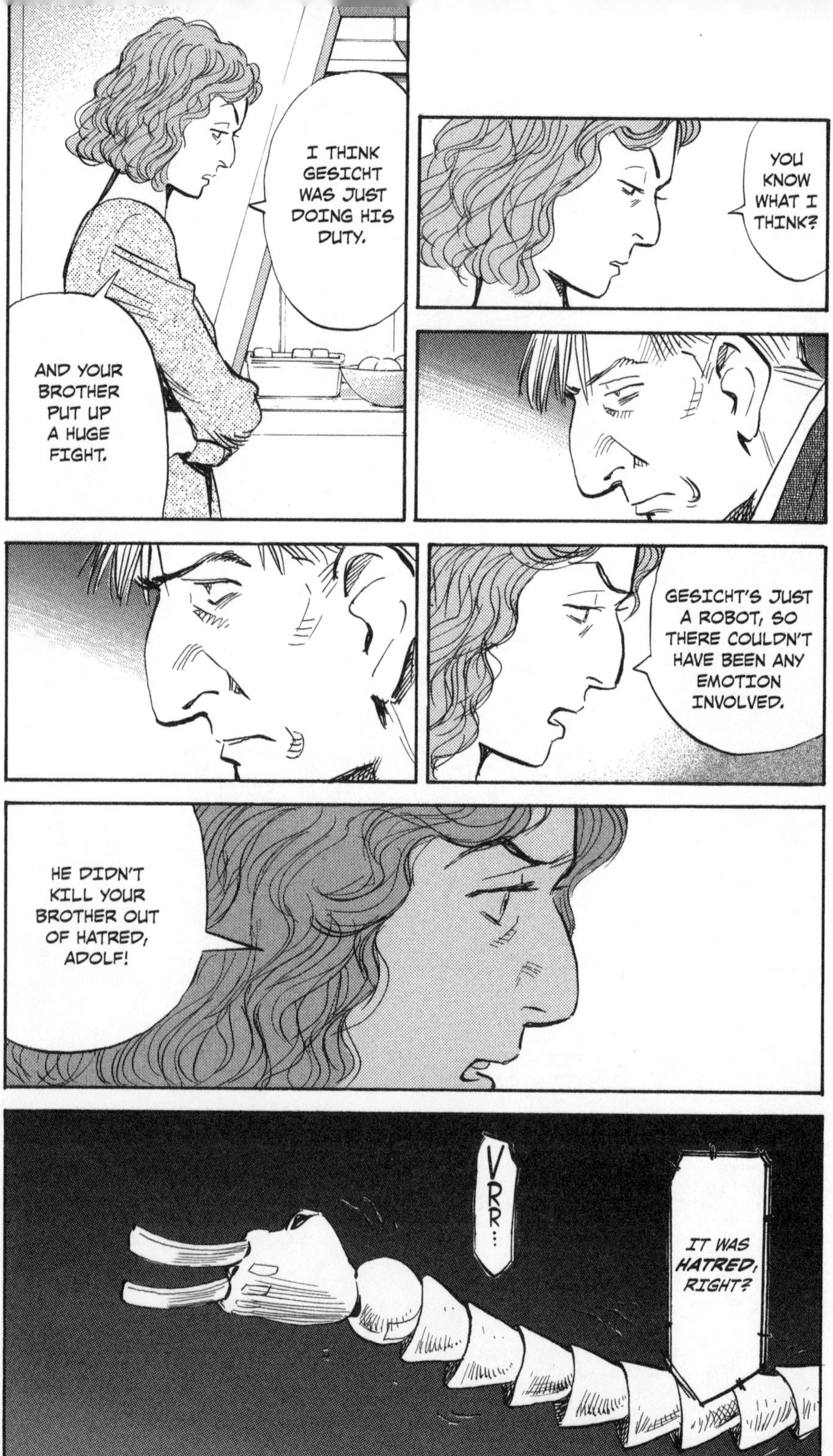
YOU KNOW WHAT I THINK?
I THINK GESICHT WAS JUST DOING HIS DUTY.
AND YOUR BROTHER PUT UP A HUGE FIGHT.
GESICHT'S JUST A ROBOT, SO THERE COULDN'T HAVE BEEN ANY EMOTION INVOLVED.
HE DIDN'T KILL YOUR BROTHER OUT OF HATRED, ADOLF!
IT WAS HATRED, RIGHT?
VRR...

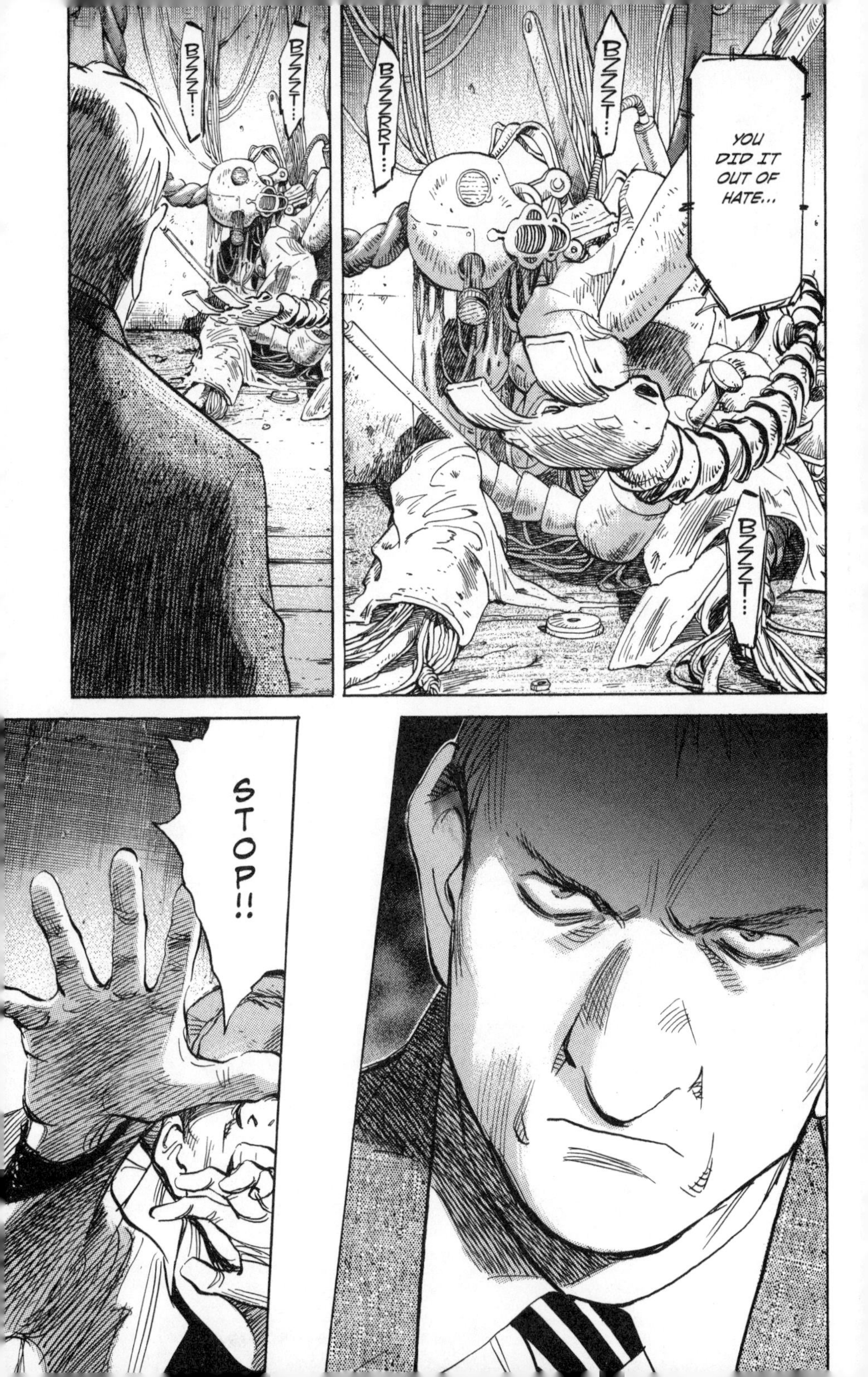
YOU DID IT OUT OF HATE...
BZZZT...
BZZZRRT...
BZZZT...
BZZZT...
BZZZT...
STOP!!

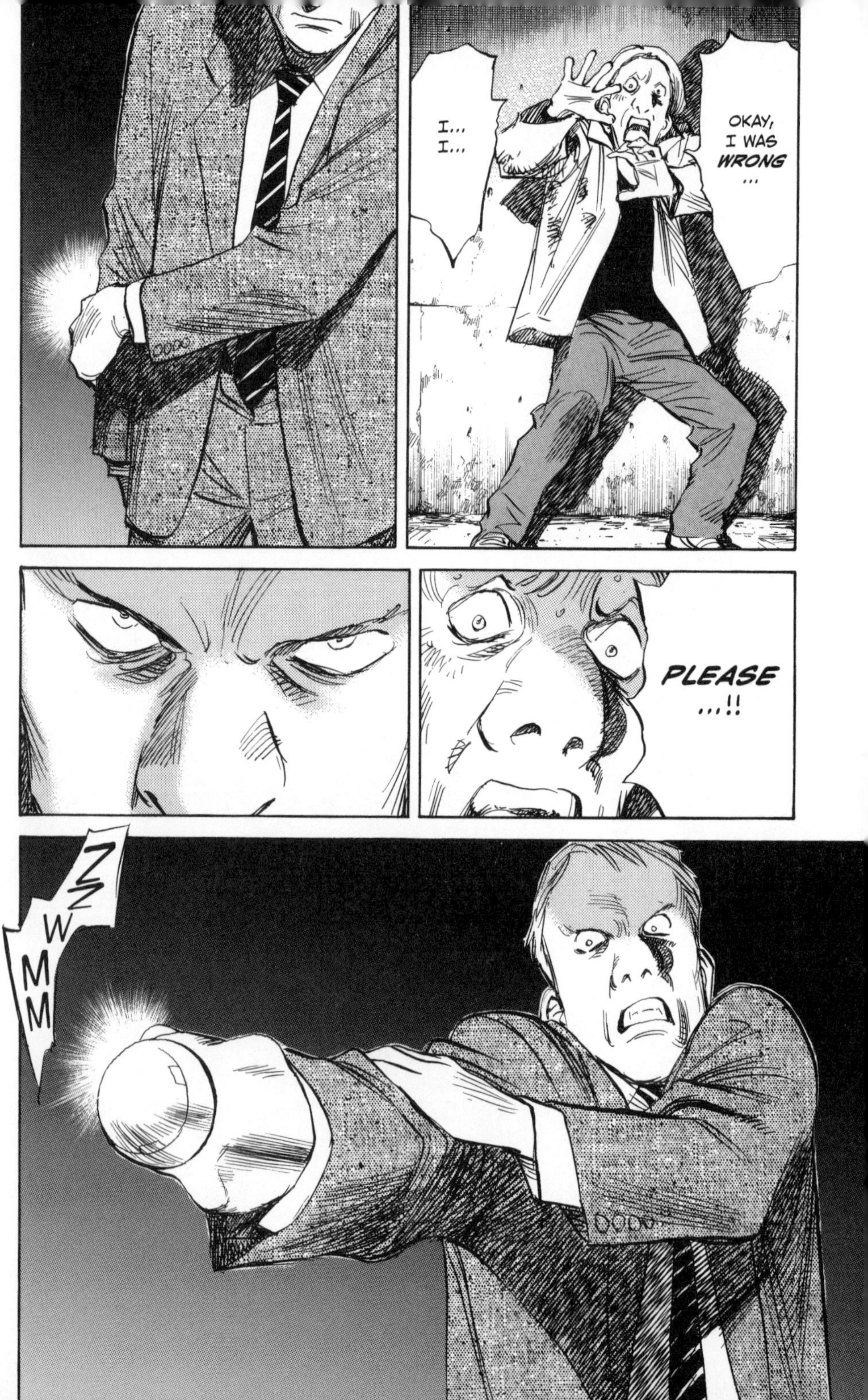
OKAY, I WAS WRONG ...
I... I...
PLEASE ...!!
ZZWMM

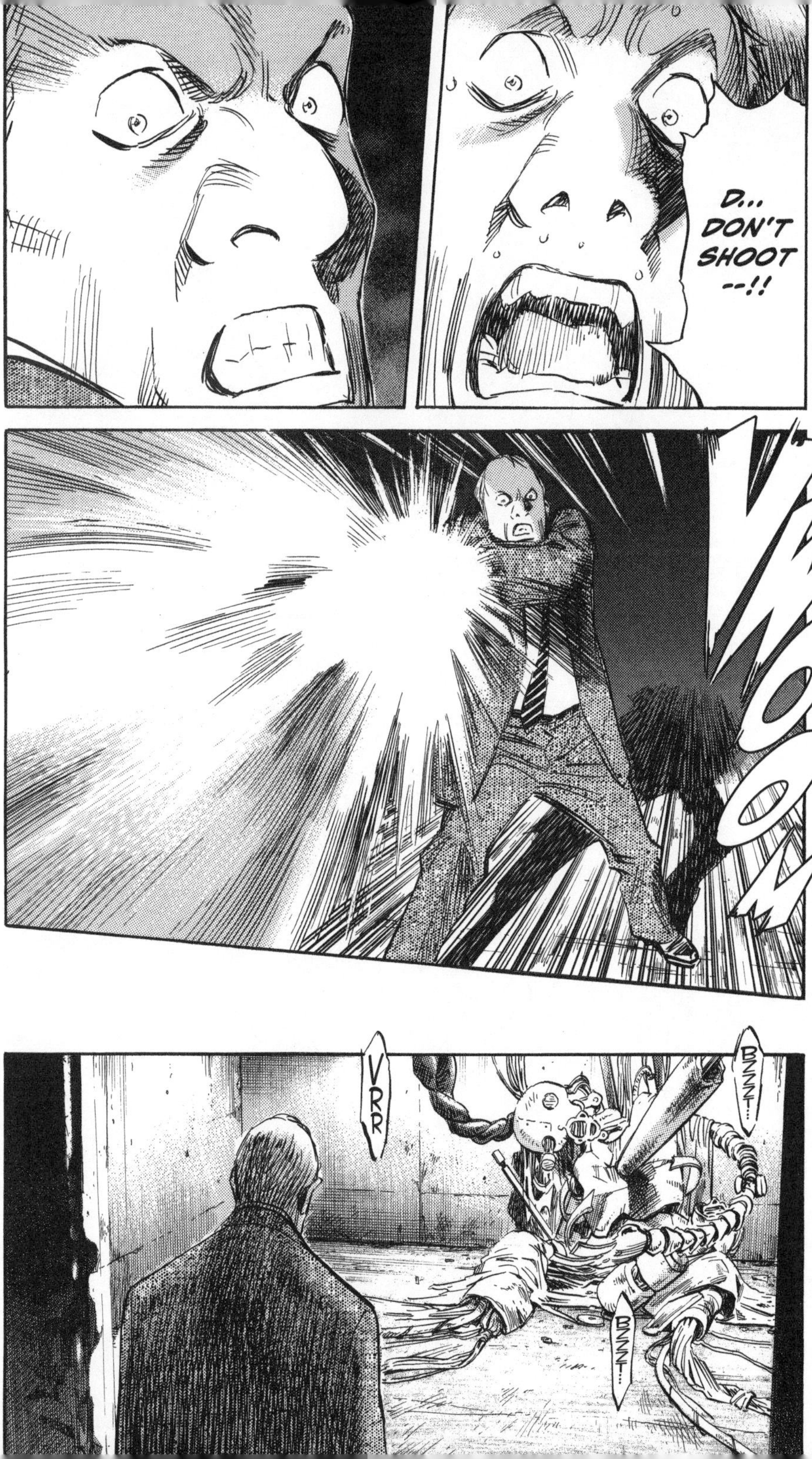
D... DON'T SHOOT --!!
VWOOOM
BZZZT...
VRR
BZZZT...

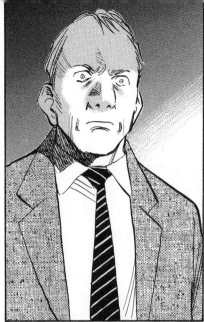

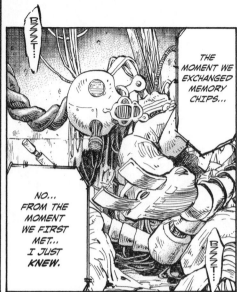

BZZZT...
THE MOMENT WE EXCHANGED MEMORY CHIPS...
NO... FROM THE MOMENT WE FIRST MET... I JUST **KNEW.**
BZZZT...
YOU AND I...
BZZZT...
BZZZT...
...WE'RE TWO OF A KIND...
AND TRY AS THEY MIGHT TO WIPE AWAY THAT MEMORY...
IT WILL **NEVER** GO AWAY.

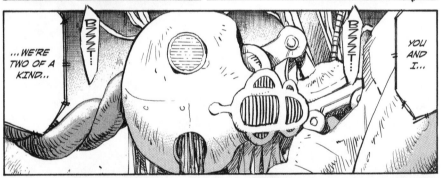

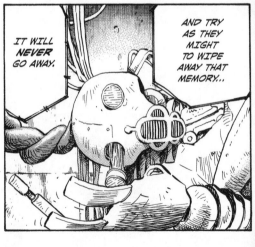

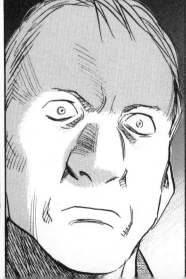

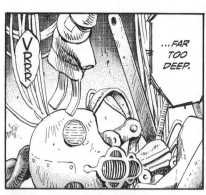

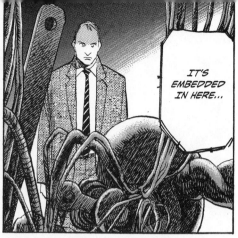

IT'S EMBEDDED IN HERE...
...FAR TOO DEEP.
VRRR
CARE TO GIVE IT A SCRATCH?
SCRAPE SCRAPE
AND DON'T YOU WORRY, IT'LL ALL COME BACK TO YOU.
THAT FEELING OF **TRUE HATE**.
HEH HEH HEH ...

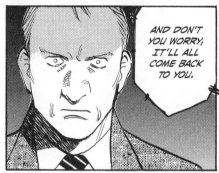

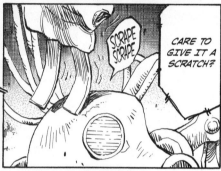

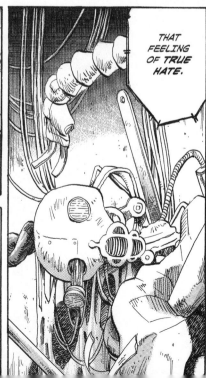

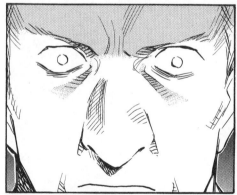

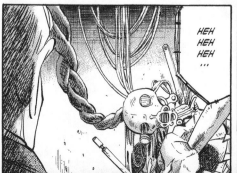

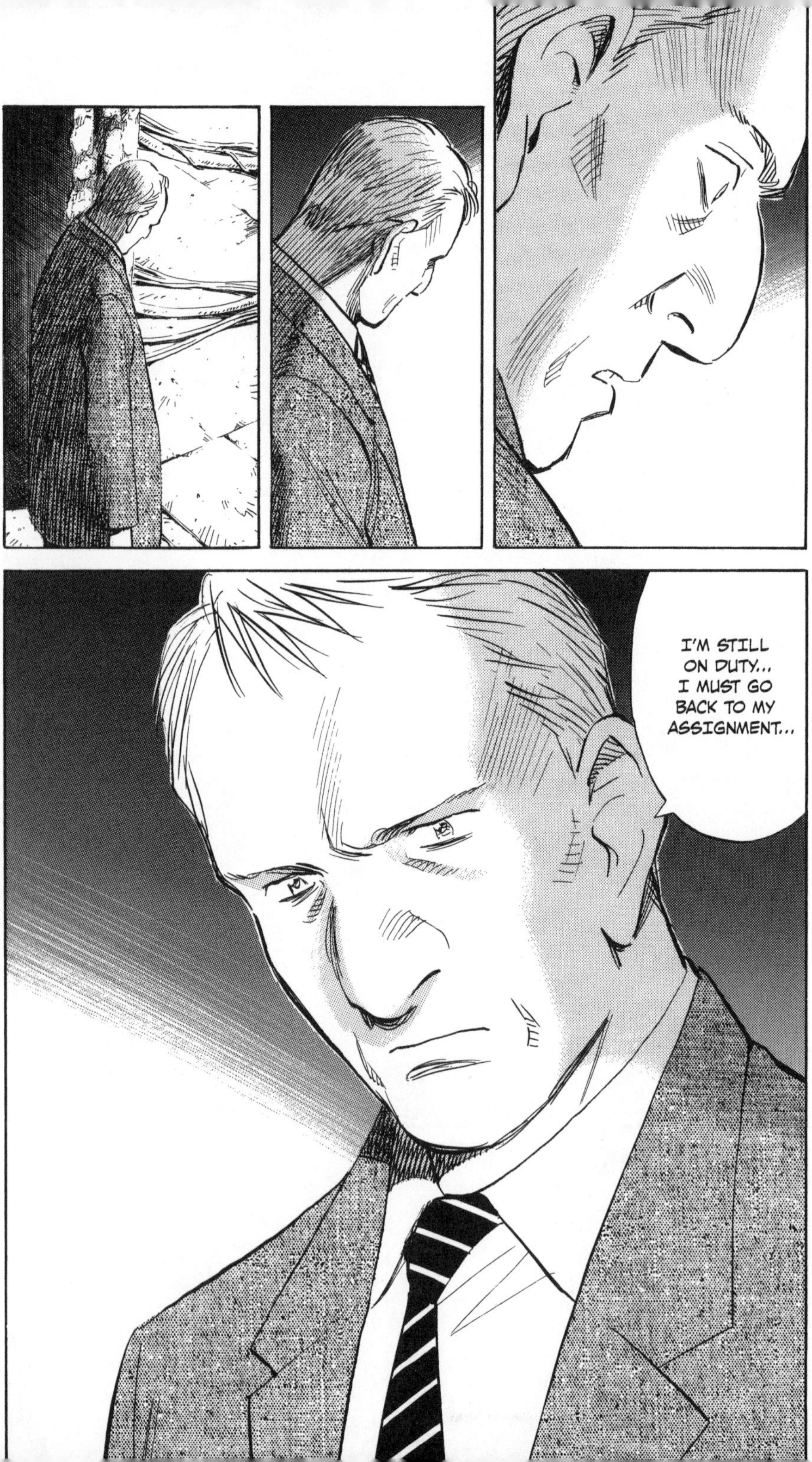
I'M STILL ON DUTY... I MUST GO BACK TO MY ASSIGNMENT...

# Act 33 Victors, Sages and Mortals

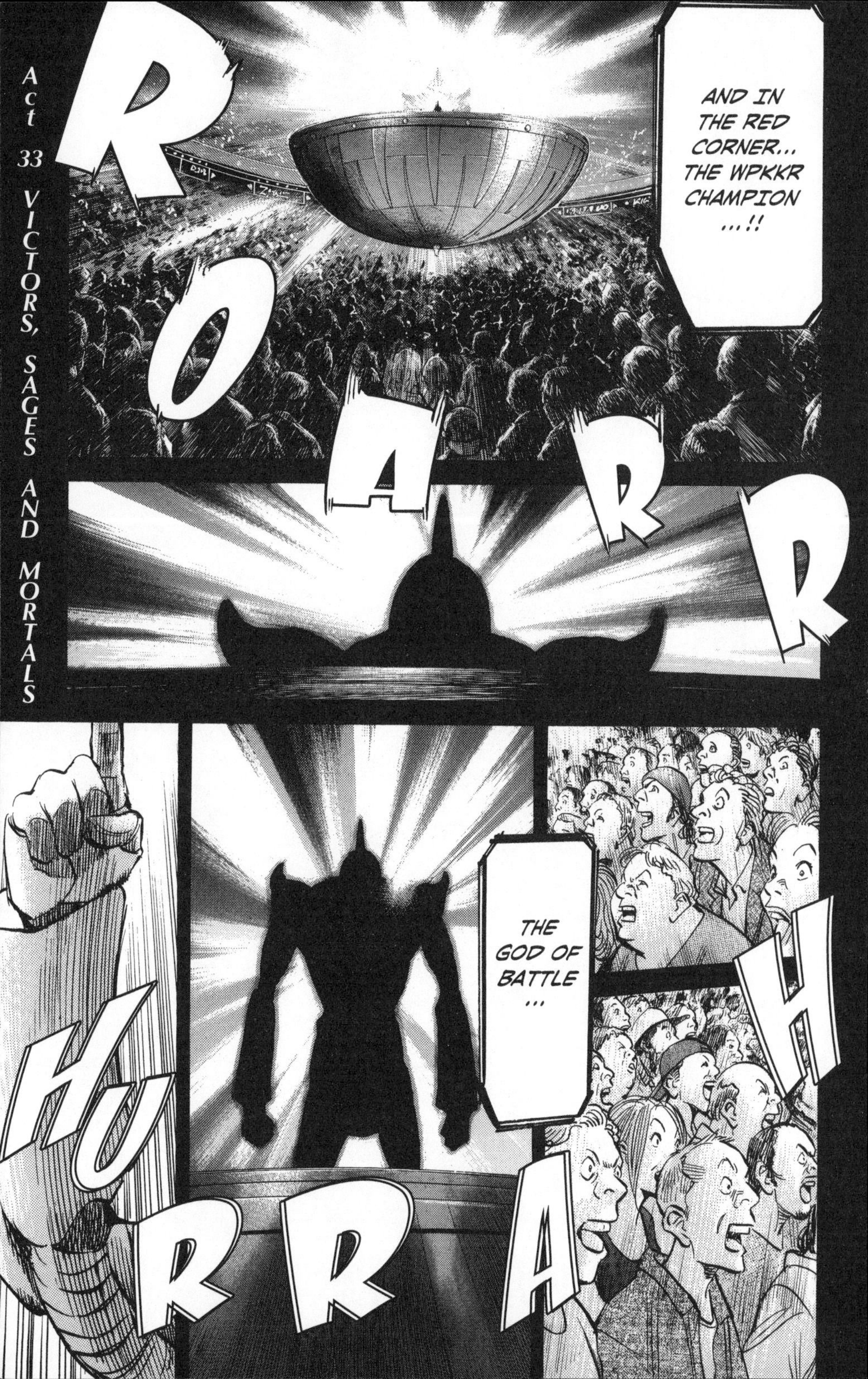
AND IN THE RED CORNER... THE WPKKR CHAMPION ...!!
ROAARR
THE GOD OF BATTLE ...
HURRAH

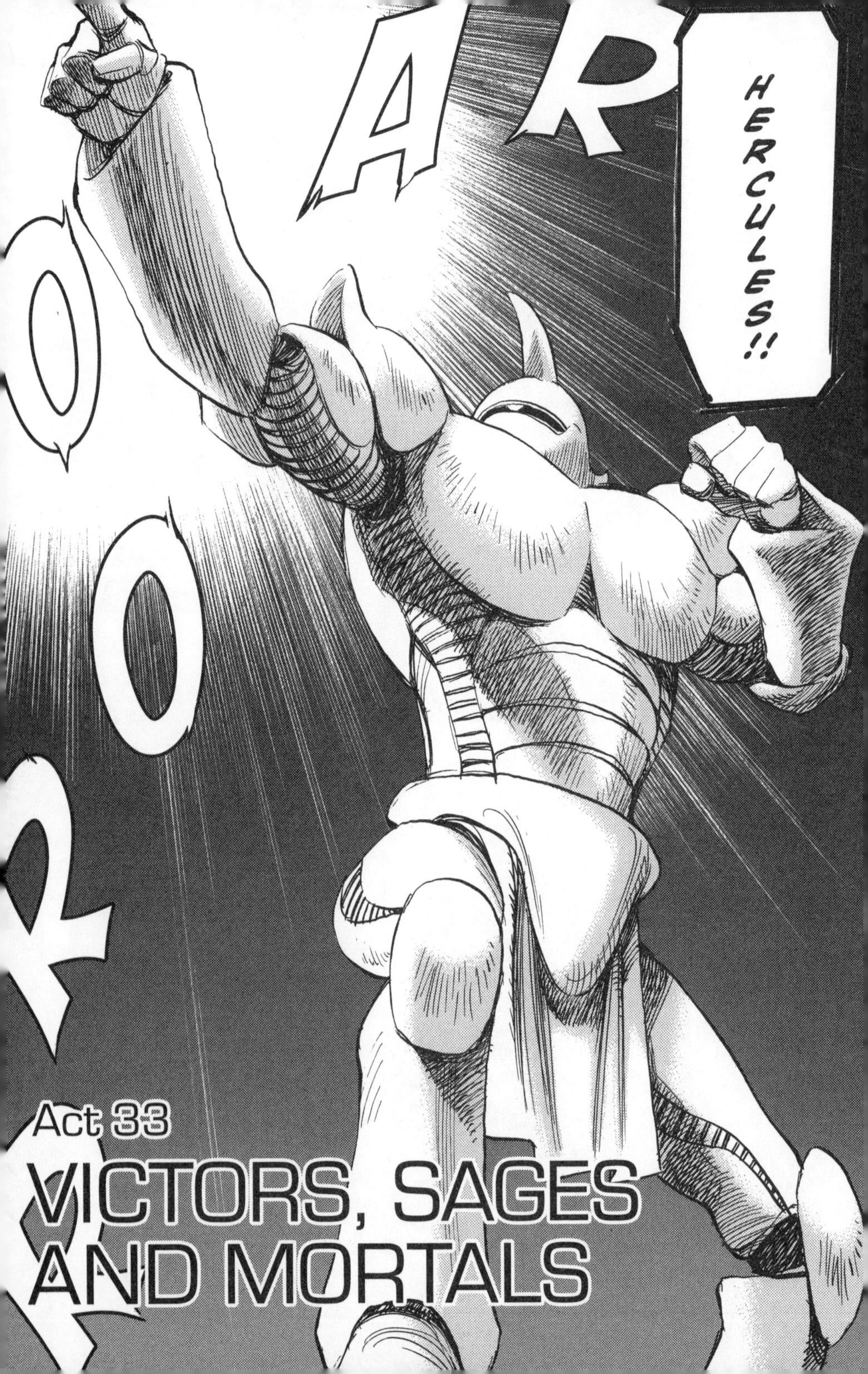
HERCULES!!
ROOAR
Act 33
VICTORS, SAGES AND MORTALS

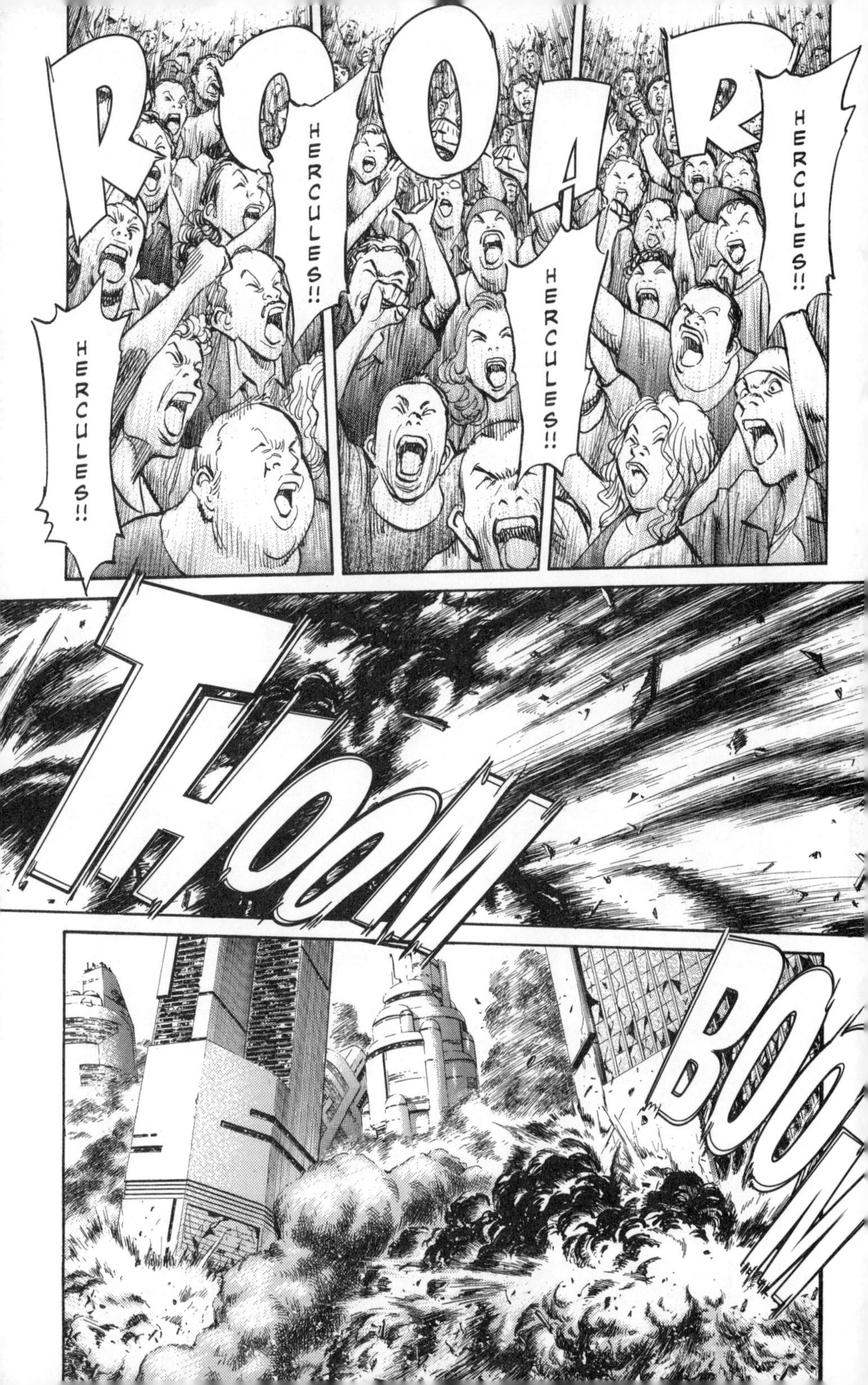
ROOAR
HERCULES!!
HERCULES!!
HERCULES!!
HERCULES!!
THOOM
BOOM

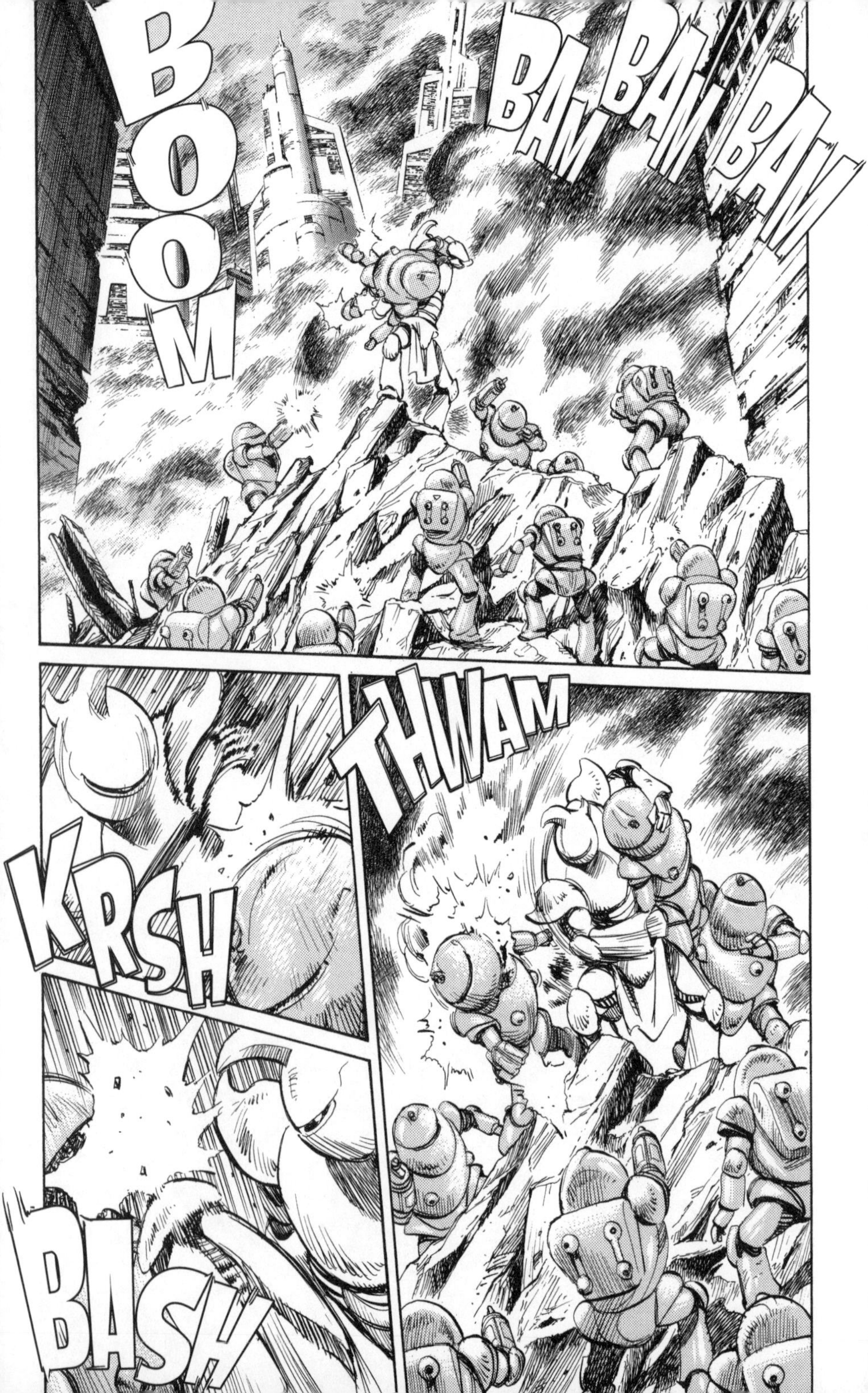
BAM BAM BAM
BOOM
THWAM
KRSH
BASH

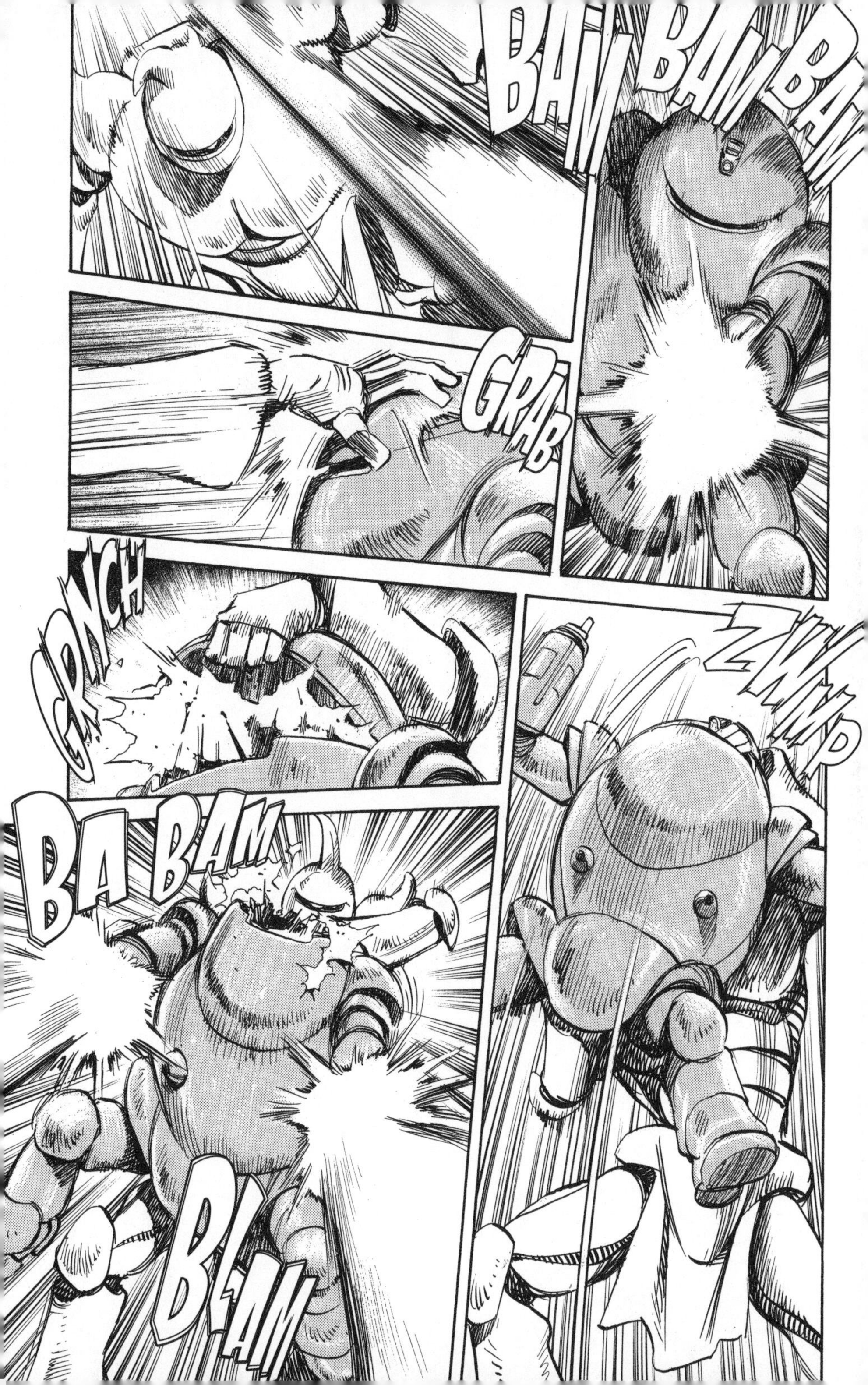
BAM BAM BAM
GRAB
ZWMP
CRNCH
BA BAM
BLAM

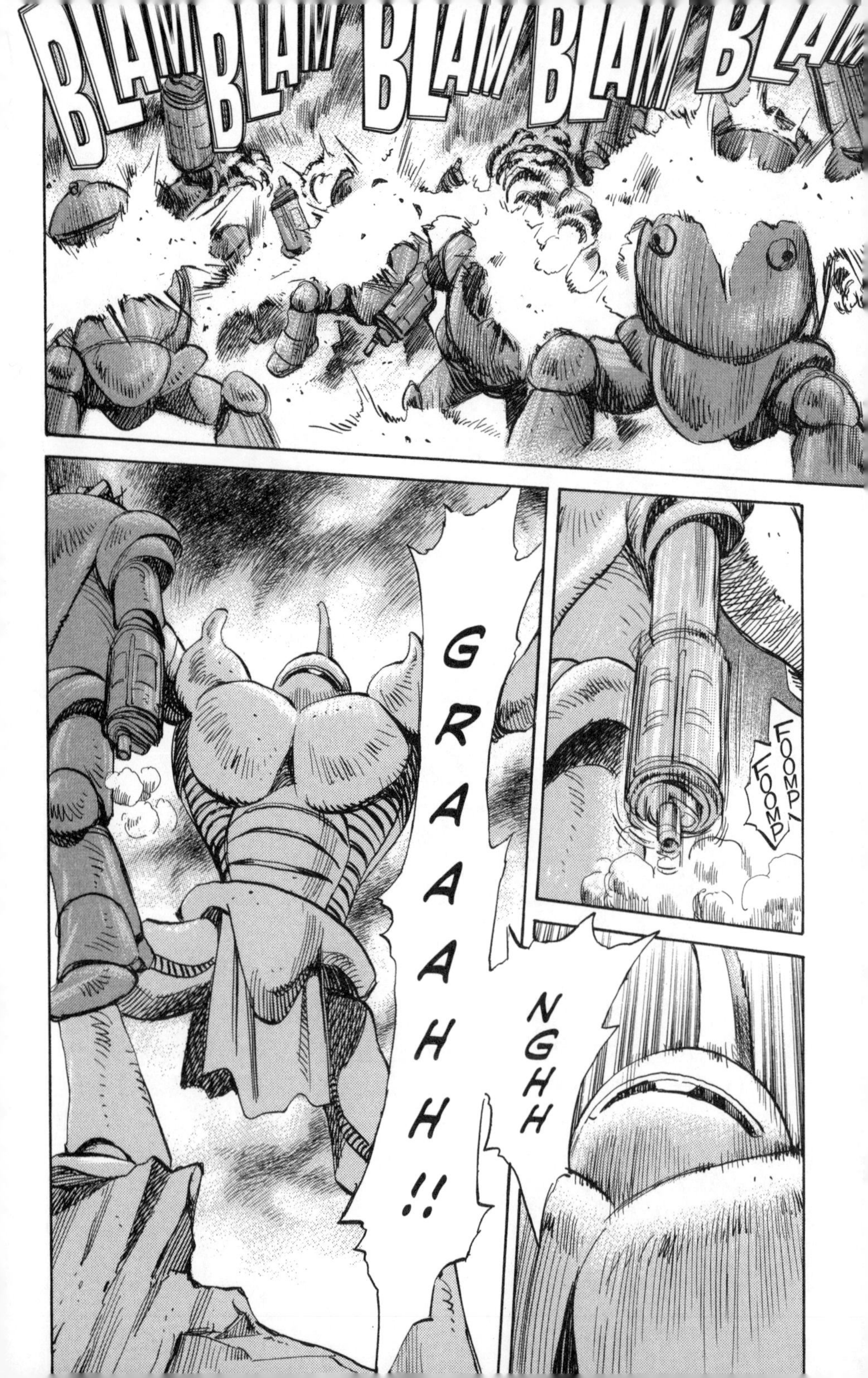
BLAM BLAM BLAM BLAM BLA
FOOMP FOOMP
NGHH
GRAAAAHHH!!

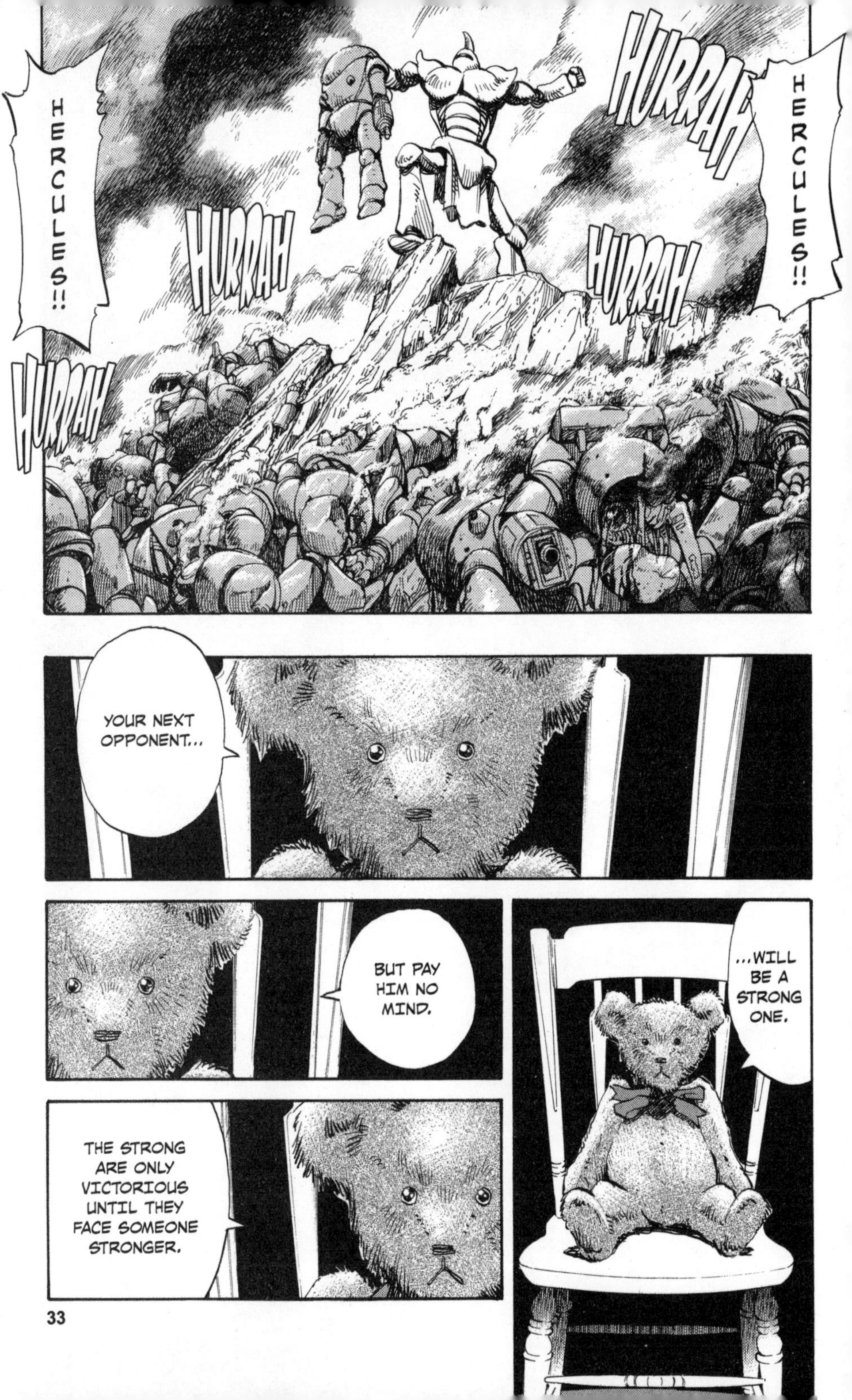
HERCULES!!
HURRAH
HURRAH
HURRAH
HURRAH
HERCULES!!
YOUR NEXT OPPONENT...
...WILL BE A STRONG ONE.
BUT PAY HIM NO MIND.
THE STRONG ARE ONLY VICTORIOUS UNTIL THEY FACE SOMEONE STRONGER.

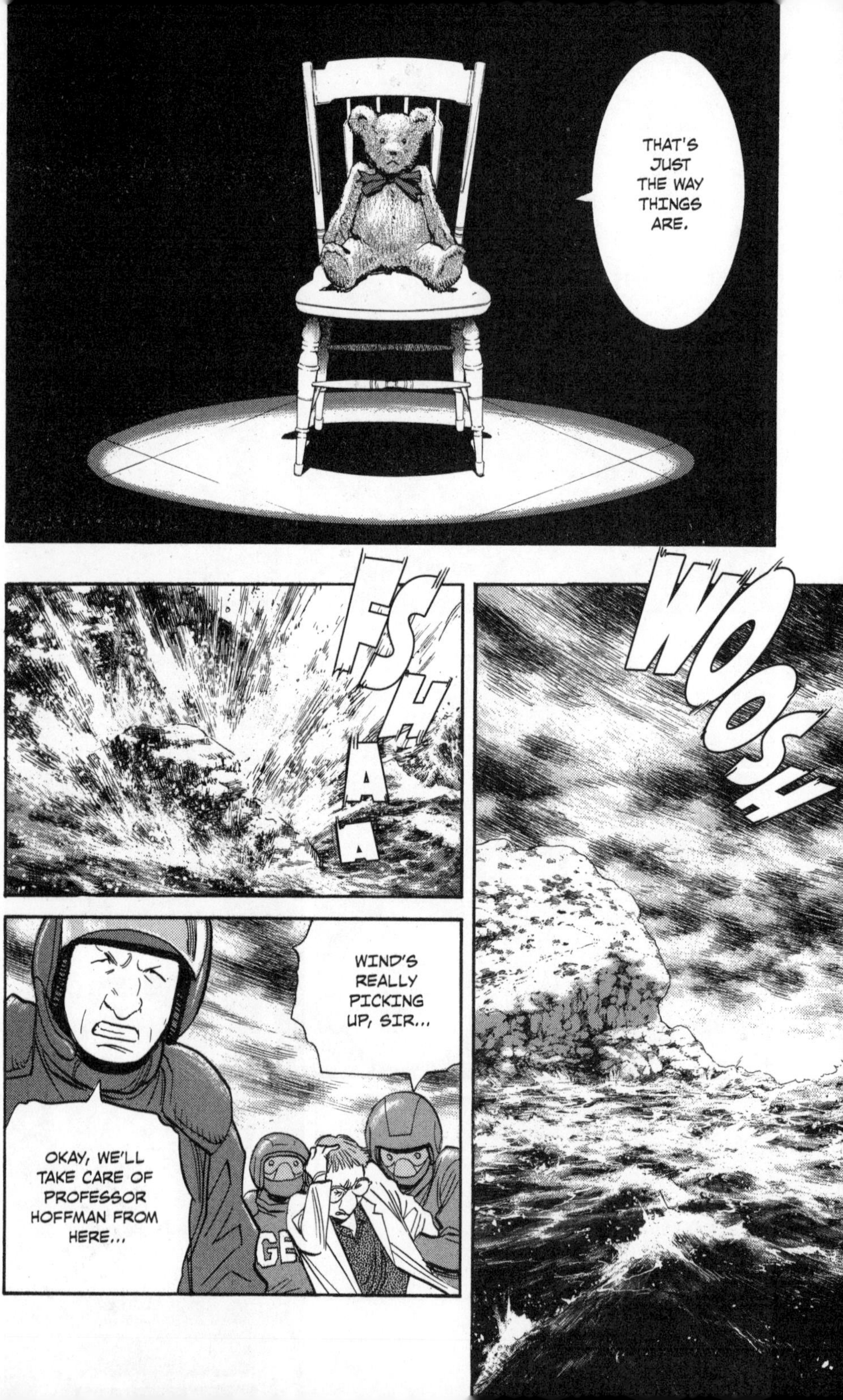
THAT'S JUST THE WAY THINGS ARE.
WOOSH
FSHAA
WIND'S REALLY PICKING UP, SIR...
OKAY, WE'LL TAKE CARE OF PROFESSOR HOFFMAN FROM HERE...
GE

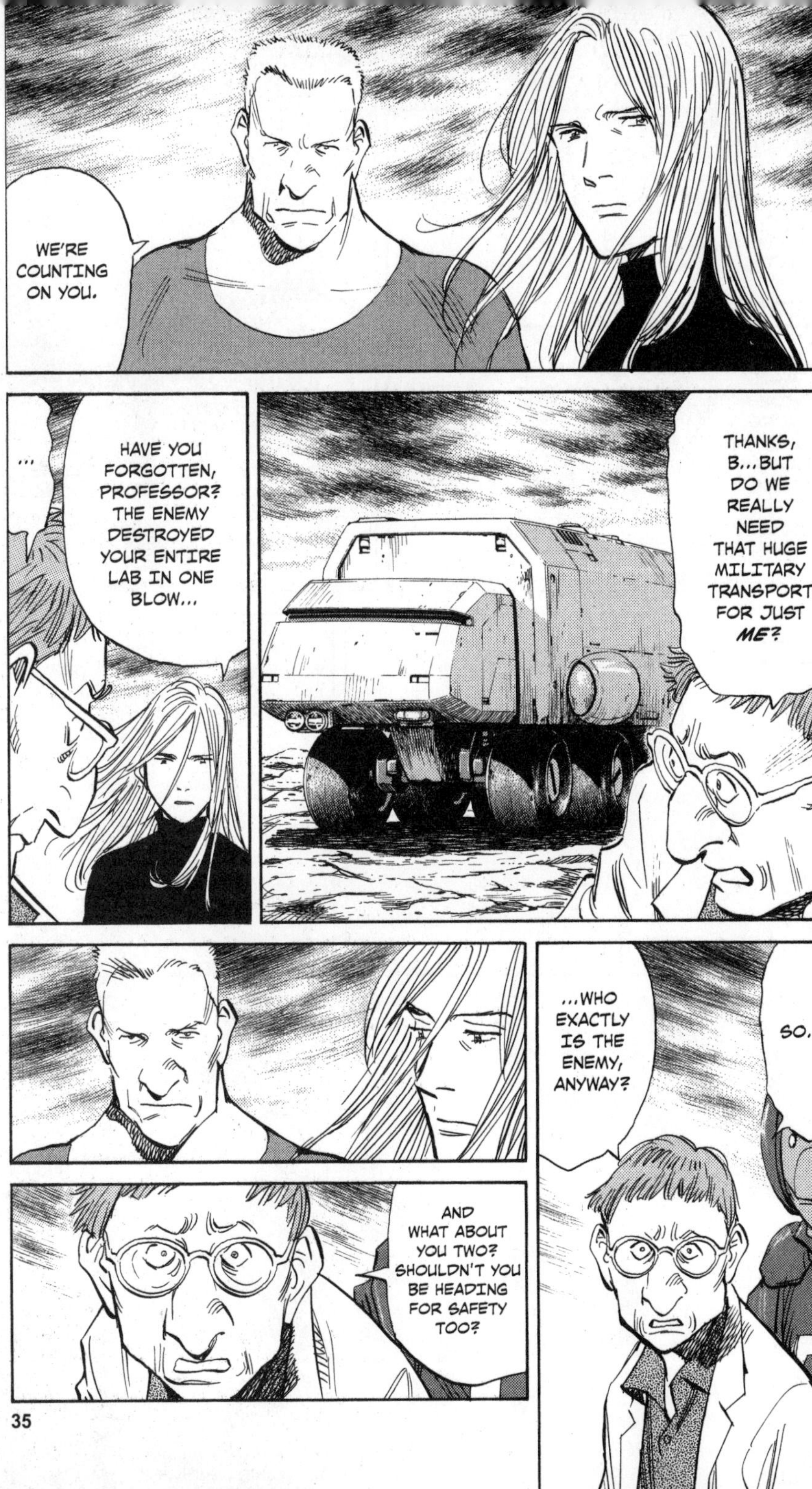
WE'RE COUNTING ON YOU.
THANKS, B...BUT DO WE REALLY NEED THAT HUGE MILITARY TRANSPORT FOR JUST *ME*?
HAVE YOU FORGOTTEN, PROFESSOR? THE ENEMY DESTROYED YOUR ENTIRE LAB IN ONE BLOW...
...
SO...
...WHO EXACTLY IS THE ENEMY, ANYWAY?
AND WHAT ABOUT YOU TWO? SHOULDN'T YOU BE HEADING FOR SAFETY TOO?

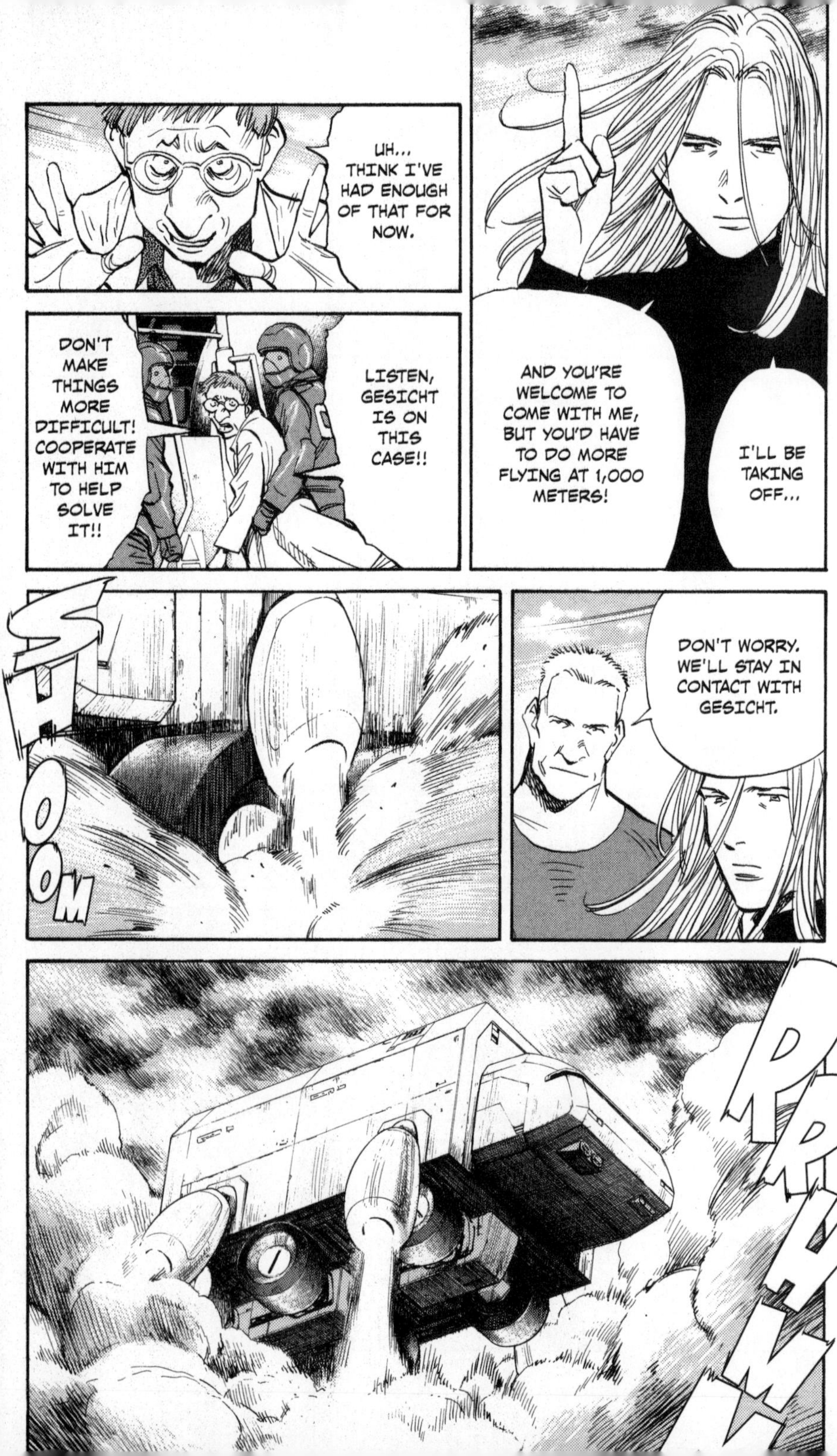
I'LL BE TAKING OFF...
AND YOU'RE WELCOME TO COME WITH ME, BUT YOU'D HAVE TO DO MORE FLYING AT 1,000 METERS!
UH... THINK I'VE HAD ENOUGH OF THAT FOR NOW.
LISTEN, GESICHT IS ON THIS CASE!!
DON'T MAKE THINGS MORE DIFFICULT! COOPERATE WITH HIM TO HELP SOLVE IT!!
DON'T WORRY. WE'LL STAY IN CONTACT WITH GESICHT.
SHOOOM
RRHM

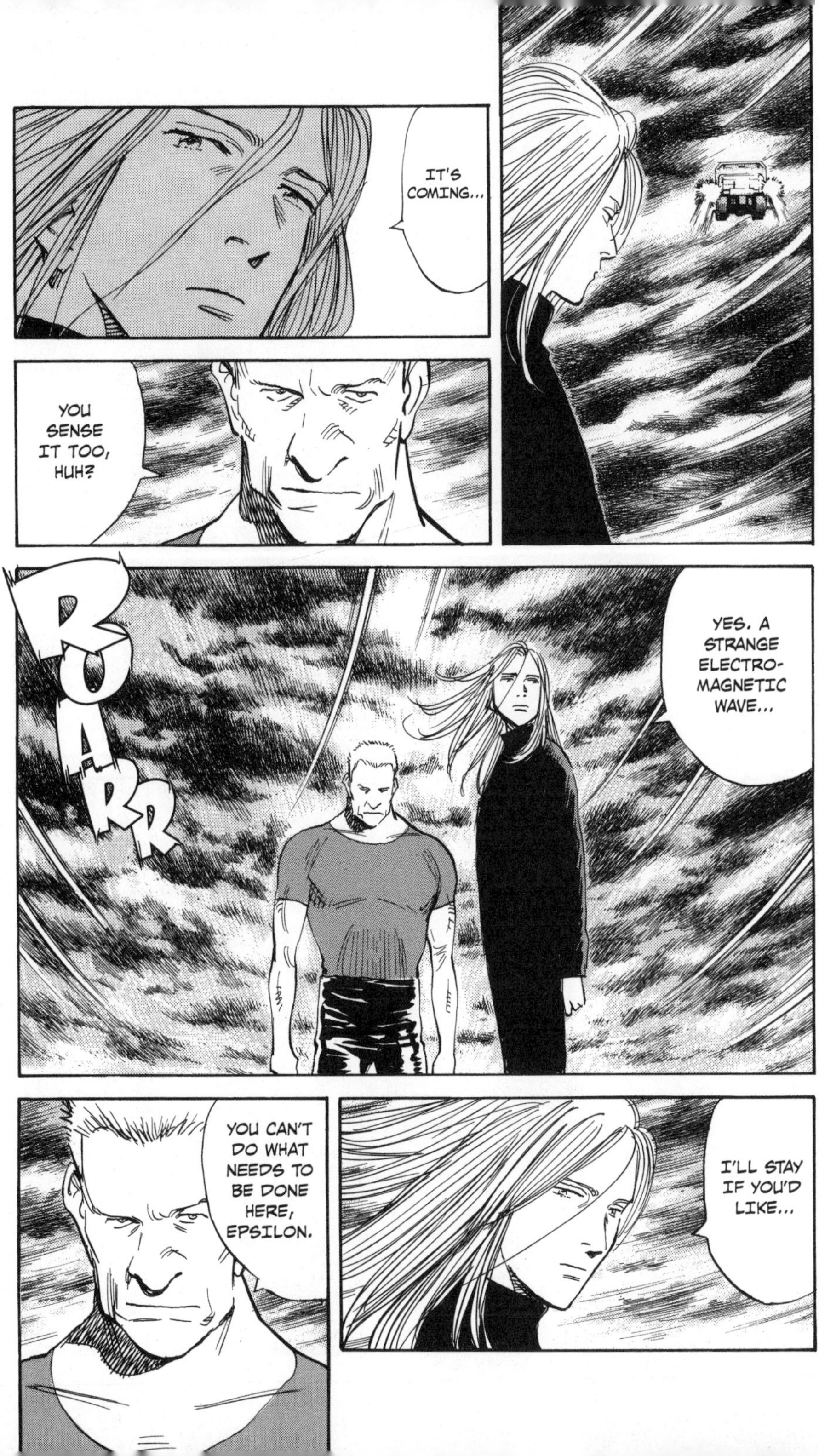
IT'S COMING...
YOU SENSE IT TOO, HUH?
YES. A STRANGE ELECTRO-MAGNETIC WAVE...
ROARR
I'LL STAY IF YOU'D LIKE...
YOU CAN'T DO WHAT NEEDS TO BE DONE HERE, EPSILON.

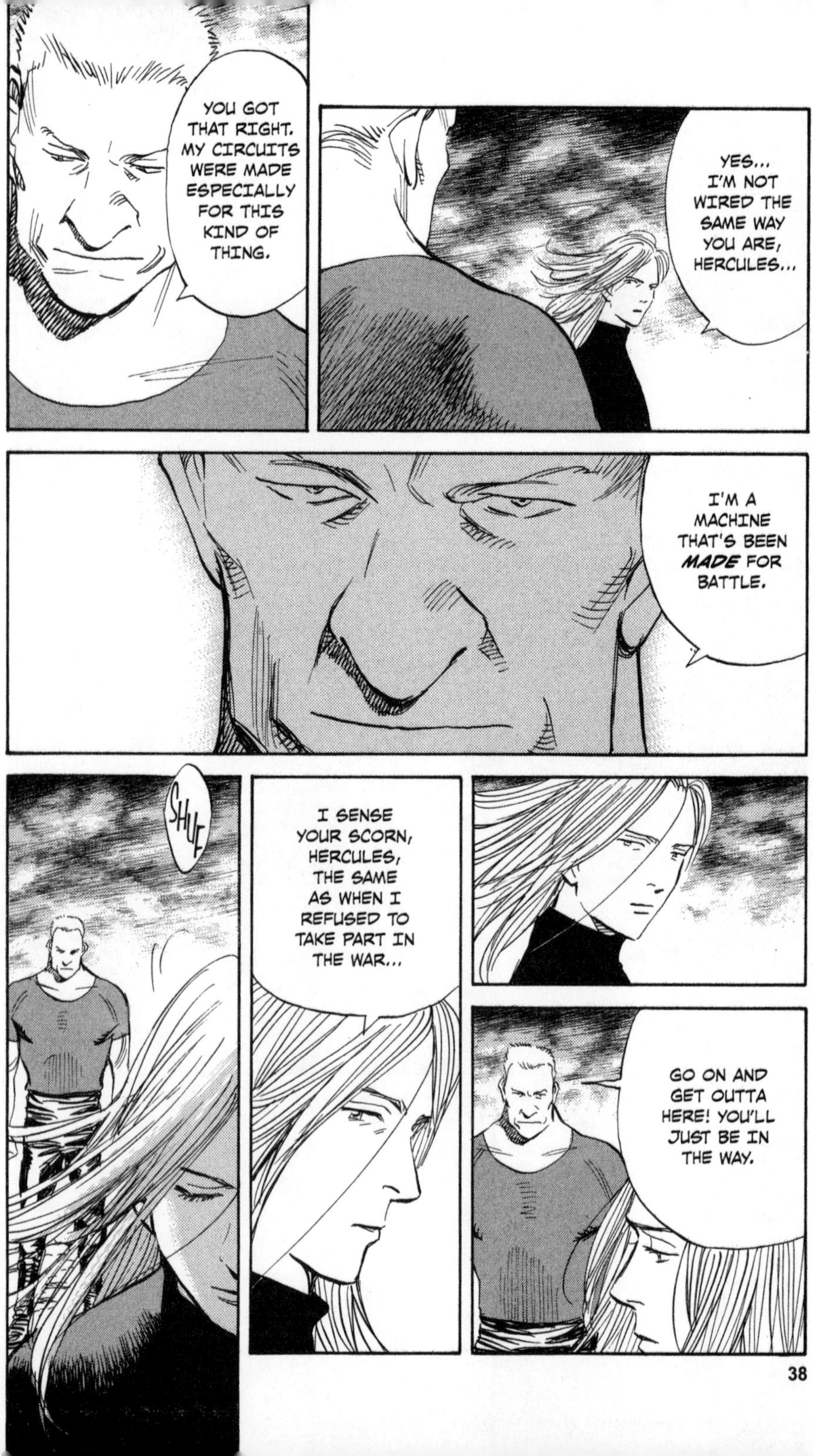
YES... I'M NOT WIRED THE SAME WAY YOU ARE, HERCULES...
YOU GOT THAT RIGHT. MY CIRCUITS WERE MADE ESPECIALLY FOR THIS KIND OF THING.
I'M A MACHINE THAT'S BEEN *MADE* FOR BATTLE.
GO ON AND GET OUTTA HERE! YOU'LL JUST BE IN THE WAY.
I SENSE YOUR SCORN, HERCULES, THE SAME AS WHEN I REFUSED TO TAKE PART IN THE WAR...
SHUF

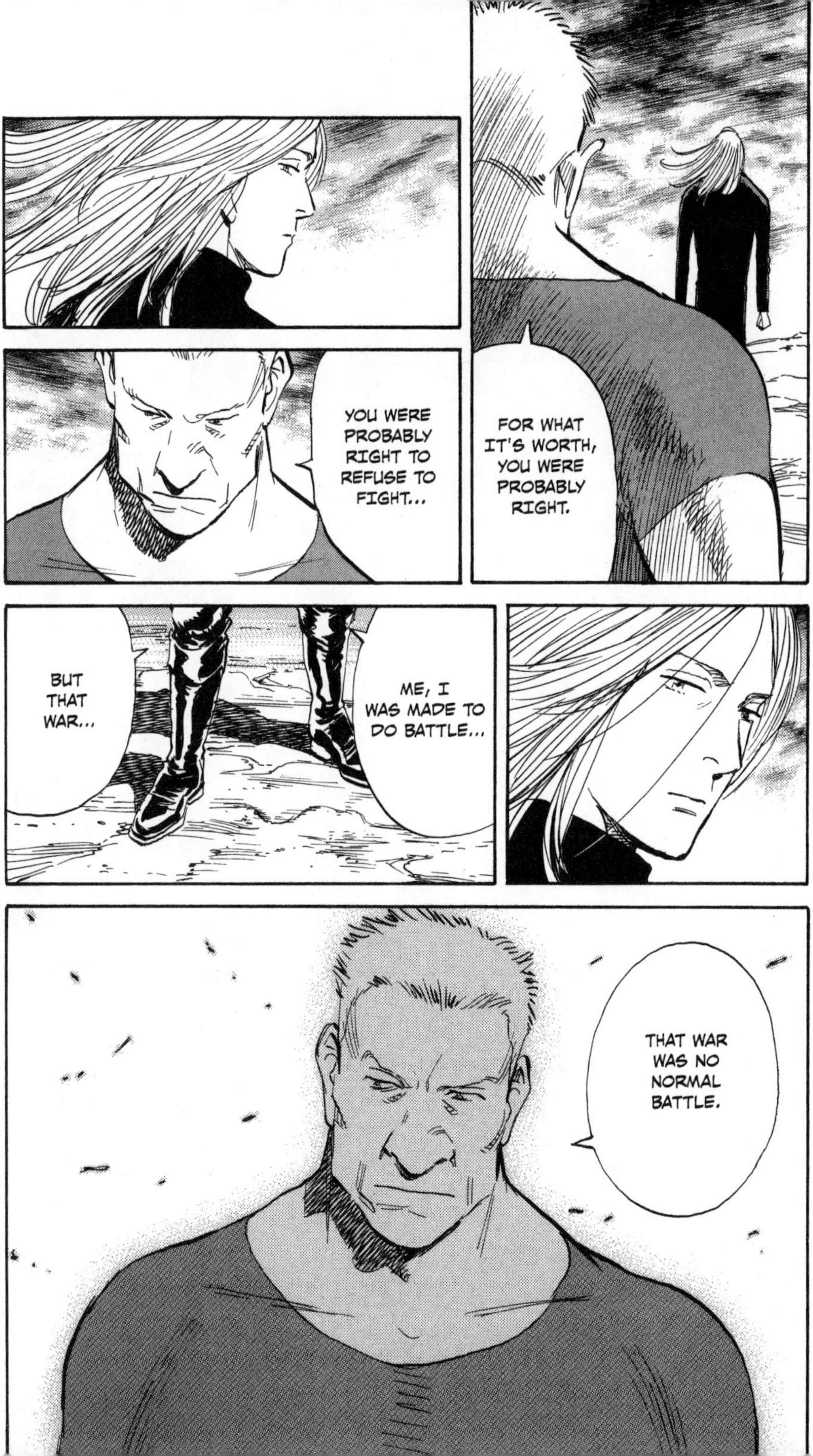
FOR WHAT IT'S WORTH, YOU WERE PROBABLY RIGHT.
YOU WERE PROBABLY RIGHT TO REFUSE TO FIGHT...
ME, I WAS MADE TO DO BATTLE...
BUT THAT WAR...
THAT WAR WAS NO NORMAL BATTLE.

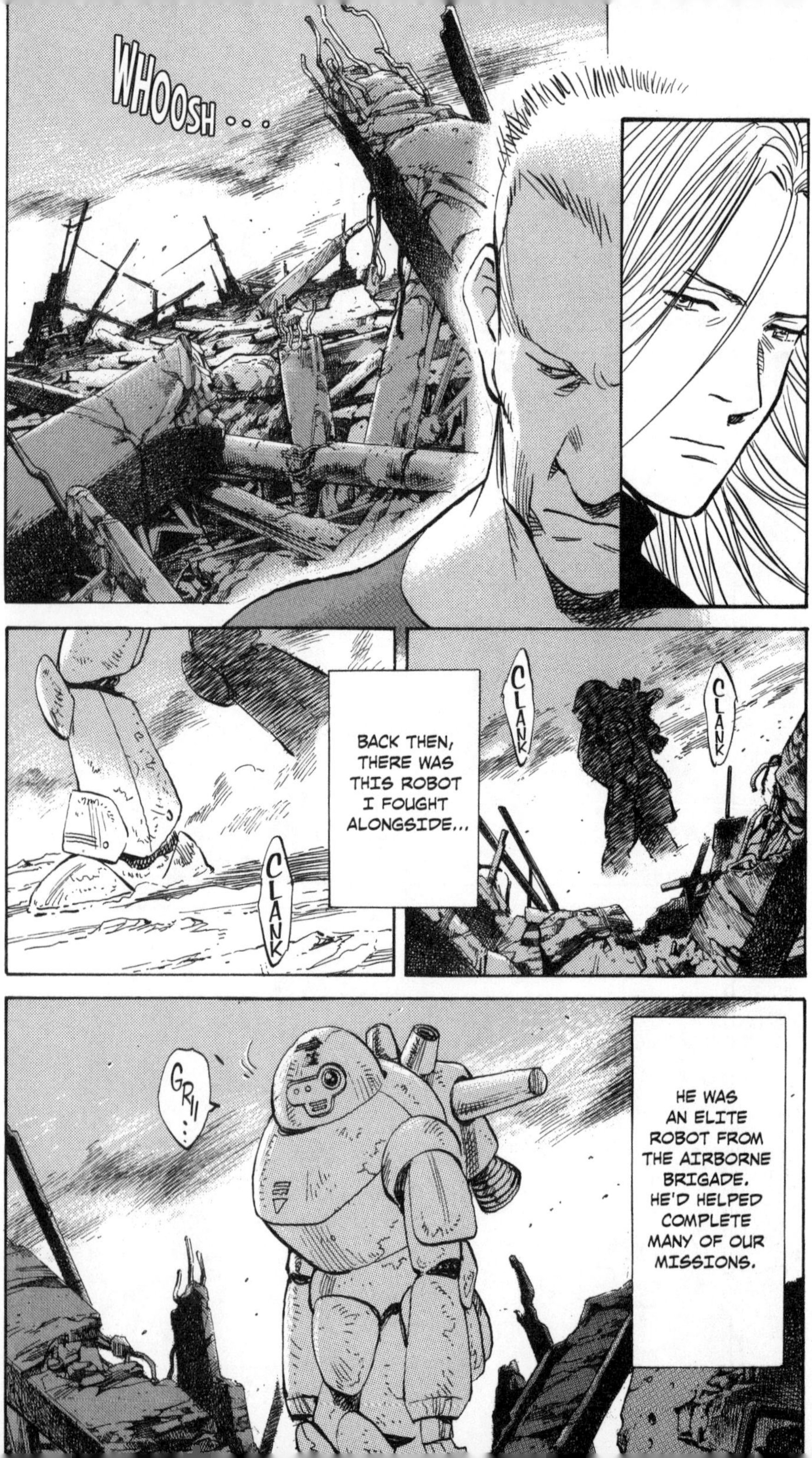
WHOOSH...
CLANK
CLANK
BACK THEN, THERE WAS THIS ROBOT I FOUGHT ALONGSIDE...
CLANK
HE WAS AN ELITE ROBOT FROM THE AIRBORNE BRIGADE. HE'D HELPED COMPLETE MANY OF OUR MISSIONS.
GRII...

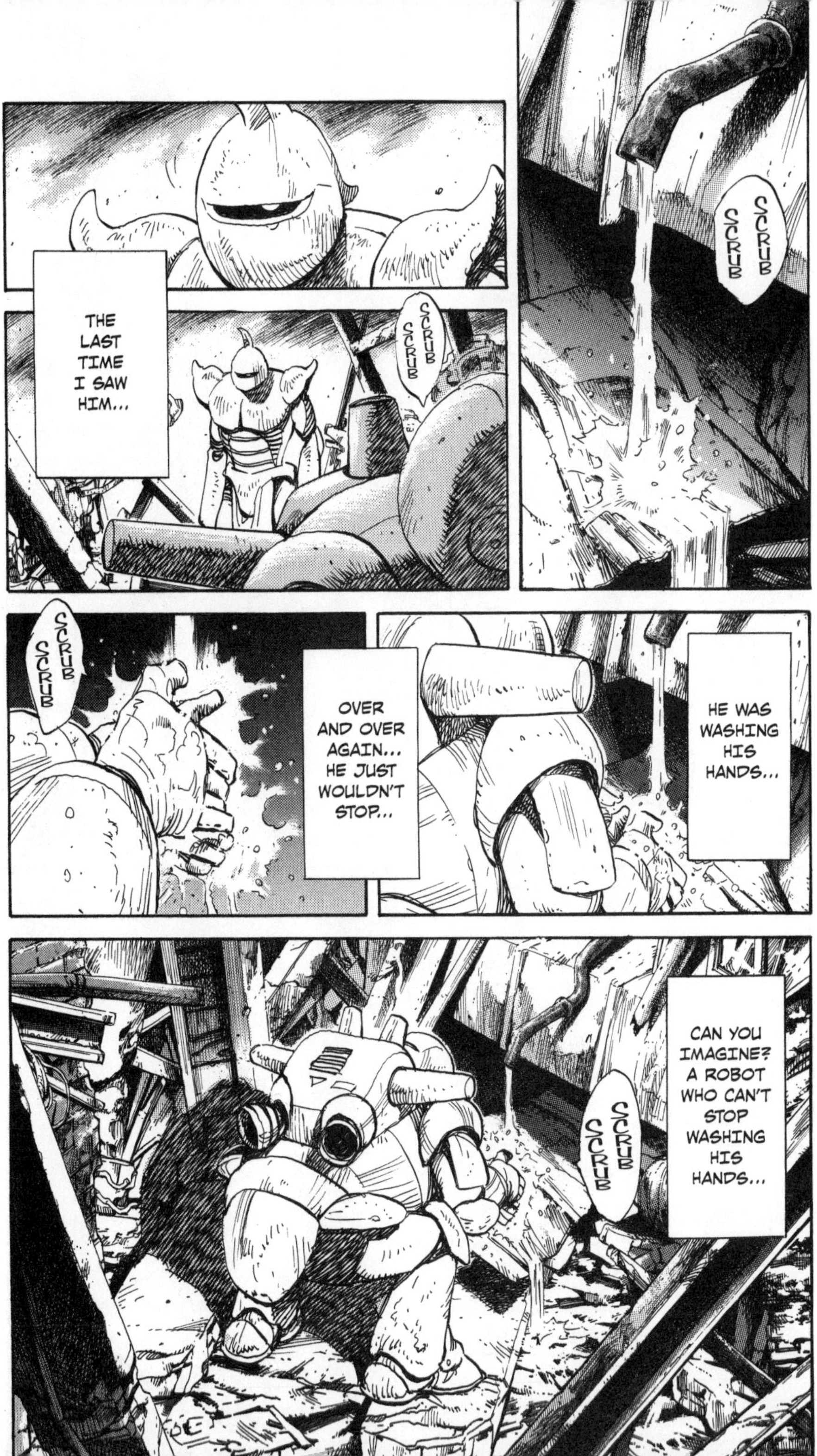
SCRUB SCRUB
THE LAST TIME I SAW HIM...
SCRUB SCRUB
HE WAS WASHING HIS HANDS...
OVER AND OVER AGAIN... HE JUST WOULDN'T STOP...
SCRUB SCRUB
CAN YOU IMAGINE? A ROBOT WHO CAN'T STOP WASHING HIS HANDS...
SCRUB SCRUB

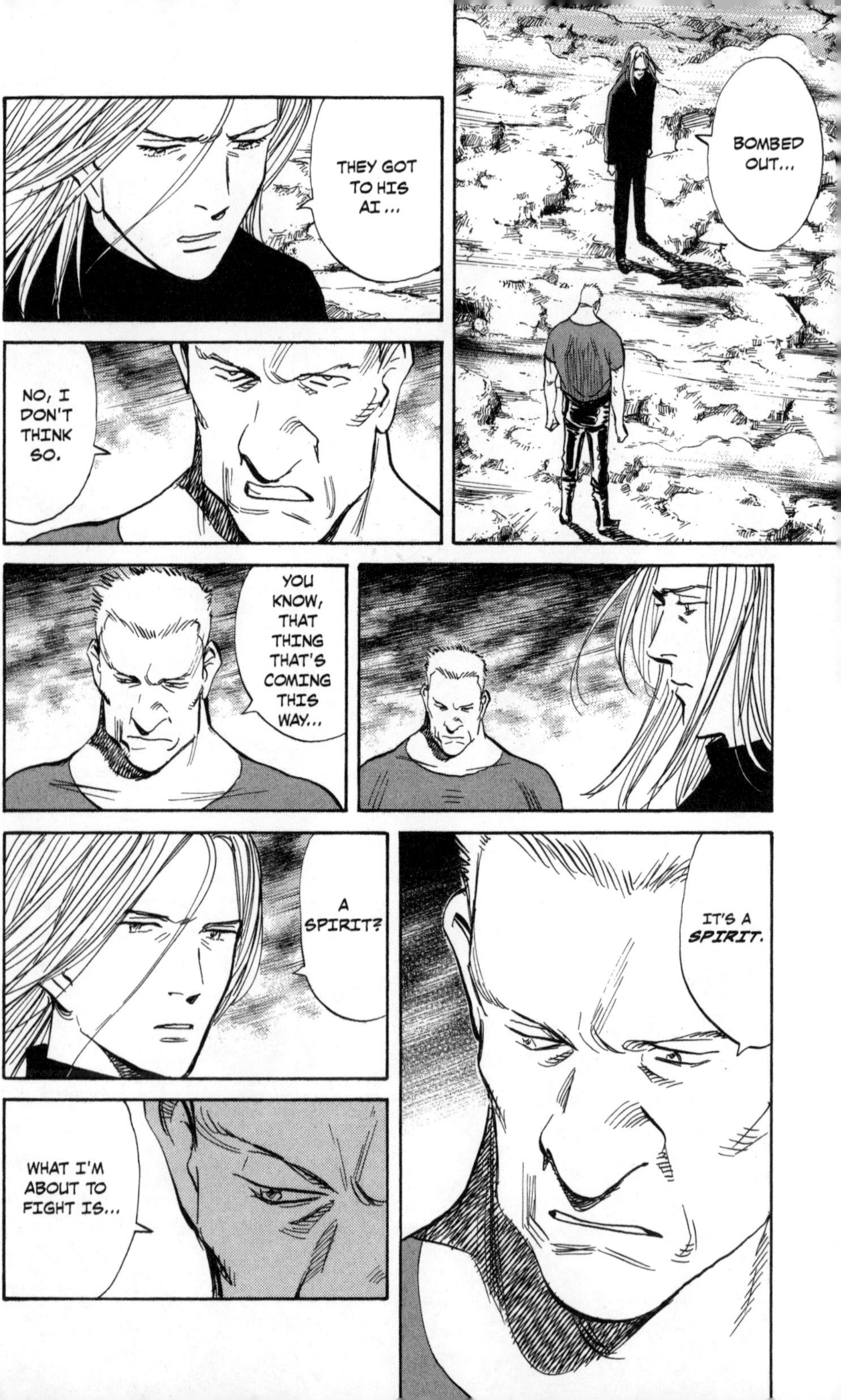
BOMBED OUT...
THEY GOT TO HIS AI...
NO, I DON'T THINK SO.
YOU KNOW, THAT THING THAT'S COMING THIS WAY...
IT'S A *SPIRIT*.
A SPIRIT?
WHAT I'M ABOUT TO FIGHT IS...

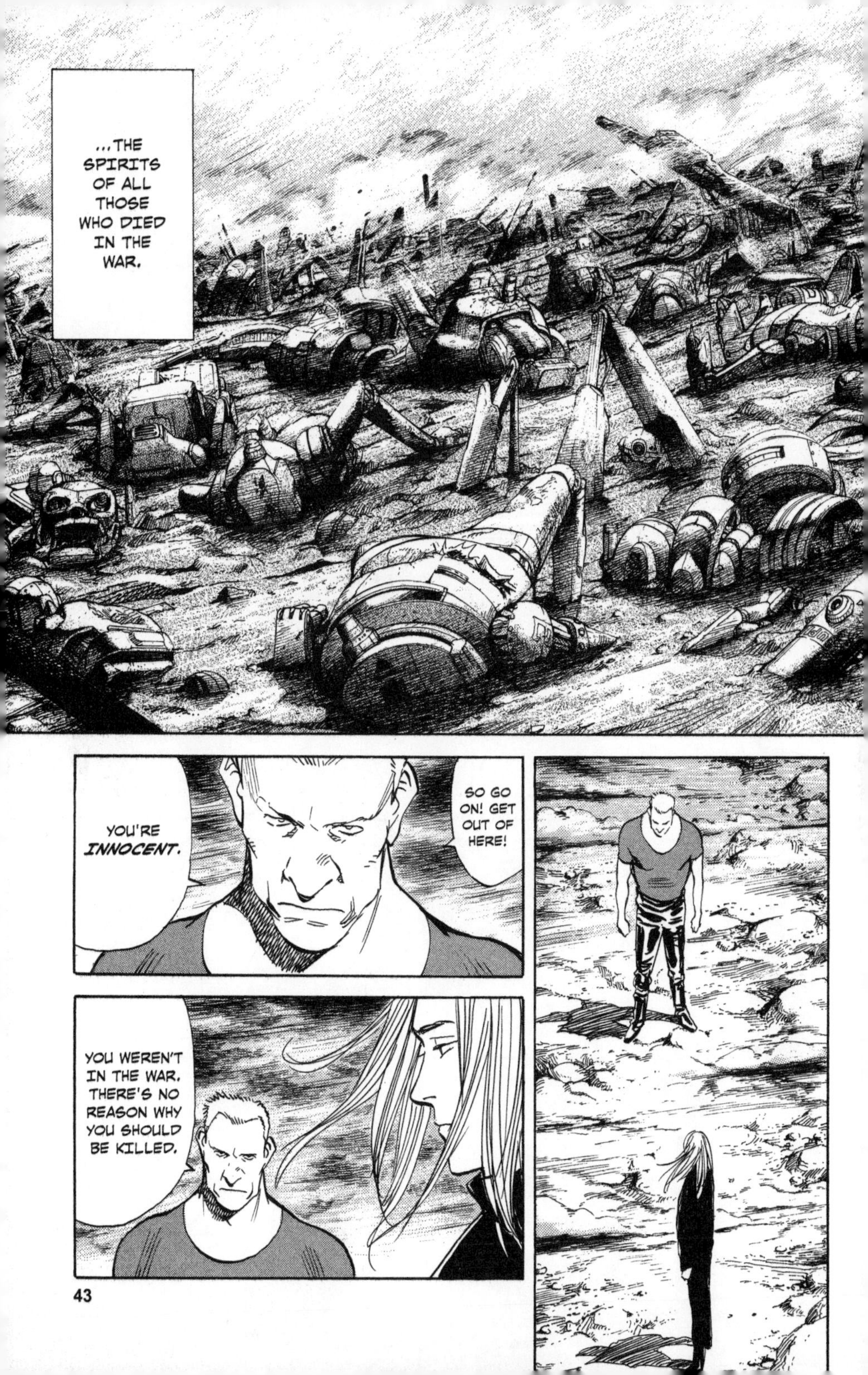
...THE SPIRITS OF ALL THOSE WHO DIED IN THE WAR.
YOU'RE *INNOCENT*.
SO GO ON! GET OUT OF HERE!
YOU WEREN'T IN THE WAR. THERE'S NO REASON WHY YOU SHOULD BE KILLED.

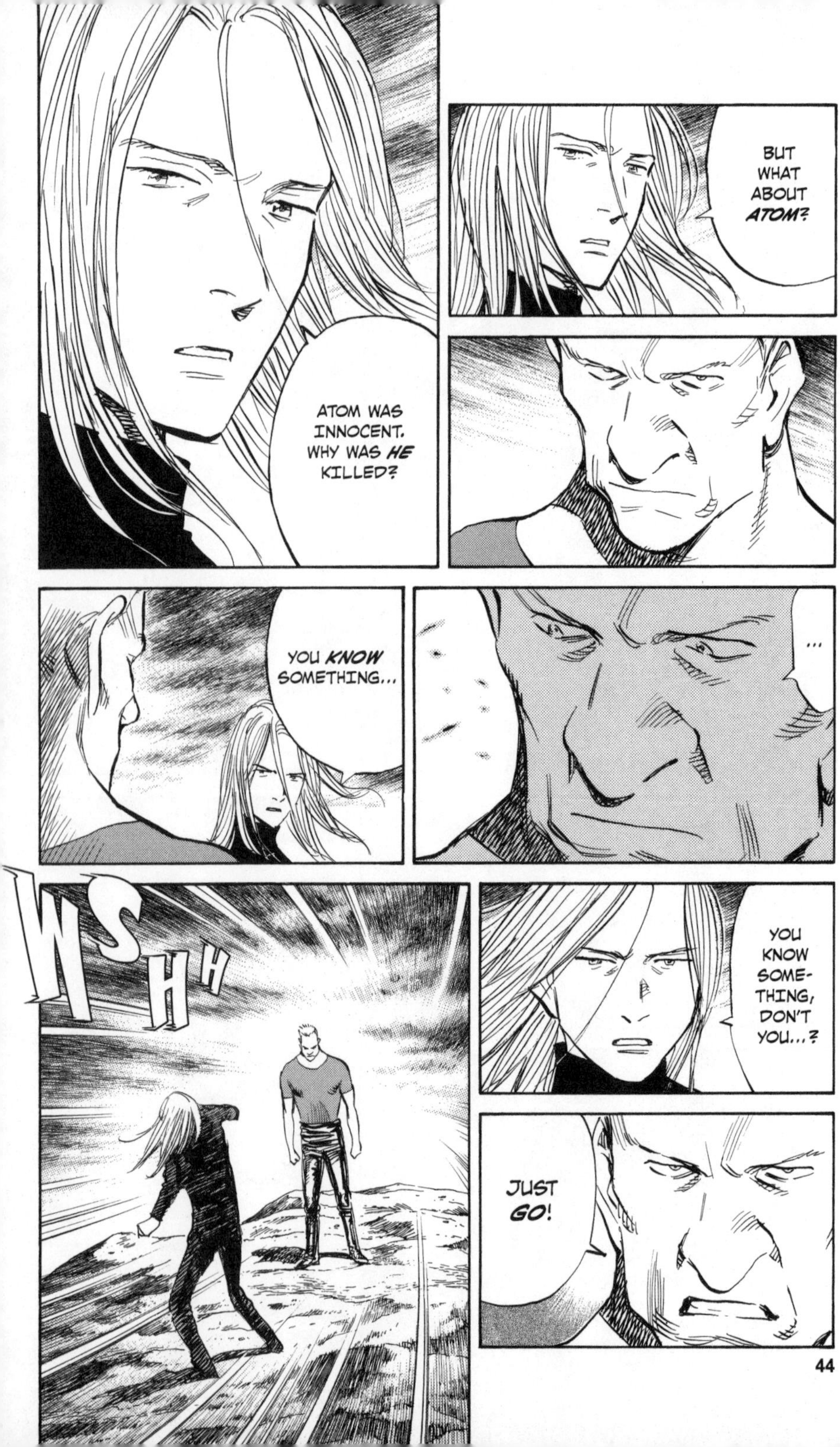
BUT WHAT ABOUT ATOM?
ATOM WAS INNOCENT. WHY WAS HE KILLED?
...
YOU KNOW SOMETHING...
YOU KNOW SOME-THING, DON'T YOU...?
JUST GO!
WSHH

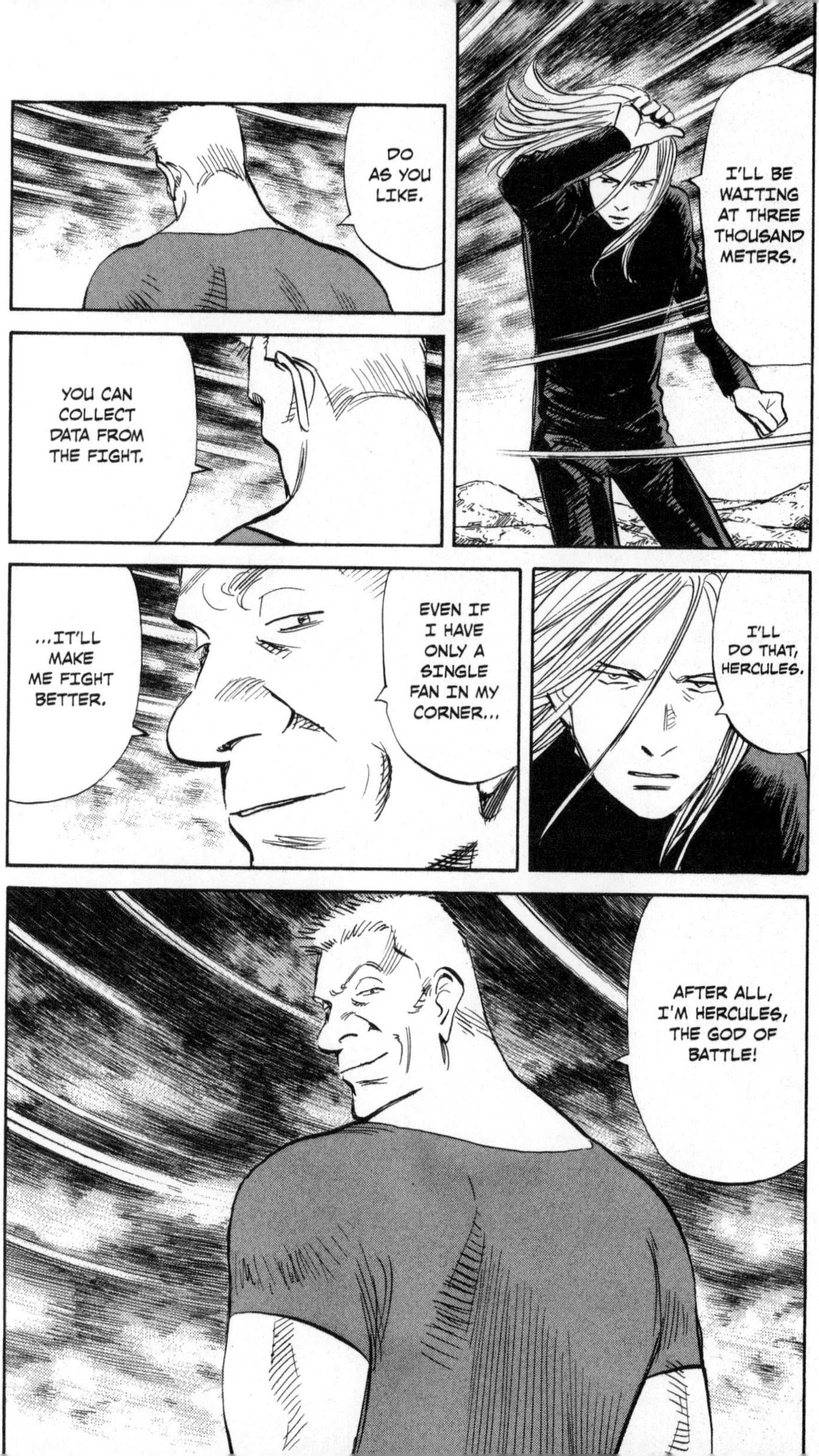
I'LL BE WAITING AT THREE THOUSAND METERS.
DO AS YOU LIKE.
YOU CAN COLLECT DATA FROM THE FIGHT.
I'LL DO THAT, HERCULES.
EVEN IF I HAVE ONLY A SINGLE FAN IN MY CORNER...
...IT'LL MAKE ME FIGHT BETTER.
AFTER ALL, I'M HERCULES, THE GOD OF BATTLE!

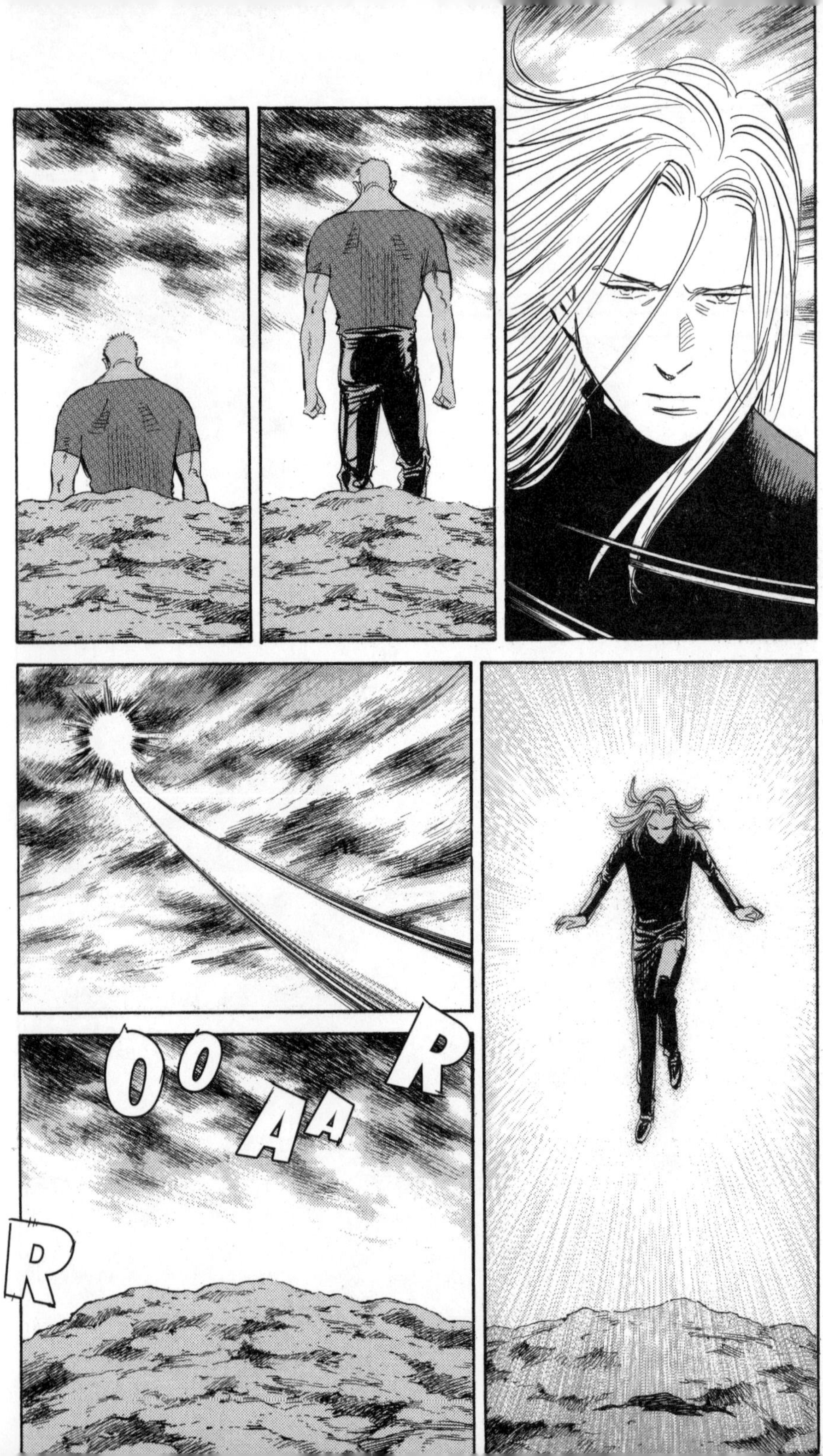
OOAARR

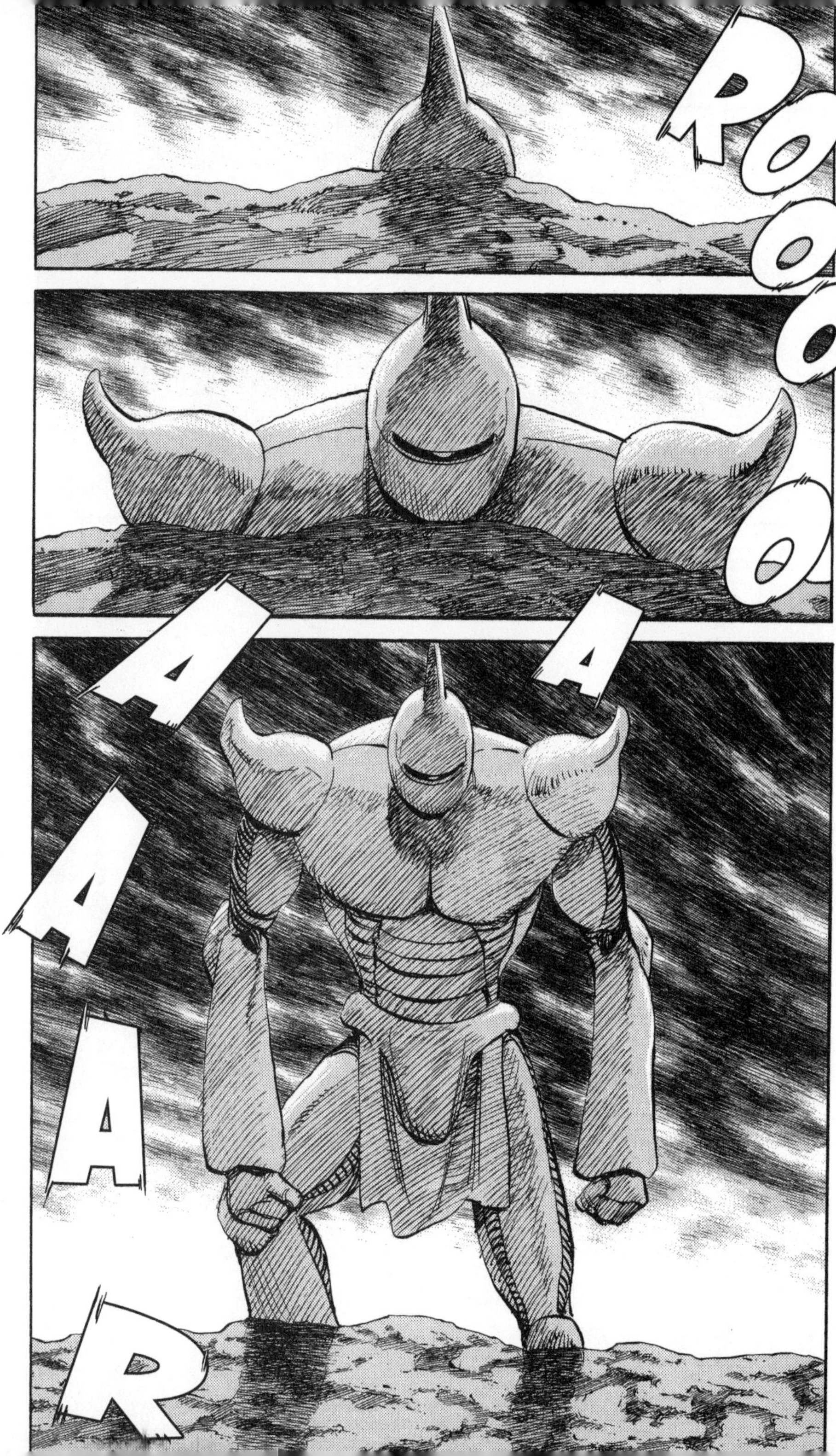
ROOOOOAAAAR

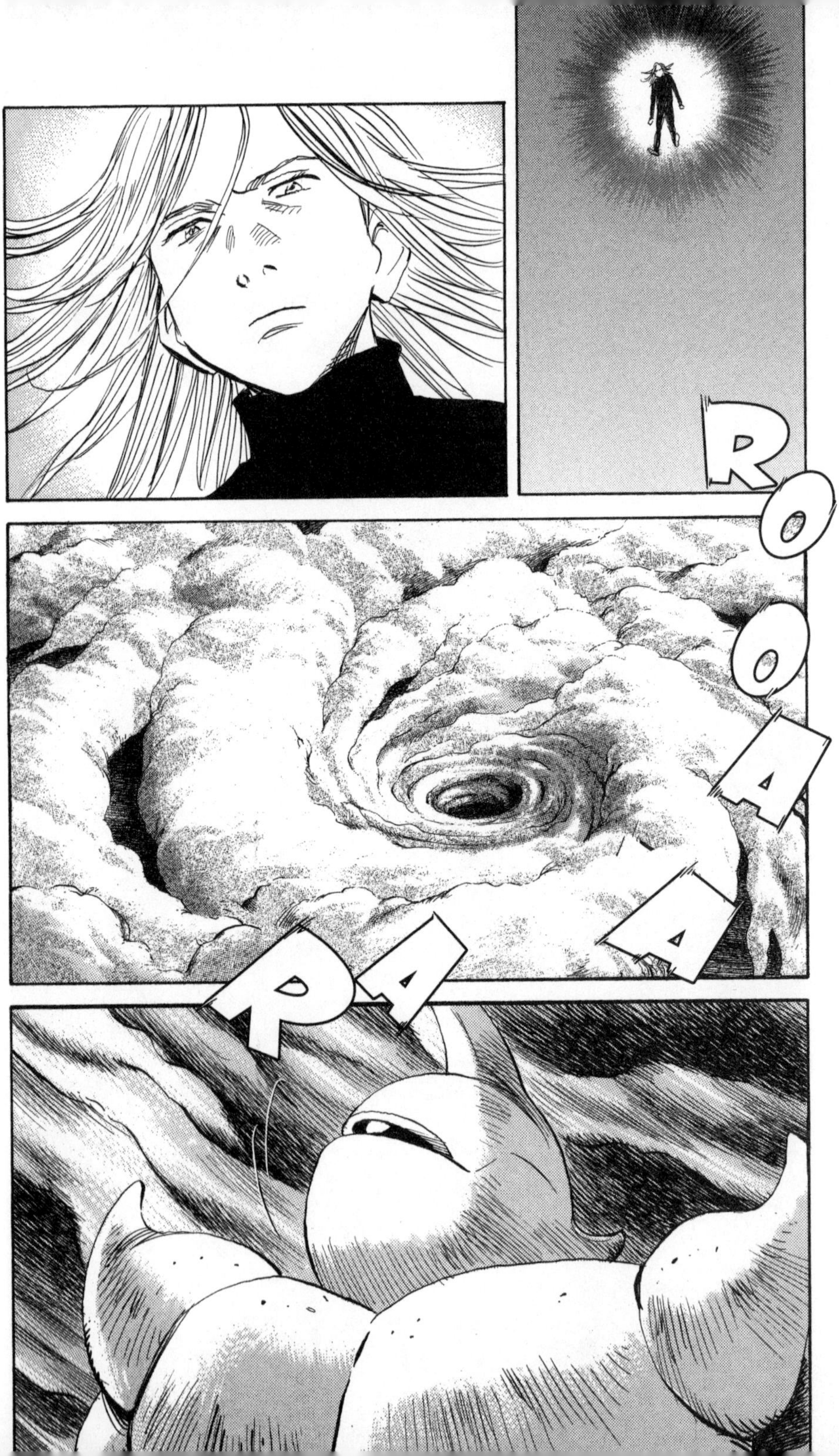
ROOAAAR

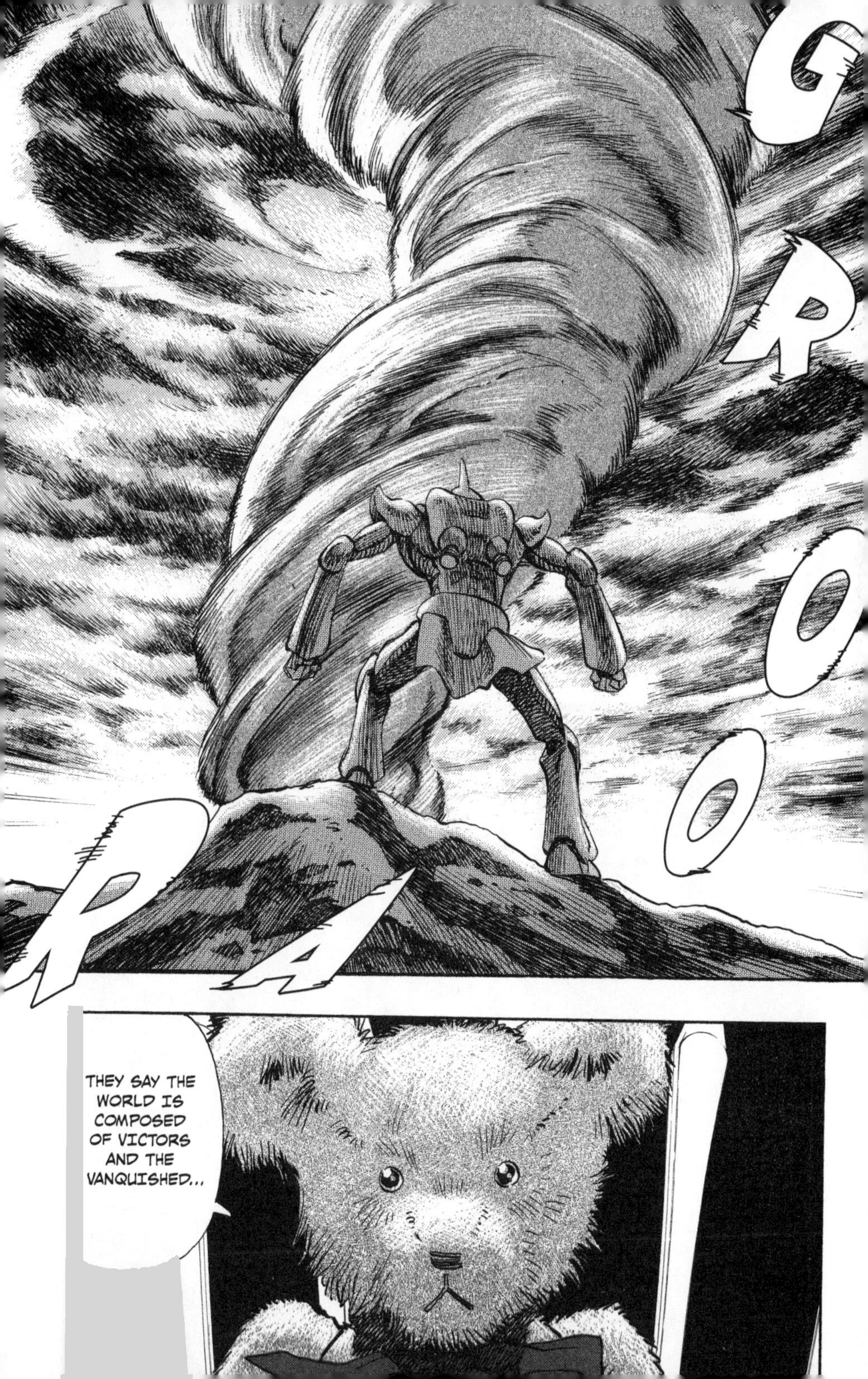
GROO
THEY SAY THE WORLD IS COMPOSED OF VICTORS AND THE VANQUISHED...

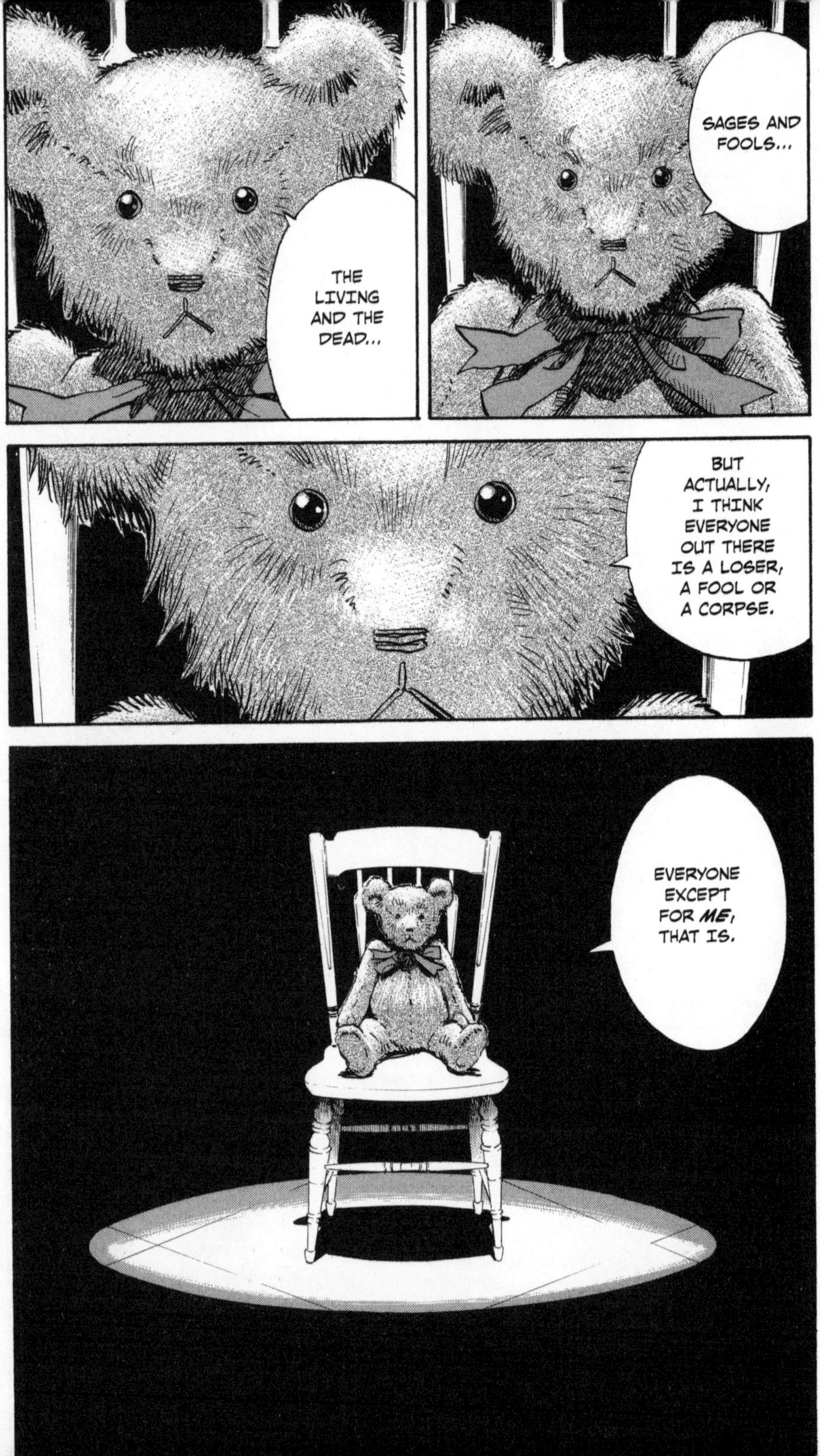
SAGES AND FOOLS...
THE LIVING AND THE DEAD...
BUT ACTUALLY, I THINK EVERYONE OUT THERE IS A LOSER, A FOOL OR A CORPSE.
EVERYONE EXCEPT FOR ***ME***, THAT IS.

# Act 34 GOD'S CHOICE

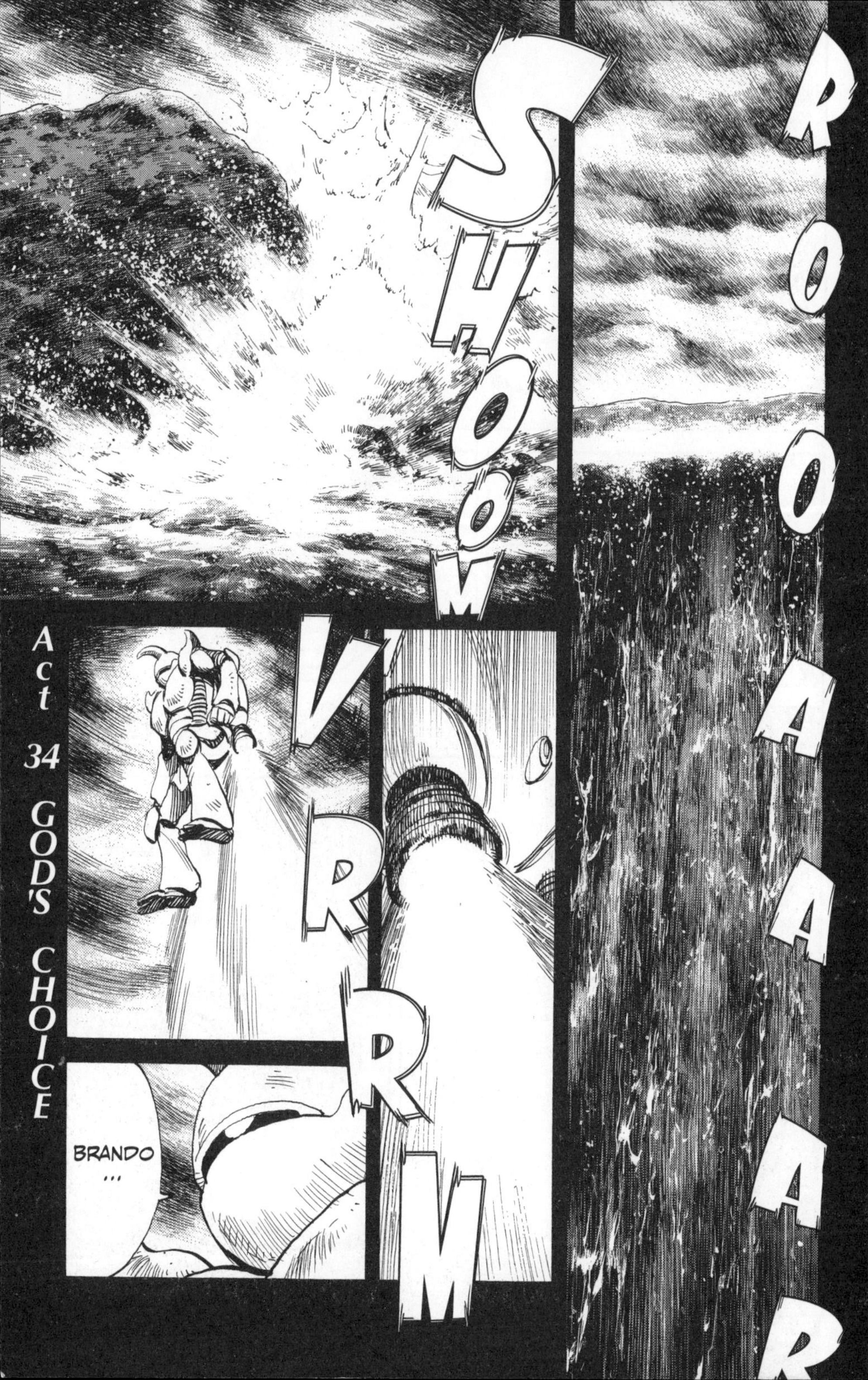
ROOAAAR
SHOOOM
VRRRM
BRANDO ...

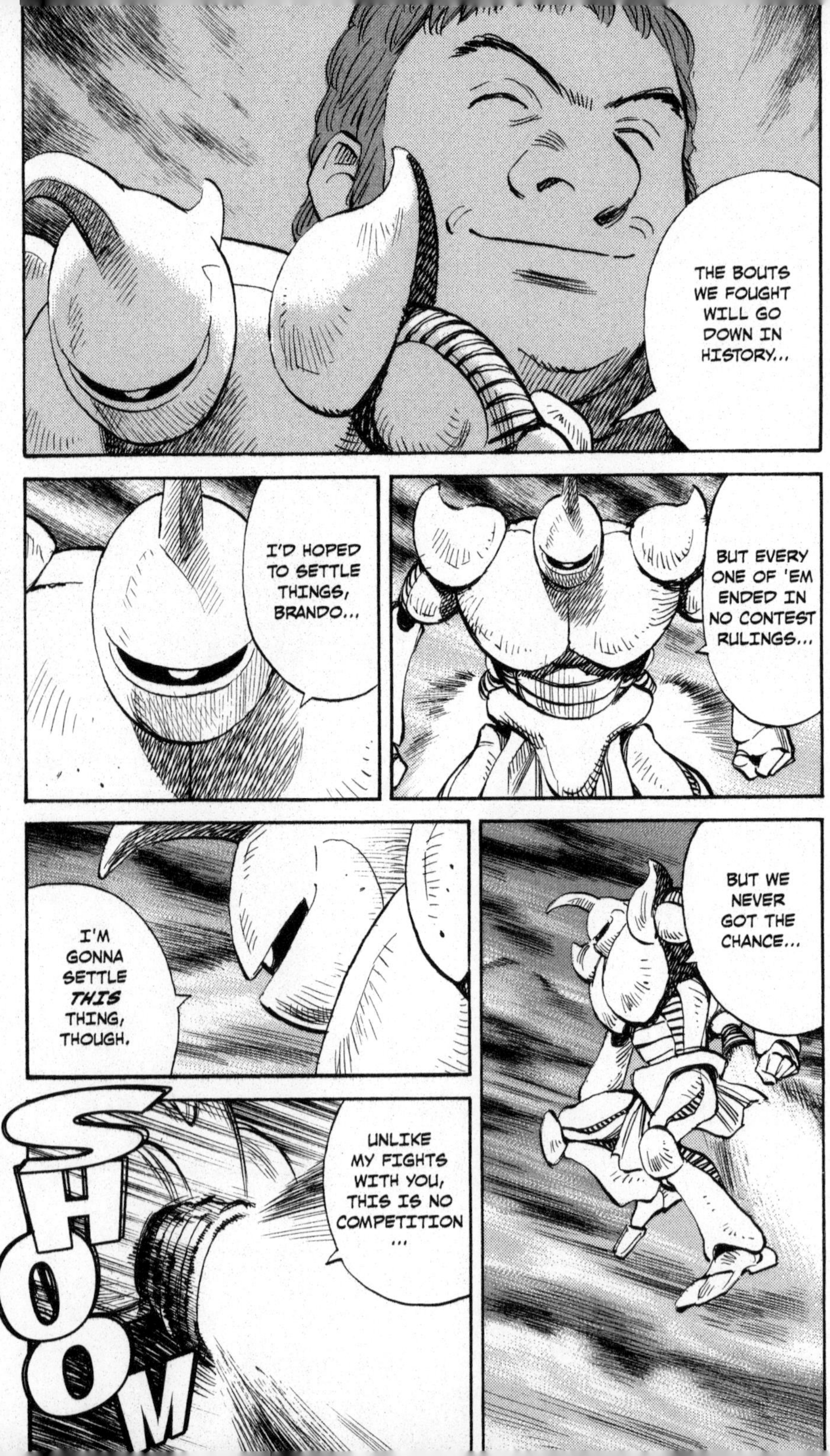
THE BOUTS WE FOUGHT WILL GO DOWN IN HISTORY...
BUT EVERY ONE OF 'EM ENDED IN NO CONTEST RULINGS...
I'D HOPED TO SETTLE THINGS, BRANDO...
BUT WE NEVER GOT THE CHANCE...
I'M GONNA SETTLE *THIS* THING, THOUGH.
UNLIKE MY FIGHTS WITH YOU, THIS IS NO COMPETITION ...
SHOOM

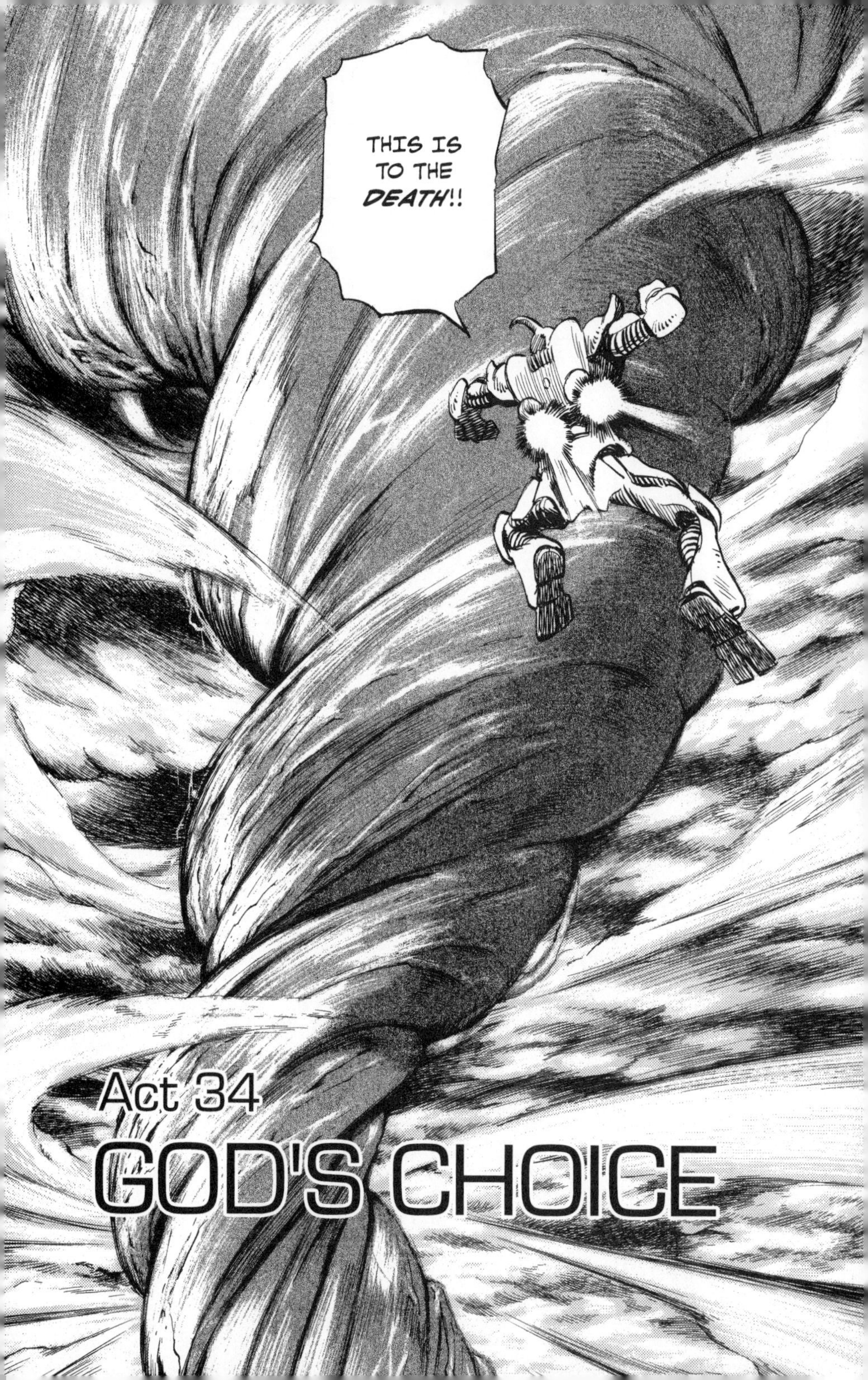
THIS IS TO THE *DEATH*!!
Act 34
GOD'S CHOICE

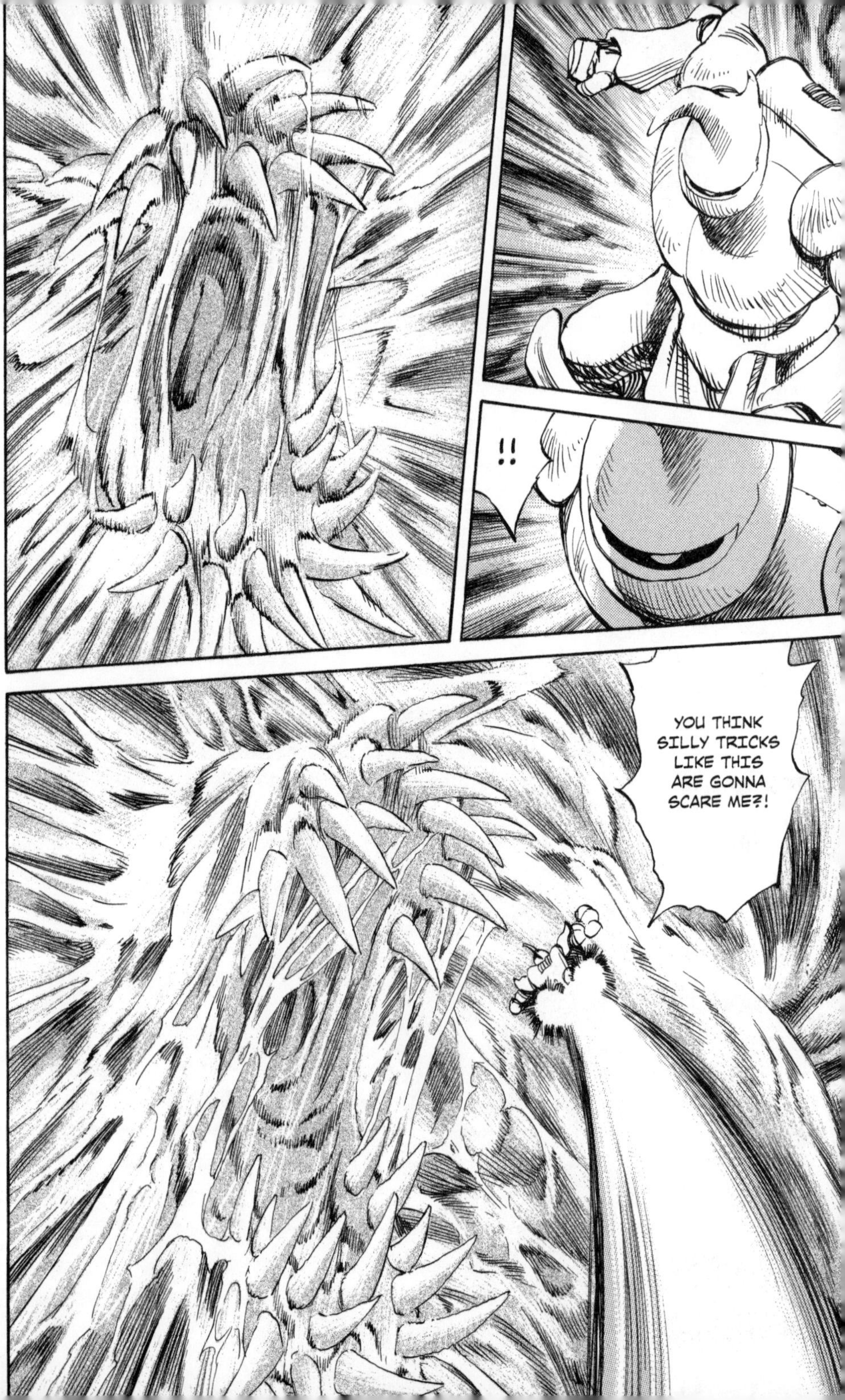
!!
YOU THINK SILLY TRICKS LIKE THIS ARE GONNA SCARE ME?!

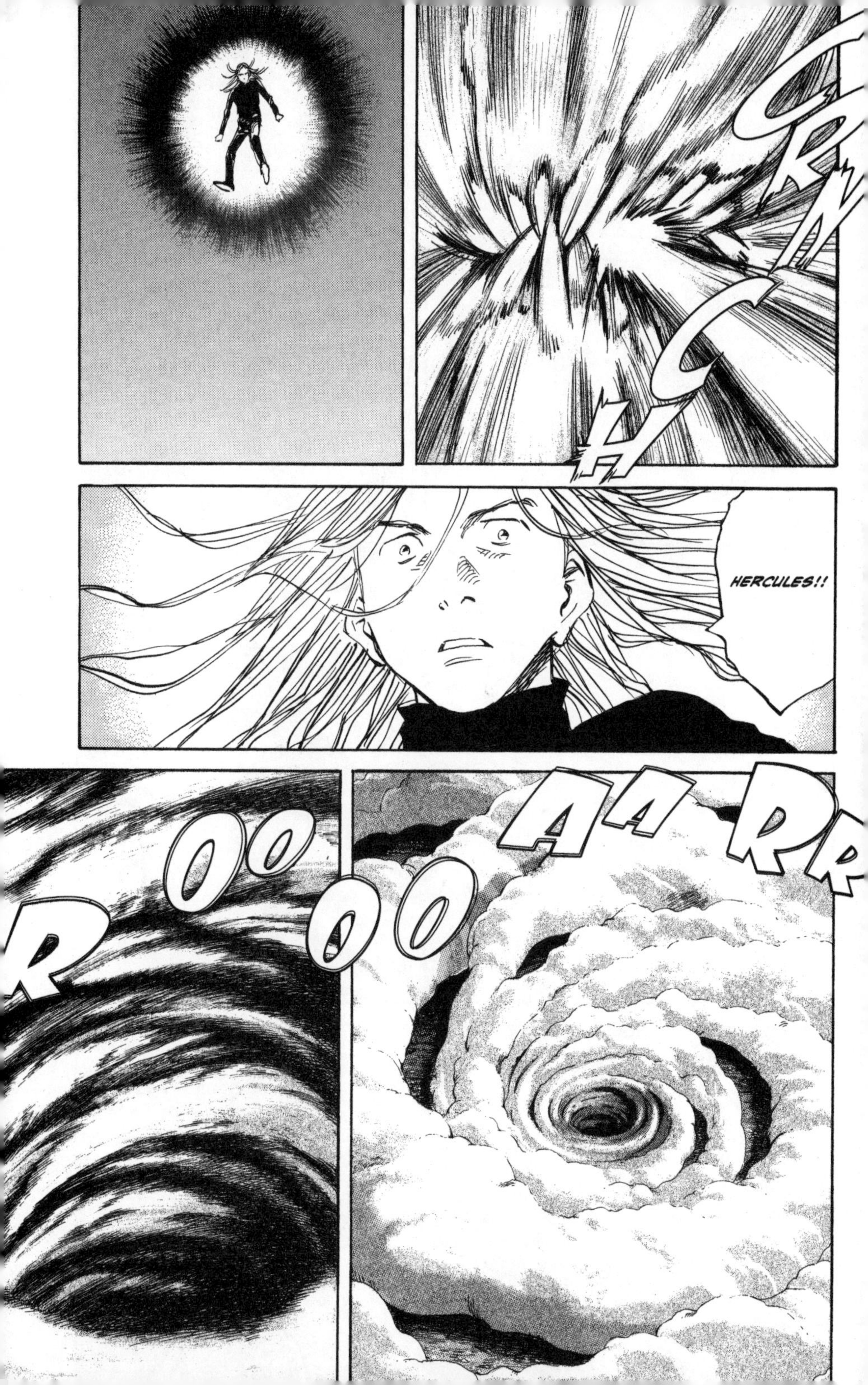
CRRNCH
HERCULES!!
ROOOOAARR

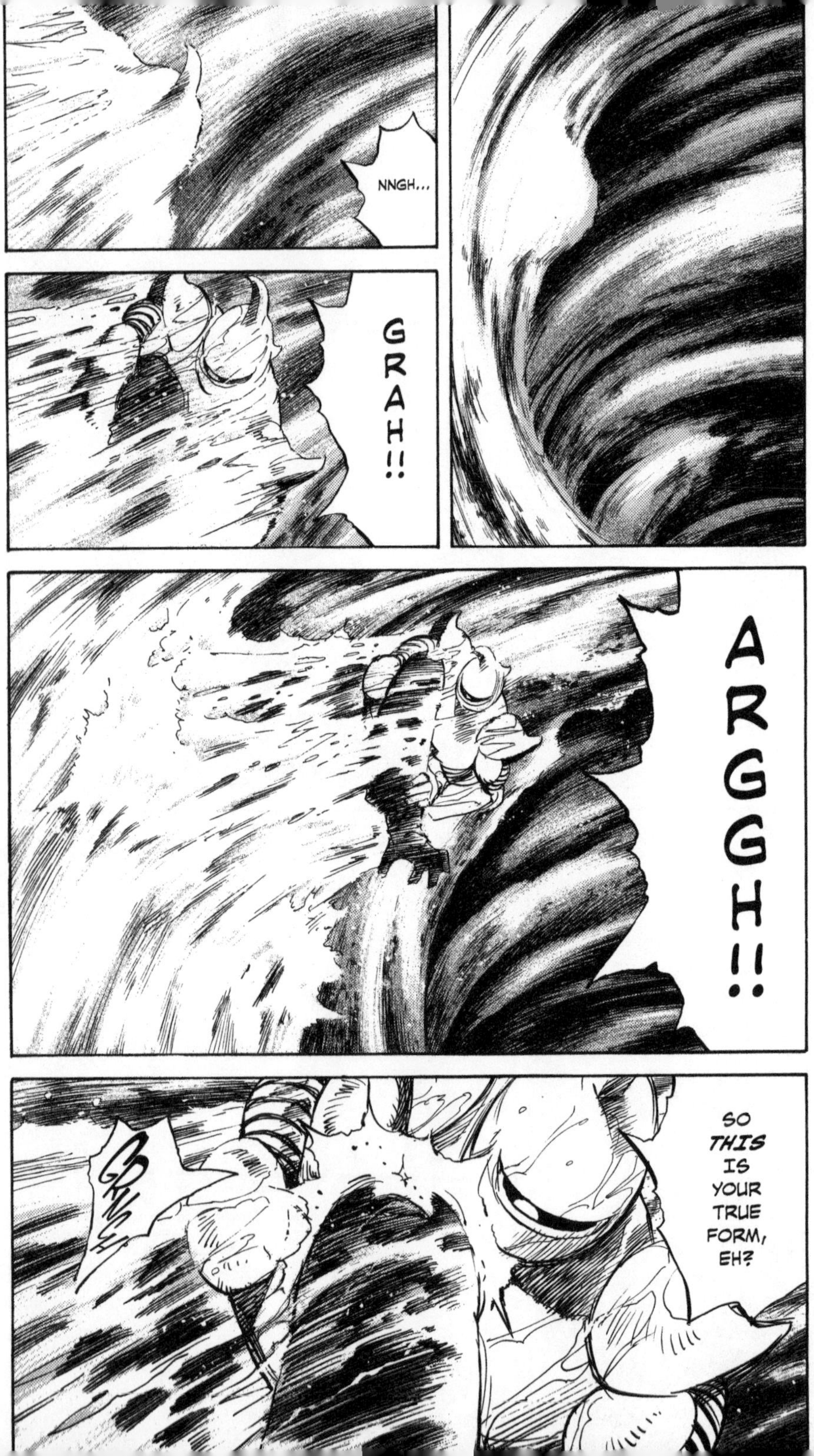
NNGH...
GRAH!!
ARGGH!!
SO *THIS* IS YOUR TRUE FORM, EH?

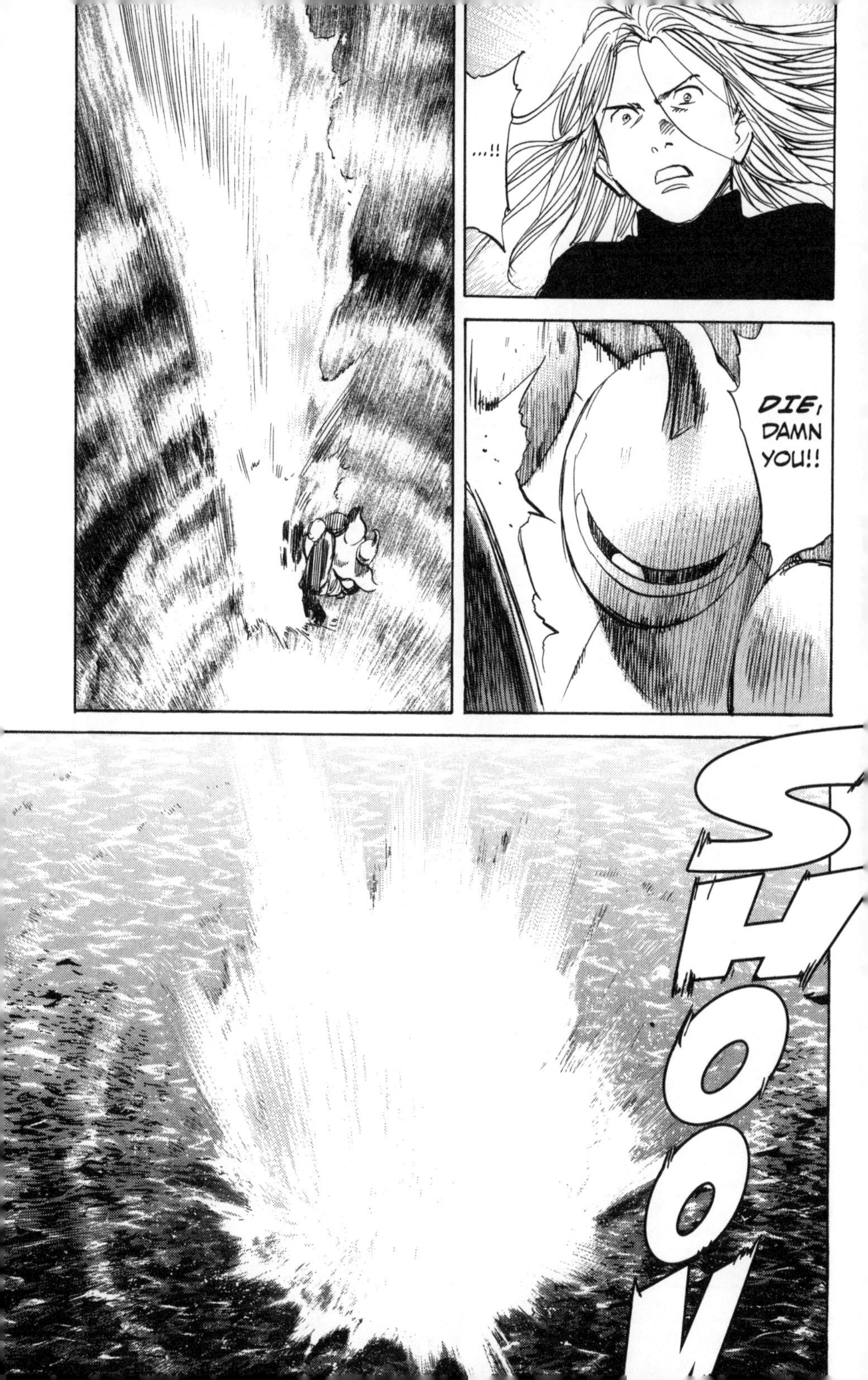
...!!
DIE, DAMN YOU!!
SHOOO

I HEREBY DECLARE THE 99TH MILITARY TRIBUNAL TO BE IN SESSION.

THE DEFENDANT SHALL NOW TAKE THE OATH.

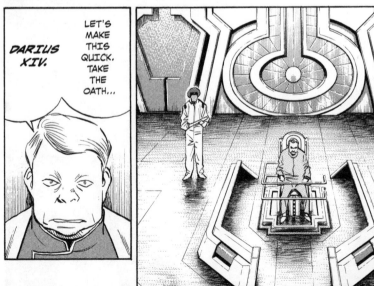

LET'S MAKE THIS QUICK. TAKE THE OATH...

*DARIUS XIV.*

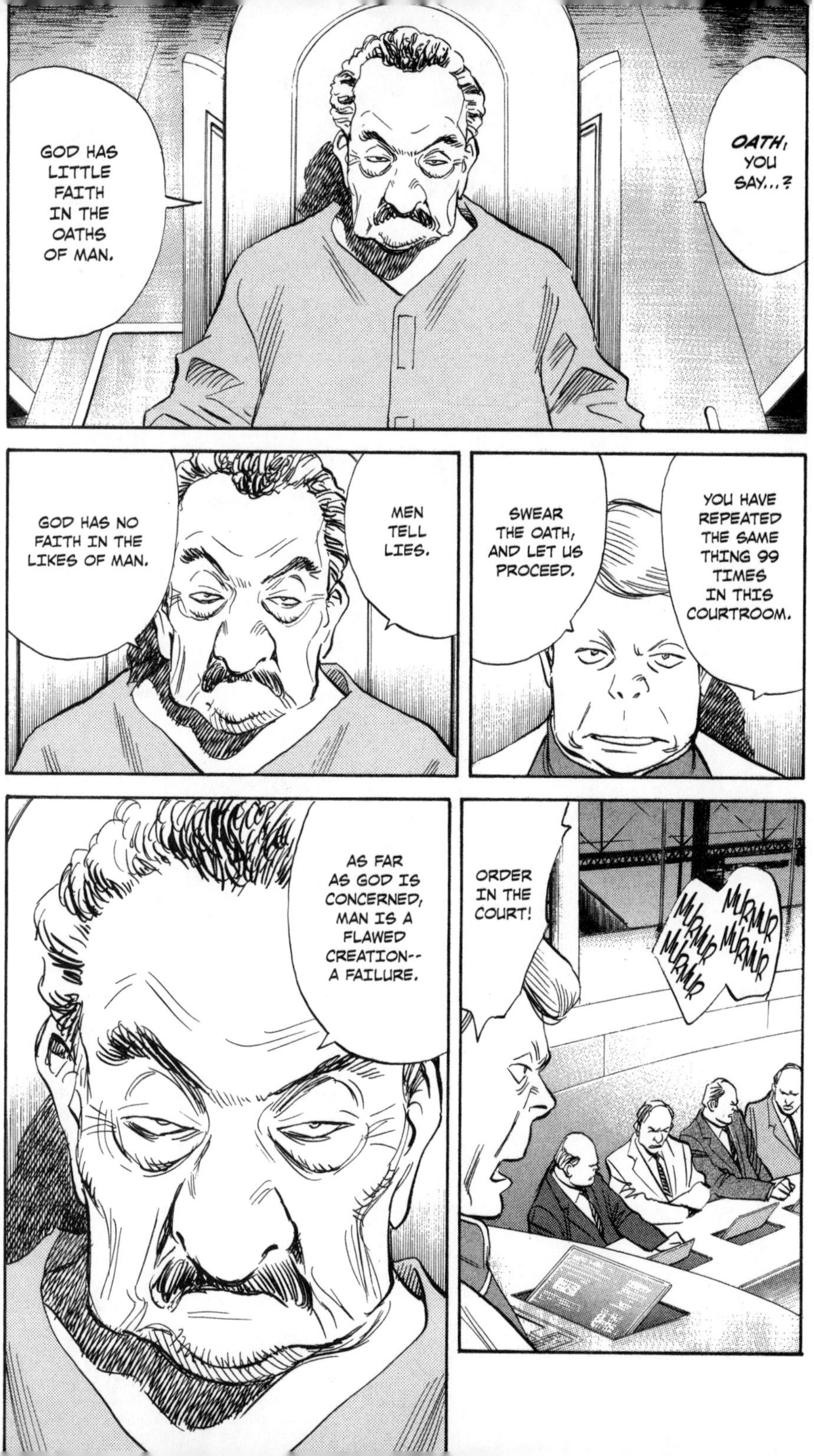
OATH, YOU SAY...?
GOD HAS LITTLE FAITH IN THE OATHS OF MAN.
YOU HAVE REPEATED THE SAME THING 99 TIMES IN THIS COURTROOM.
SWEAR THE OATH, AND LET US PROCEED.
MEN TELL LIES.
GOD HAS NO FAITH IN THE LIKES OF MAN.
MURMUR MURMUR
MURMUR MURMUR
ORDER IN THE COURT!
AS FAR AS GOD IS CONCERNED, MAN IS A FLAWED CREATION-- A FAILURE.

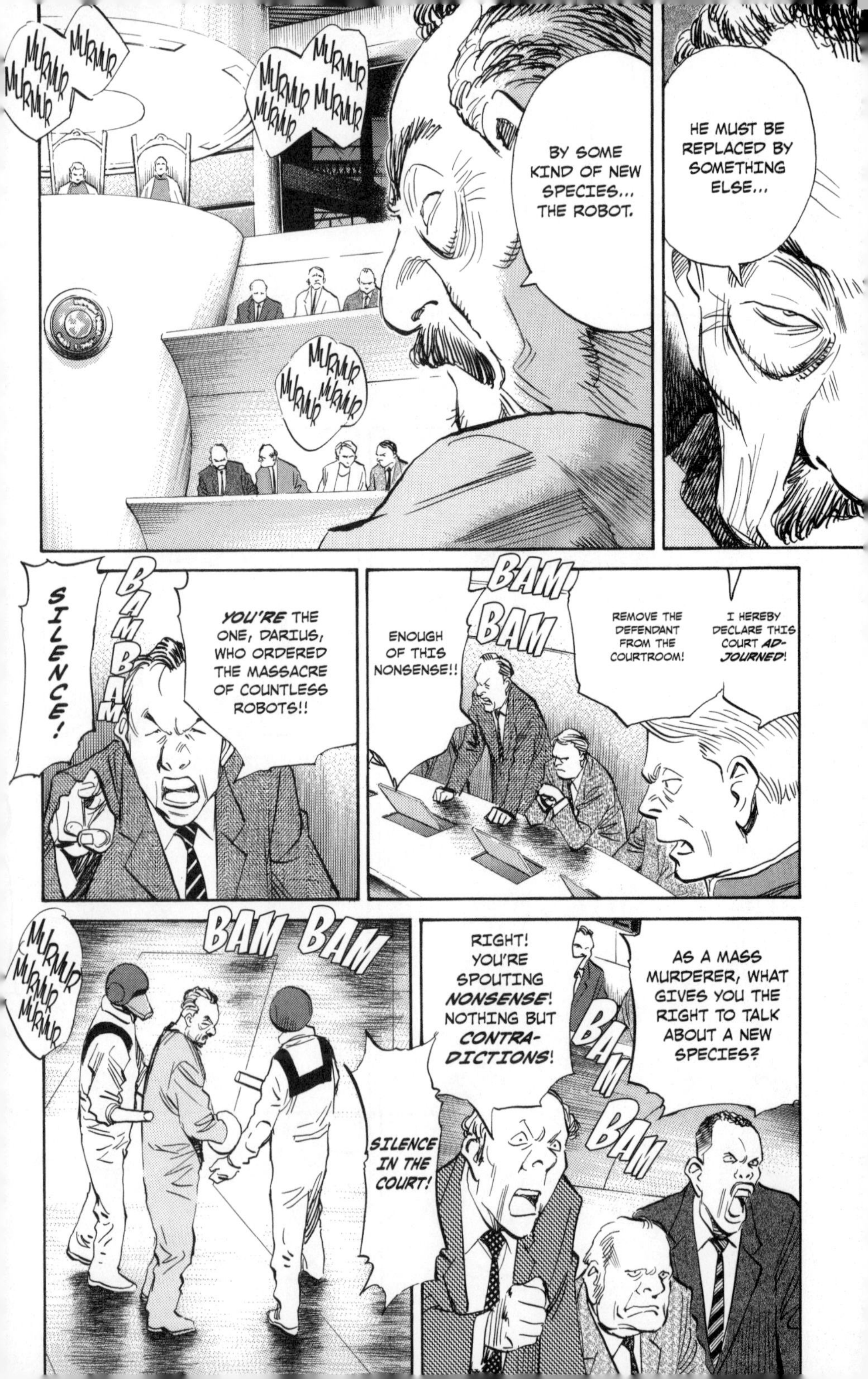
HE MUST BE REPLACED BY SOMETHING ELSE...
BY SOME KIND OF NEW SPECIES... THE ROBOT.
MURMUR MURMUR MURMUR
MURMUR MURMUR MURMUR
MURMUR MURMUR MURMUR
I HEREBY DECLARE THIS COURT *ADJOURNED*!
REMOVE THE DEFENDANT FROM THE COURTROOM!
BAM BAM
ENOUGH OF THIS NONSENSE!!
*YOU'RE* THE ONE, DARIUS, WHO ORDERED THE MASSACRE OF COUNTLESS ROBOTS!!
BAM BAM
SILENCE!
AS A MASS MURDERER, WHAT GIVES YOU THE RIGHT TO TALK ABOUT A NEW SPECIES?
BAM BAM
RIGHT! YOU'RE SPOUTING *NONSENSE*! NOTHING BUT *CONTRA-DICTIONS*!
BAM BAM
MURMUR MURMUR MURMUR
SILENCE IN THE COURT!

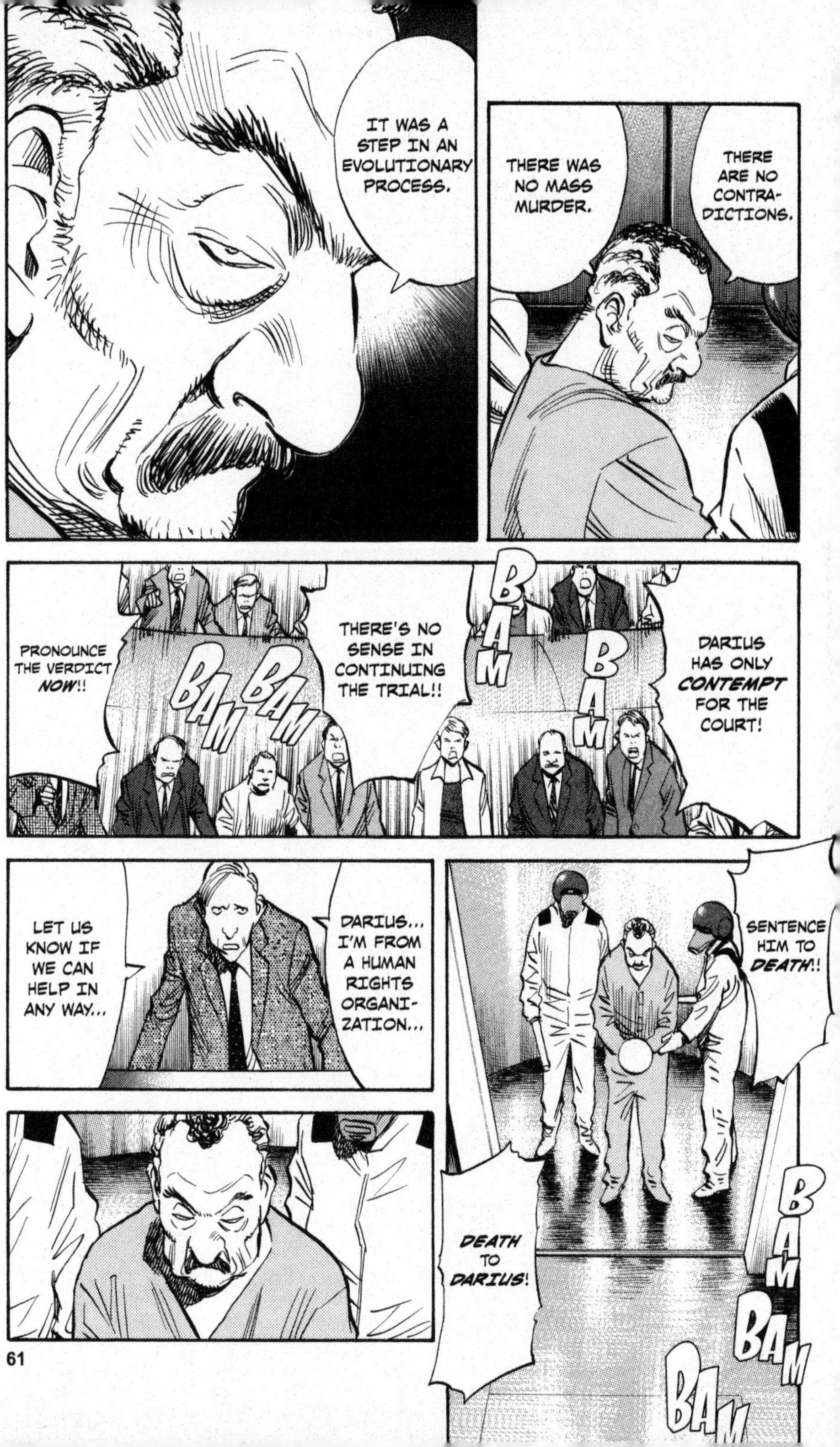
THERE ARE NO CONTRA-DICTIONS.
THERE WAS NO MASS MURDER.
IT WAS A STEP IN AN EVOLUTIONARY PROCESS.
DARIUS HAS ONLY *CONTEMPT* FOR THE COURT!
BAM
BAM
THERE'S NO SENSE IN CONTINUING THE TRIAL!!
BAM
BAM
PRONOUNCE THE VERDICT *NOW*!!
SENTENCE HIM TO *DEATH*!!
BAM
BAM
BAM
BAM
*DEATH* TO *DARIUS*!
DARIUS... I'M FROM A HUMAN RIGHTS ORGANI-ZATION...
LET US KNOW IF WE CAN HELP IN ANY WAY...

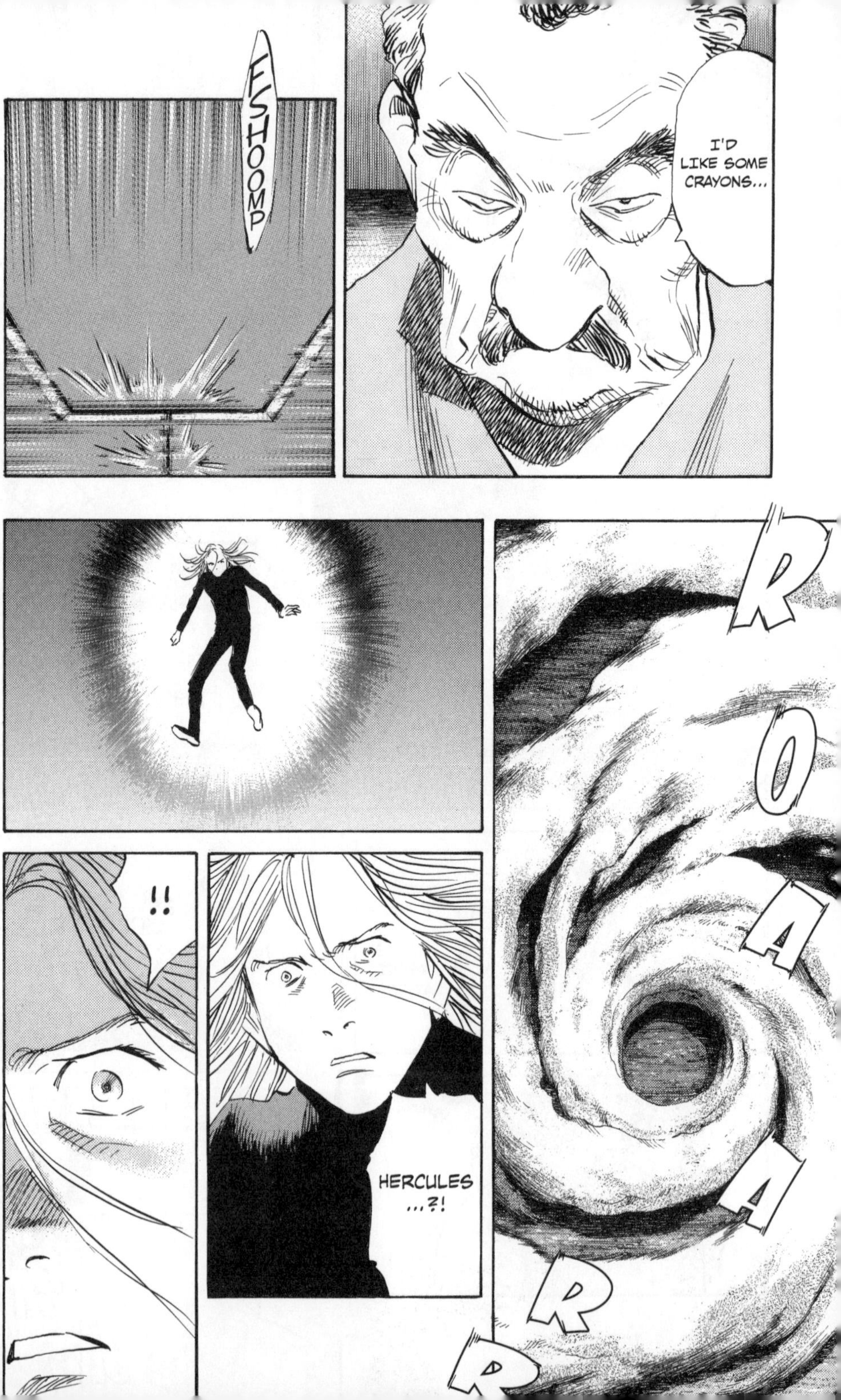
I'D LIKE SOME CRAYONS...
FSHOOOMP
ROAARR
HERCULES ...?!
!!

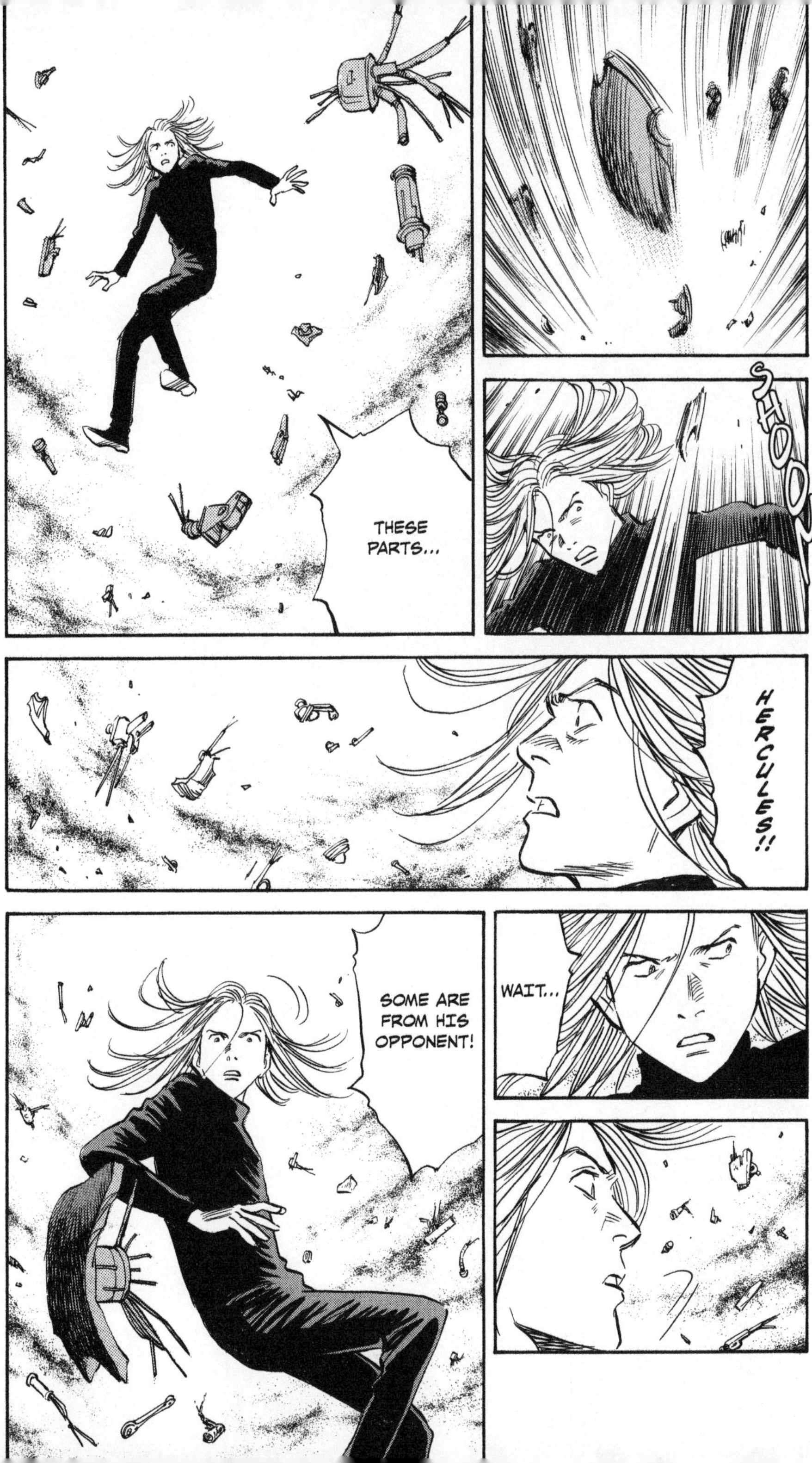
SHOOM
THESE PARTS...
HERCULES!!
WAIT...
SOME ARE FROM HIS OPPONENT!

GASP

COULD THEY HAVE DESTROYED EACH OTHER?

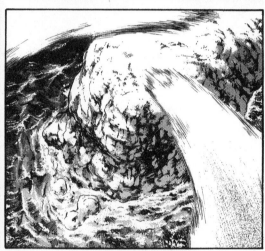

TWITCH

THERE'S HIS DAILY-LIFE BODY...

64

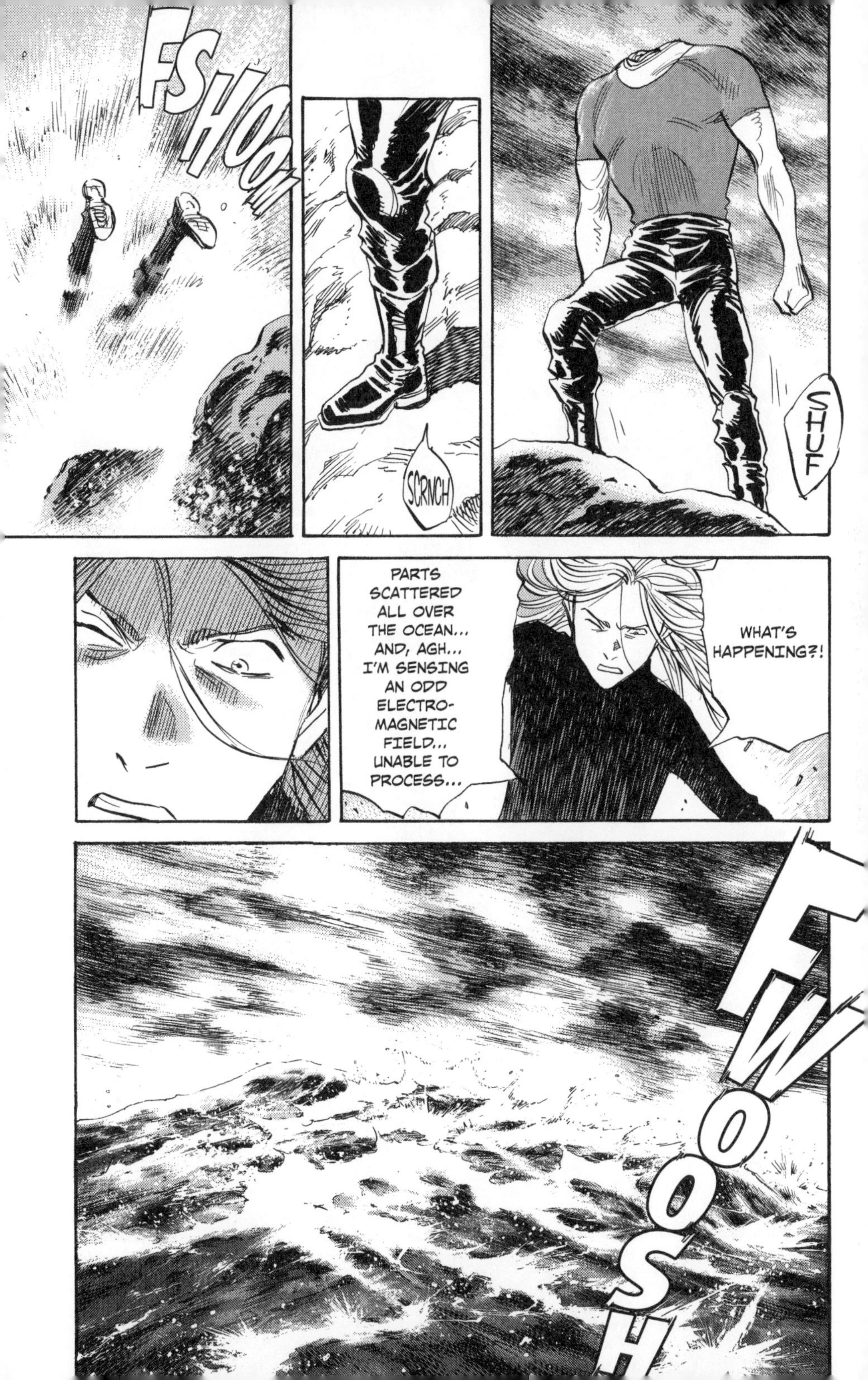
SHUF
SCRNCH
FSHOOM
WHAT'S HAPPENING?!
PARTS SCATTERED ALL OVER THE OCEAN... AND, AGH... I'M SENSING AN ODD ELECTRO-MAGNETIC FIELD... UNABLE TO PROCESS...
FWOOSH

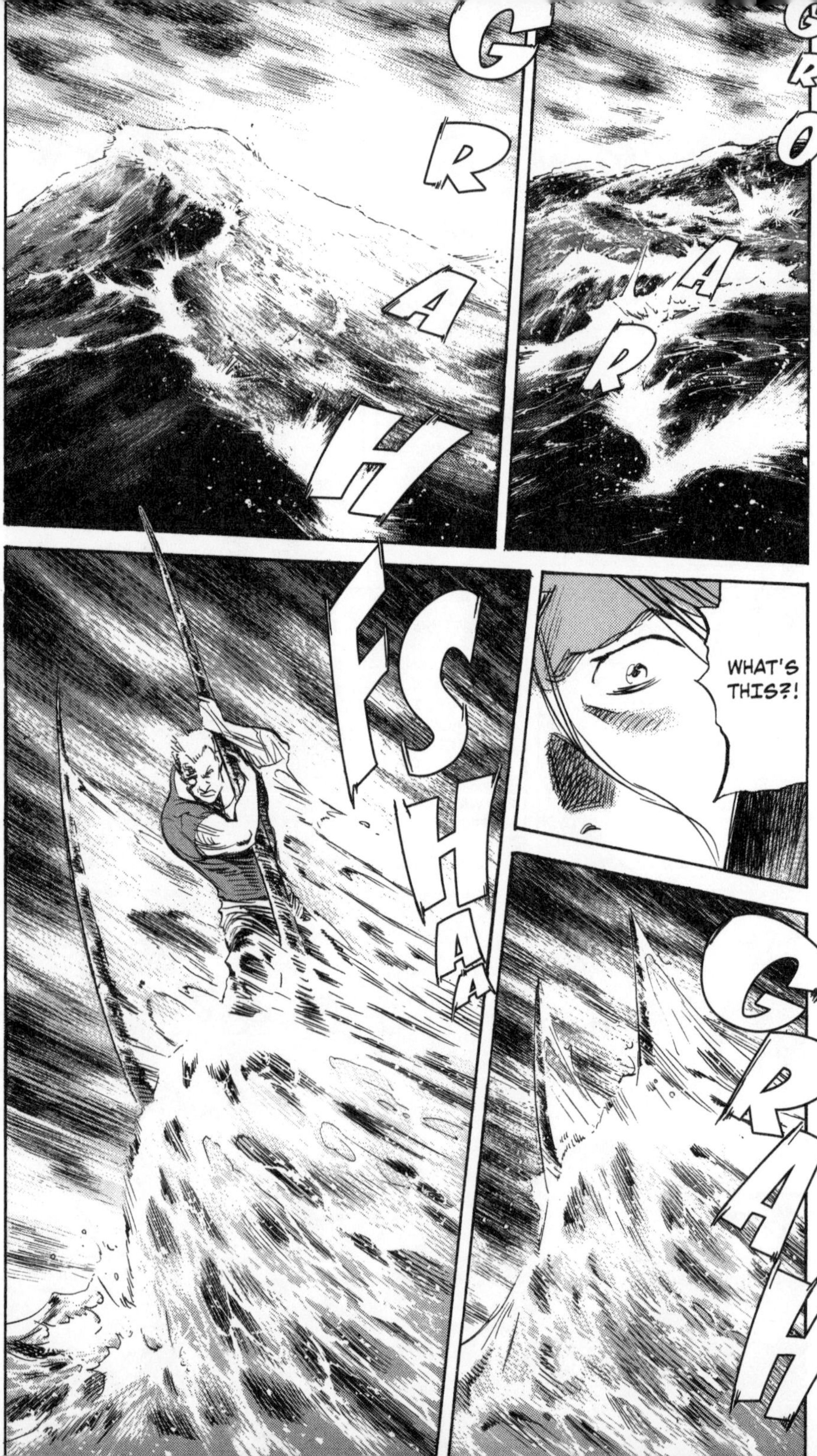
GROAR
GRAH
WHAT'S THIS?!
GRAH
FSHAA

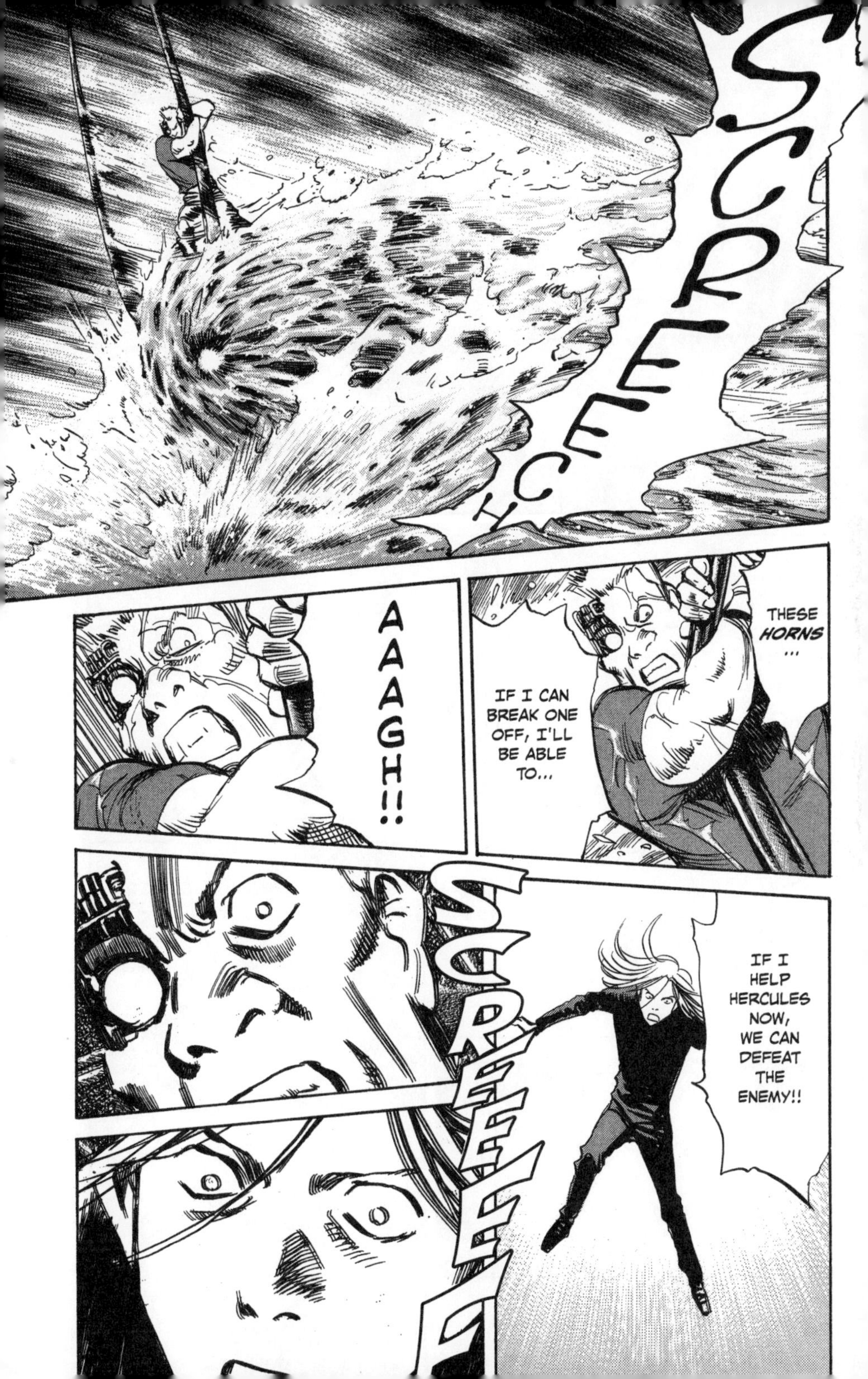
SCREEECH
THESE *HORNS* ...
IF I CAN BREAK ONE OFF, I'LL BE ABLE TO...
AAAAGH!!
IF I HELP HERCULES NOW, WE CAN DEFEAT THE ENEMY!!
SCREEEEEE

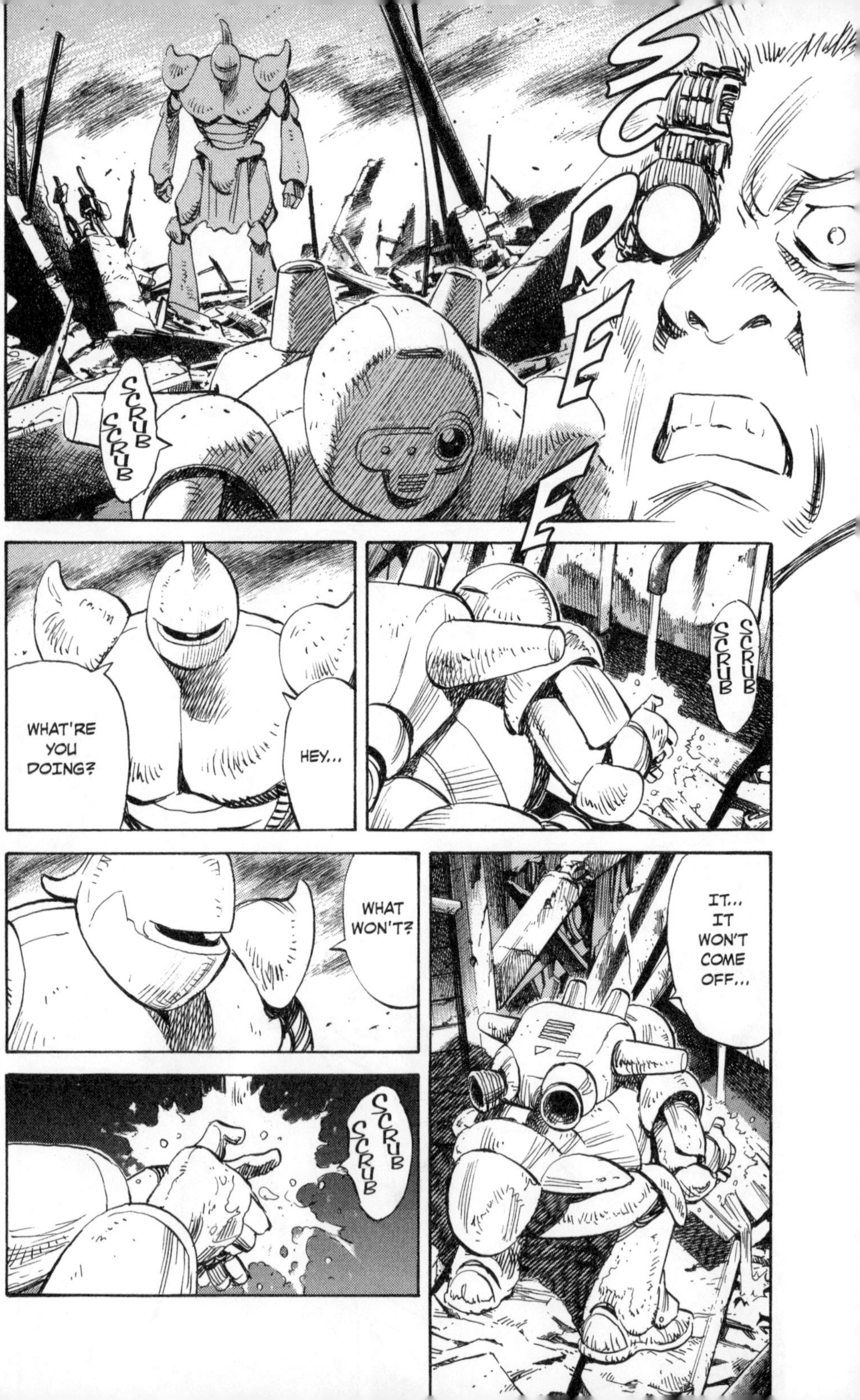
SCREEE
SCRUB SCRUB
SCRUB SCRUB
HEY...
WHAT'RE YOU DOING?
IT... IT WON'T COME OFF...
WHAT WON'T?
SCRUB SCRUB

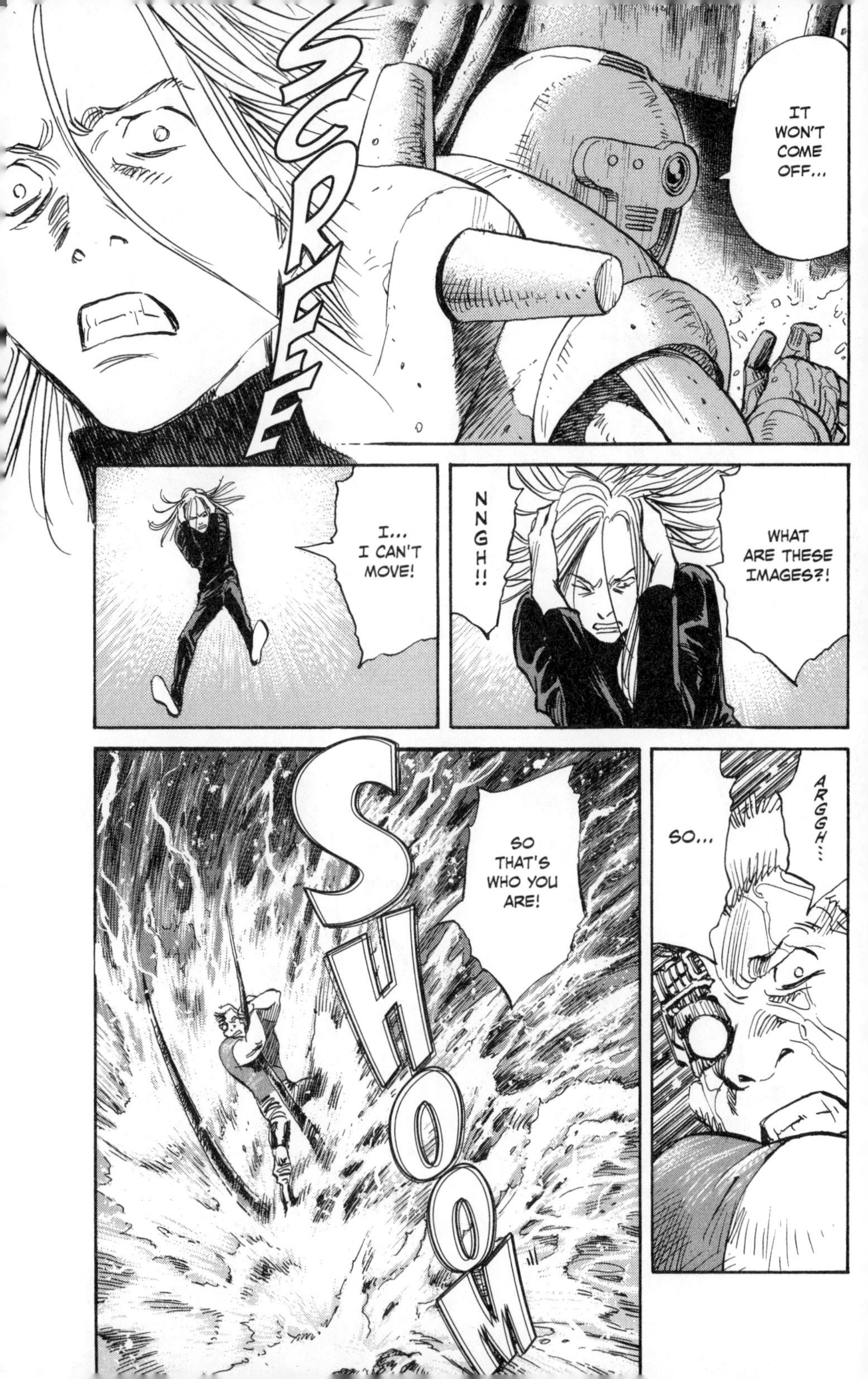
IT WON'T COME OFF...
SCREEE
WHAT ARE THESE IMAGES?!
NNGH!!
I... I CAN'T MOVE!
ARGGH...
SO...
SO THAT'S WHO YOU ARE!
SHOOOM

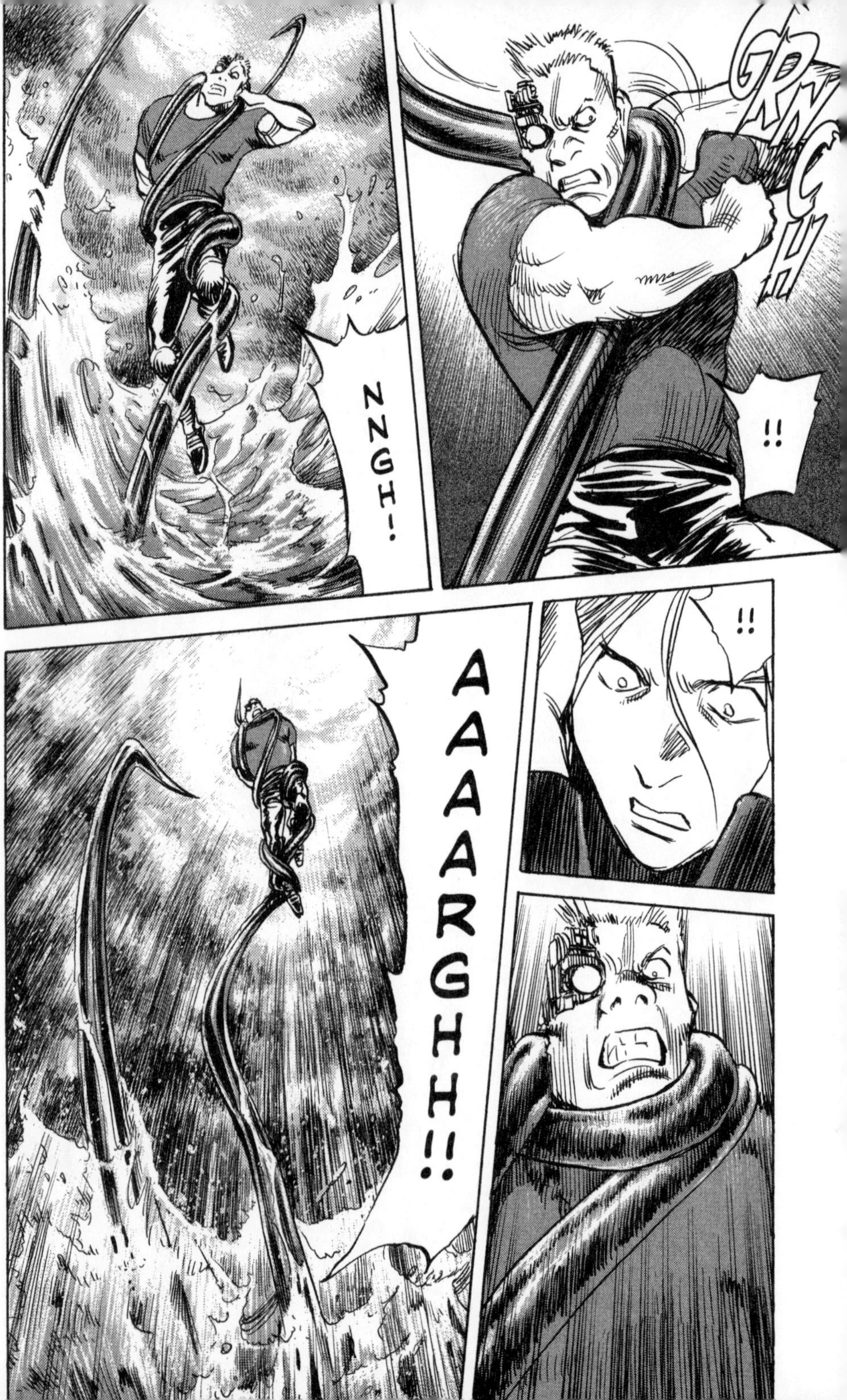
GRNCH
!!
NNGH!
!!
AAAARGHH!!

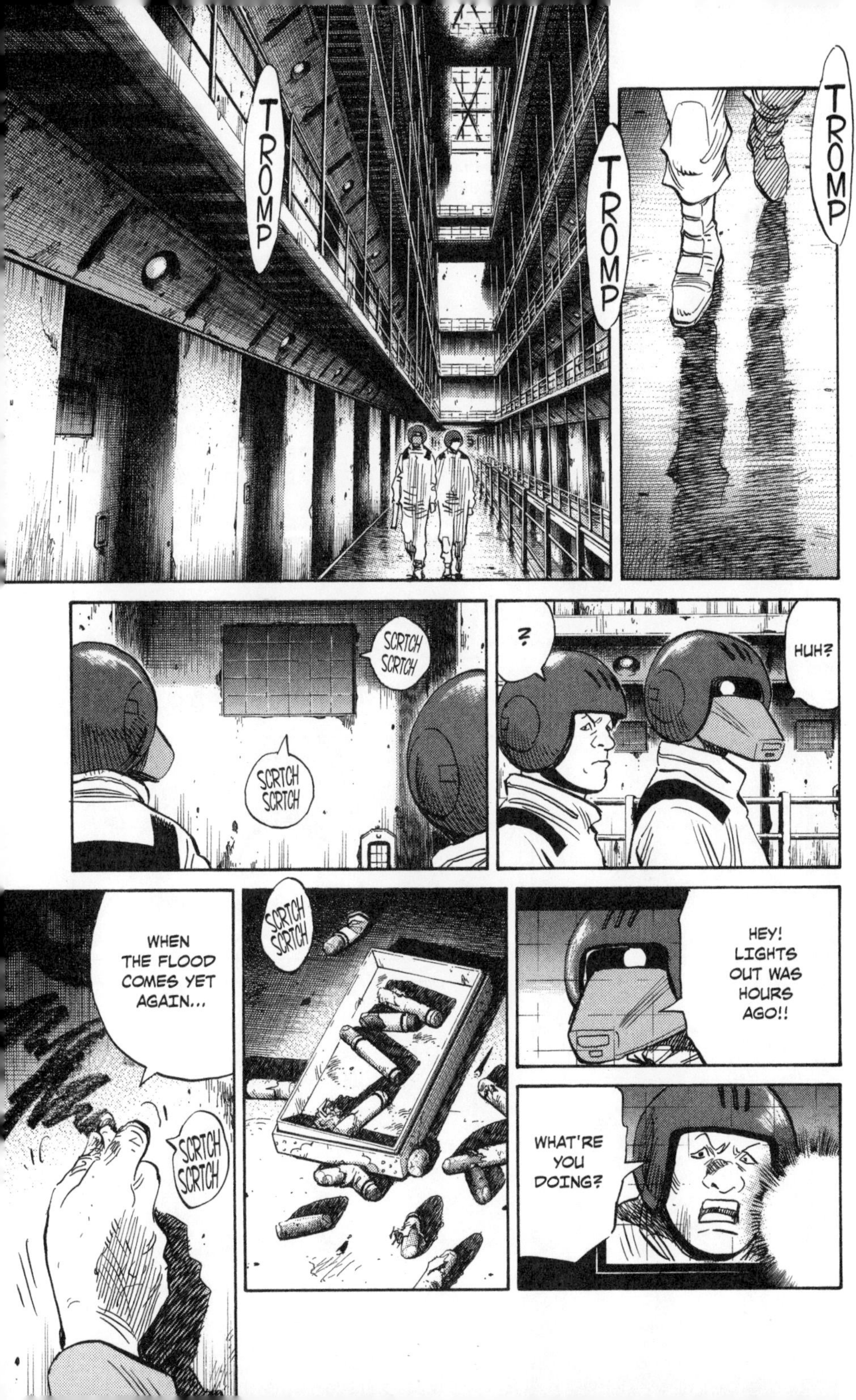
TROMP
TROMP
TROMP
HUH?
?
SCRTCH SCRTCH
SCRTCH SCRTCH
HEY! LIGHTS OUT WAS HOURS AGO!!
WHAT'RE YOU DOING?
SCRTCH SCRTCH
WHEN THE FLOOD COMES YET AGAIN...
SCRTCH SCRTCH

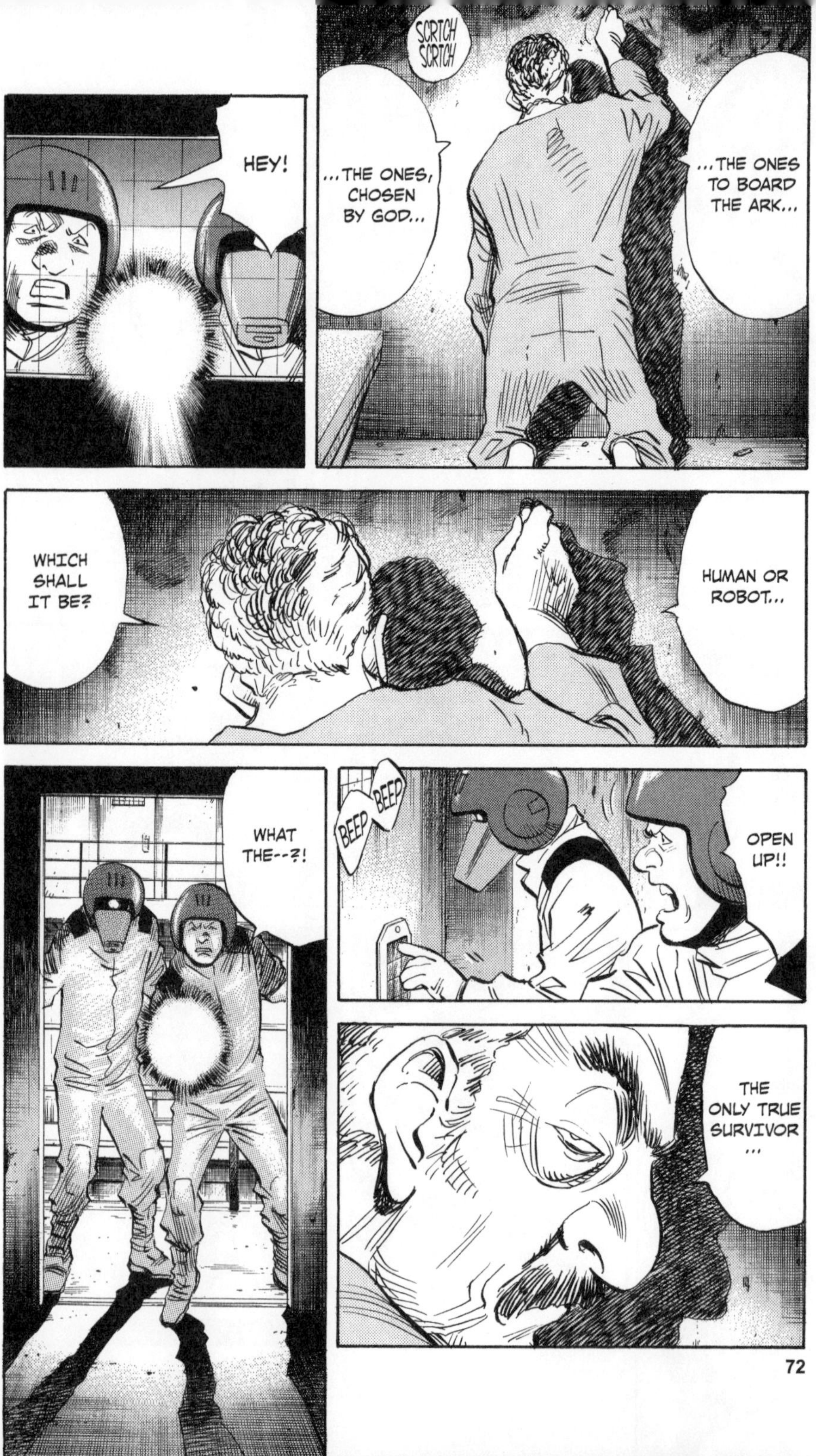

SCRTCH SCRTCH
...THE ONES TO BOARD THE ARK...
...THE ONES, CHOSEN BY GOD...
HEY!
HUMAN OR ROBOT...
WHICH SHALL IT BE?
BEEP BEEP
OPEN UP!!
THE ONLY TRUE SURVIVOR ...
WHAT THE--?!

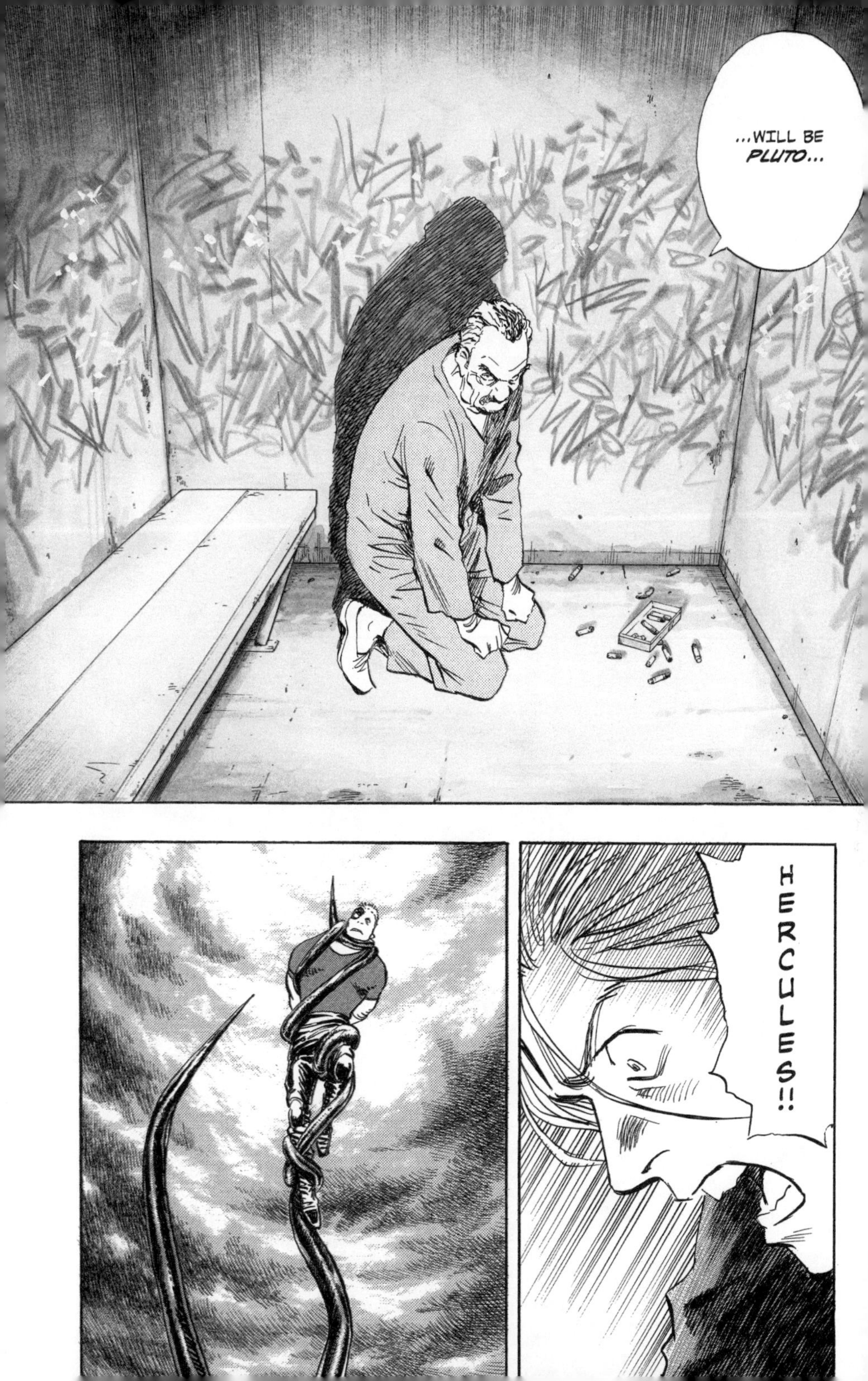
...WILL BE PLUTO...
HERCULES!!

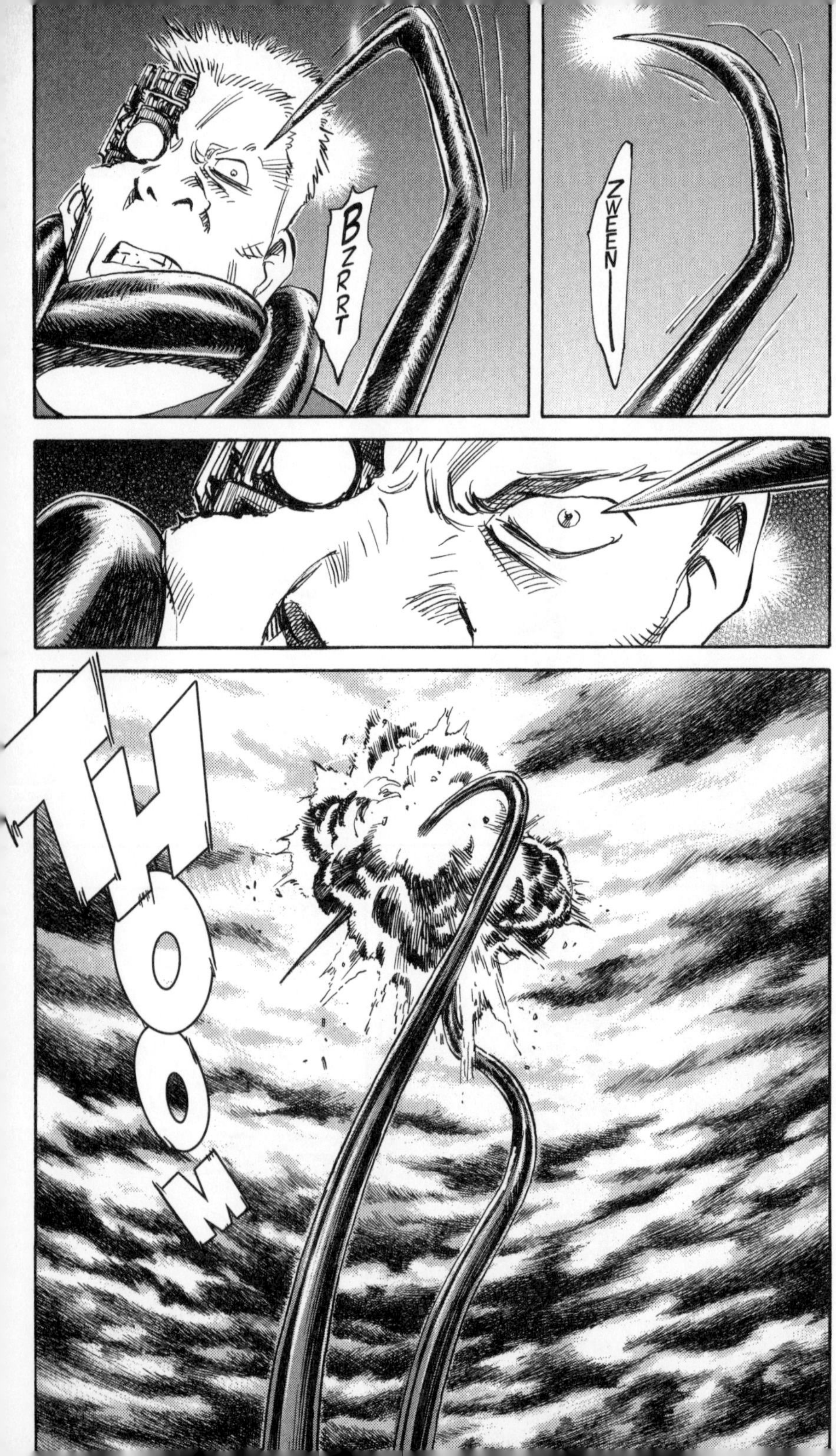
ZWEEN
BZRRT
THOOOM

# Act 35 GESICHT, DO YOU COPY?

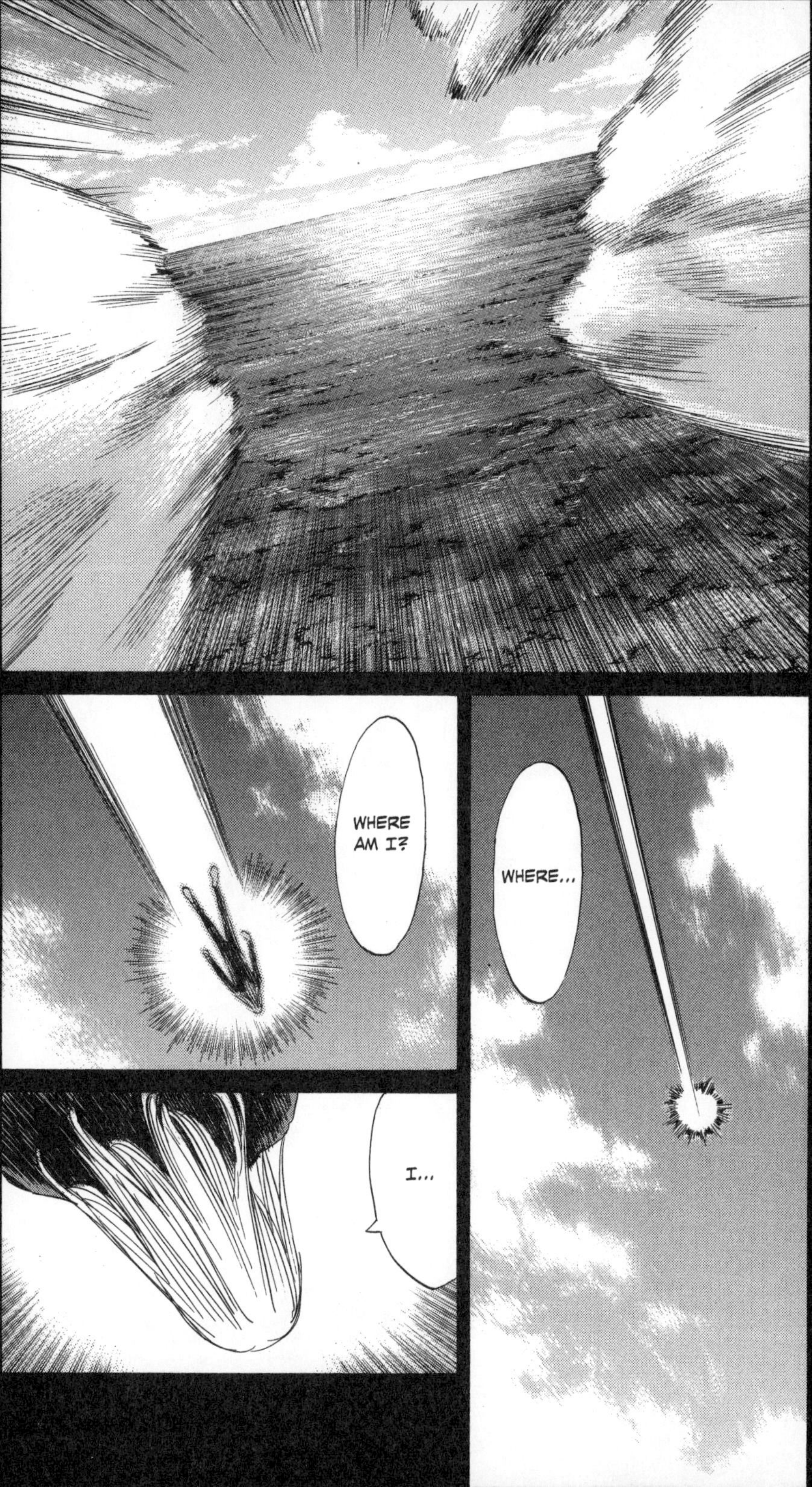
WHERE...
WHERE AM I?
I...

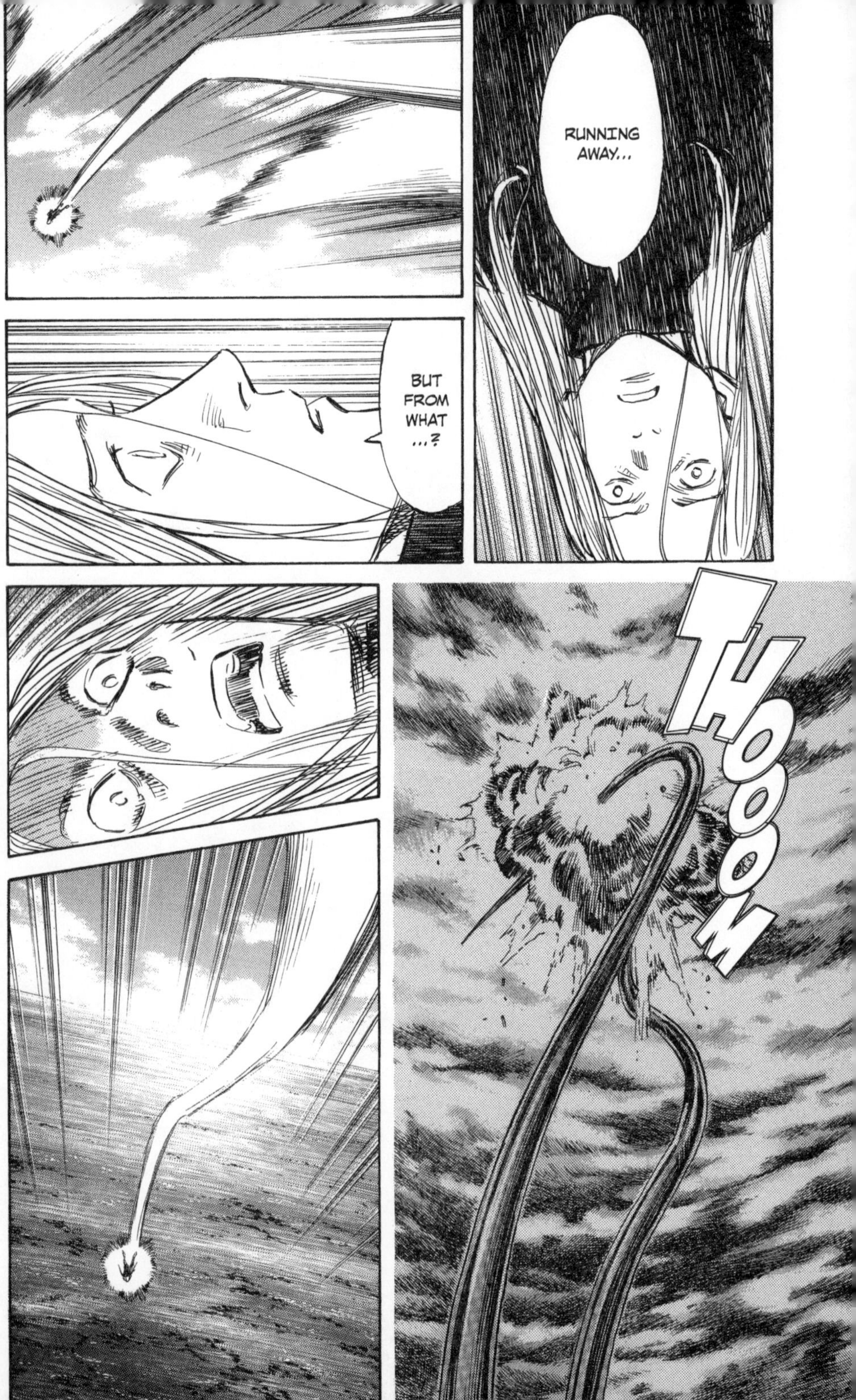
RUNNING AWAY...
BUT FROM WHAT ...?
THOOOM

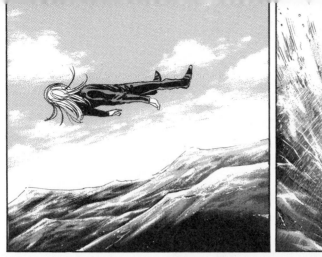

HERCULES IS *DEAD*!

Act 35
GESICHT,
DO YOU COPY?

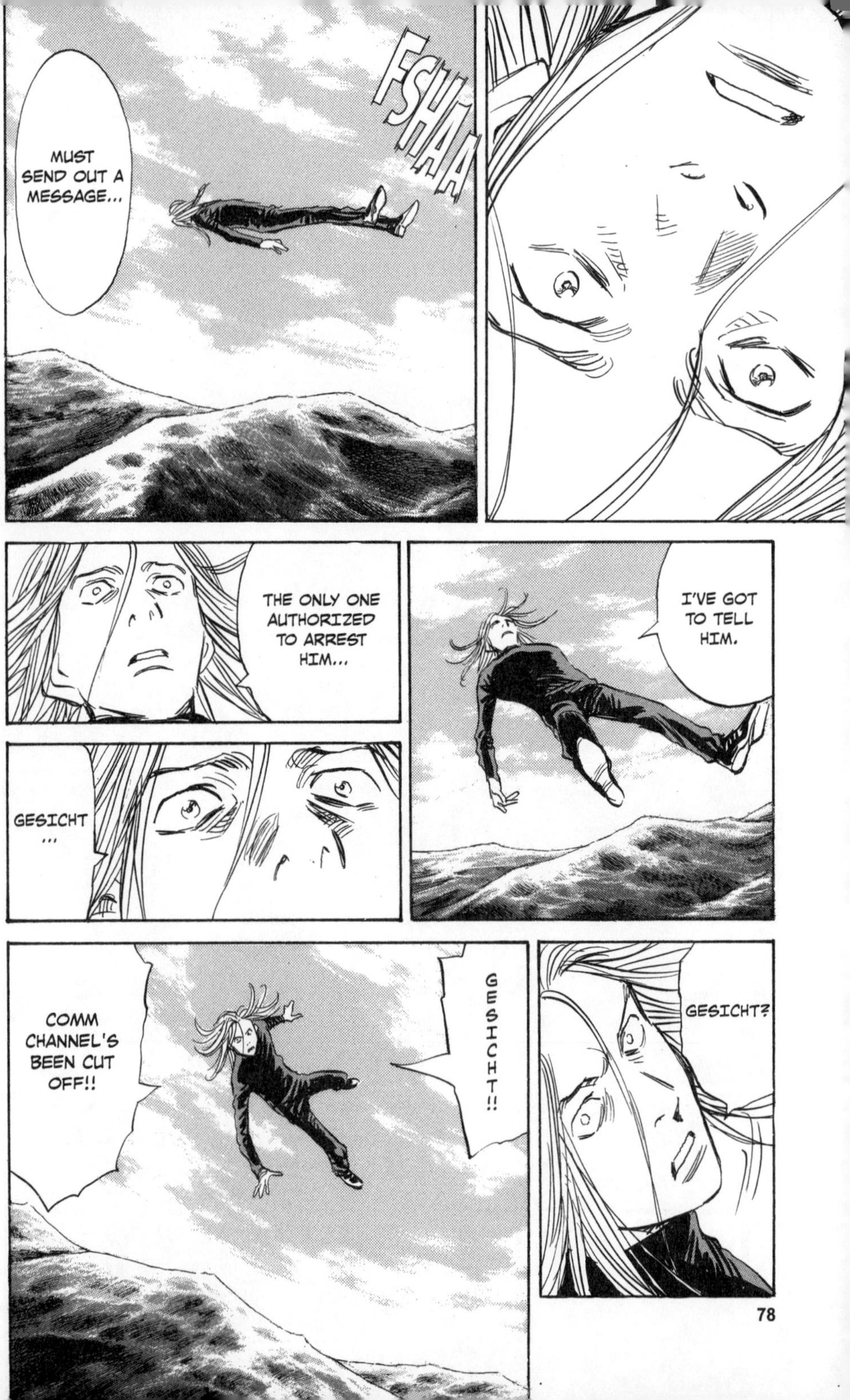
FSHAA
MUST SEND OUT A MESSAGE...
I'VE GOT TO TELL HIM.
THE ONLY ONE AUTHORIZED TO ARREST HIM...
GESICHT ...
GESICHT?
GESICHT!!
COMM CHANNEL'S BEEN CUT OFF!!

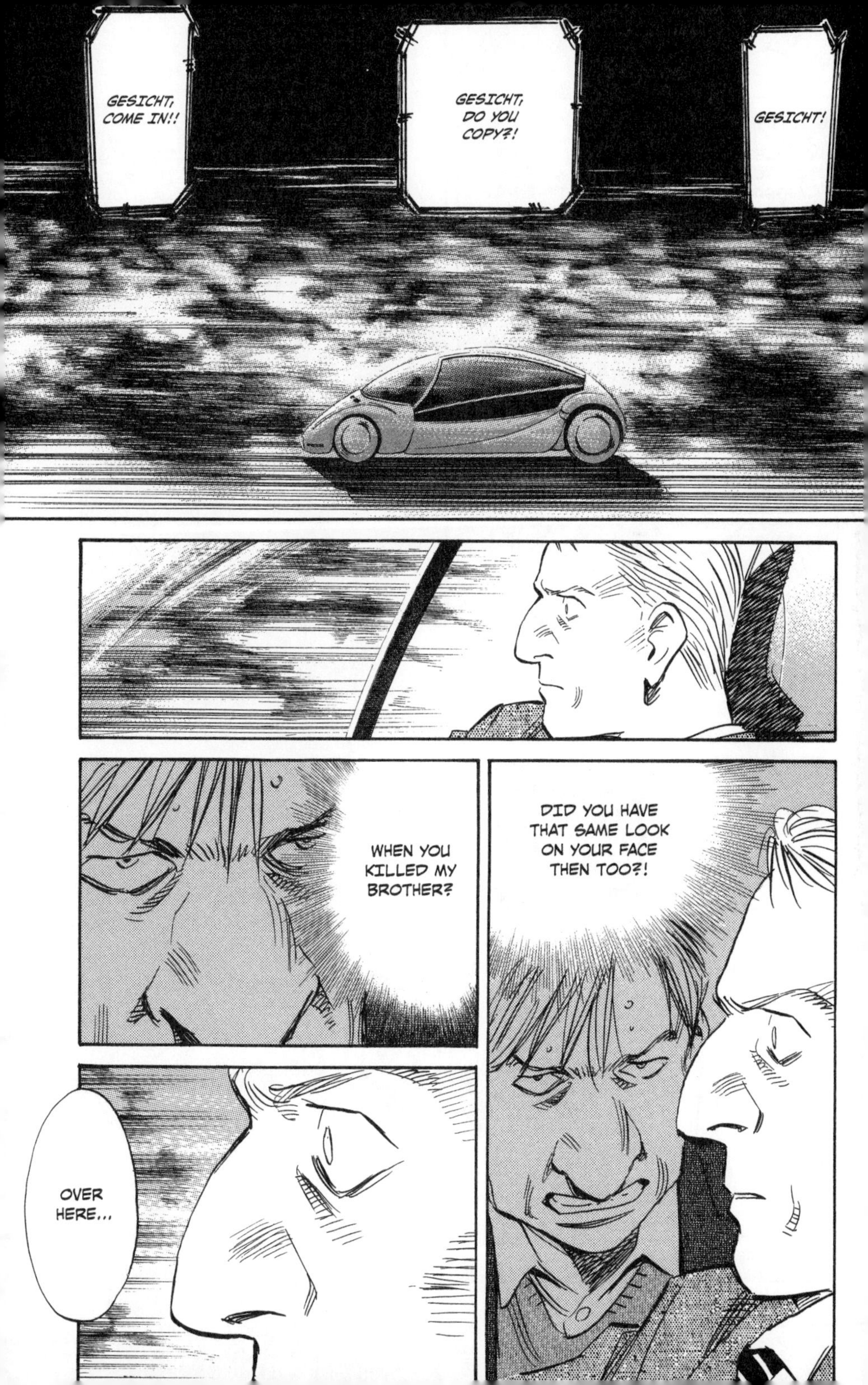
GESICHT!
GESICHT, DO YOU COPY?!
GESICHT, COME IN!!
DID YOU HAVE THAT SAME LOOK ON YOUR FACE THEN TOO?!
WHEN YOU KILLED MY BROTHER?
OVER HERE...

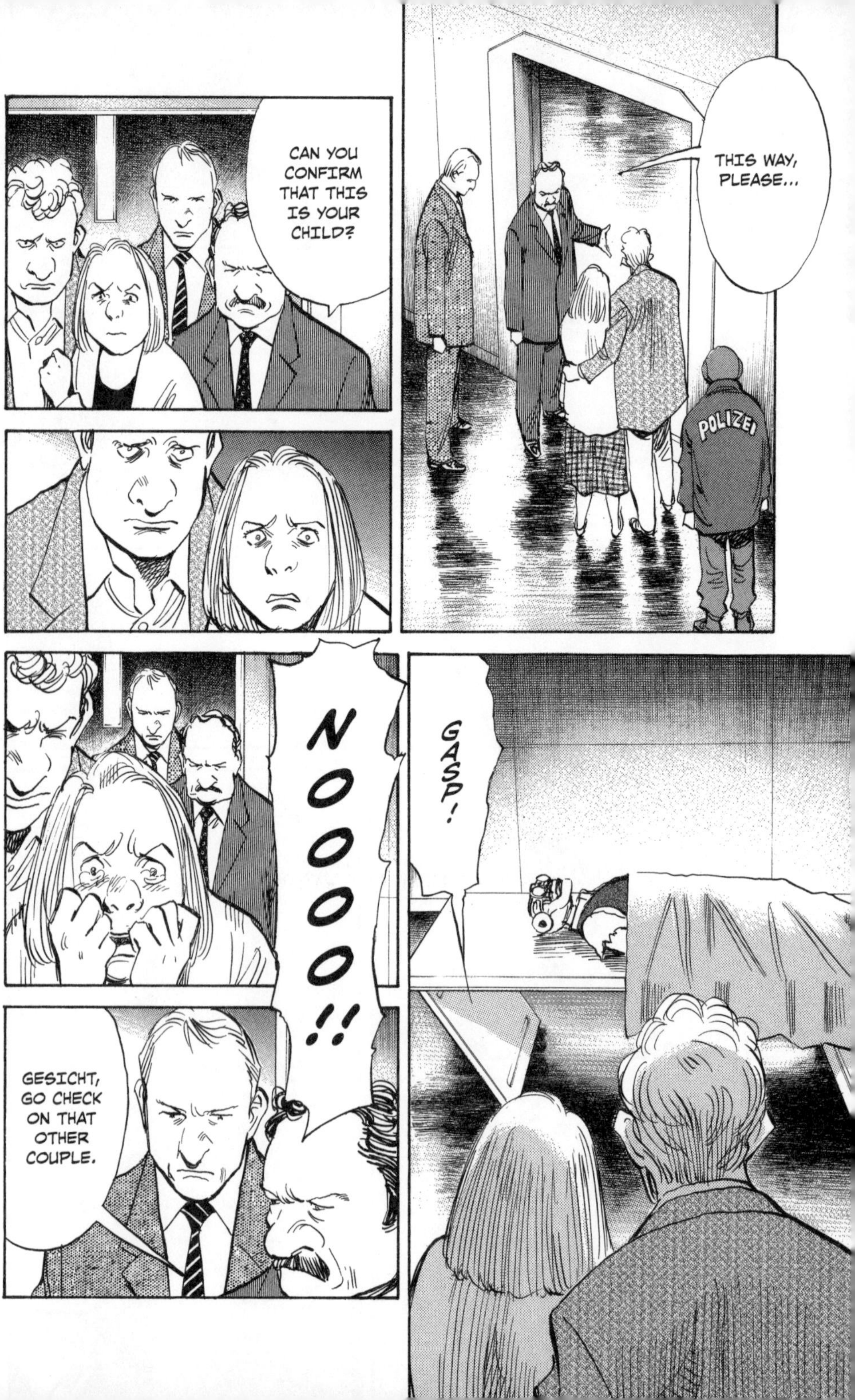
THIS WAY, PLEASE...
POLIZEI
CAN YOU CONFIRM THAT THIS IS YOUR CHILD?
GASP!
NOOOOO!!
GESICHT, GO CHECK ON THAT OTHER COUPLE.

KLAK

NOOO!!

KLAK

KLAK

YES, THAT'S OUR CHILD.

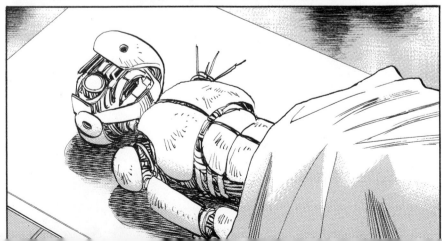

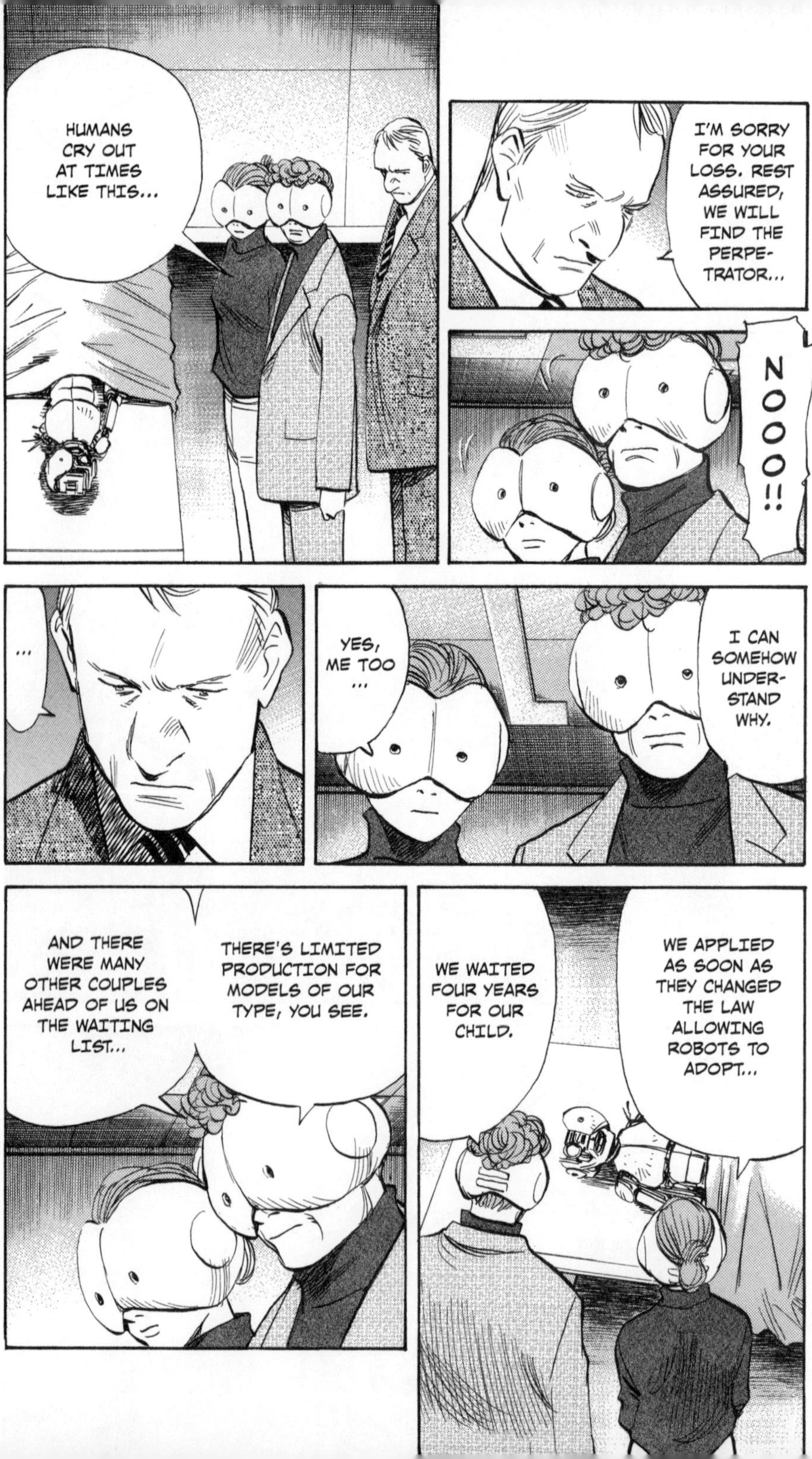
I'M SORRY FOR YOUR LOSS. REST ASSURED, WE WILL FIND THE PERPETRATOR...
NOOO!!
HUMANS CRY OUT AT TIMES LIKE THIS...
I CAN SOMEHOW UNDERSTAND WHY.
YES, ME TOO ...
...
WE APPLIED AS SOON AS THEY CHANGED THE LAW ALLOWING ROBOTS TO ADOPT...
WE WAITED FOUR YEARS FOR OUR CHILD.
THERE'S LIMITED PRODUCTION FOR MODELS OF OUR TYPE, YOU SEE.
AND THERE WERE MANY OTHER COUPLES AHEAD OF US ON THE WAITING LIST...

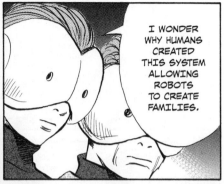

I WONDER WHY HUMANS CREATED THIS SYSTEM ALLOWING ROBOTS TO CREATE FAMILIES.
IF IT WEREN'T FOR THIS SYSTEM...
...WE WOULDN'T BE HAVING THESE FEELINGS RIGHT NOW.
MY NAME IS GESICHT, AND I'VE BEEN ASKED TO JOIN THE INVESTIGATION STARTING TODAY.

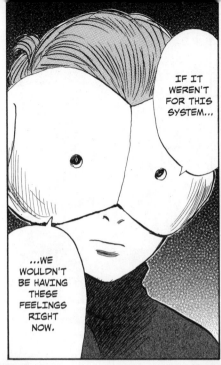

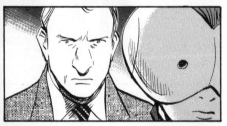

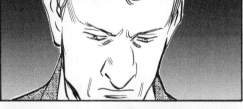

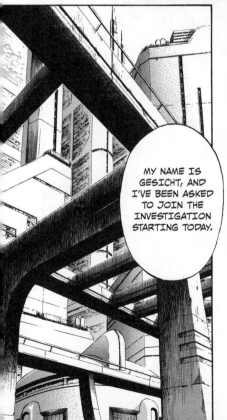

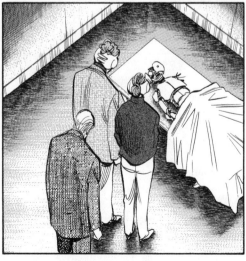

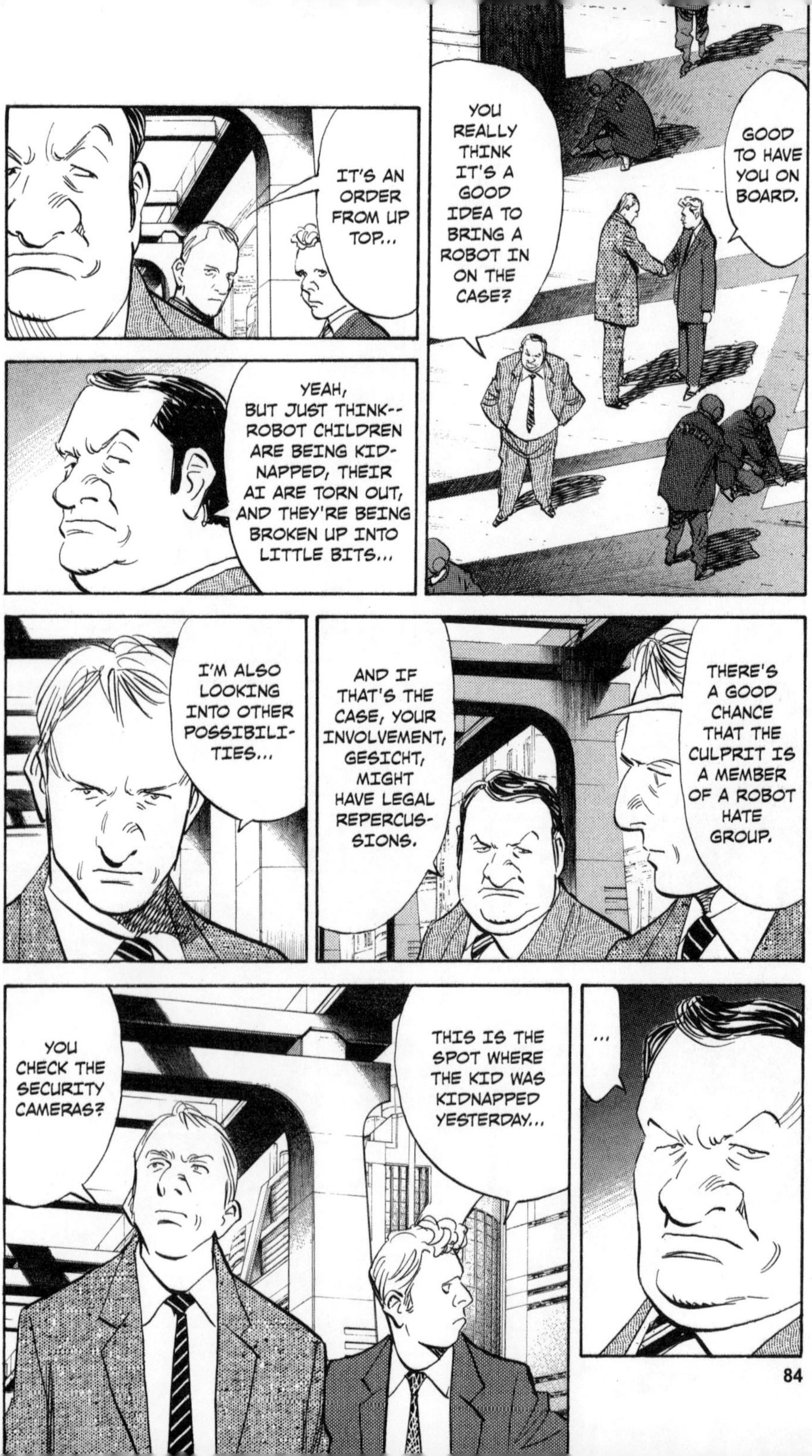
GOOD TO HAVE YOU ON BOARD.
YOU REALLY THINK IT'S A GOOD IDEA TO BRING A ROBOT IN ON THE CASE?
IT'S AN ORDER FROM UP TOP...
YEAH, BUT JUST THINK-- ROBOT CHILDREN ARE BEING KID-NAPPED, THEIR AI ARE TORN OUT, AND THEY'RE BEING BROKEN UP INTO LITTLE BITS...
THERE'S A GOOD CHANCE THAT THE CULPRIT IS A MEMBER OF A ROBOT HATE GROUP.
AND IF THAT'S THE CASE, YOUR INVOLVEMENT, GESICHT, MIGHT HAVE LEGAL REPERCUS-SIONS.
I'M ALSO LOOKING INTO OTHER POSSIBILI-TIES...
...
THIS IS THE SPOT WHERE THE KID WAS KIDNAPPED YESTERDAY...
YOU CHECK THE SECURITY CAMERAS?

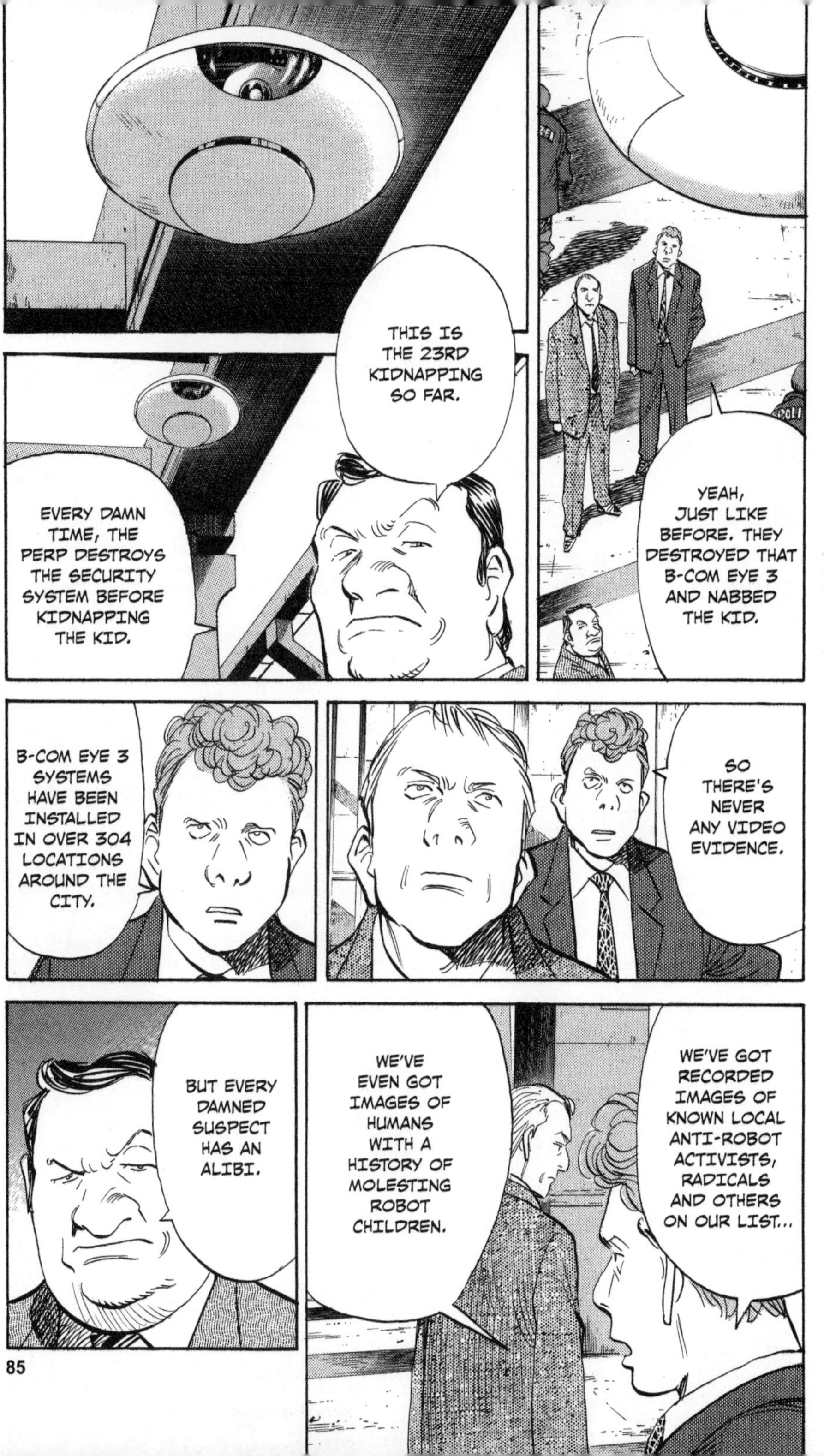
YEAH, JUST LIKE BEFORE. THEY DESTROYED THAT B-COM EYE 3 AND NABBED THE KID.
THIS IS THE 23RD KIDNAPPING SO FAR.
EVERY DAMN TIME, THE PERP DESTROYS THE SECURITY SYSTEM BEFORE KIDNAPPING THE KID.
SO THERE'S NEVER ANY VIDEO EVIDENCE.
B-COM EYE 3 SYSTEMS HAVE BEEN INSTALLED IN OVER 304 LOCATIONS AROUND THE CITY.
WE'VE GOT RECORDED IMAGES OF KNOWN LOCAL ANTI-ROBOT ACTIVISTS, RADICALS AND OTHERS ON OUR LIST...
WE'VE EVEN GOT IMAGES OF HUMANS WITH A HISTORY OF MOLESTING ROBOT CHILDREN.
BUT EVERY DAMNED SUSPECT HAS AN ALIBI.

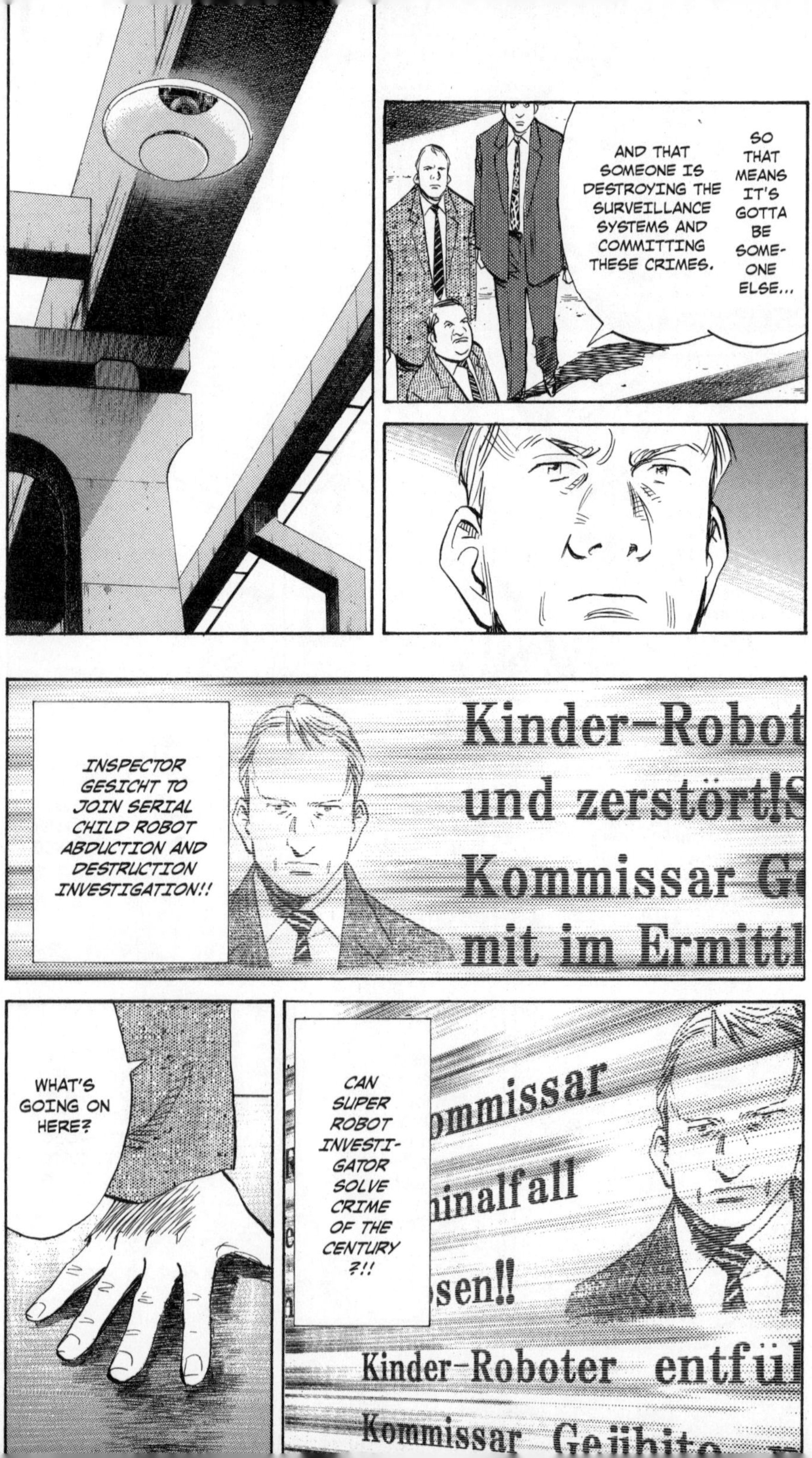
SO THAT MEANS IT'S GOTTA BE SOME-ONE ELSE...
AND THAT SOMEONE IS DESTROYING THE SURVEILLANCE SYSTEMS AND COMMITTING THESE CRIMES.
Kinder-Robot
und zerstört!S
Kommissar G
mit im Ermittl
INSPECTOR GESICHT TO JOIN SERIAL CHILD ROBOT ABDUCTION AND DESTRUCTION INVESTIGATION!!
ommissar
inalfall
osen!!
Kinder-Roboter entfü
CAN SUPER ROBOT INVESTI-GATOR SOLVE CRIME OF THE CENTURY ?!!
WHAT'S GOING ON HERE?

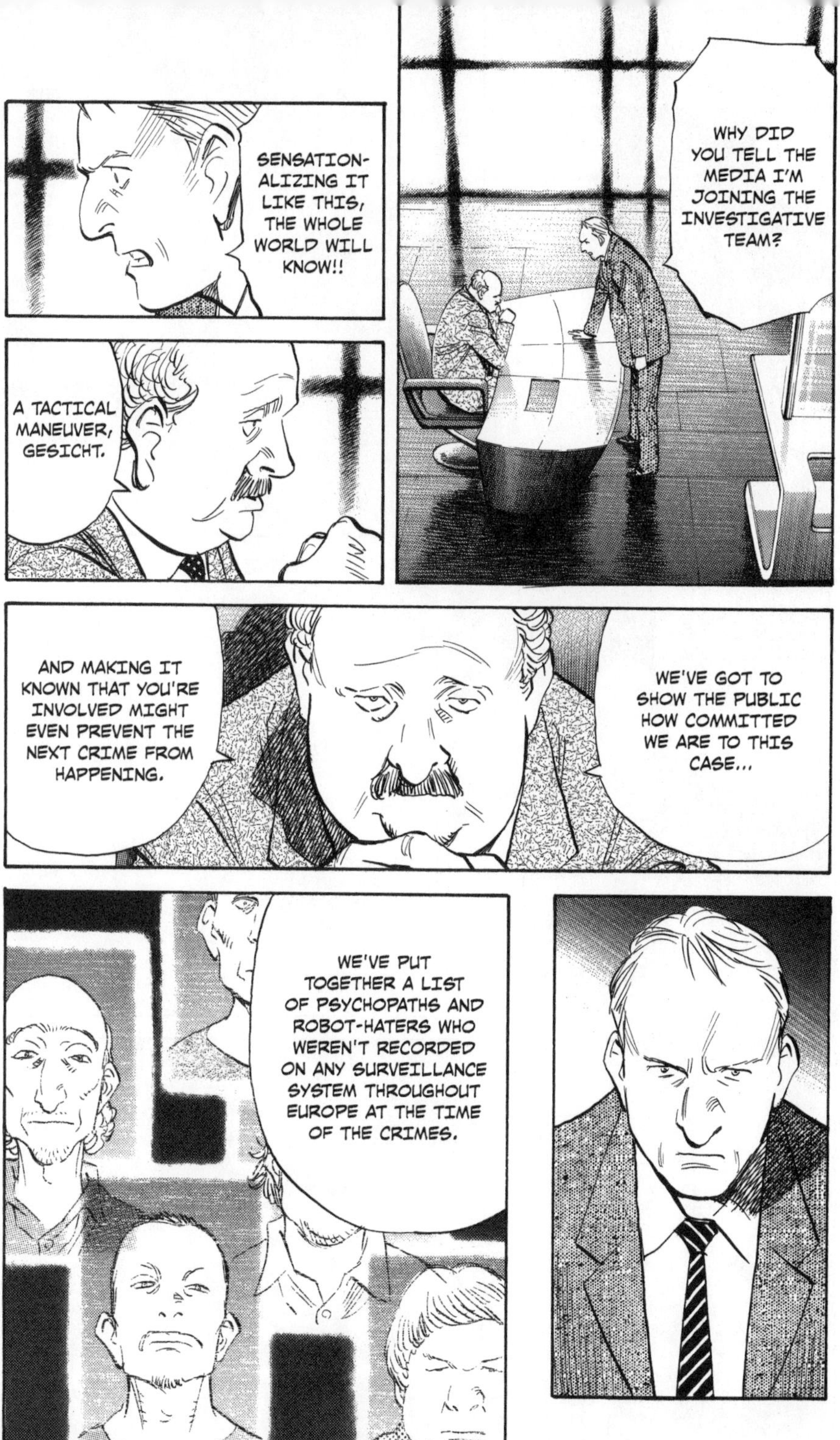
WHY DID YOU TELL THE MEDIA I'M JOINING THE INVESTIGATIVE TEAM?
SENSATION-ALIZING IT LIKE THIS, THE WHOLE WORLD WILL KNOW!!
A TACTICAL MANEUVER, GESICHT.
WE'VE GOT TO SHOW THE PUBLIC HOW COMMITTED WE ARE TO THIS CASE...
AND MAKING IT KNOWN THAT YOU'RE INVOLVED MIGHT EVEN PREVENT THE NEXT CRIME FROM HAPPENING.
WE'VE PUT TOGETHER A LIST OF PSYCHOPATHS AND ROBOT-HATERS WHO WEREN'T RECORDED ON ANY SURVEILLANCE SYSTEM THROUGHOUT EUROPE AT THE TIME OF THE CRIMES.

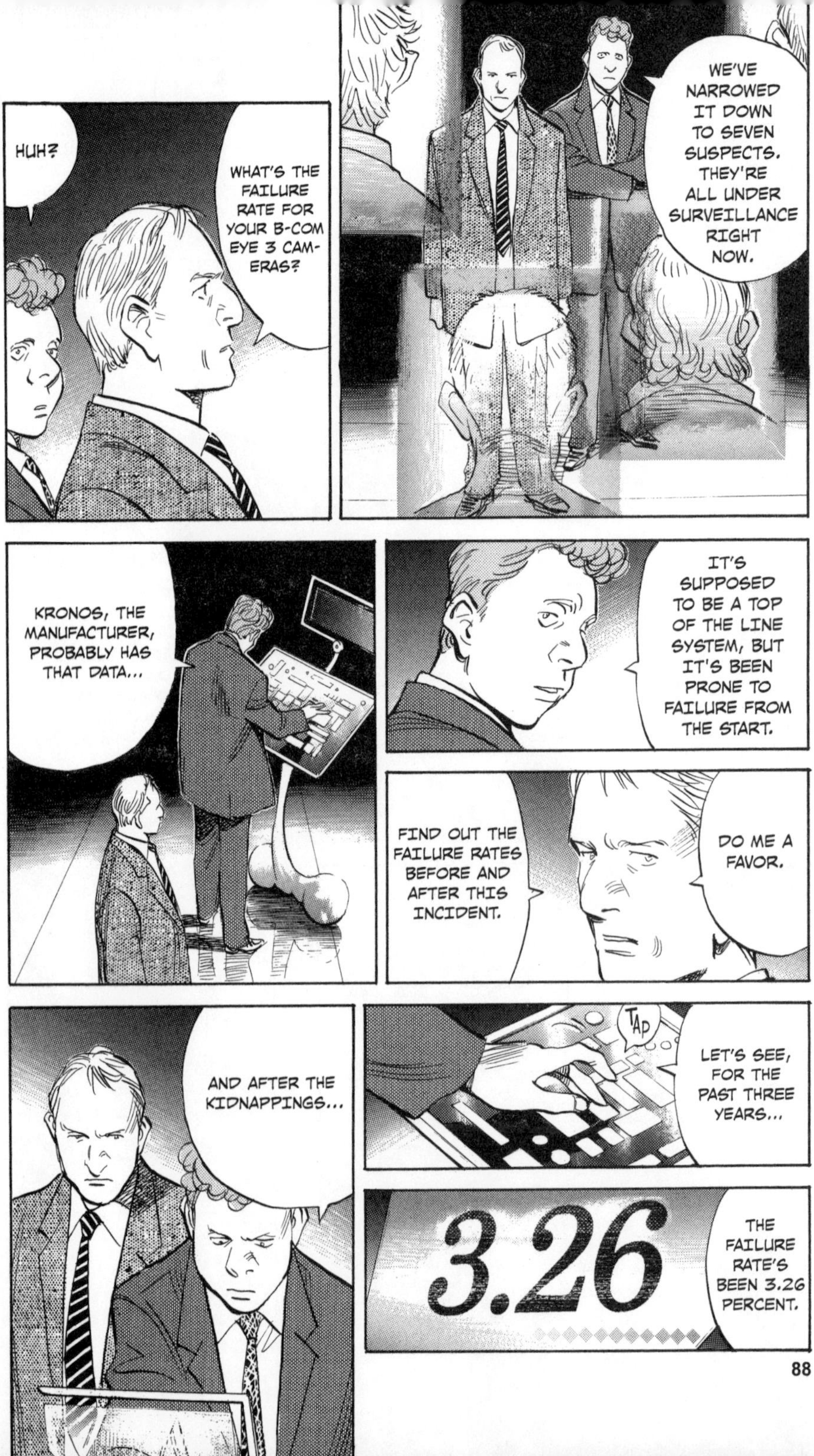
WE'VE NARROWED IT DOWN TO SEVEN SUSPECTS. THEY'RE ALL UNDER SURVEILLANCE RIGHT NOW.
WHAT'S THE FAILURE RATE FOR YOUR B-COM EYE 3 CAMERAS?
HUH?
IT'S SUPPOSED TO BE A TOP OF THE LINE SYSTEM, BUT IT'S BEEN PRONE TO FAILURE FROM THE START.
DO ME A FAVOR.
FIND OUT THE FAILURE RATES BEFORE AND AFTER THIS INCIDENT.
KRONOS, THE MANUFACTURER, PROBABLY HAS THAT DATA...
TAP
LET'S SEE, FOR THE PAST THREE YEARS...
3.26
THE FAILURE RATE'S BEEN 3.26 PERCENT.
AND AFTER THE KIDNAPPINGS...

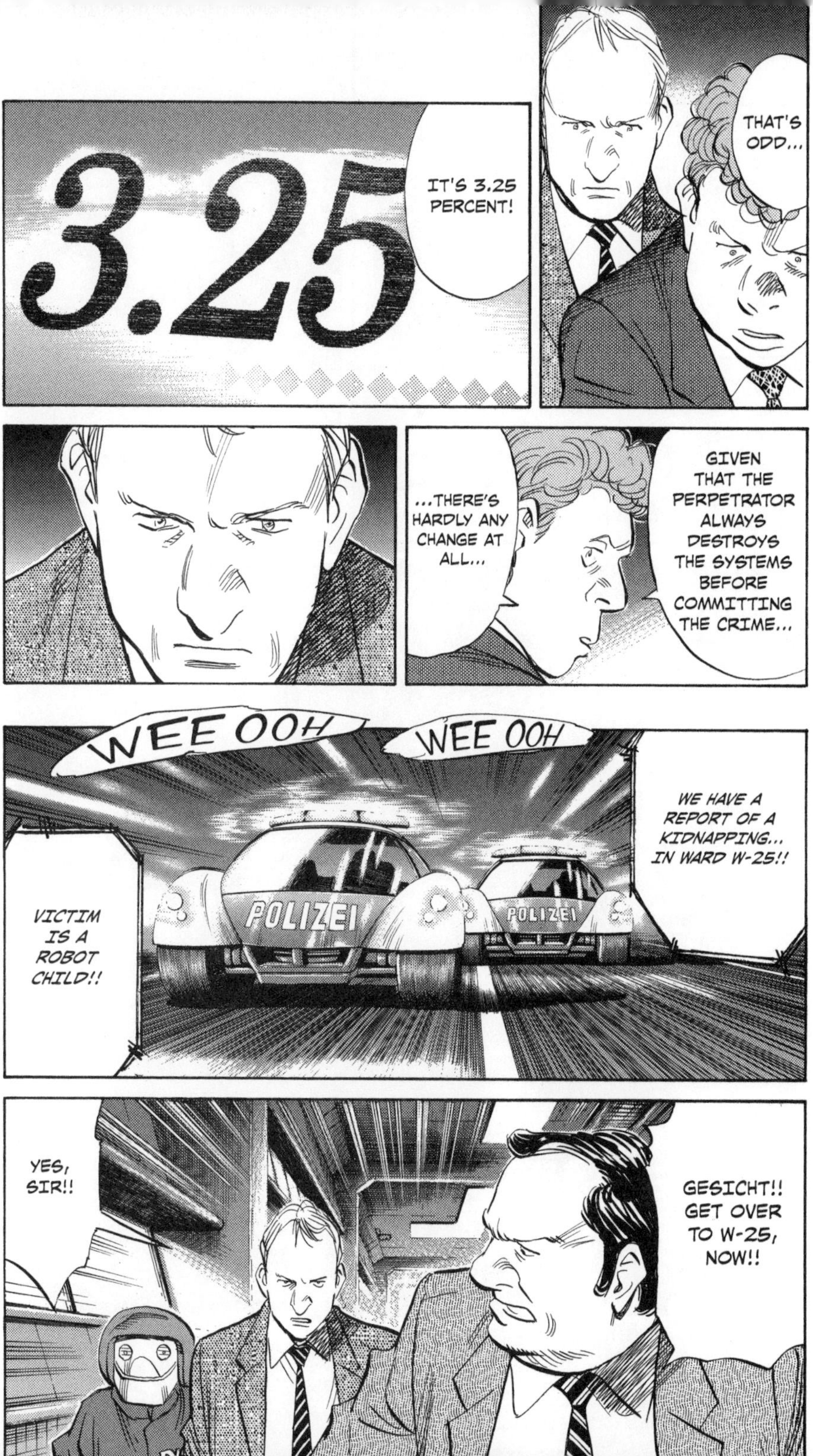
THAT'S ODD...
3.25
IT'S 3.25 PERCENT!
GIVEN THAT THE PERPETRATOR ALWAYS DESTROYS THE SYSTEMS BEFORE COMMITTING THE CRIME...
...THERE'S HARDLY ANY CHANGE AT ALL...
WEE OOH
WEE OOH
WE HAVE A REPORT OF A KIDNAPPING... IN WARD W-25!!
POLIZEI
POLIZEI
VICTIM IS A ROBOT CHILD!!
GESICHT!! GET OVER TO W-25, NOW!!
YES, SIR!!

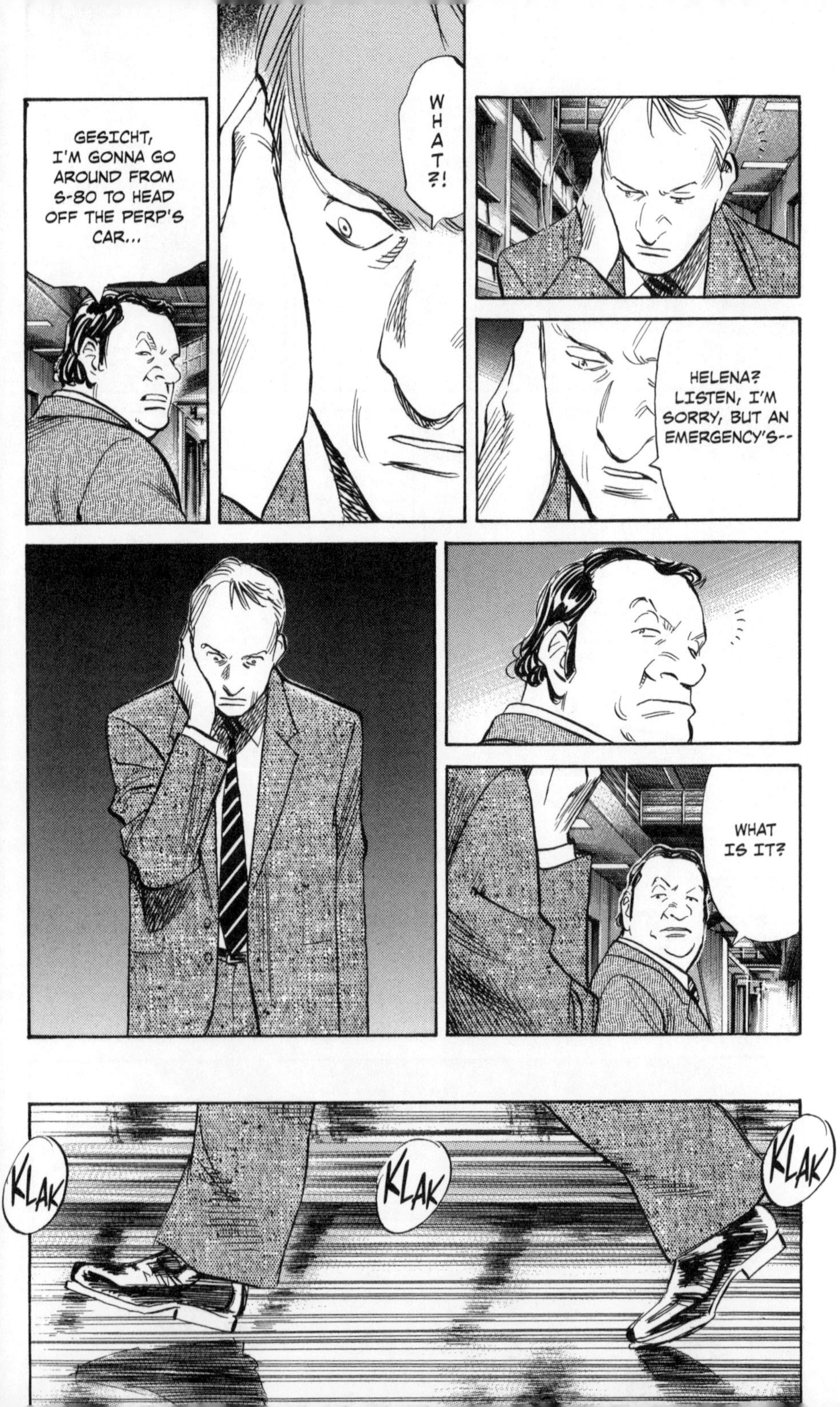
HELENA? LISTEN, I'M SORRY, BUT AN EMERGENCY'S--
WHAT?!
GESICHT, I'M GONNA GO AROUND FROM S-80 TO HEAD OFF THE PERP'S CAR...
WHAT IS IT?
KLAK
KLAK
KLAK

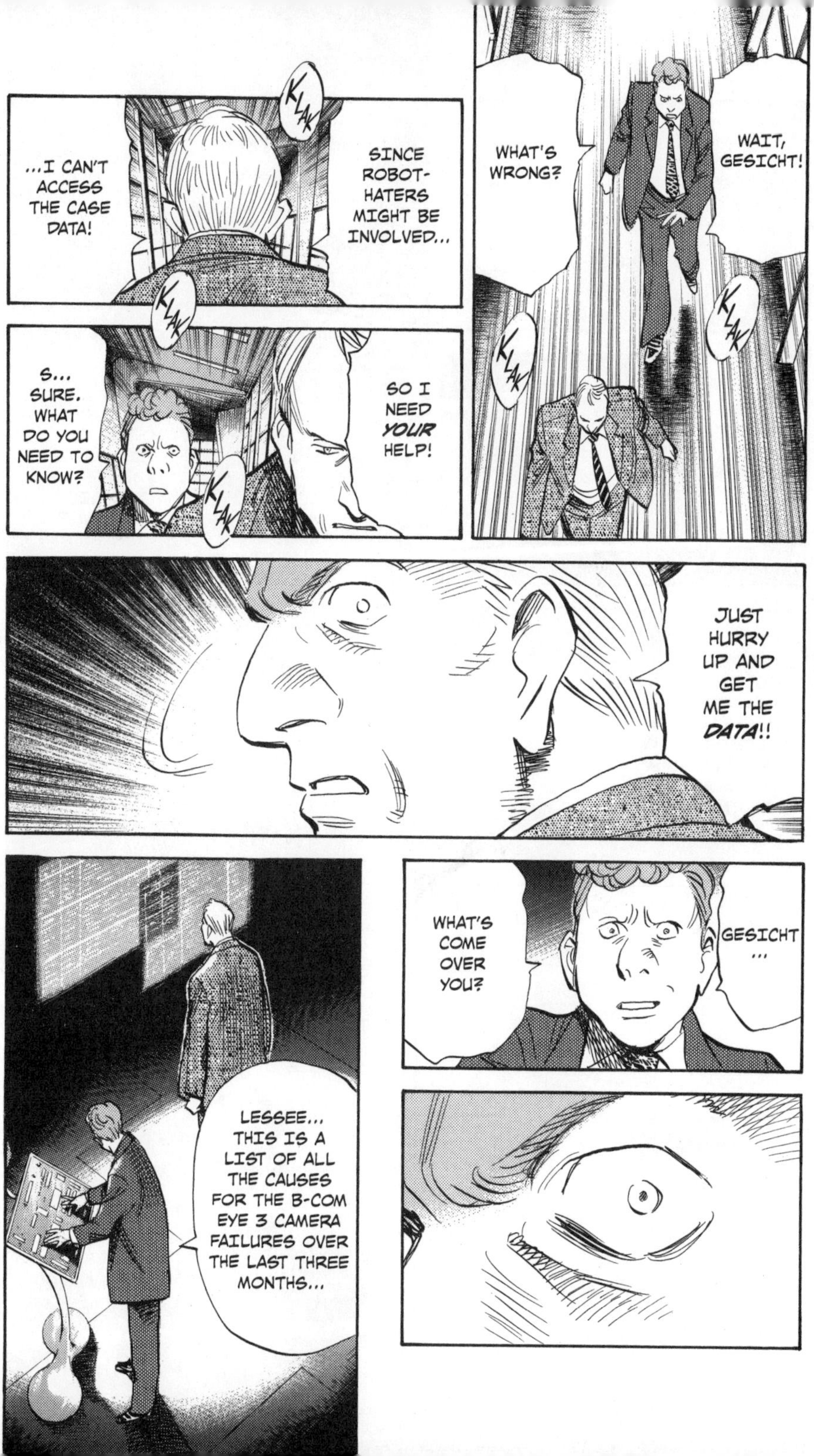
WAIT, GESICHT!
WHAT'S WRONG?
KLAK
KLAK
SINCE ROBOT-HATERS MIGHT BE INVOLVED...
...I CAN'T ACCESS THE CASE DATA!
KLAK
KLAK
SO I NEED YOUR HELP!
S... SURE. WHAT DO YOU NEED TO KNOW?
KLAK
JUST HURRY UP AND GET ME THE DATA!!
GESICHT...
WHAT'S COME OVER YOU?
LESSEE... THIS IS A LIST OF ALL THE CAUSES FOR THE B-COM EYE 3 CAMERA FAILURES OVER THE LAST THREE MONTHS...

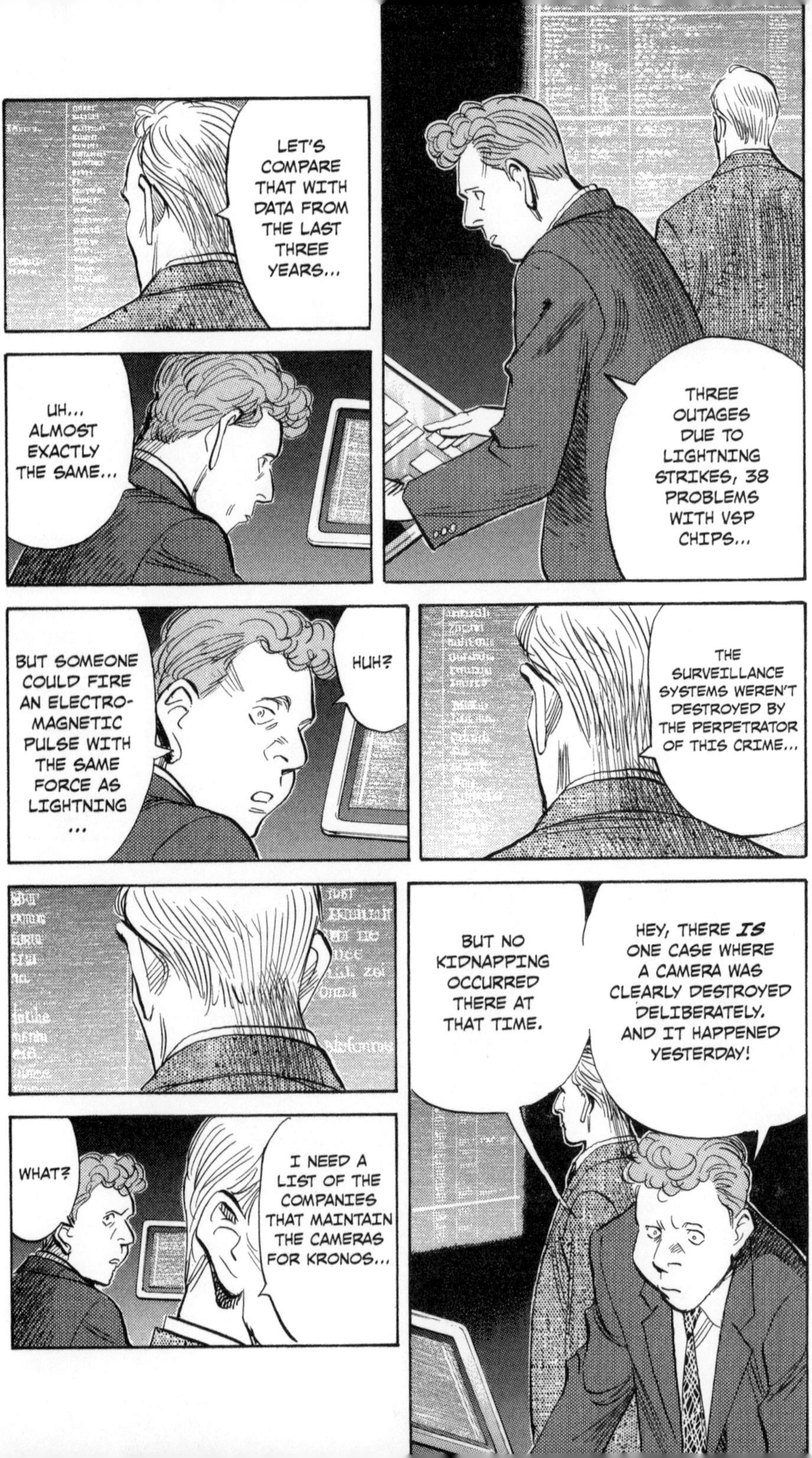
THREE OUTAGES DUE TO LIGHTNING STRIKES, 38 PROBLEMS WITH VSP CHIPS...
LET'S COMPARE THAT WITH DATA FROM THE LAST THREE YEARS...
UH... ALMOST EXACTLY THE SAME...
THE SURVEILLANCE SYSTEMS WEREN'T DESTROYED BY THE PERPETRATOR OF THIS CRIME...
HUH?
BUT SOMEONE COULD FIRE AN ELECTRO-MAGNETIC PULSE WITH THE SAME FORCE AS LIGHTNING...
HEY, THERE *IS* ONE CASE WHERE A CAMERA WAS CLEARLY DESTROYED DELIBERATELY. AND IT HAPPENED YESTERDAY!
BUT NO KIDNAPPING OCCURRED THERE AT THAT TIME.
I NEED A LIST OF THE COMPANIES THAT MAINTAIN THE CAMERAS FOR KRONOS...
WHAT?

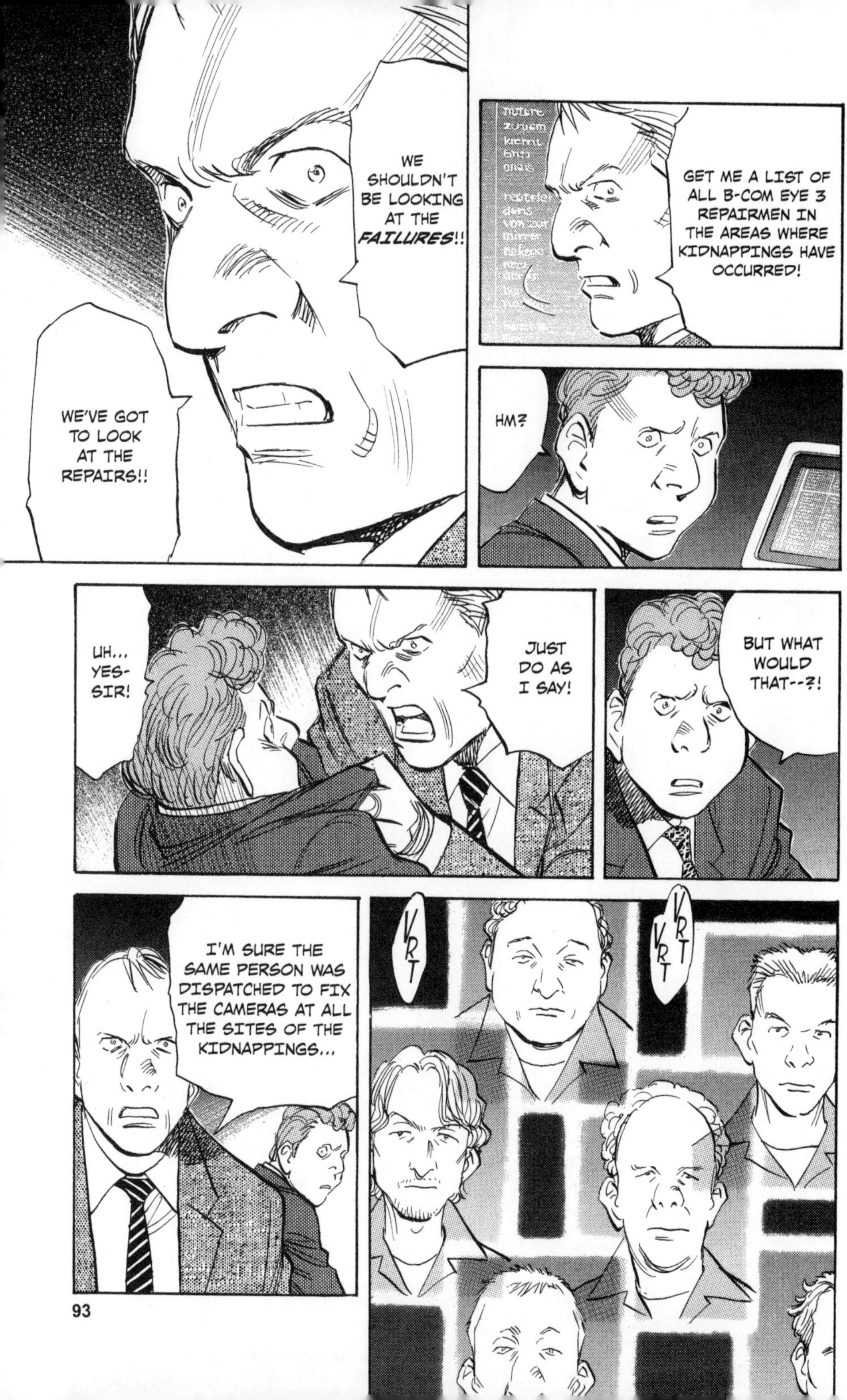
GET ME A LIST OF ALL B-COM EYE 3 REPAIRMEN IN THE AREAS WHERE KIDNAPPINGS HAVE OCCURRED!
HM?
WE SHOULDN'T BE LOOKING AT THE *FAILURES*!!
WE'VE GOT TO LOOK AT THE REPAIRS!!
BUT WHAT WOULD THAT--?!
JUST DO AS I SAY!
UH... YES-SIR!
VRT
VRT
VRT
I'M SURE THE SAME PERSON WAS DISPATCHED TO FIX THE CAMERAS AT ALL THE SITES OF THE KIDNAPPINGS...

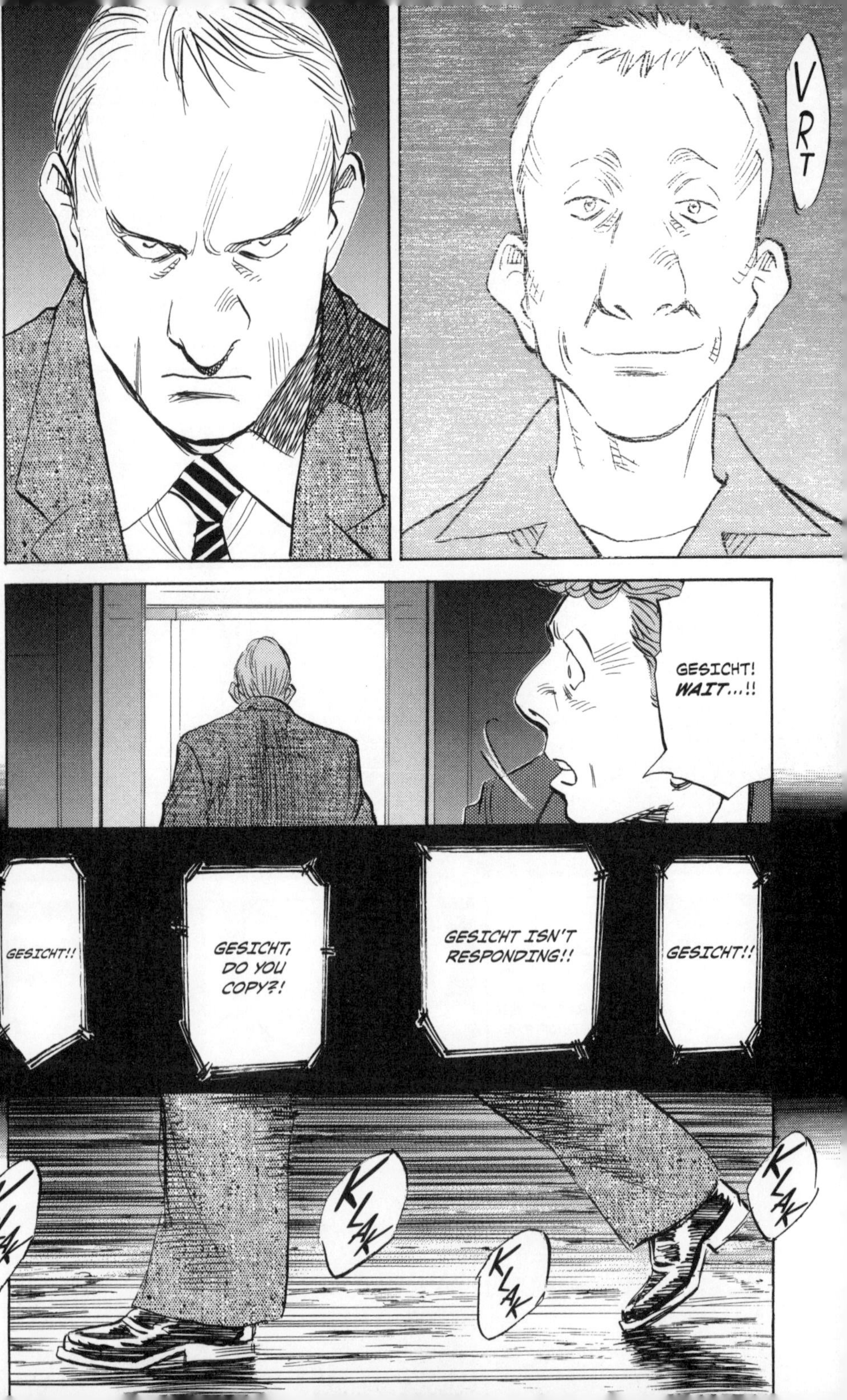
VRT
GESICHT! WAIT...!!
GESICHT!!
GESICHT ISN'T RESPONDING!!
GESICHT, DO YOU COPY?!
GESICHT!!
KLAK
KLAK
KLAK
KLAK

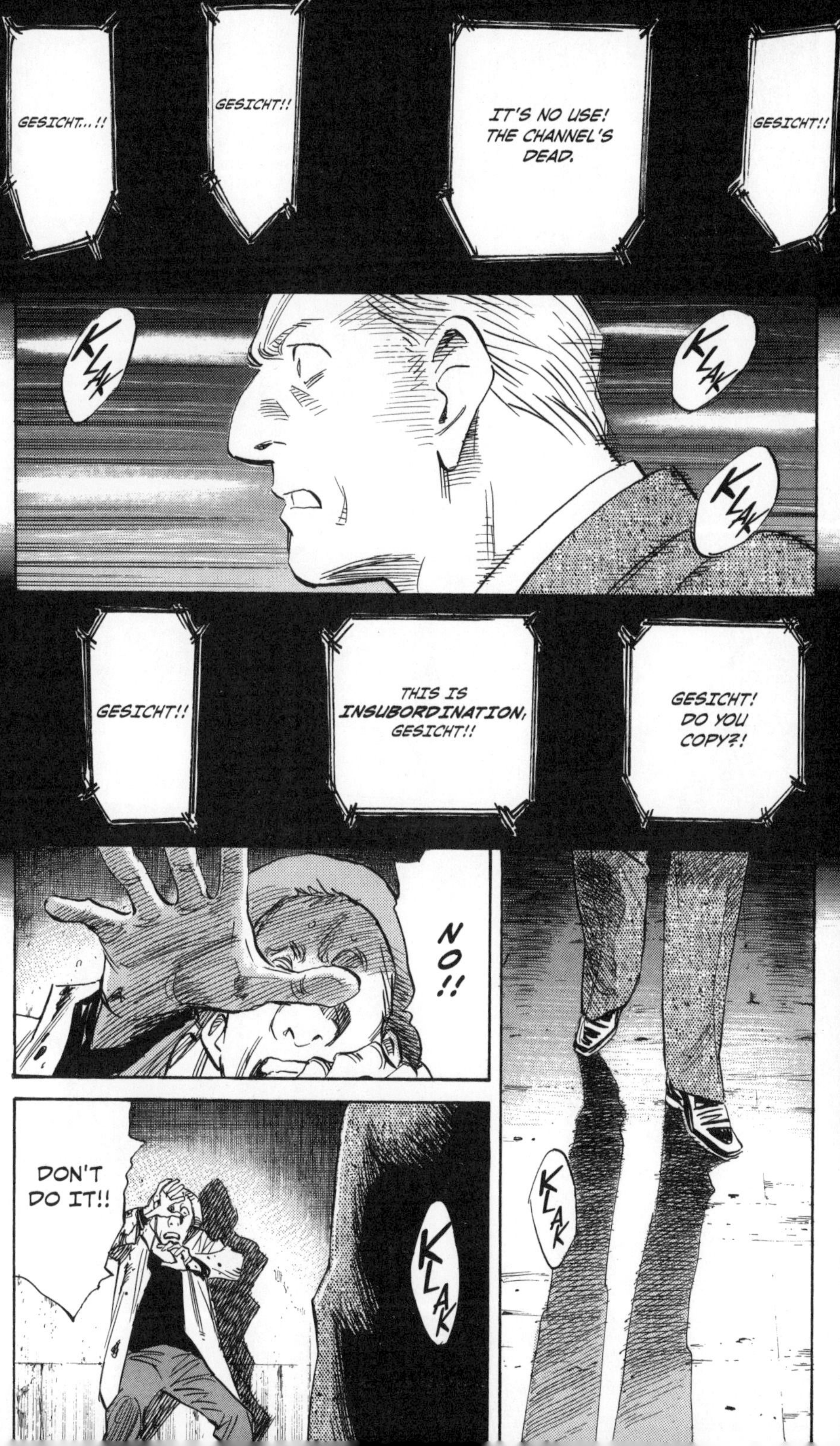
GESICHT!!
IT'S NO USE! THE CHANNEL'S DEAD.
GESICHT!!
GESICHT...!!
KLAK
KLAK
KLAK
GESICHT! DO YOU COPY?!
THIS IS INSUBORDINATION, GESICHT!!
GESICHT!!
KLAK
NO!!
KLAK
DON'T DO IT!!

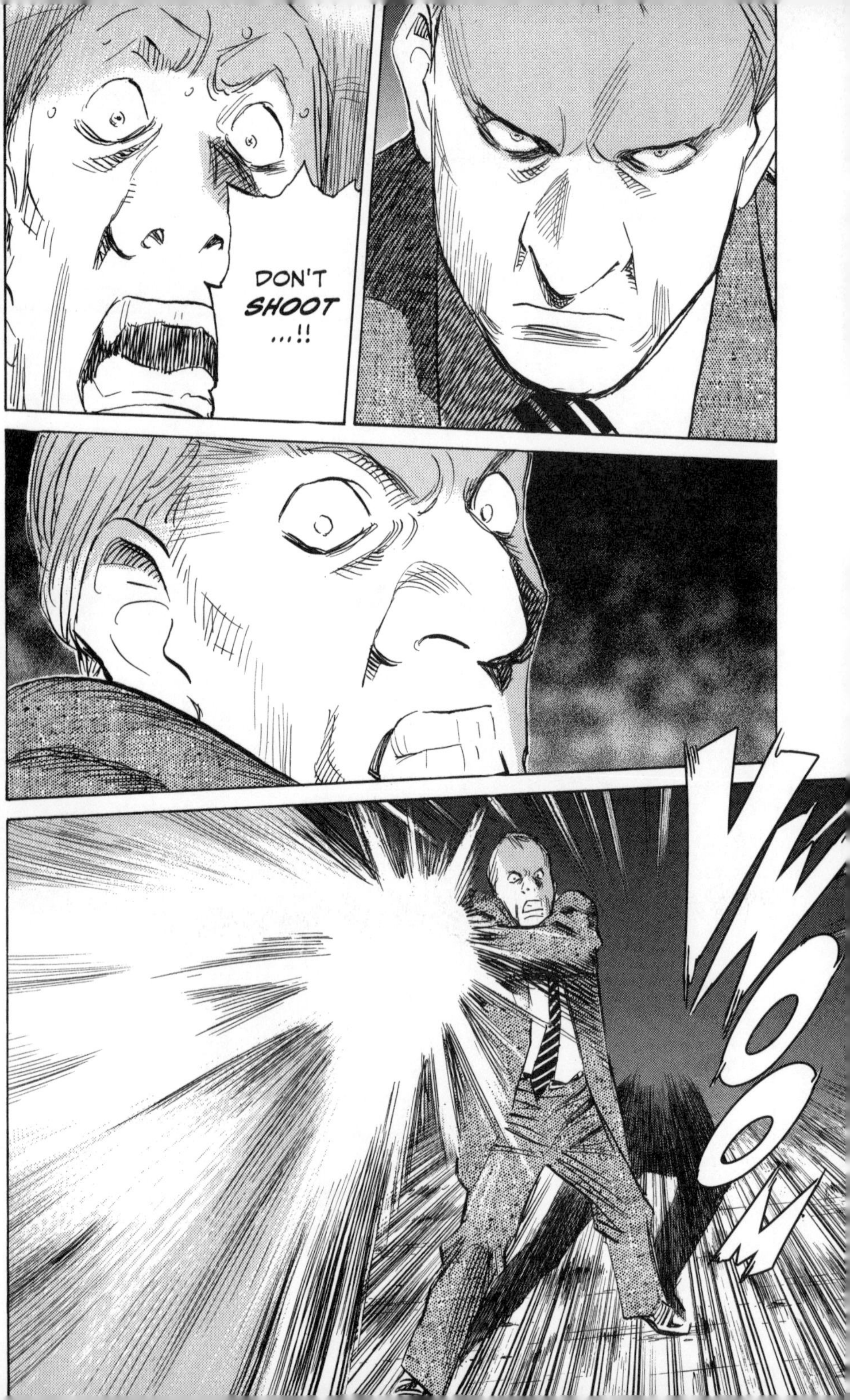
DON'T SHOOT ...!!
VWOOM

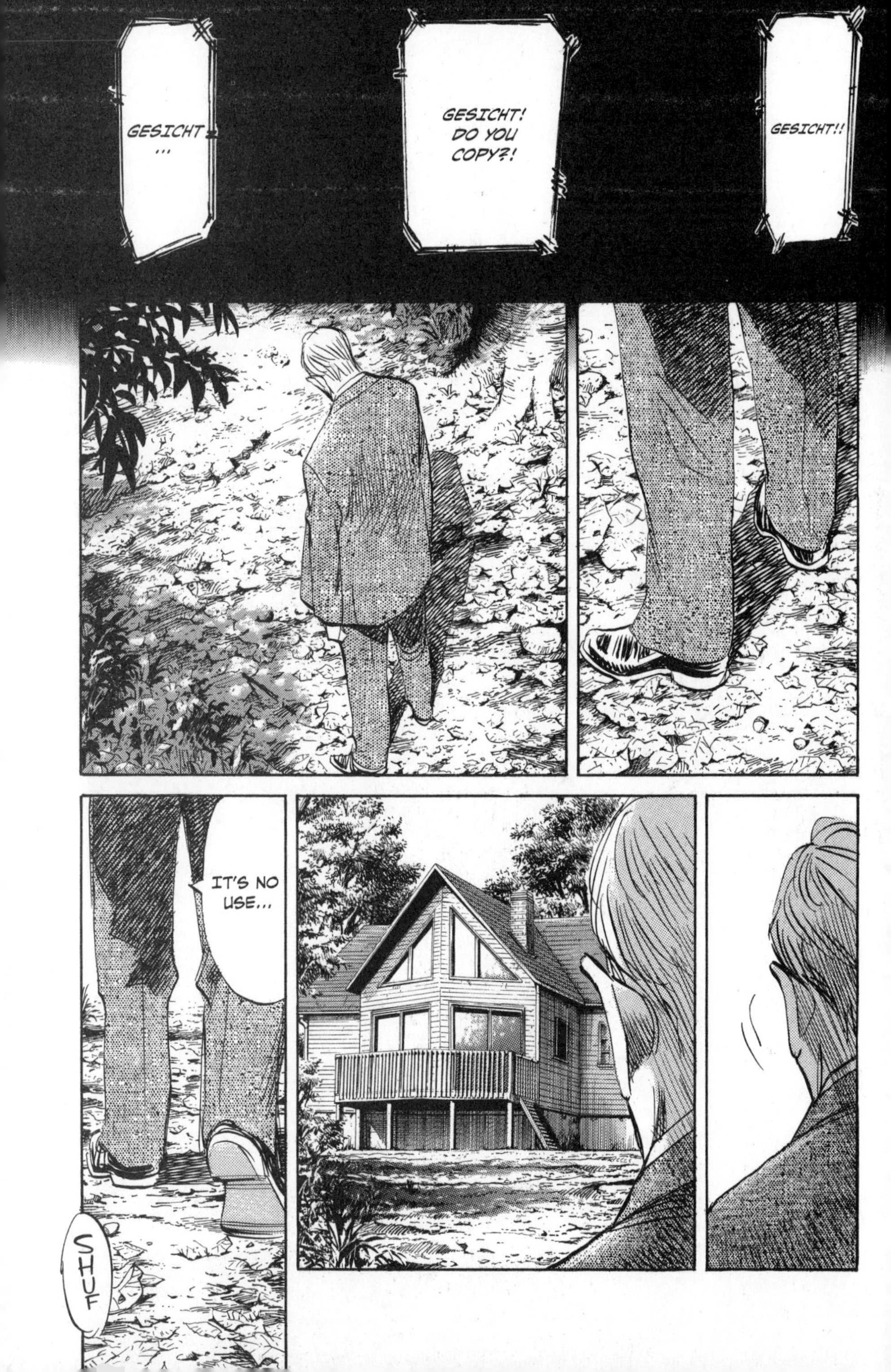
GESICHT!!
GESICHT! DO YOU COPY?!
GESICHT ...
IT'S NO USE...
SHUF

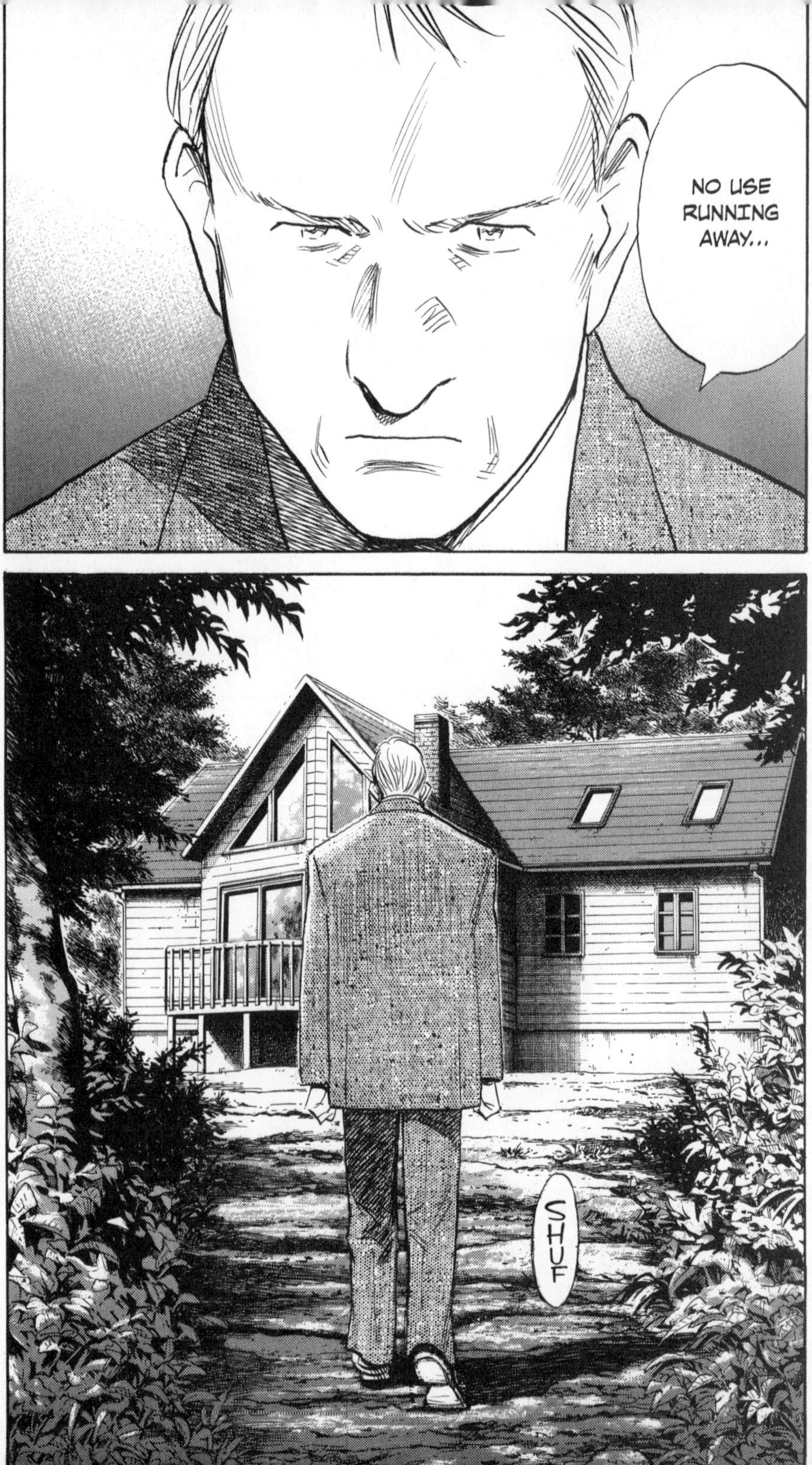
NO USE RUNNING AWAY...
SHUF

# Act 36 PURSUIT OF HATE

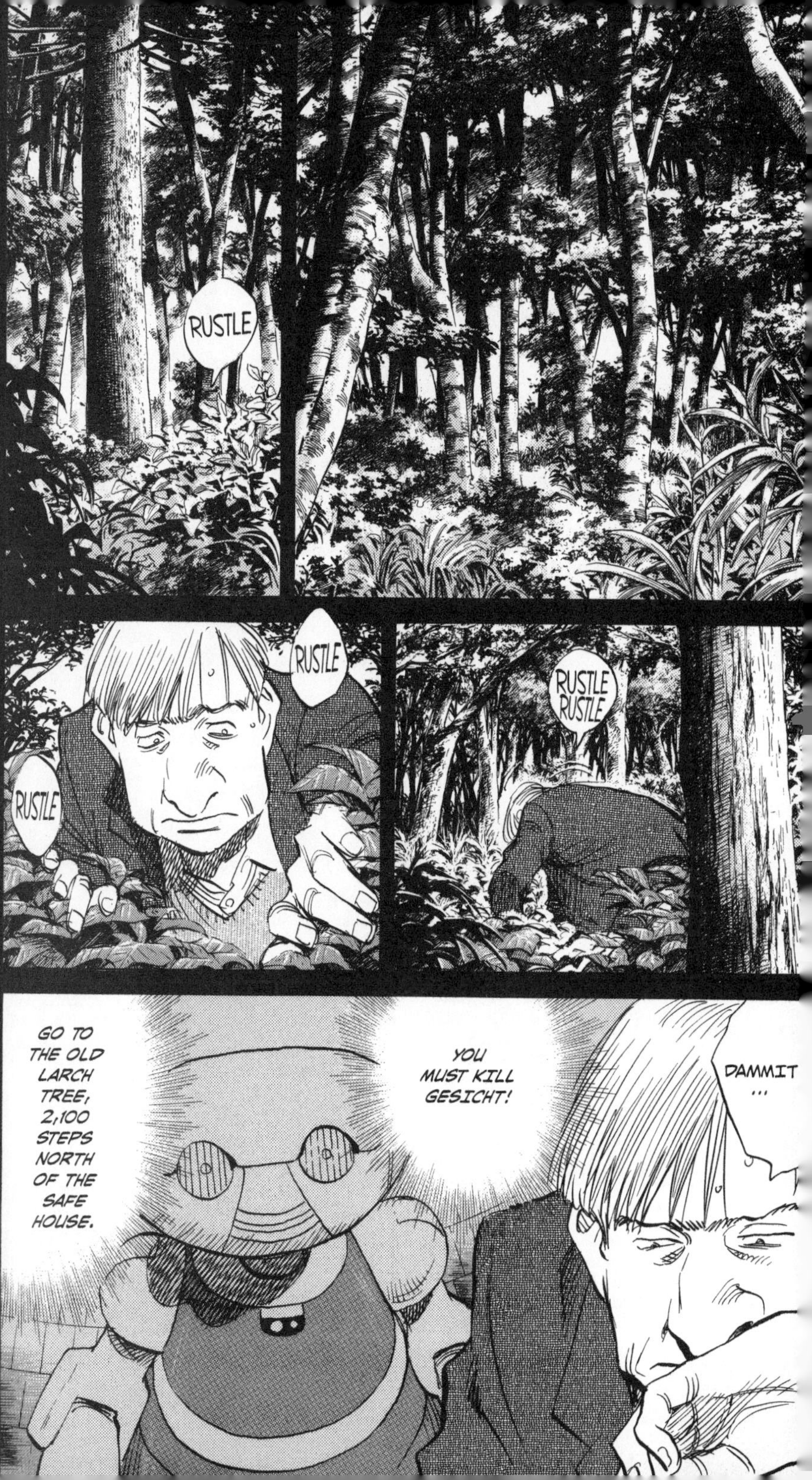
RUSTLE
RUSTLE RUSTLE
RUSTLE
RUSTLE
DAMMIT ...
YOU MUST KILL GESICHT!
GO TO THE OLD LARCH TREE, 2,100 STEPS NORTH OF THE SAFE HOUSE.

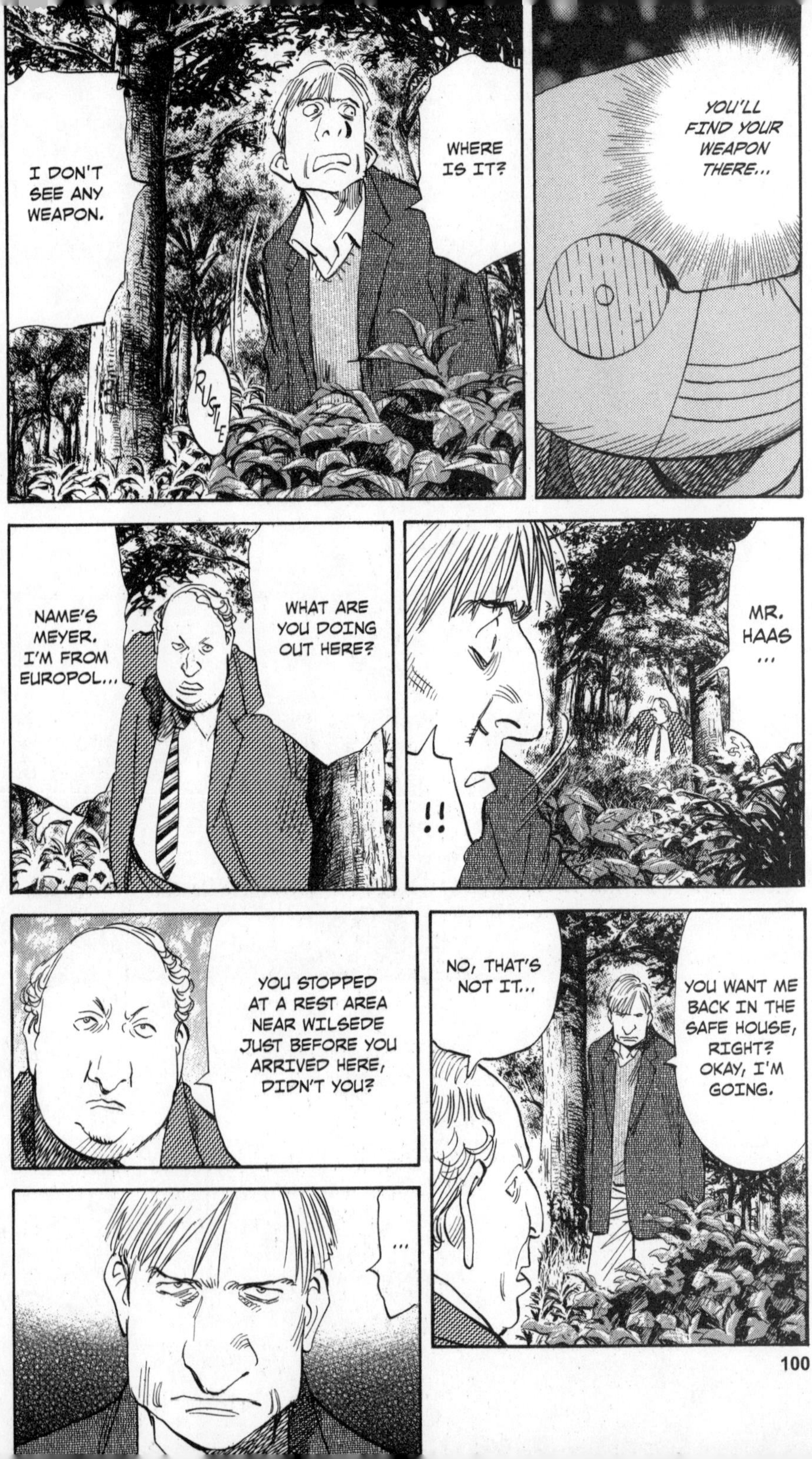
YOU'LL FIND YOUR WEAPON THERE...
WHERE IS IT?
I DON'T SEE ANY WEAPON.
RUSTLE
MR. HAAS ...
!!
WHAT ARE YOU DOING OUT HERE?
NAME'S MEYER. I'M FROM EUROPOL...
YOU WANT ME BACK IN THE SAFE HOUSE, RIGHT? OKAY, I'M GOING.
NO, THAT'S NOT IT...
YOU STOPPED AT A REST AREA NEAR WILSEDE JUST BEFORE YOU ARRIVED HERE, DIDN'T YOU?
...

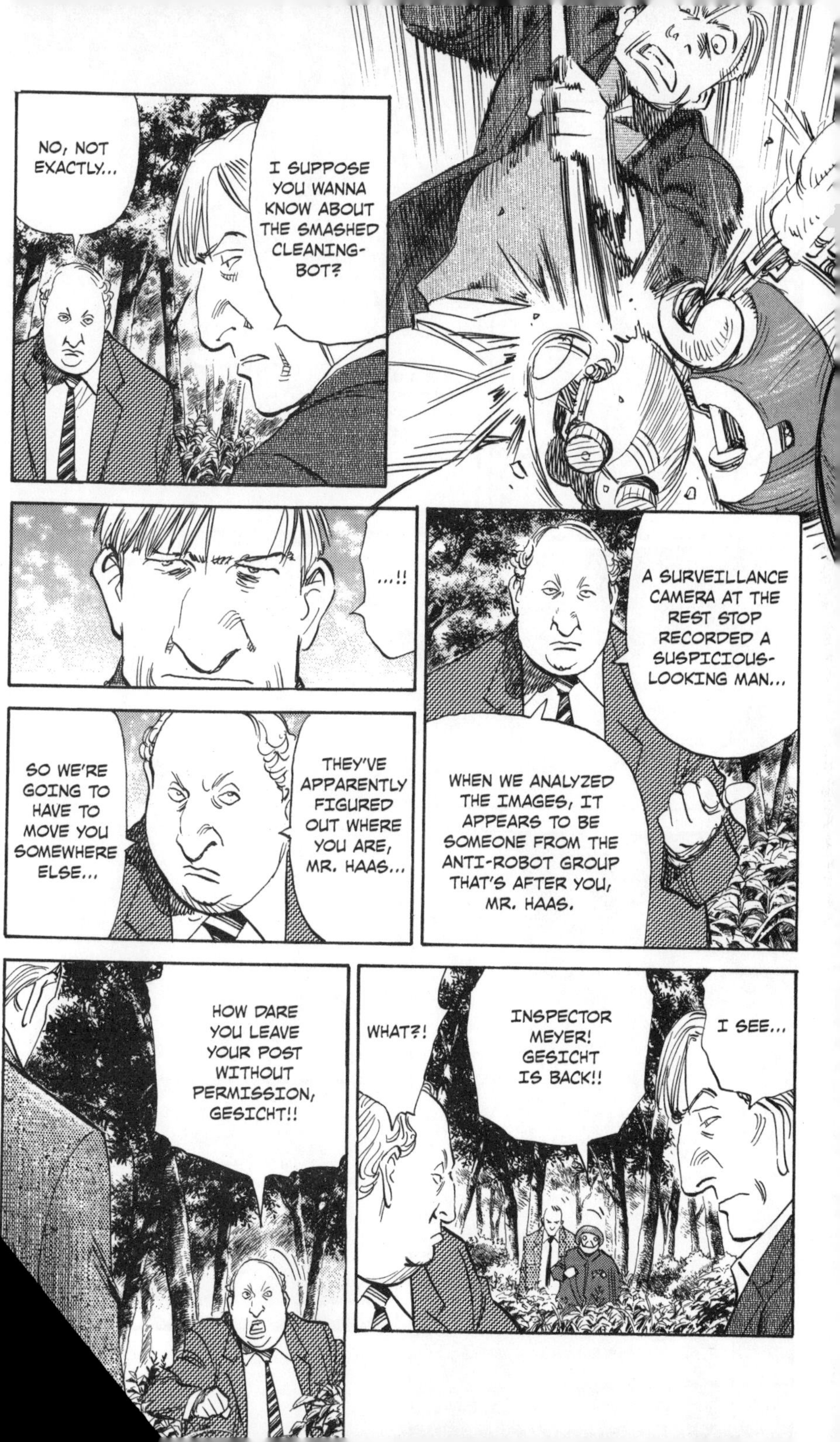
I SUPPOSE YOU WANNA KNOW ABOUT THE SMASHED CLEANING-BOT?
NO, NOT EXACTLY...
A SURVEILLANCE CAMERA AT THE REST STOP RECORDED A SUSPICIOUS-LOOKING MAN...
WHEN WE ANALYZED THE IMAGES, IT APPEARS TO BE SOMEONE FROM THE ANTI-ROBOT GROUP THAT'S AFTER YOU, MR. HAAS.
...!!
THEY'VE APPARENTLY FIGURED OUT WHERE YOU ARE, MR. HAAS...
SO WE'RE GOING TO HAVE TO MOVE YOU SOMEWHERE ELSE...
I SEE...
INSPECTOR MEYER! GESICHT IS BACK!!
WHAT?!
HOW DARE YOU LEAVE YOUR POST WITHOUT PERMISSION, GESICHT!!

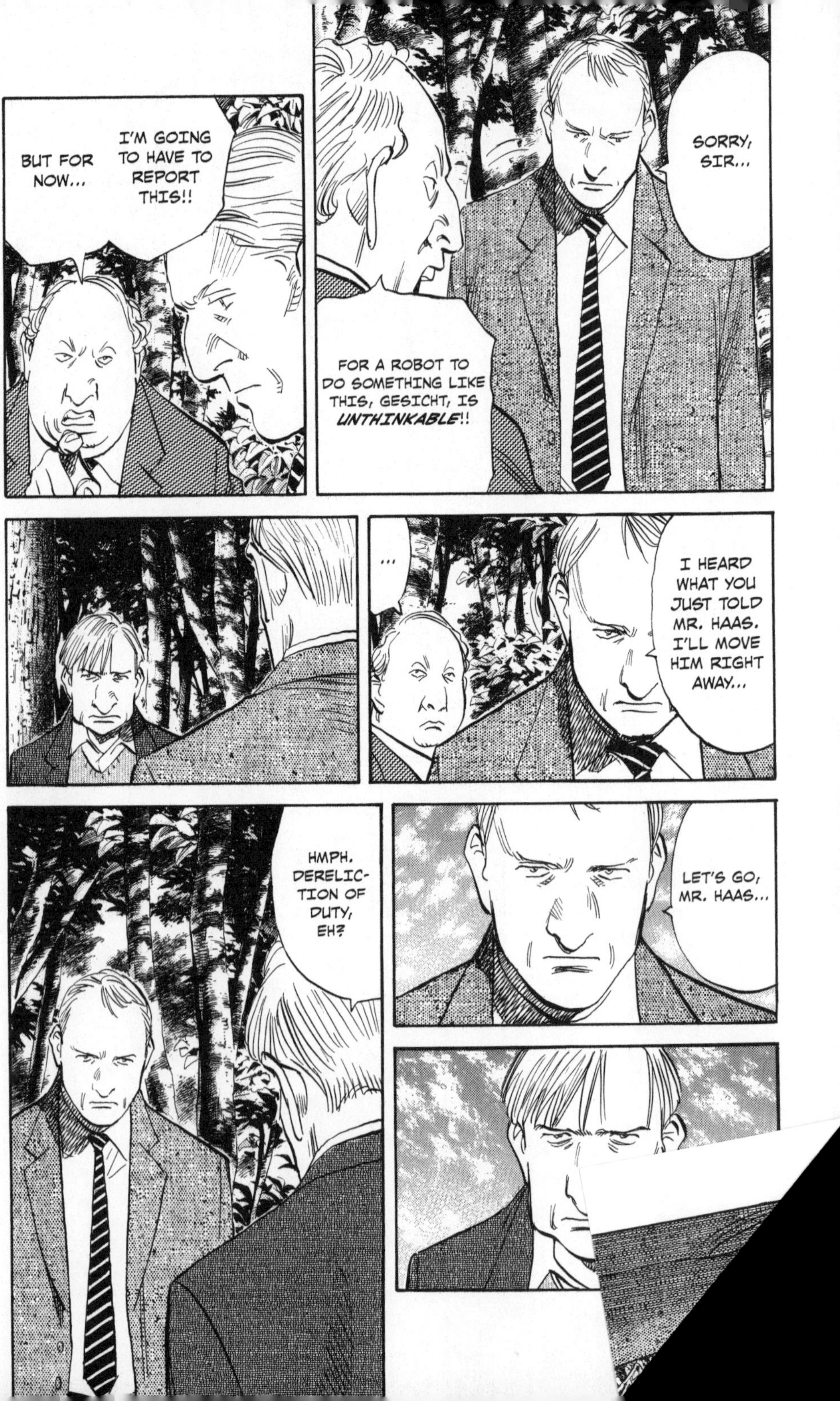
SORRY, SIR...
FOR A ROBOT TO DO SOMETHING LIKE THIS, GESICHT, IS *UNTHINKABLE*!!
I'M GOING TO HAVE TO REPORT THIS!!
BUT FOR NOW...
I HEARD WHAT YOU JUST TOLD MR. HAAS. I'LL MOVE HIM RIGHT AWAY...
...
LET'S GO, MR. HAAS...
HMPH. DERELICTION OF DUTY, EH?

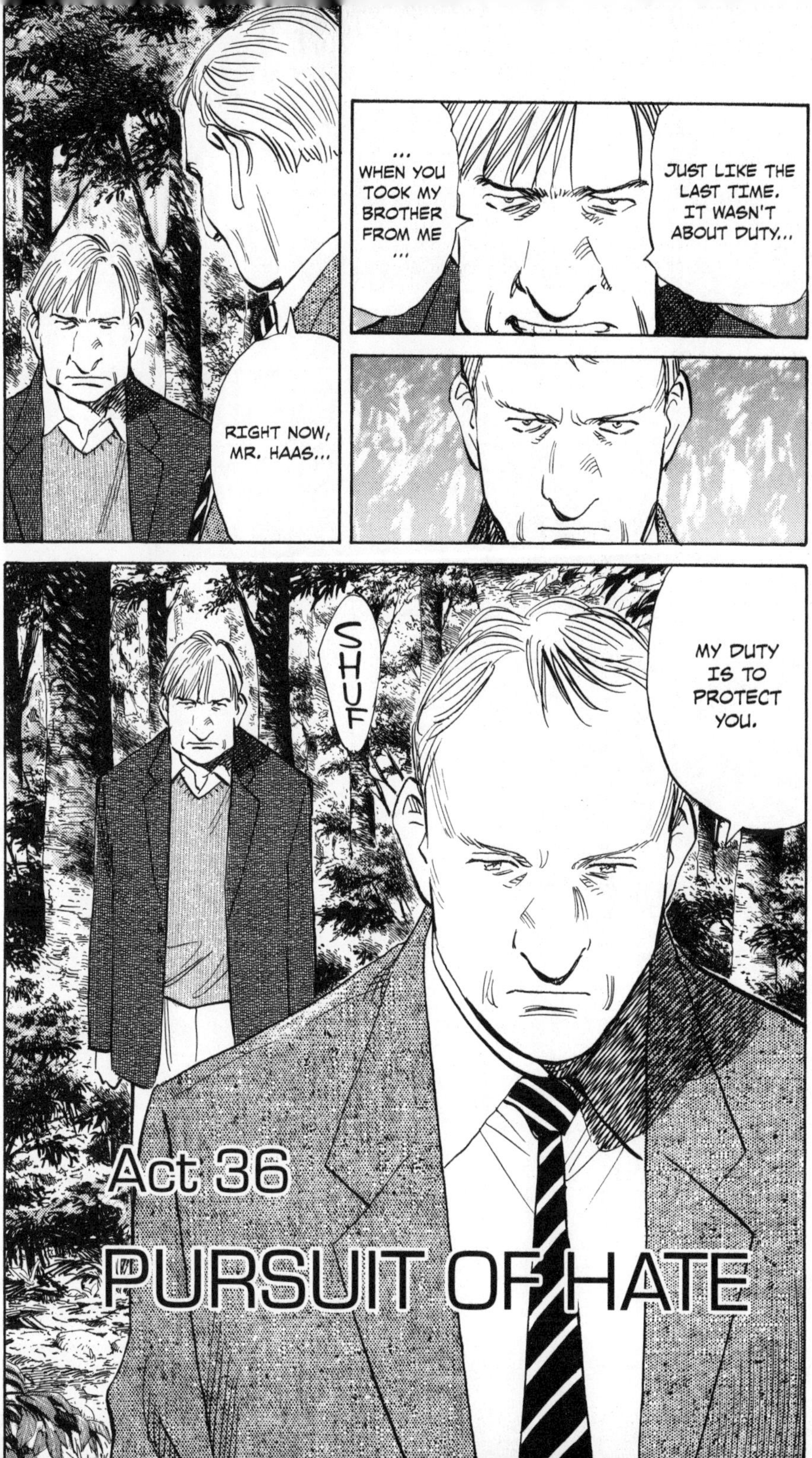
JUST LIKE THE LAST TIME. IT WASN'T ABOUT DUTY...
... WHEN YOU TOOK MY BROTHER FROM ME ...
RIGHT NOW, MR. HAAS...
MY DUTY IS TO PROTECT YOU.
SHUF

# Act 36
# PURSUIT OF HATE

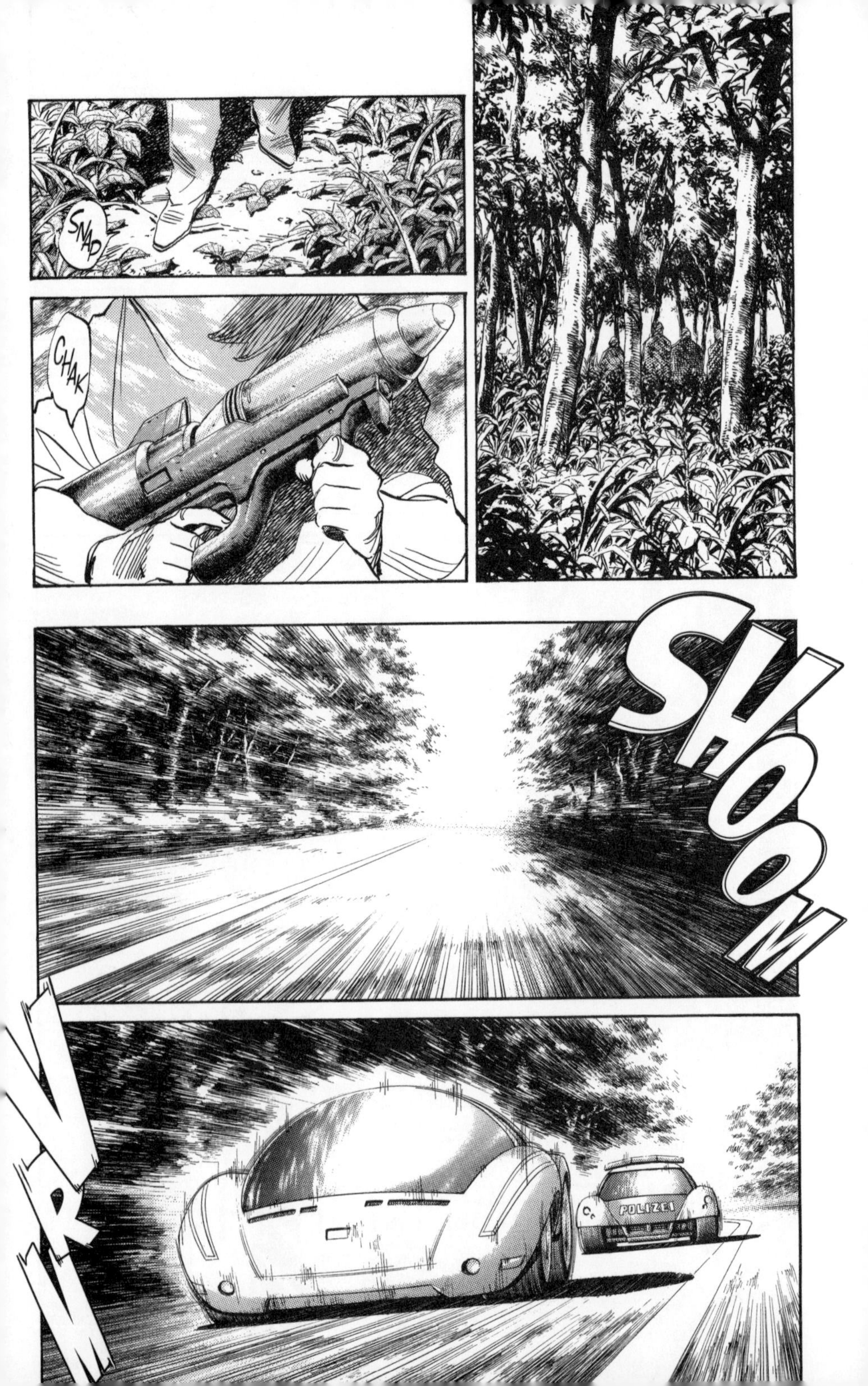
SNAP
CHAK
SHOOM
VRM
POLIZEI

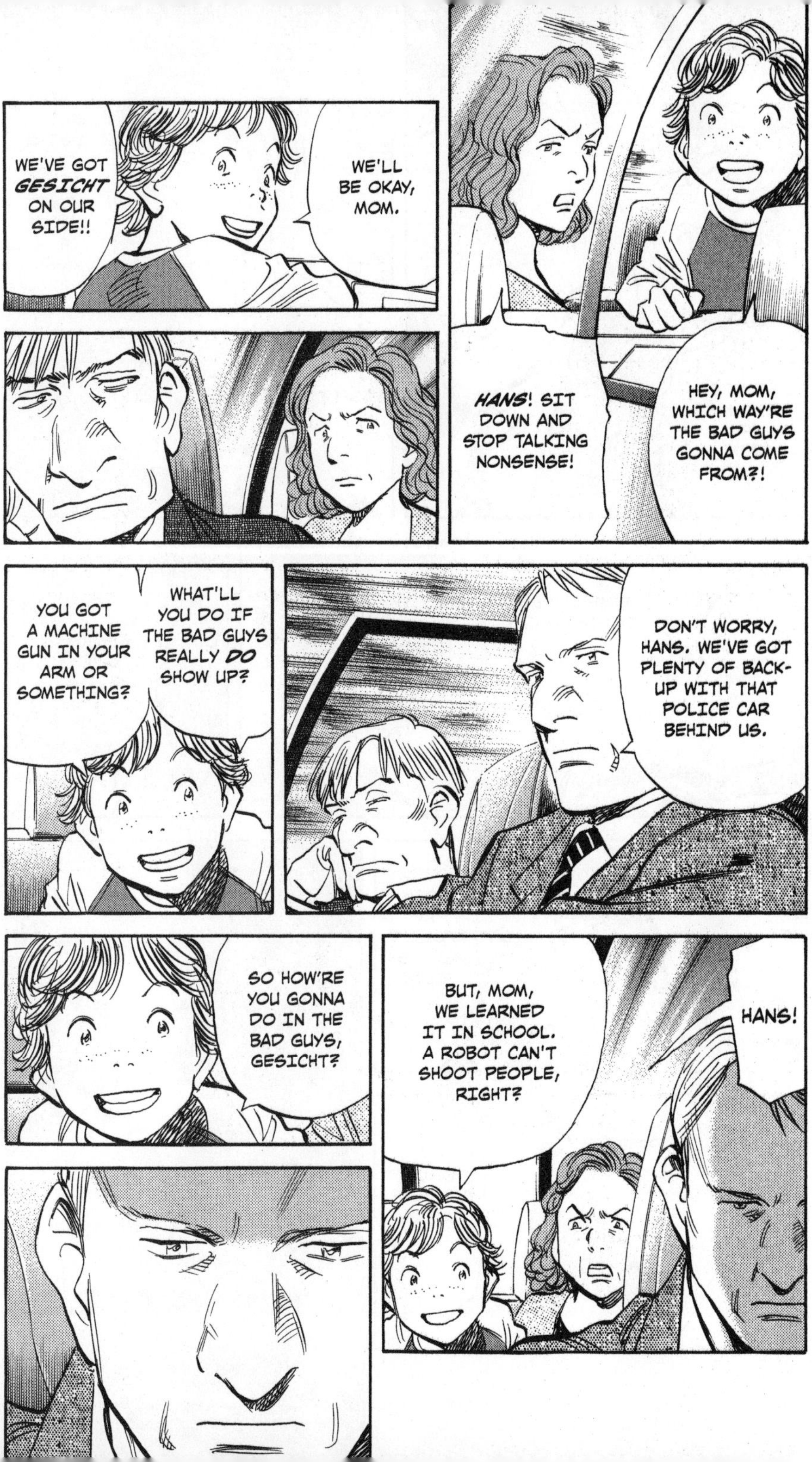
HEY, MOM, WHICH WAY'RE THE BAD GUYS GONNA COME FROM?!
HANS! SIT DOWN AND STOP TALKING NONSENSE!
WE'LL BE OKAY, MOM.
WE'VE GOT GESICHT ON OUR SIDE!!
DON'T WORRY, HANS. WE'VE GOT PLENTY OF BACK-UP WITH THAT POLICE CAR BEHIND US.
WHAT'LL YOU DO IF THE BAD GUYS REALLY DO SHOW UP?
YOU GOT A MACHINE GUN IN YOUR ARM OR SOMETHING?
HANS!
BUT, MOM, WE LEARNED IT IN SCHOOL. A ROBOT CAN'T SHOOT PEOPLE, RIGHT?
SO HOW'RE YOU GONNA DO IN THE BAD GUYS, GESICHT?

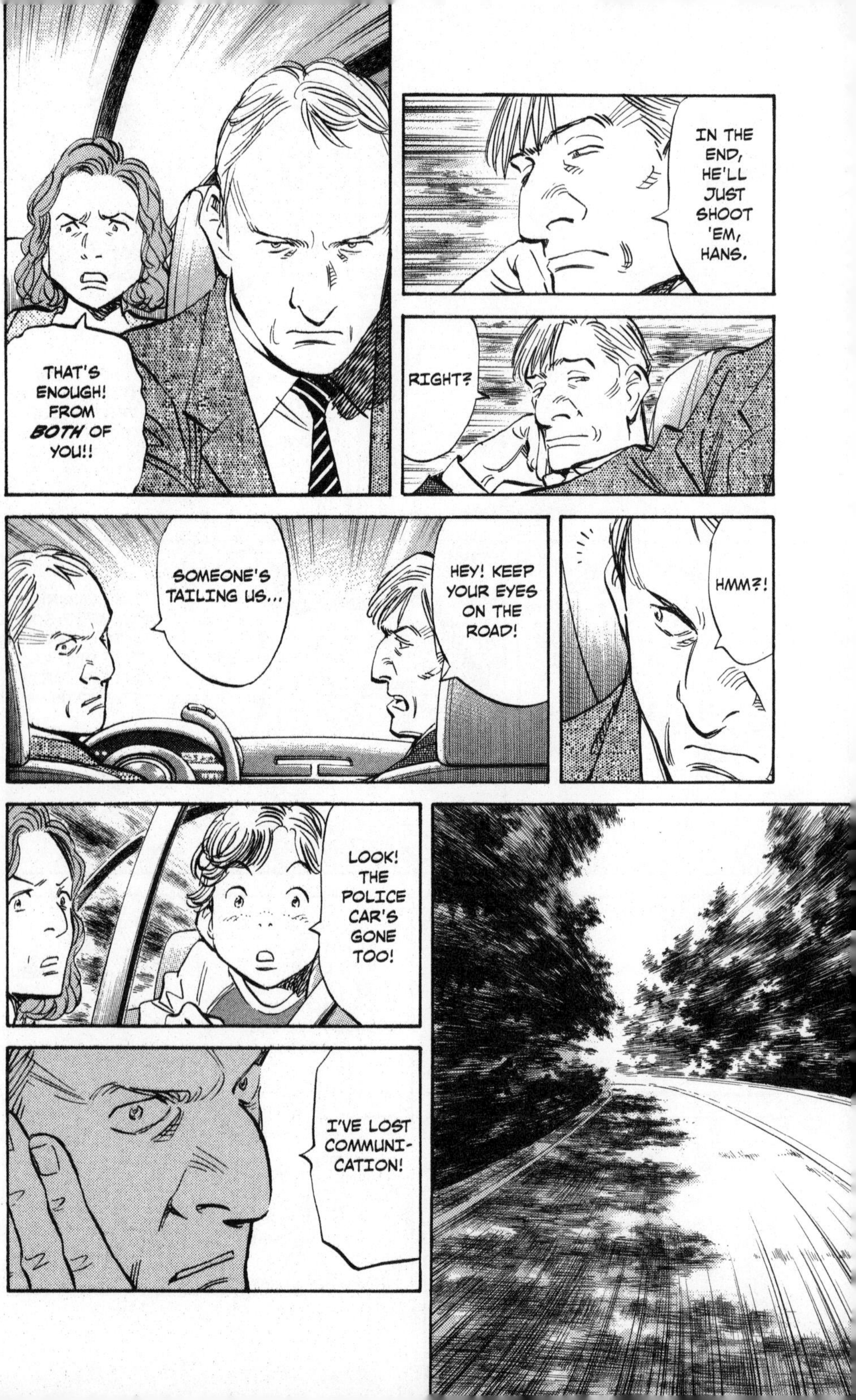
IN THE END, HE'LL JUST SHOOT 'EM, HANS.
RIGHT?
THAT'S ENOUGH! FROM *BOTH* OF YOU!!
HMM?!
HEY! KEEP YOUR EYES ON THE ROAD!
SOMEONE'S TAILING US...
LOOK! THE POLICE CAR'S GONE TOO!
I'VE LOST COMMUNICATION!

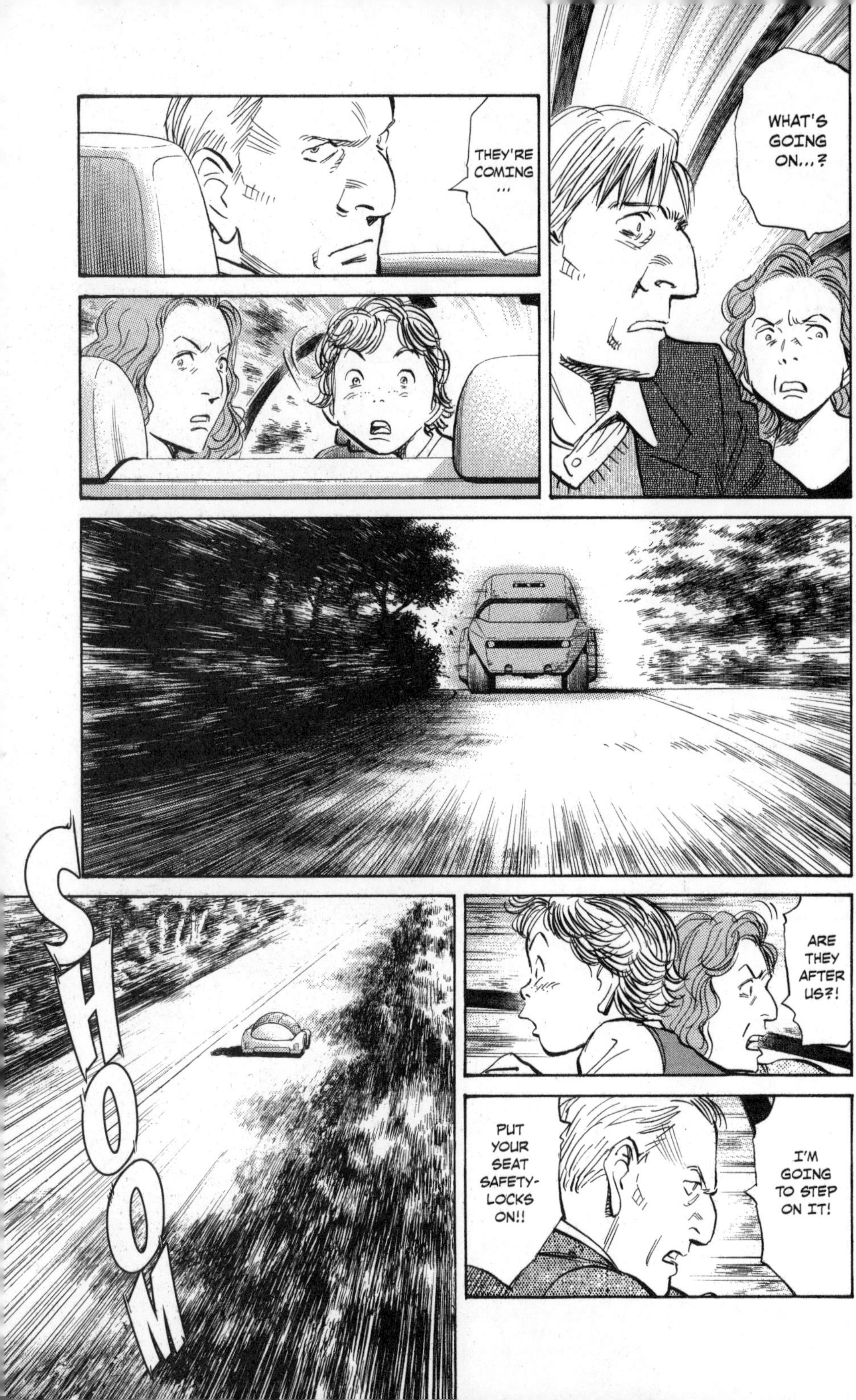
WHAT'S GOING ON...?
THEY'RE COMING ...
ARE THEY AFTER US?!
I'M GOING TO STEP ON IT!
PUT YOUR SEAT SAFETY-LOCKS ON!!
SHOOM

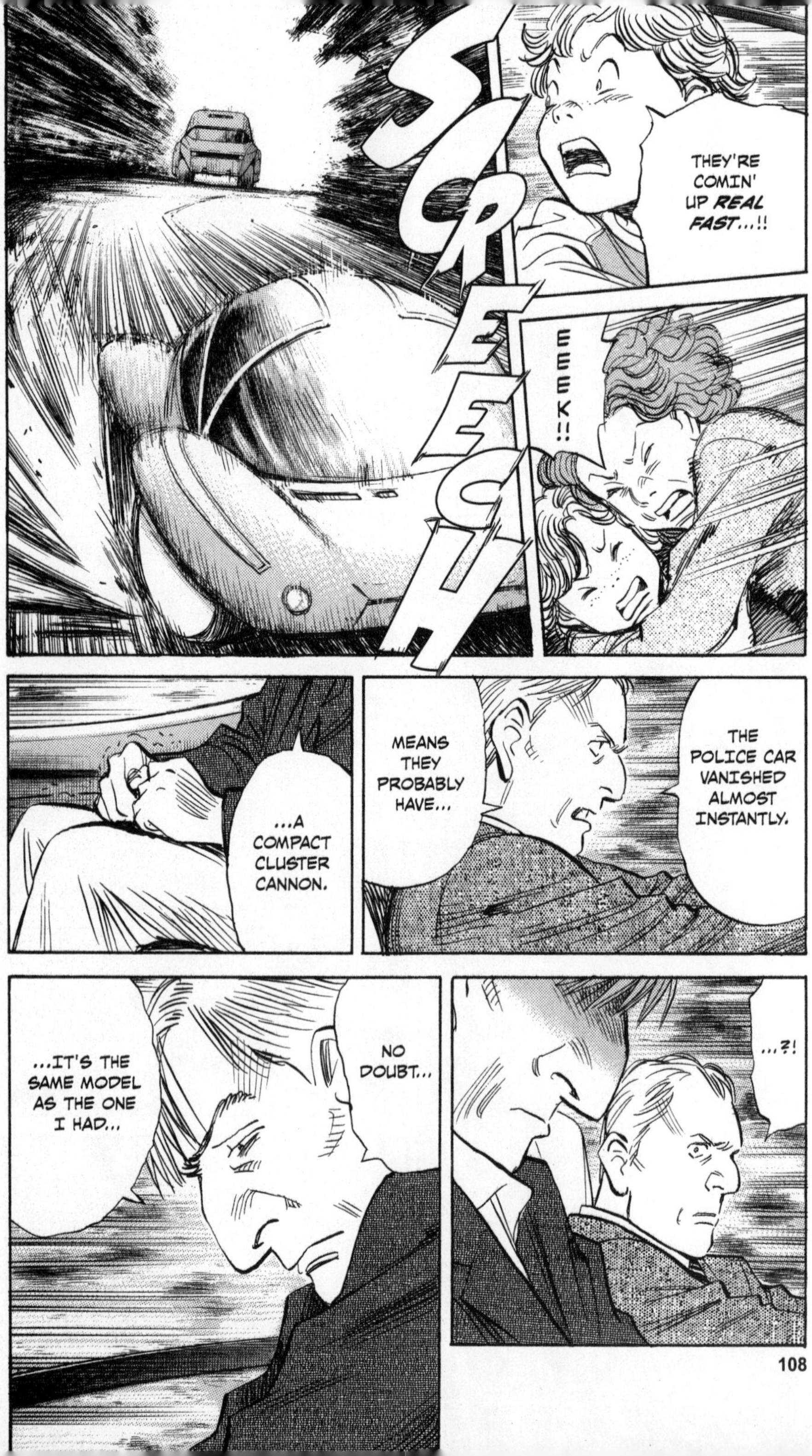
THEY'RE COMIN' UP REAL FAST...!!
SCREEEECH
EEEEK!!
THE POLICE CAR VANISHED ALMOST INSTANTLY.
MEANS THEY PROBABLY HAVE...
...A COMPACT CLUSTER CANNON.
...?!
NO DOUBT...
...IT'S THE SAME MODEL AS THE ONE I HAD...

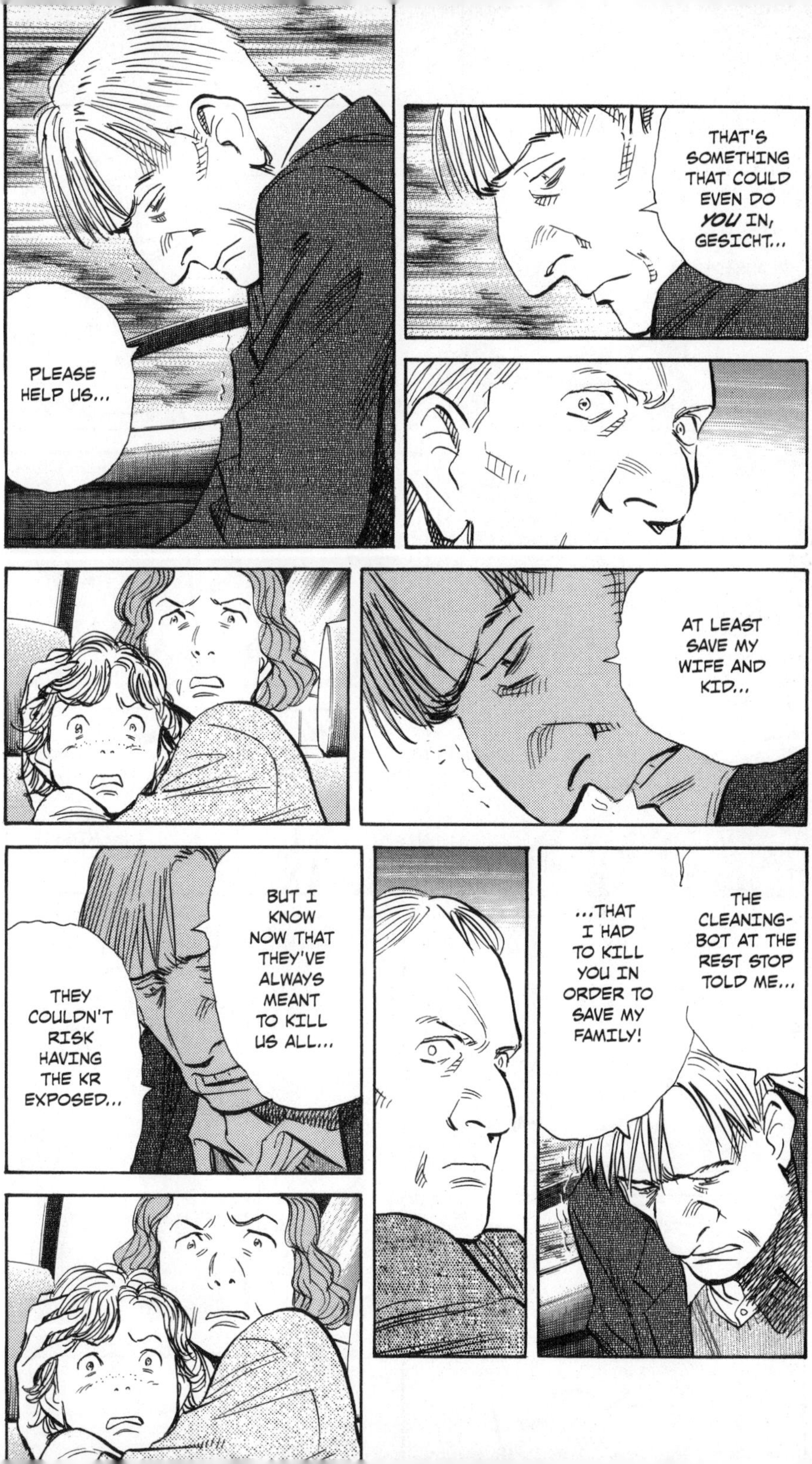
THAT'S SOMETHING THAT COULD EVEN DO *YOU* IN, GESICHT...
PLEASE HELP US...
AT LEAST SAVE MY WIFE AND KID...
THE CLEANING-BOT AT THE REST STOP TOLD ME...
...THAT I HAD TO KILL YOU IN ORDER TO SAVE MY FAMILY!
BUT I KNOW NOW THAT THEY'VE ALWAYS MEANT TO KILL US ALL...
THEY COULDN'T RISK HAVING THE KR EXPOSED...

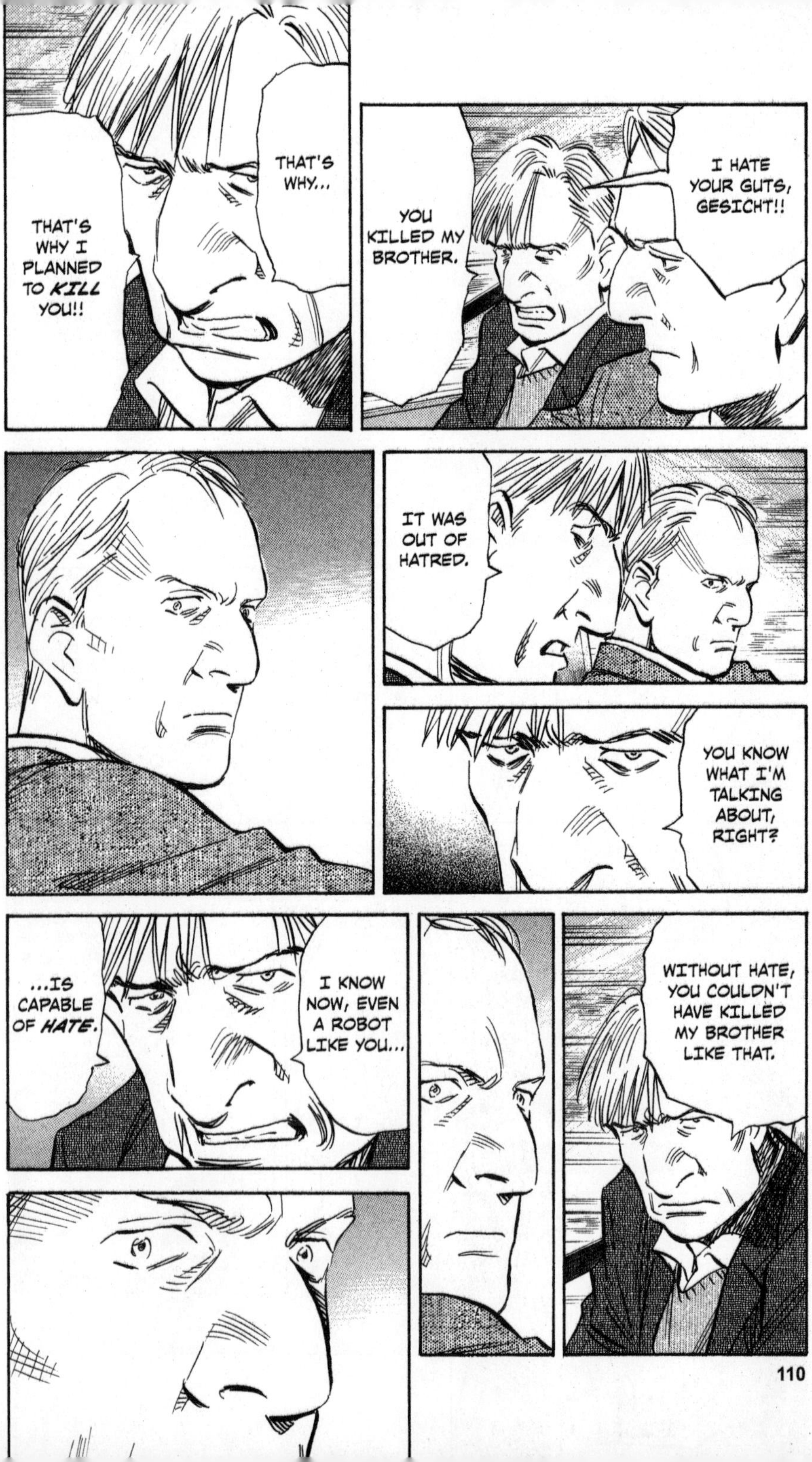
I HATE YOUR GUTS, GESICHT!!
YOU KILLED MY BROTHER.
THAT'S WHY...
THAT'S WHY I PLANNED TO KILL YOU!!
IT WAS OUT OF HATRED.
YOU KNOW WHAT I'M TALKING ABOUT, RIGHT?
WITHOUT HATE, YOU COULDN'T HAVE KILLED MY BROTHER LIKE THAT.
I KNOW NOW, EVEN A ROBOT LIKE YOU...
...IS CAPABLE OF HATE.

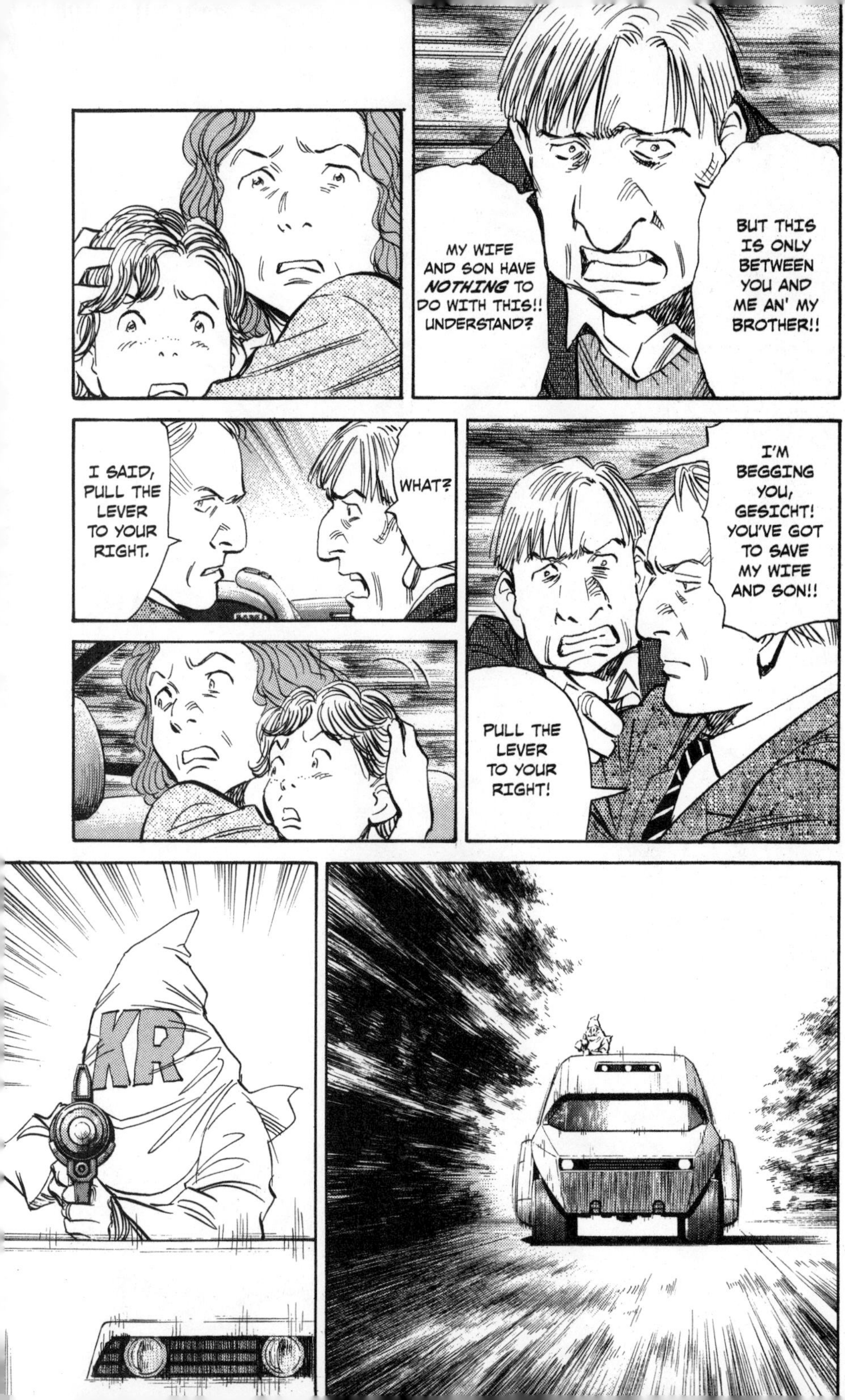
BUT THIS IS ONLY BETWEEN YOU AND ME AN' MY BROTHER!!
MY WIFE AND SON HAVE *NOTHING* TO DO WITH THIS!! UNDERSTAND?
I'M BEGGING YOU, GESICHT! YOU'VE GOT TO SAVE MY WIFE AND SON!!
PULL THE LEVER TO YOUR RIGHT!
WHAT?
I SAID, PULL THE LEVER TO YOUR RIGHT.
KR

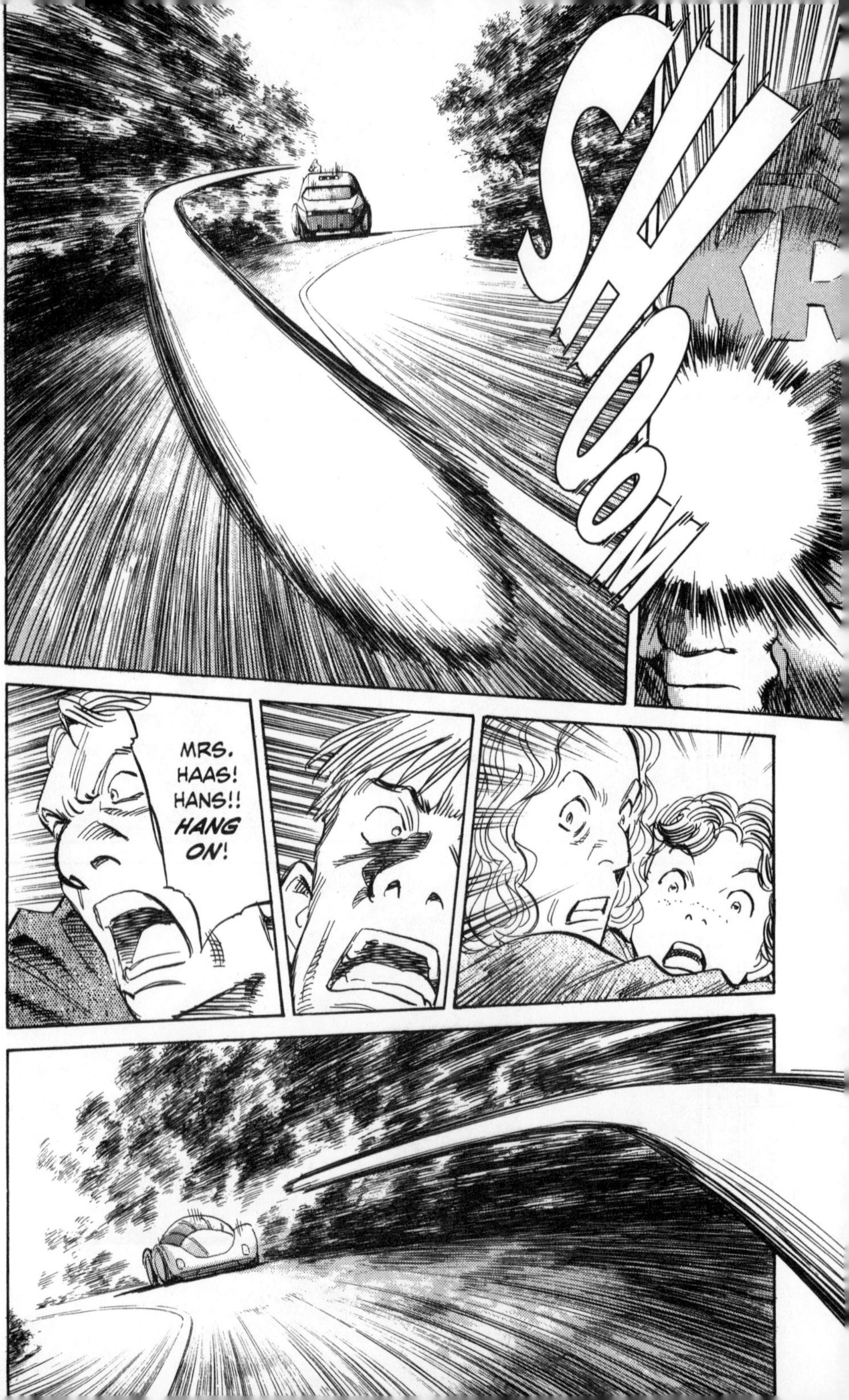
KR
SHOOOM
MRS. HAAS! HANS!! *HANG ON*!

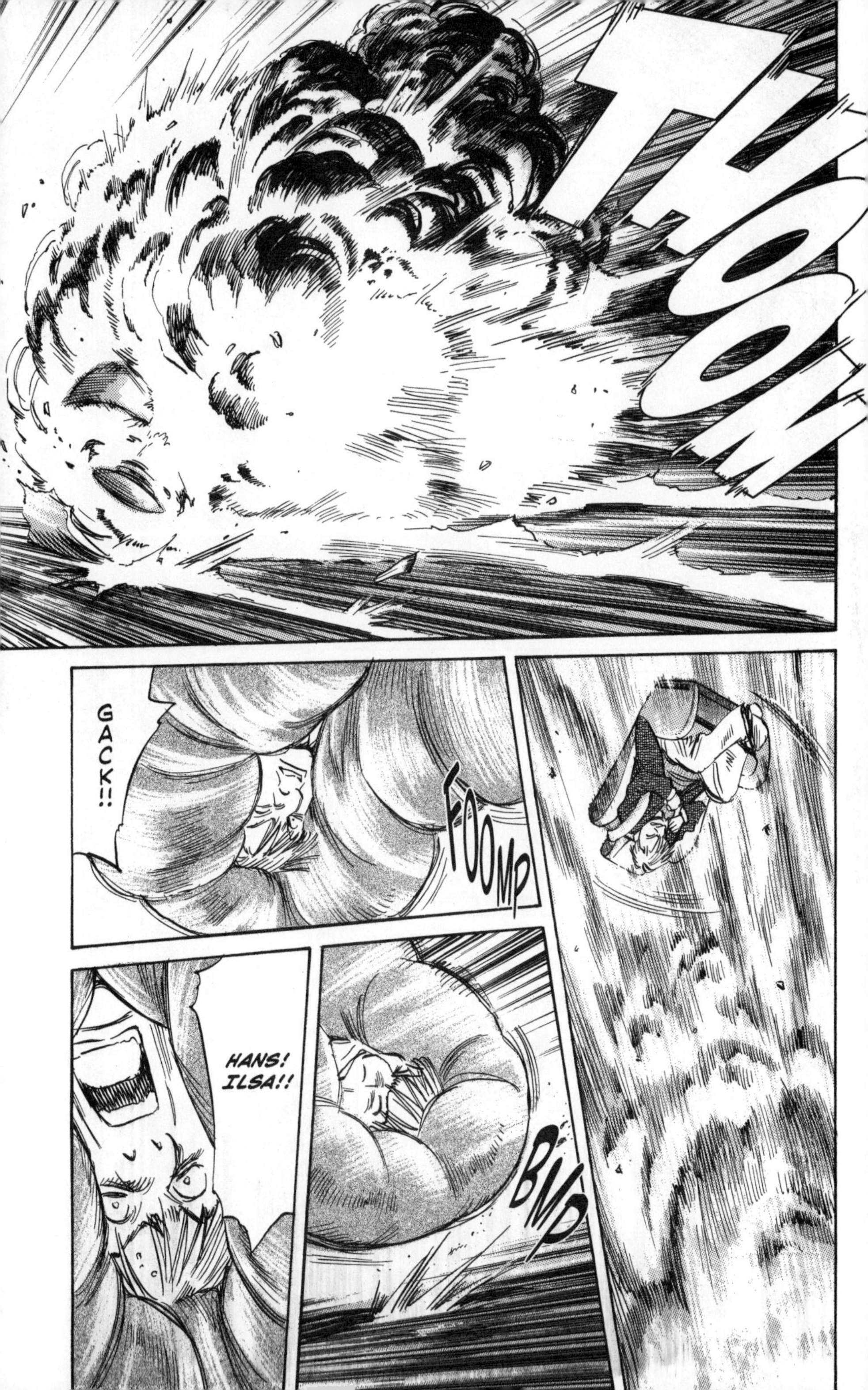
THOOM
GACK!!
FOOMP
BMP
HANS! ILSA!!

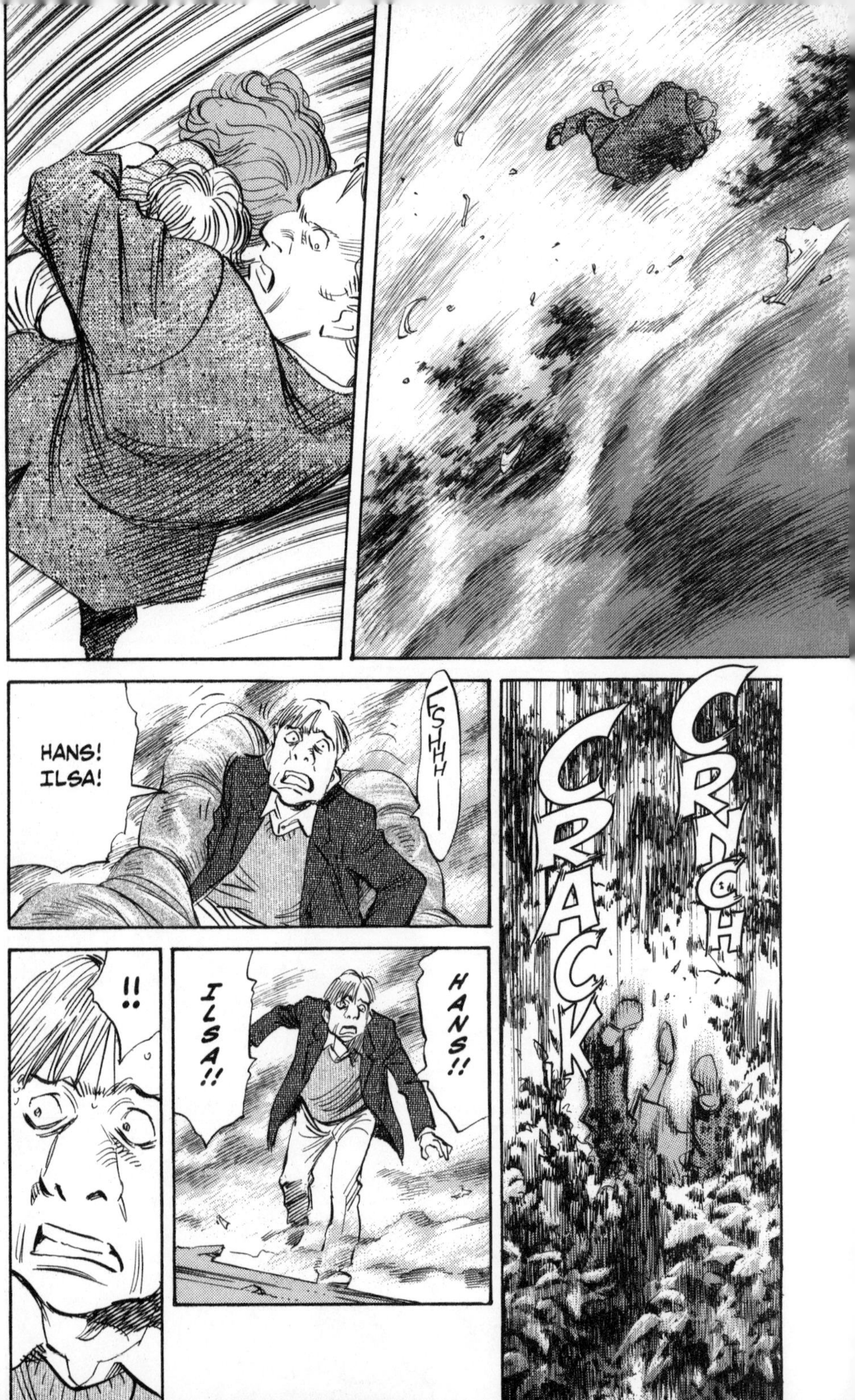
CRNCH
CRACK
FSHHH
HANS!
ILSA!
HANS!!
ILSA!!
!!

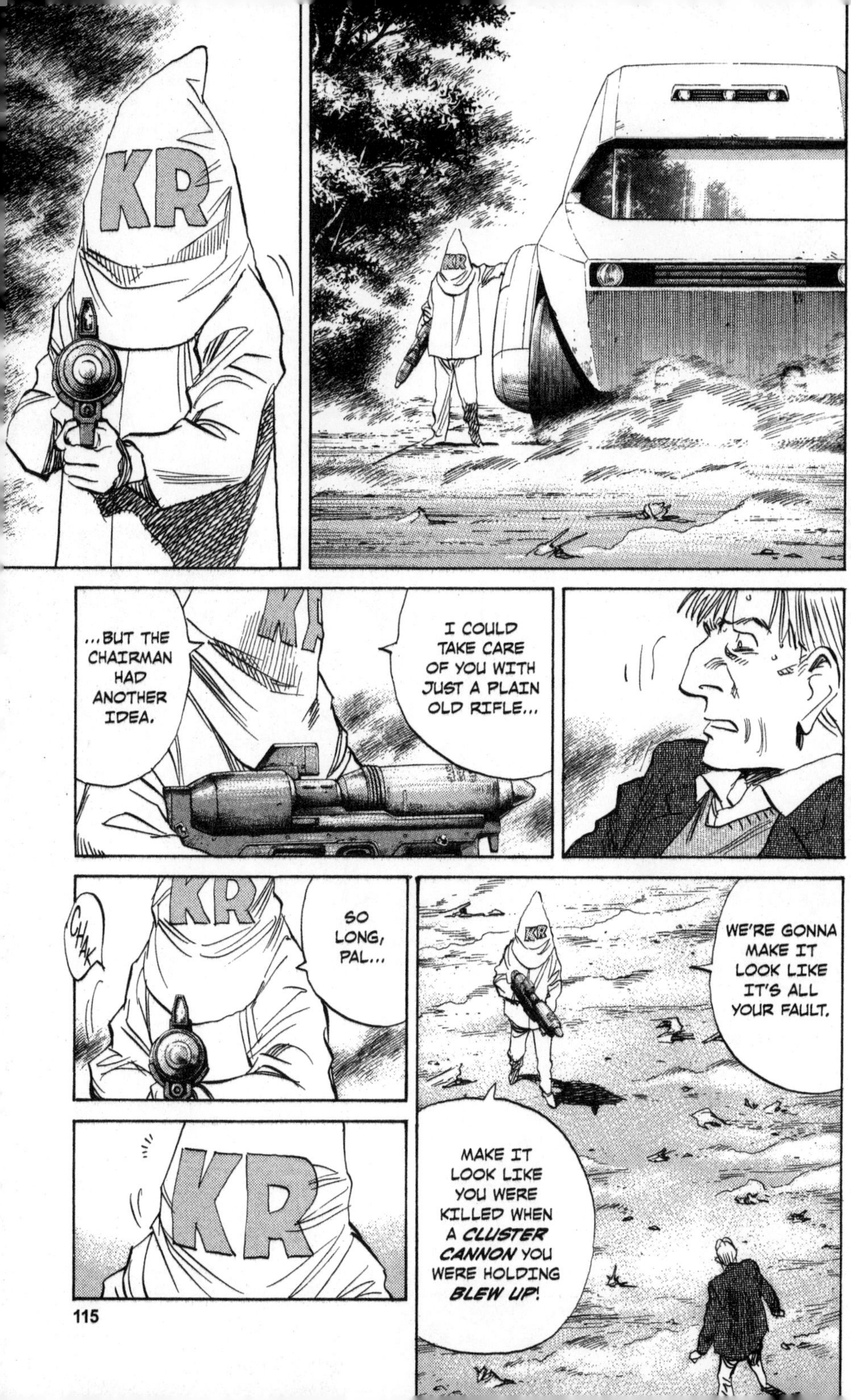
I COULD TAKE CARE OF YOU WITH JUST A PLAIN OLD RIFLE...
...BUT THE CHAIRMAN HAD ANOTHER IDEA.
WE'RE GONNA MAKE IT LOOK LIKE IT'S ALL YOUR FAULT.
MAKE IT LOOK LIKE YOU WERE KILLED WHEN A ***CLUSTER CANNON*** YOU WERE HOLDING ***BLEW UP***!
SO LONG, PAL...
CHAK

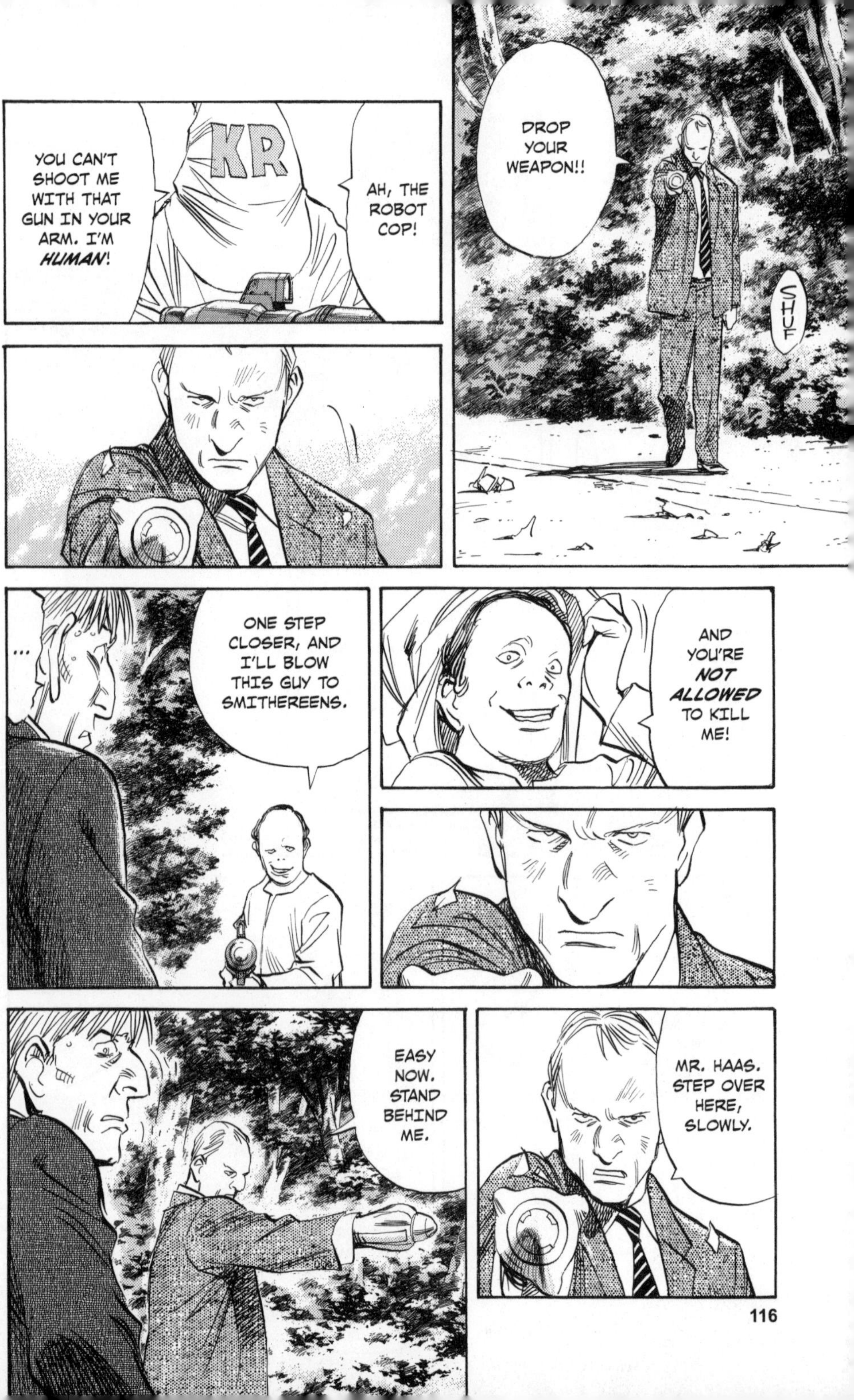

DROP YOUR WEAPON!!
SHUF
AH, THE ROBOT COP!
YOU CAN'T SHOOT ME WITH THAT GUN IN YOUR ARM. I'M ***HUMAN***!
KR
AND YOU'RE ***NOT ALLOWED*** TO KILL ME!
ONE STEP CLOSER, AND I'LL BLOW THIS GUY TO SMITHEREENS.
...
MR. HAAS. STEP OVER HERE, SLOWLY.
EASY NOW. STAND BEHIND ME.

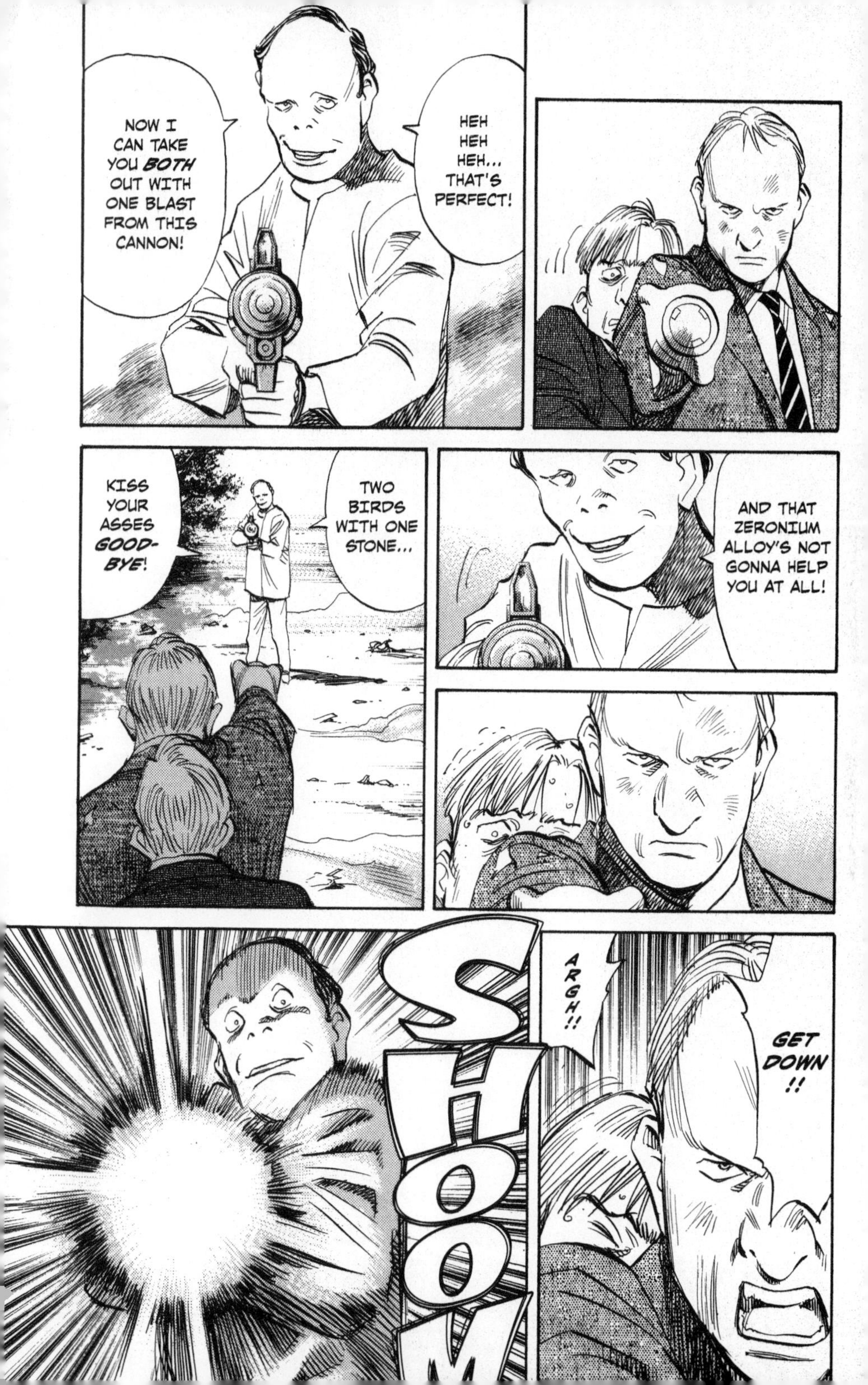
HEH HEH HEH... THAT'S PERFECT!
NOW I CAN TAKE YOU *BOTH* OUT WITH ONE BLAST FROM THIS CANNON!
AND THAT ZERONIUM ALLOY'S NOT GONNA HELP YOU AT ALL!
TWO BIRDS WITH ONE STONE...
KISS YOUR ASSES *GOOD-BYE*!
*ARGH!!*
*GET DOWN!!*
SHOOM

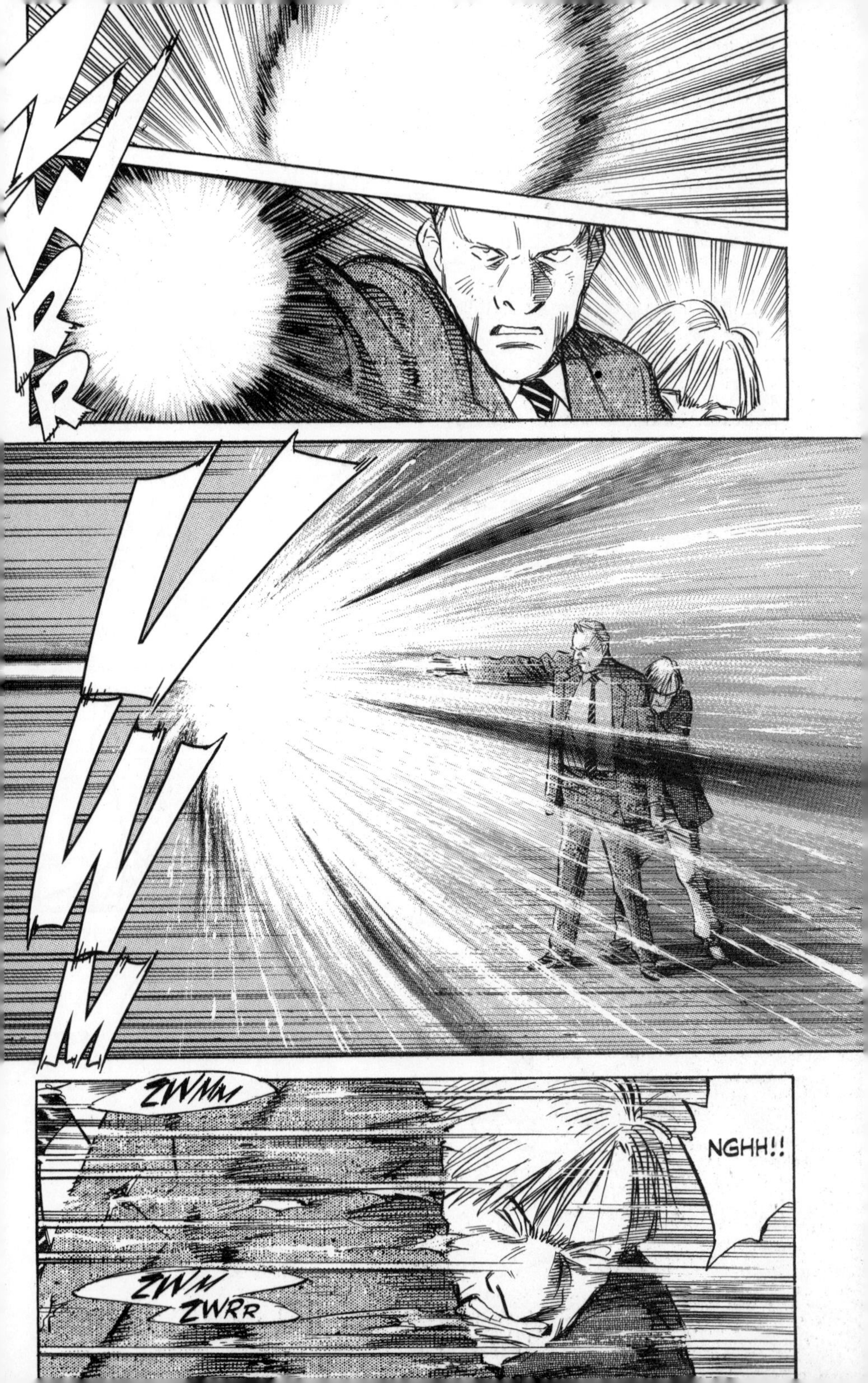
ZWRR
VWWM
NGHH!!
ZWMM
ZWM
ZWRr

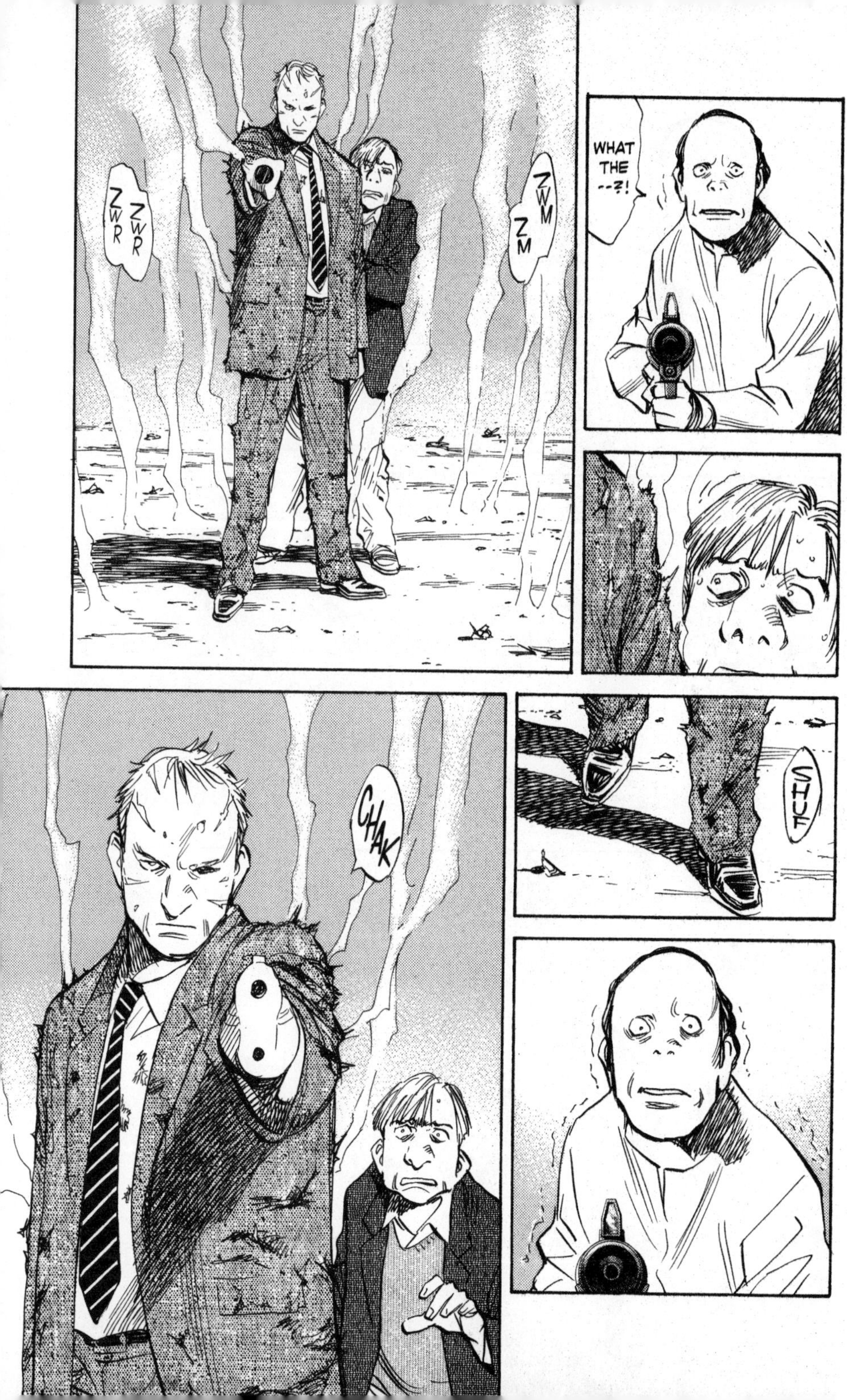
WHAT THE --?!
ZWR ZWR
ZWM ZM
SHUF
CHAK

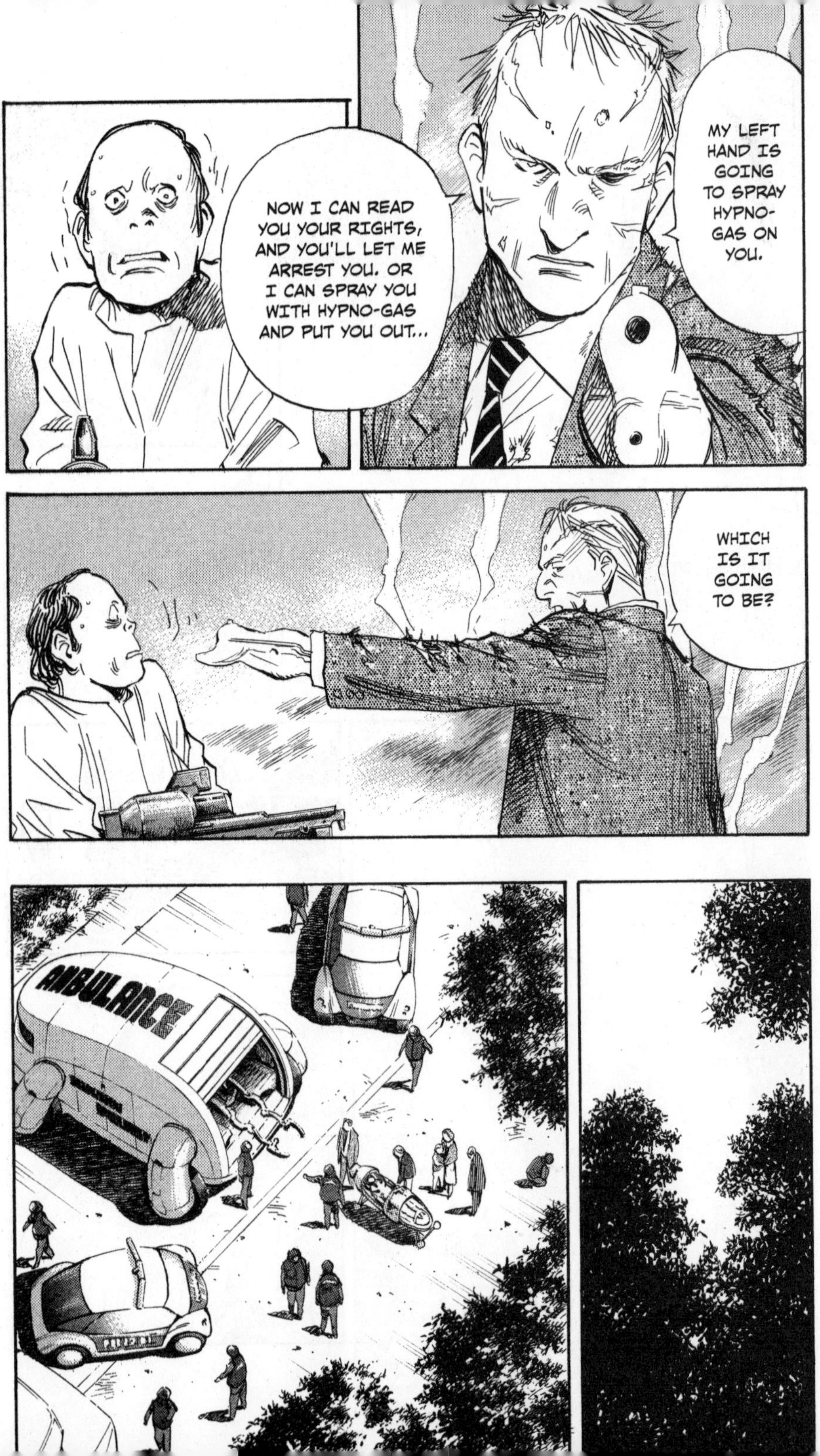
MY LEFT HAND IS GOING TO SPRAY HYPNO-GAS ON YOU.
NOW I CAN READ YOU YOUR RIGHTS, AND YOU'LL LET ME ARREST YOU. OR I CAN SPRAY YOU WITH HYPNO-GAS AND PUT YOU OUT...
WHICH IS IT GOING TO BE?
AMBULANCE

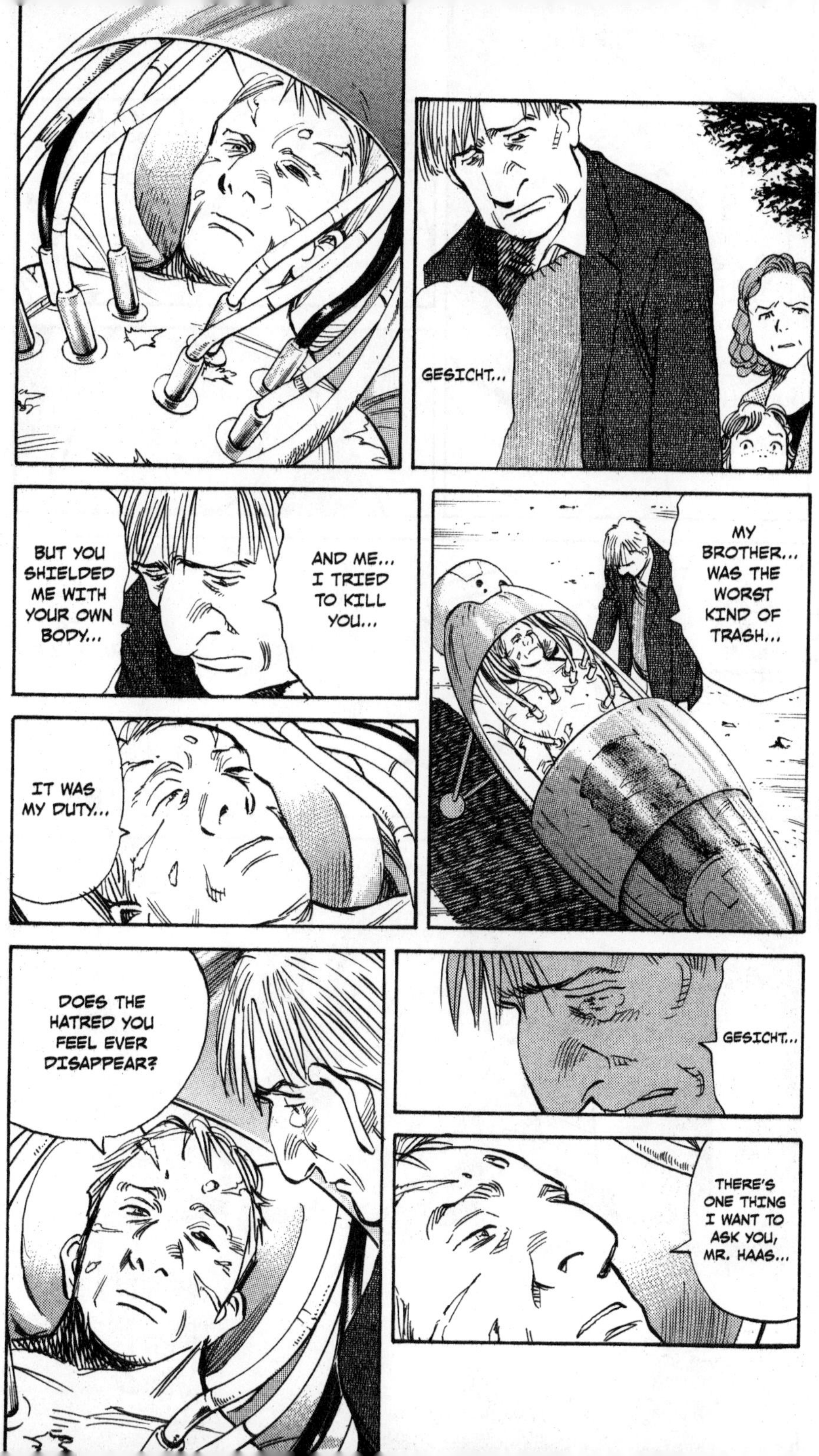
GESICHT...
MY BROTHER... WAS THE WORST KIND OF TRASH...
AND ME... I TRIED TO KILL YOU...
BUT YOU SHIELDED ME WITH YOUR OWN BODY...
IT WAS MY DUTY...
GESICHT...
THERE'S ONE THING I WANT TO ASK YOU, MR. HAAS...
DOES THE HATRED YOU FEEL EVER DISAPPEAR?

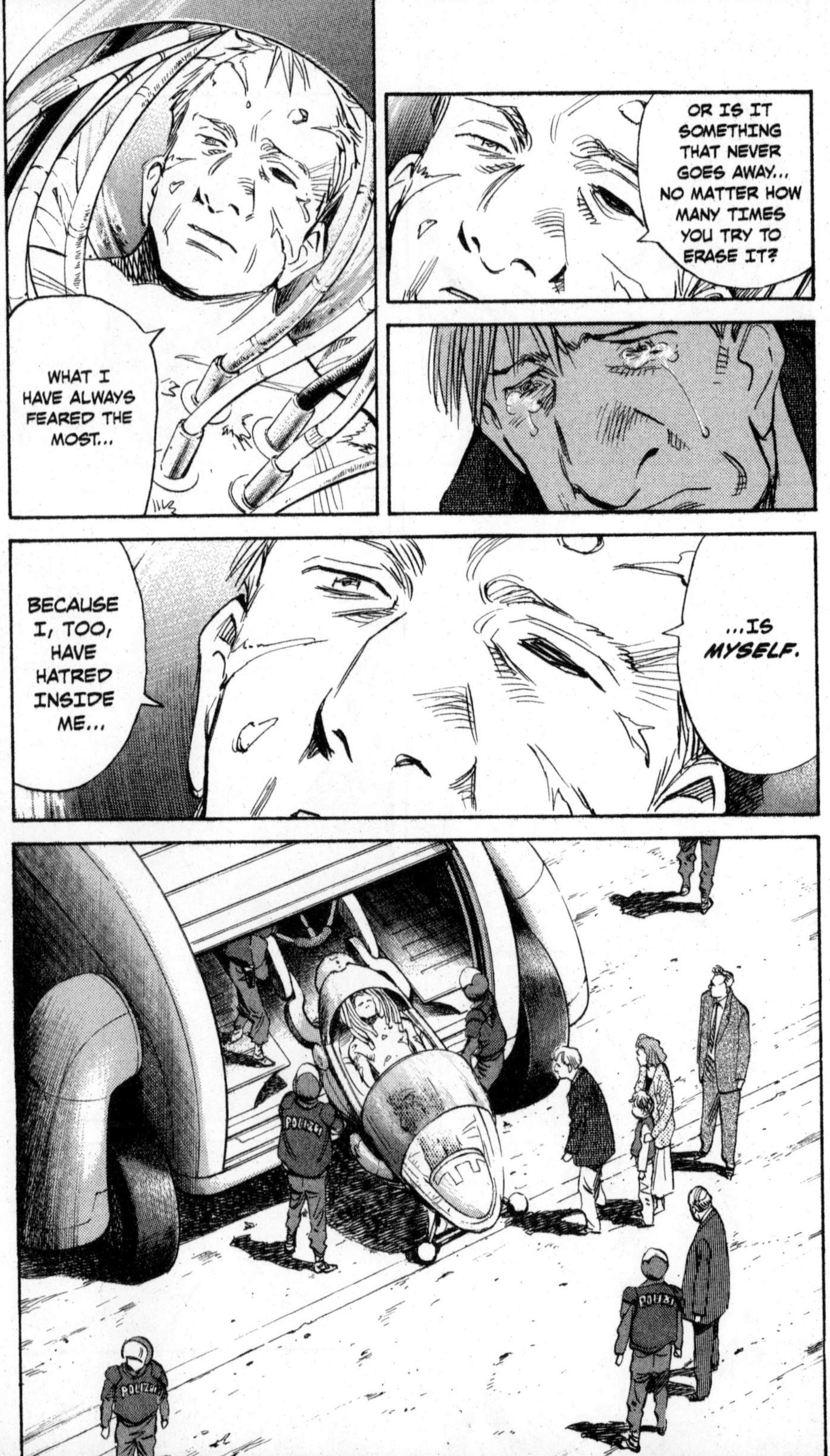
OR IS IT SOMETHING THAT NEVER GOES AWAY... NO MATTER HOW MANY TIMES YOU TRY TO ERASE IT?
WHAT I HAVE ALWAYS FEARED THE MOST...
...IS *MYSELF*.
BECAUSE I, TOO, HAVE HATRED INSIDE ME...
POLIZEI
POLIZEI
POLIZEI

# Act 37 SAD VISITOR

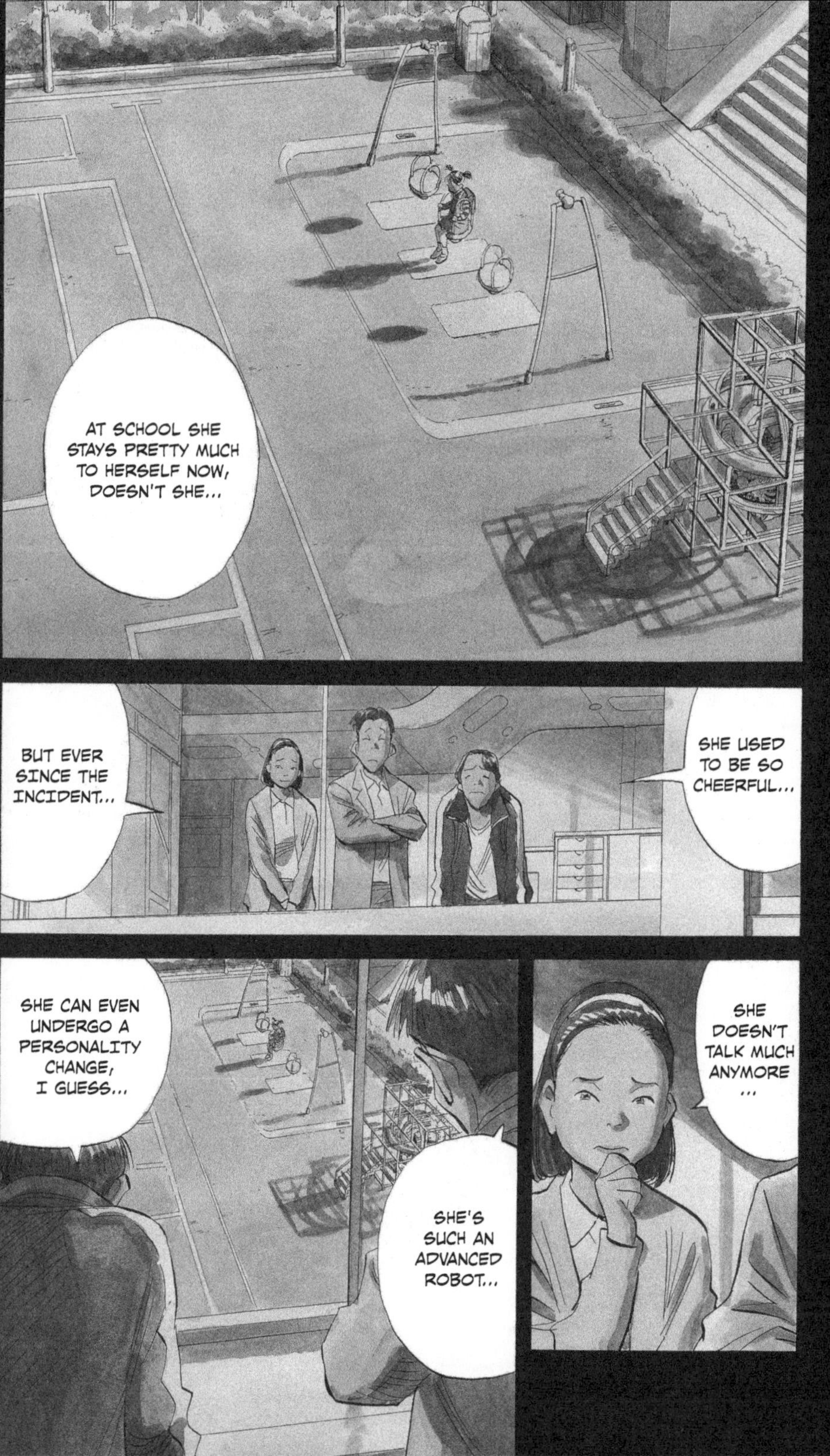

AT SCHOOL SHE STAYS PRETTY MUCH TO HERSELF NOW, DOESN'T SHE...
SHE USED TO BE SO CHEERFUL...
BUT EVER SINCE THE INCIDENT...
SHE DOESN'T TALK MUCH ANYMORE...
SHE'S SUCH AN ADVANCED ROBOT...
SHE CAN EVEN UNDERGO A PERSONALITY CHANGE, I GUESS...

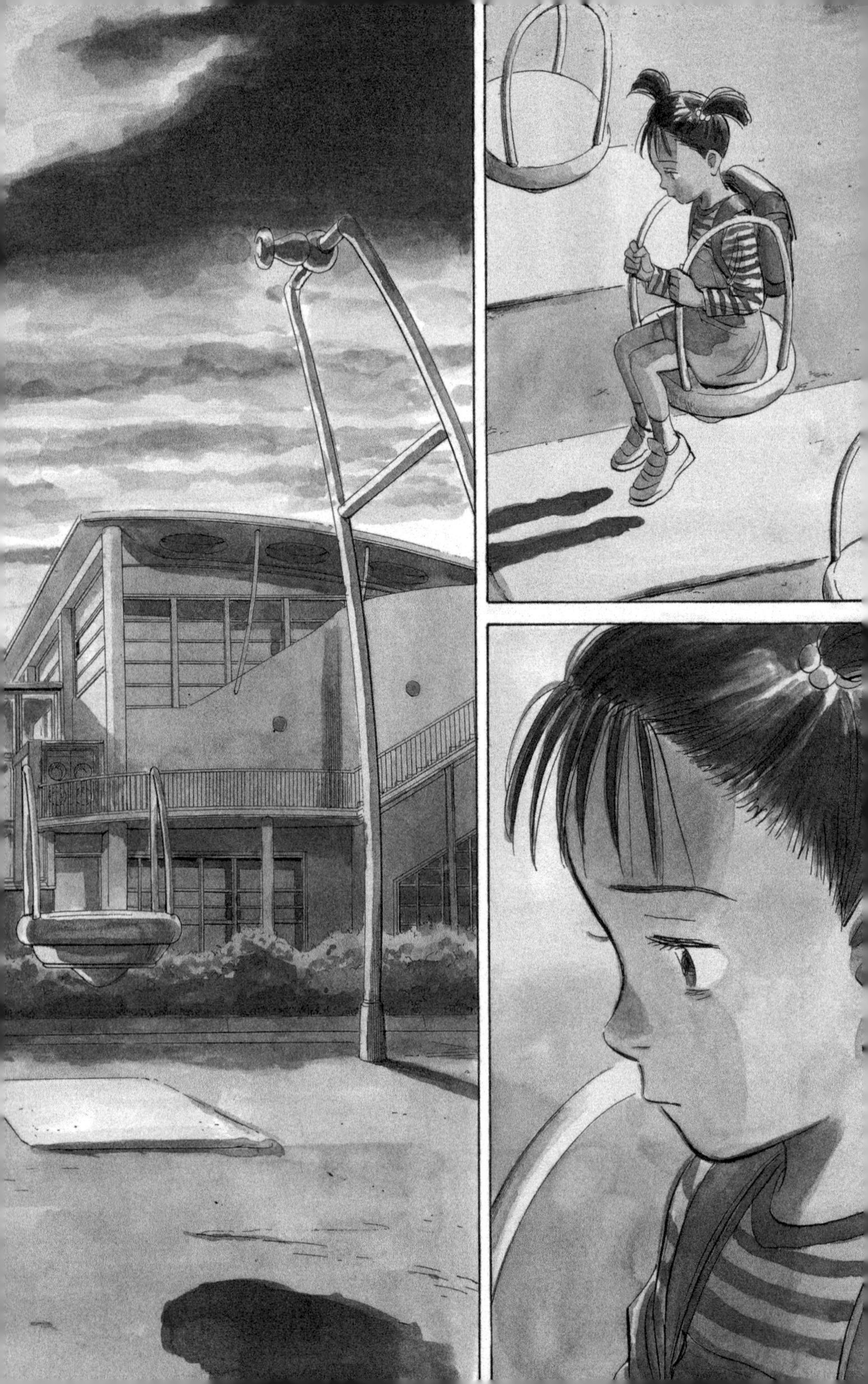

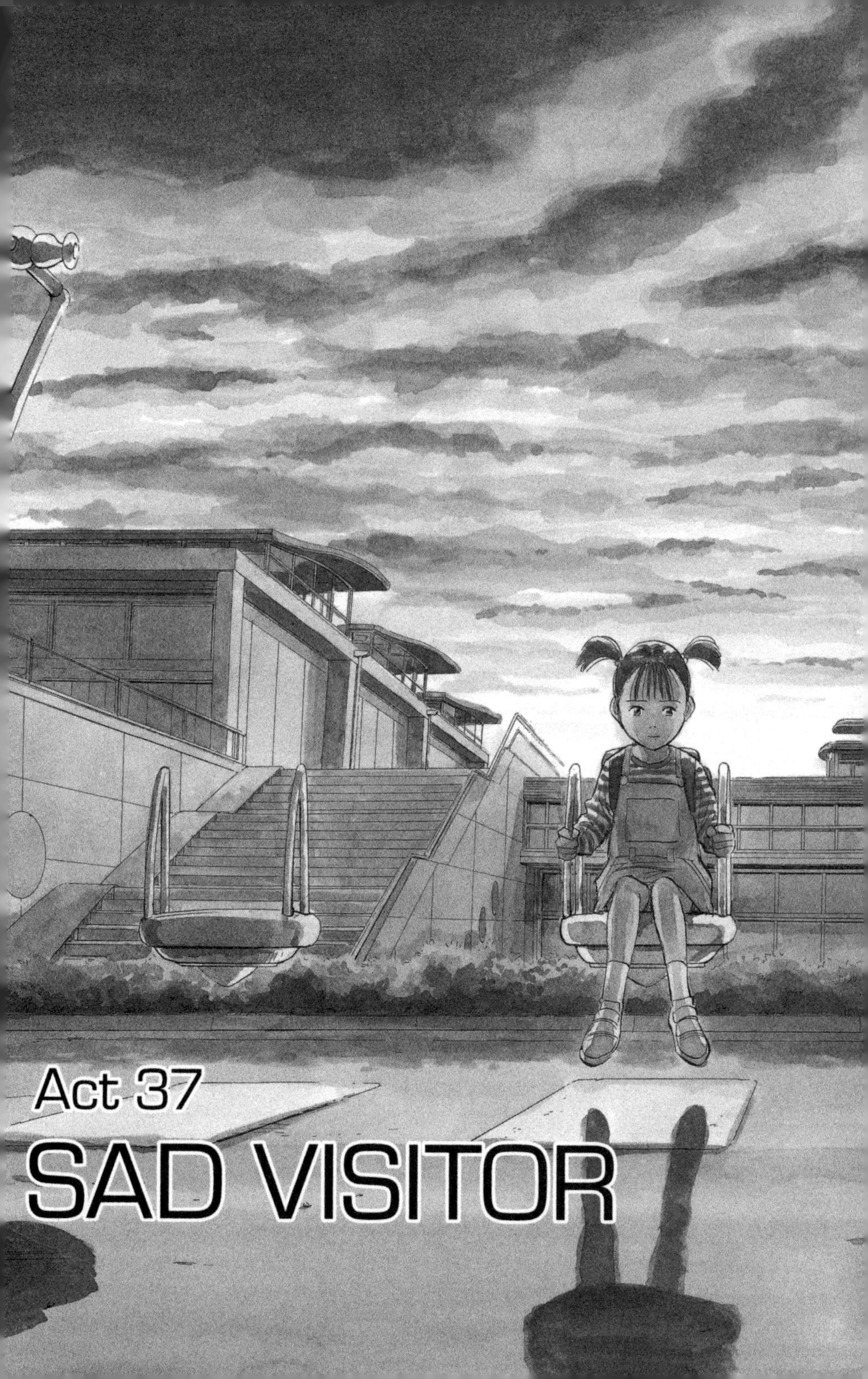
Act 37
SAD VISITOR

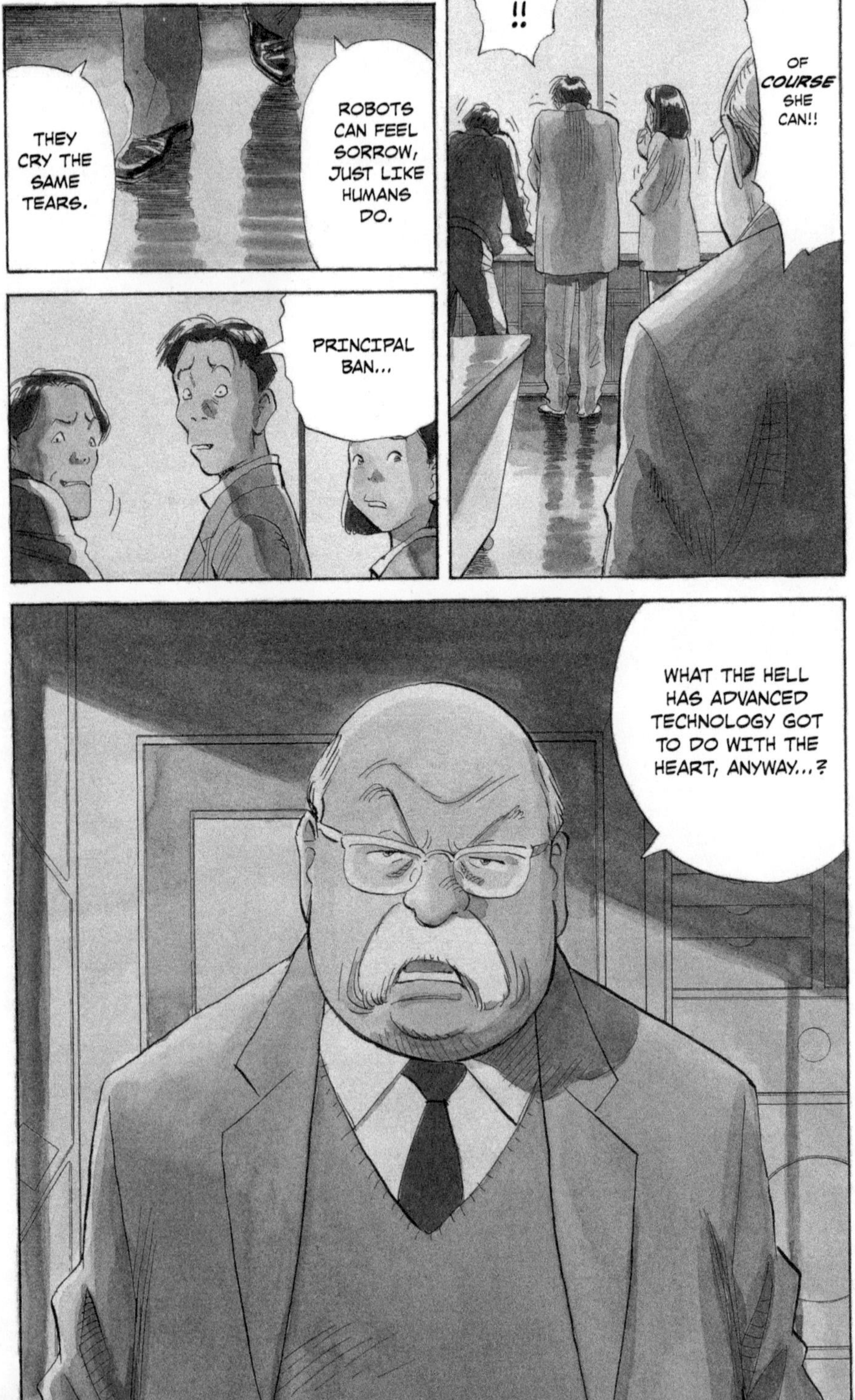

OF COURSE SHE CAN!!
!!
ROBOTS CAN FEEL SORROW, JUST LIKE HUMANS DO.
THEY CRY THE SAME TEARS.
PRINCIPAL BAN...
WHAT THE HELL HAS ADVANCED TECHNOLOGY GOT TO DO WITH THE HEART, ANYWAY...?

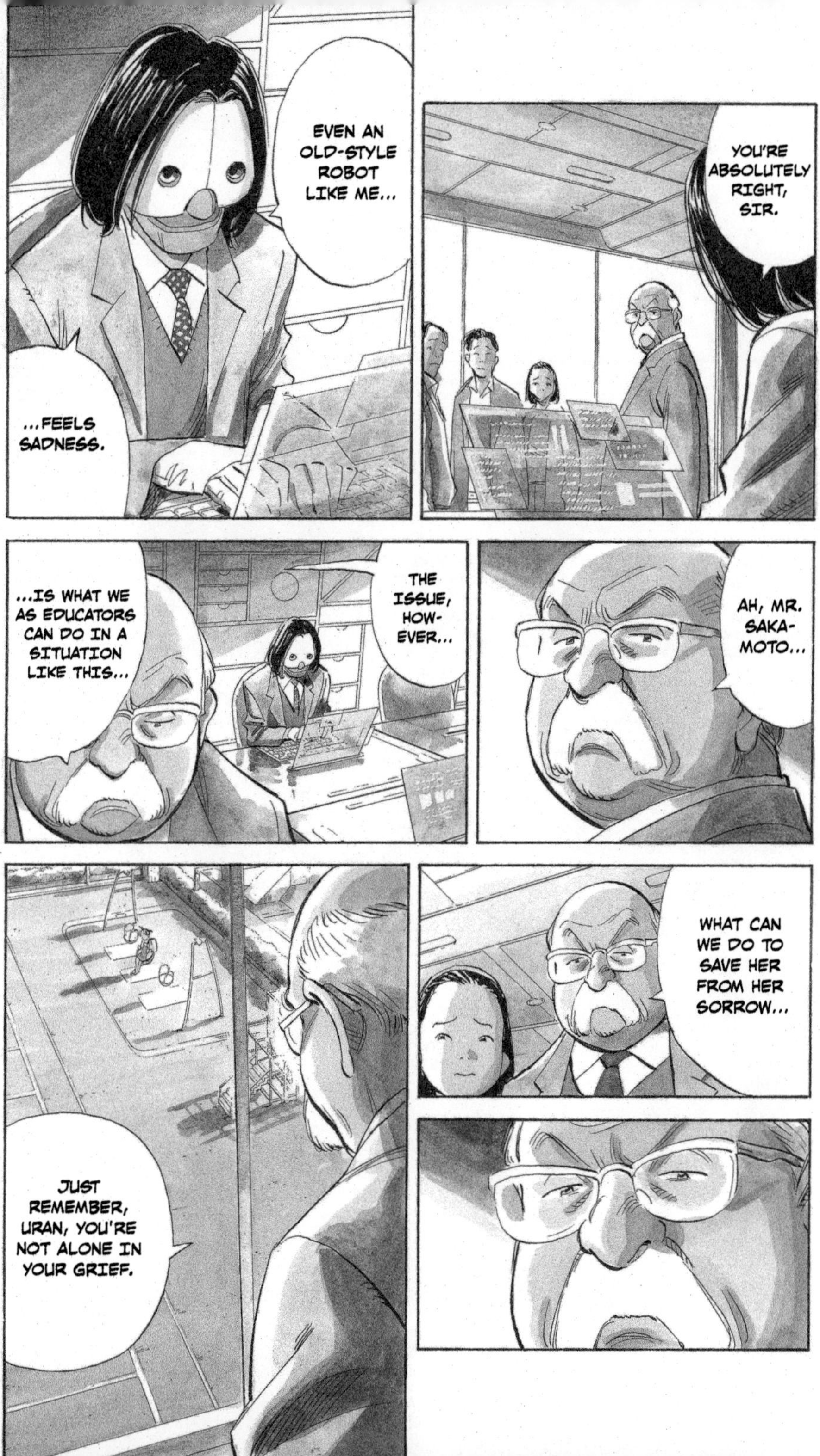
EVEN AN OLD-STYLE ROBOT LIKE ME...
...FEELS SADNESS.
YOU'RE ABSOLUTELY RIGHT, SIR.
THE ISSUE, HOW-EVER...
...IS WHAT WE AS EDUCATORS CAN DO IN A SITUATION LIKE THIS...
AH, MR. SAKA-MOTO...
WHAT CAN WE DO TO SAVE HER FROM HER SORROW...
JUST REMEMBER, URAN, YOU'RE NOT ALONE IN YOUR GRIEF.

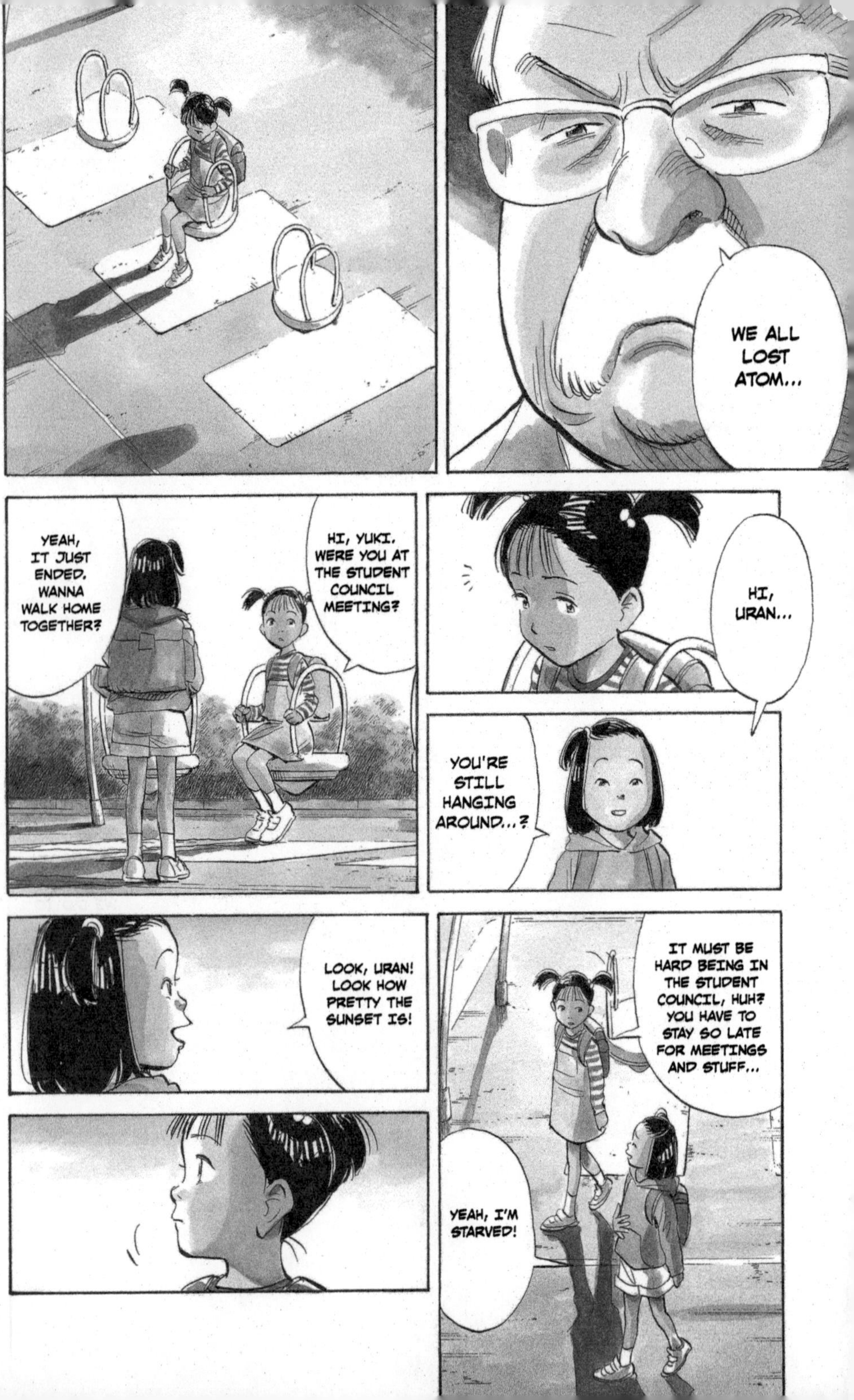
WE ALL LOST ATOM...
HI, URAN...
YOU'RE STILL HANGING AROUND...?
HI, YUKI. WERE YOU AT THE STUDENT COUNCIL MEETING?
YEAH, IT JUST ENDED. WANNA WALK HOME TOGETHER?
IT MUST BE HARD BEING IN THE STUDENT COUNCIL, HUH? YOU HAVE TO STAY SO LATE FOR MEETINGS AND STUFF...
YEAH, I'M STARVED!
LOOK, URAN! LOOK HOW PRETTY THE SUNSET IS!

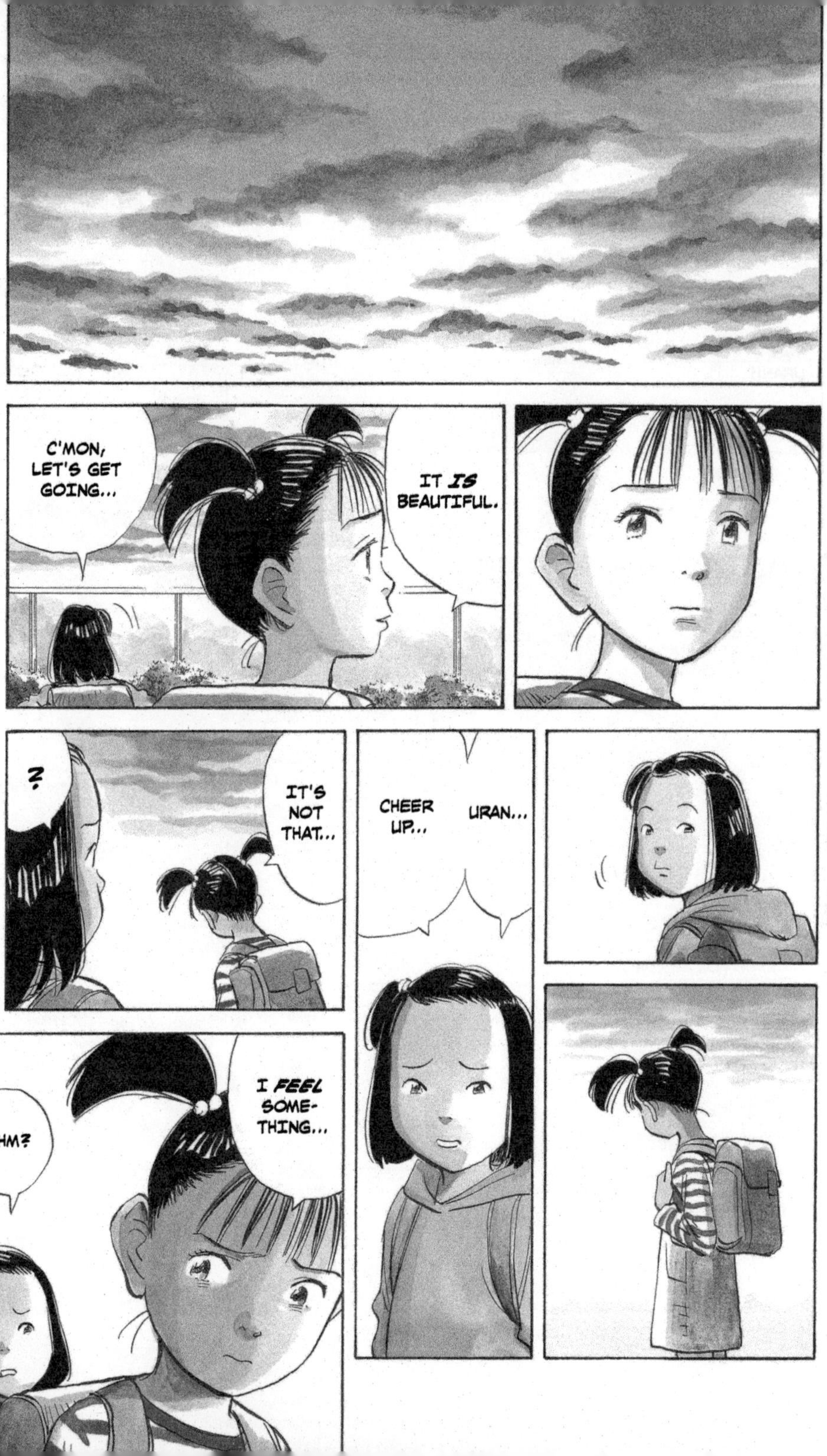
IT *IS* BEAUTIFUL.
C'MON, LET'S GET GOING...
URAN...
CHEER UP...
IT'S NOT THAT...
?
I *FEEL* SOME-THING...
HM?

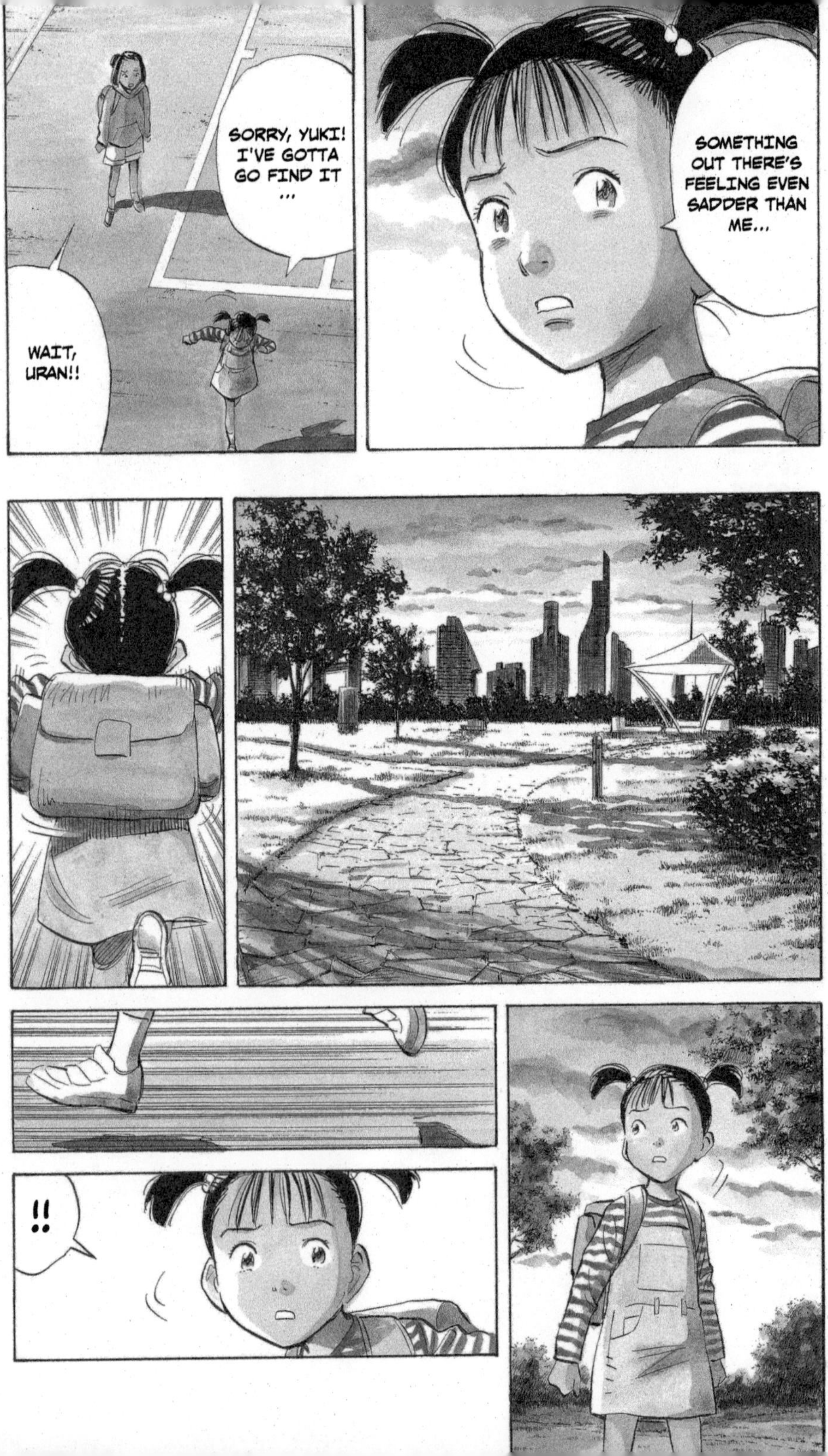
SOMETHING OUT THERE'S FEELING EVEN SADDER THAN ME...
SORRY, YUKI! I'VE GOTTA GO FIND IT ...
WAIT, URAN!!
!!

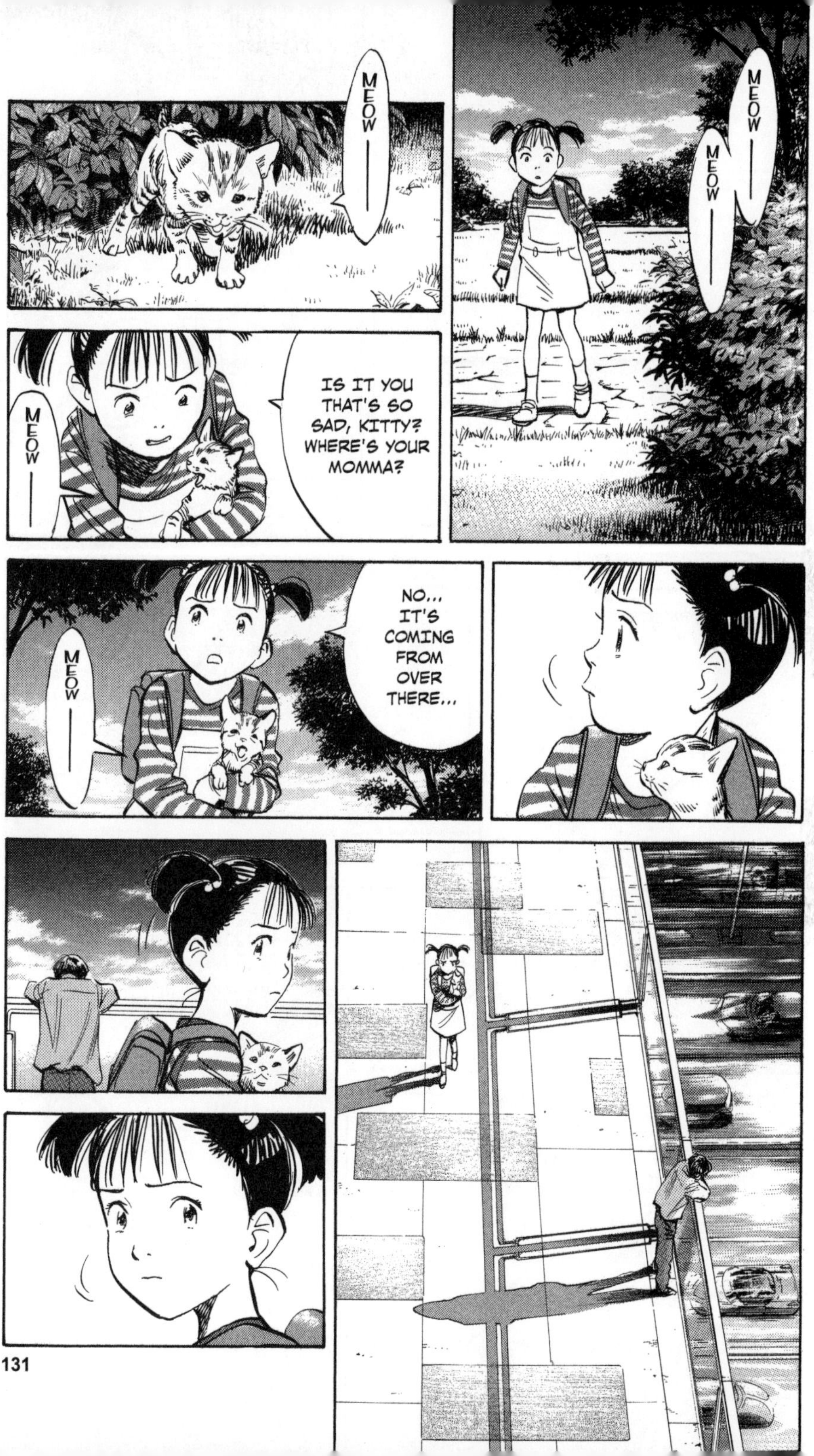
MEOW ——
MEOW ——
MEOW ——
IS IT YOU THAT'S SO SAD, KITTY? WHERE'S YOUR MOMMA?
MEOW ——
NO... IT'S COMING FROM OVER THERE...
MEOW ——

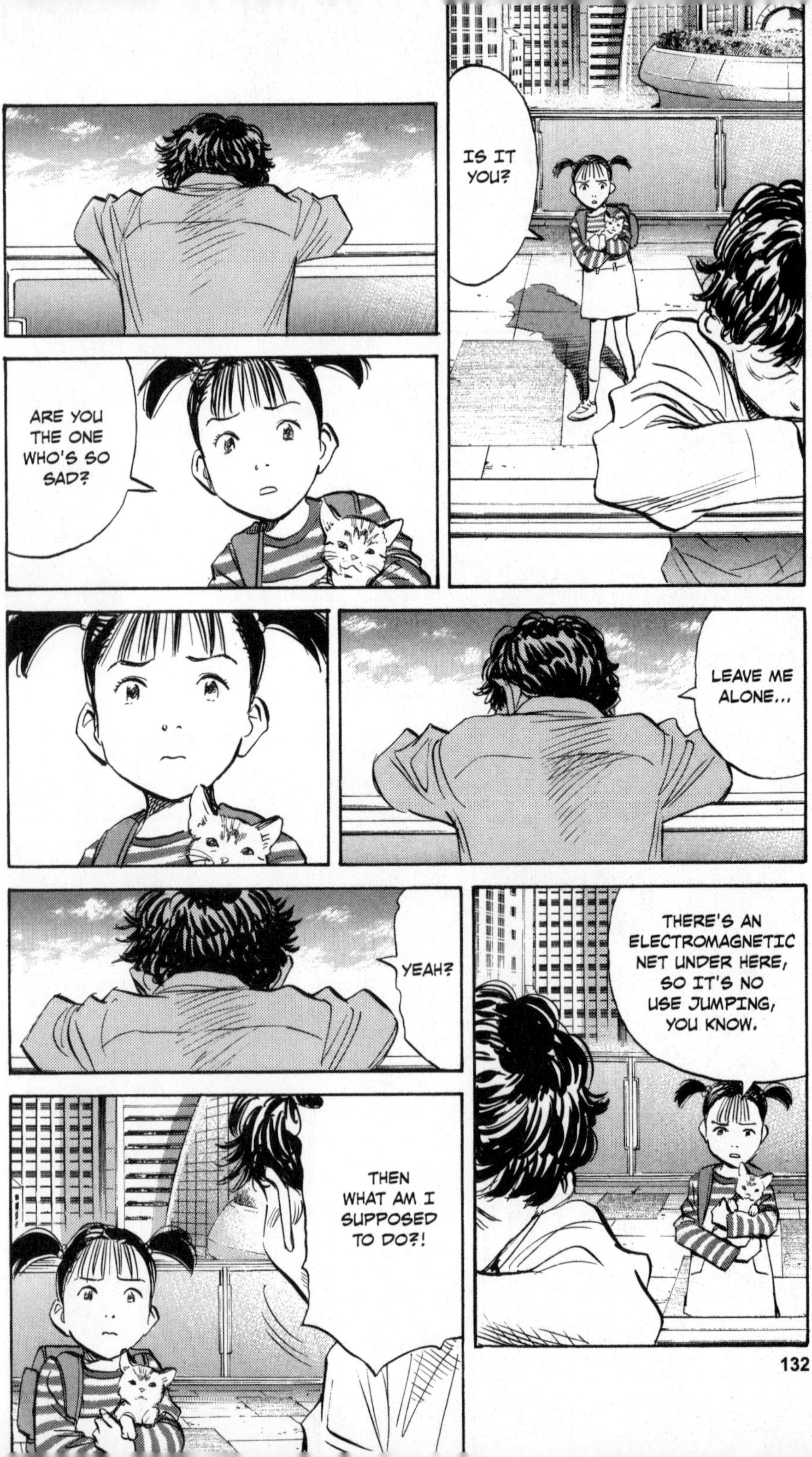
IS IT YOU?
ARE YOU THE ONE WHO'S SO SAD?
LEAVE ME ALONE...
THERE'S AN ELECTROMAGNETIC NET UNDER HERE, SO IT'S NO USE JUMPING, YOU KNOW.
YEAH?
THEN WHAT AM I SUPPOSED TO DO?!

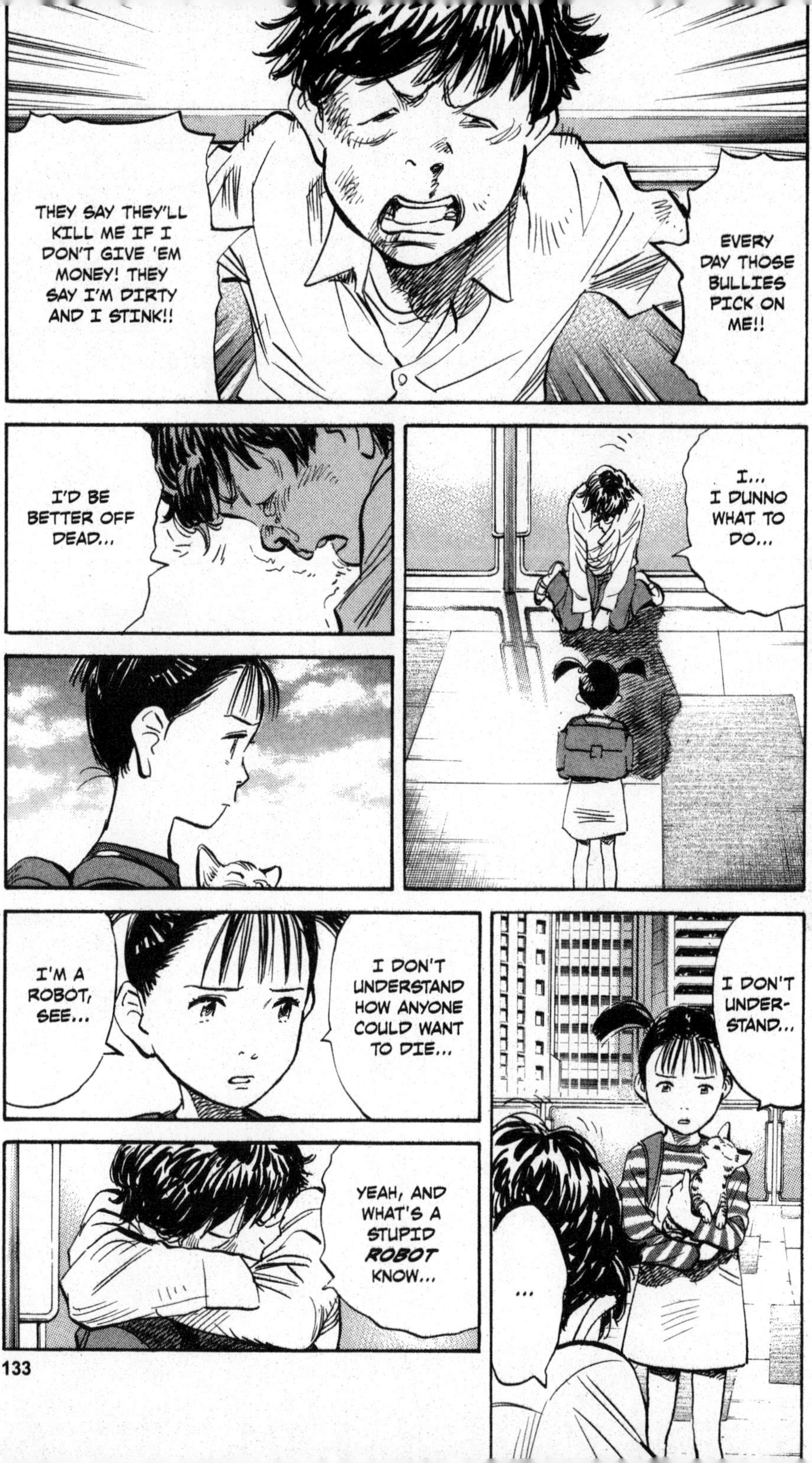
EVERY DAY THOSE BULLIES PICK ON ME!!
THEY SAY THEY'LL KILL ME IF I DON'T GIVE 'EM MONEY! THEY SAY I'M DIRTY AND I STINK!!
I... I DUNNO WHAT TO DO...
I'D BE BETTER OFF DEAD...
I DON'T UNDER-STAND...
...
I DON'T UNDERSTAND HOW ANYONE COULD WANT TO DIE...
I'M A ROBOT, SEE...
YEAH, AND WHAT'S A STUPID *ROBOT* KNOW...

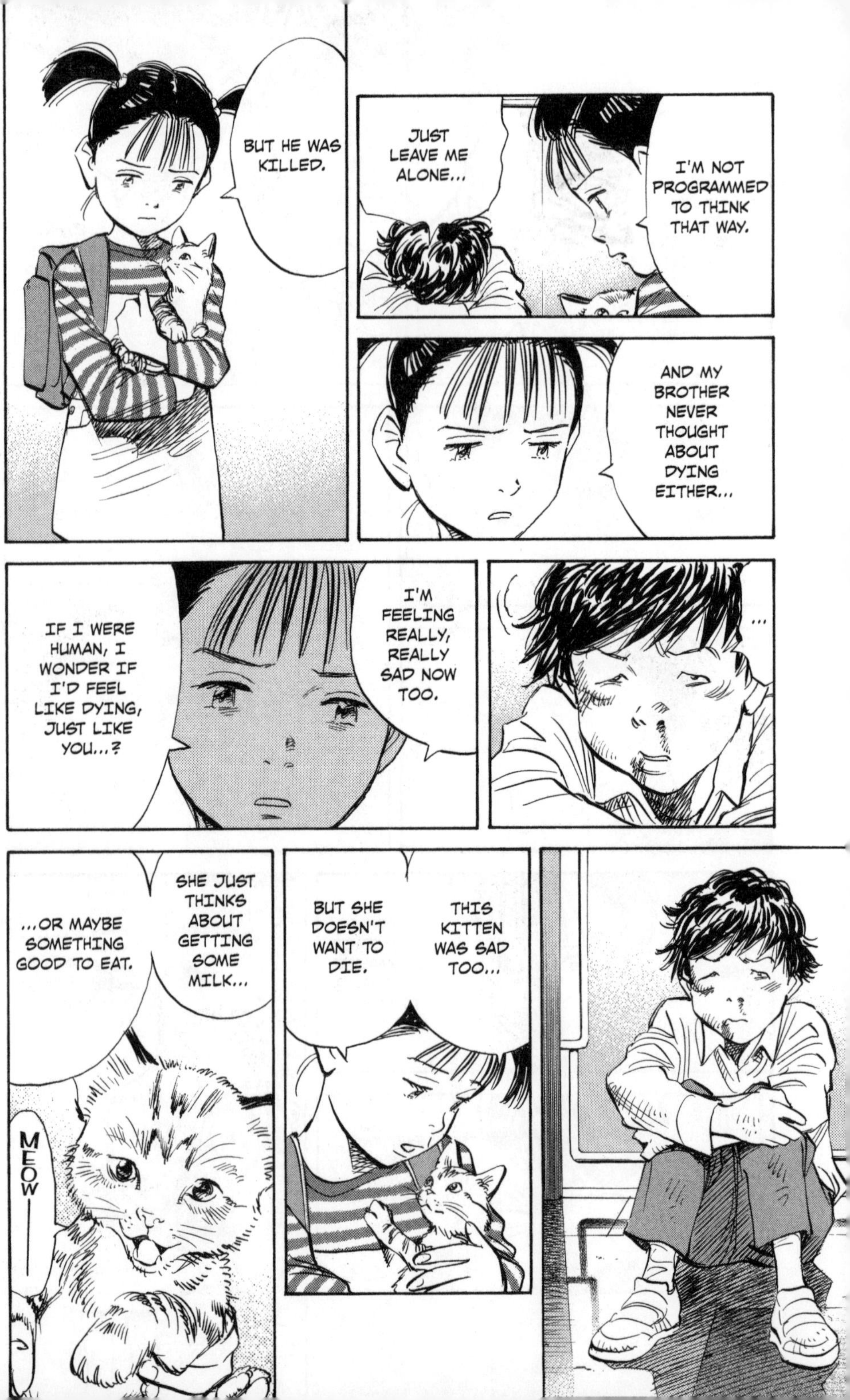
I'M NOT PROGRAMMED TO THINK THAT WAY.
JUST LEAVE ME ALONE...
AND MY BROTHER NEVER THOUGHT ABOUT DYING EITHER...
BUT HE WAS KILLED.
...
I'M FEELING REALLY, REALLY SAD NOW TOO.
IF I WERE HUMAN, I WONDER IF I'D FEEL LIKE DYING, JUST LIKE YOU...?
THIS KITTEN WAS SAD TOO...
BUT SHE DOESN'T WANT TO DIE.
SHE JUST THINKS ABOUT GETTING SOME MILK...
...OR MAYBE SOMETHING GOOD TO EAT.
MEOW——

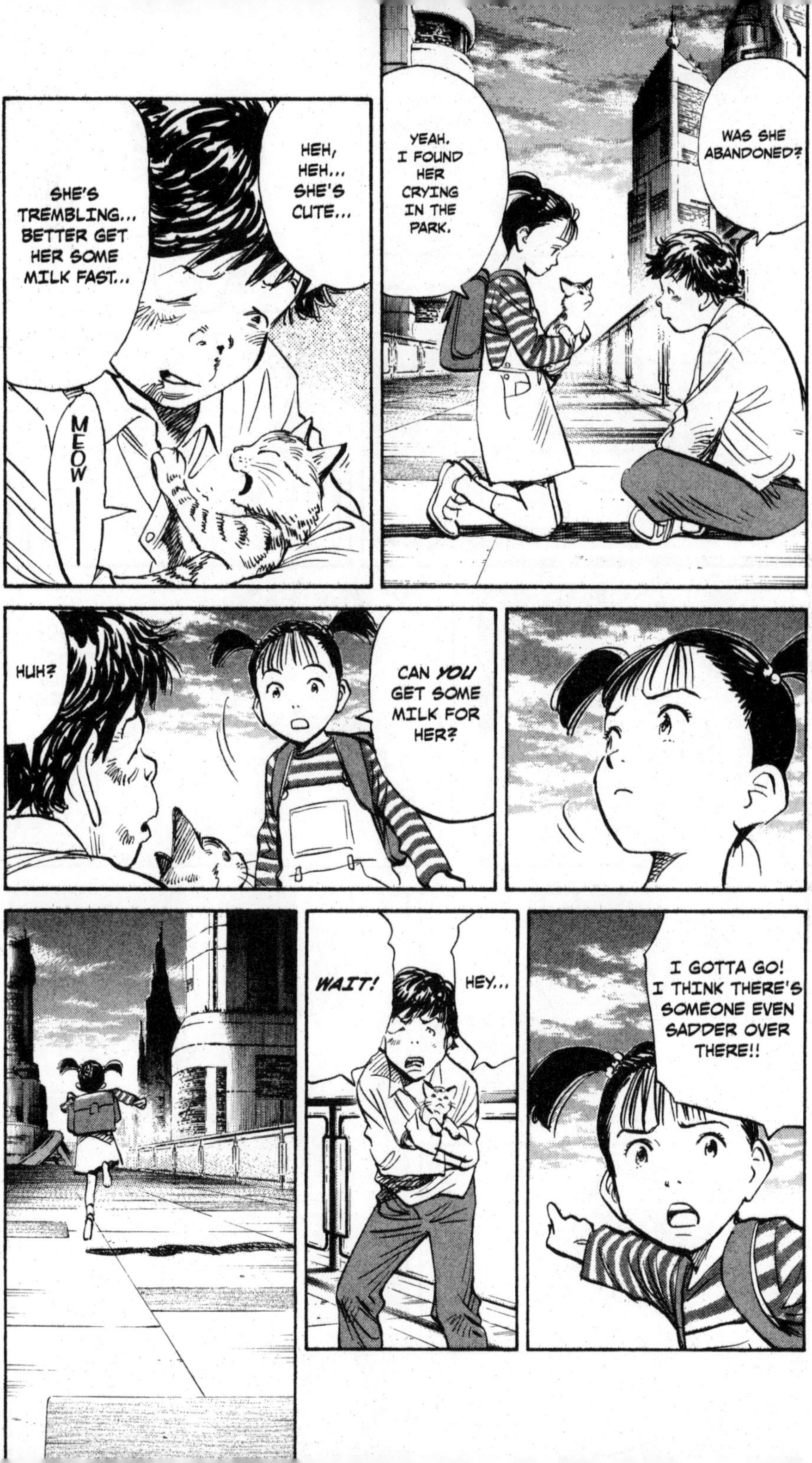
WAS SHE ABANDONED?
YEAH. I FOUND HER CRYING IN THE PARK.
HEH, HEH... SHE'S CUTE...
SHE'S TREMBLING... BETTER GET HER SOME MILK FAST...
MEOW—
CAN *YOU* GET SOME MILK FOR HER?
HUH?
I GOTTA GO! I THINK THERE'S SOMEONE EVEN SADDER OVER THERE!!
HEY...
*WAIT!*

THIS IS YOUR DOG, RIGHT?

YEAH, SO WHAT?

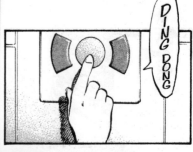

DING DONG

WHAT IS IT?!

HUH?!

HE'S CRYING BECAUSE YOU DON'T WALK HIM ENOUGH.

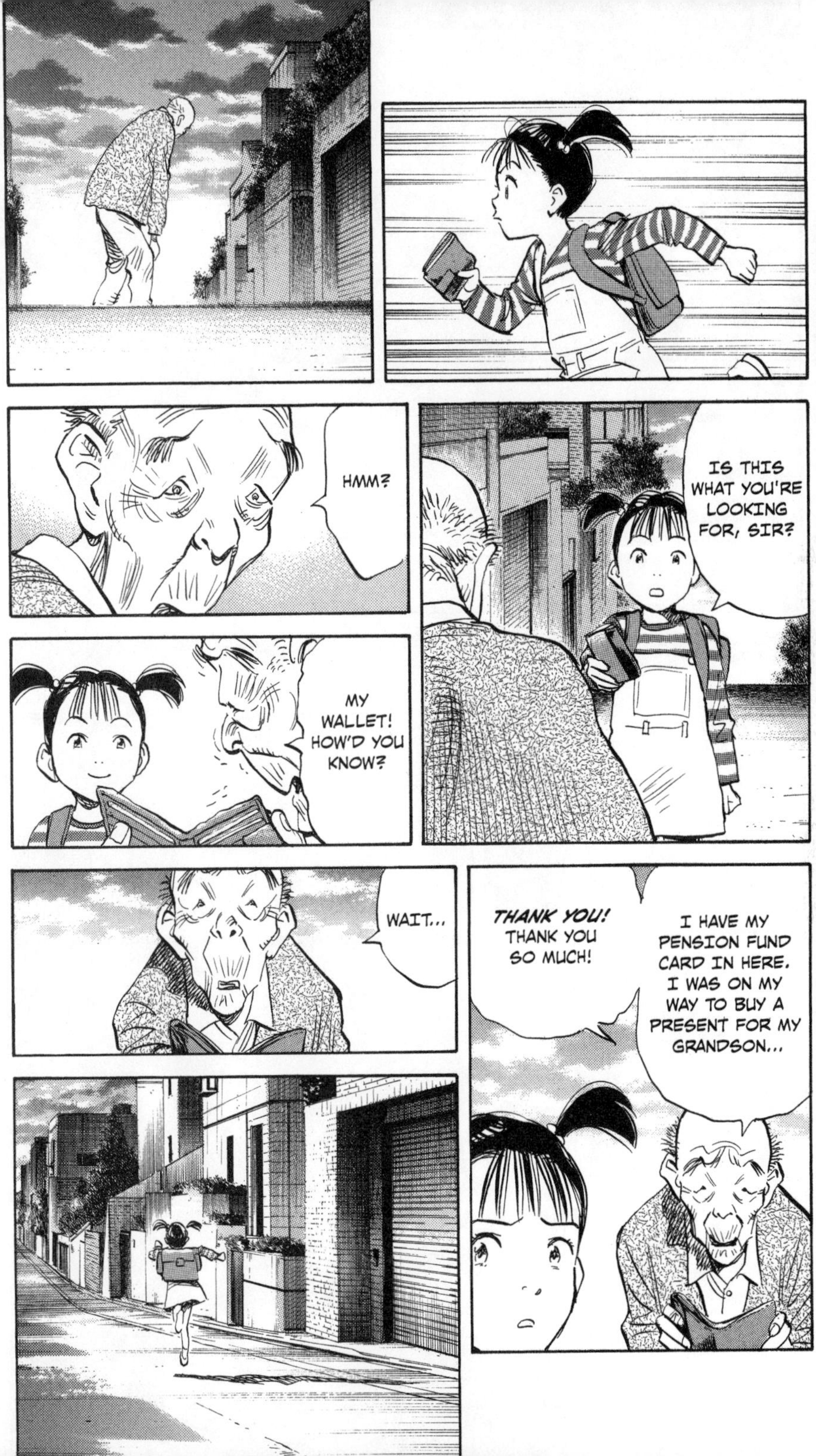
IS THIS WHAT YOU'RE LOOKING FOR, SIR?
HMM?
MY WALLET! HOW'D YOU KNOW?
I HAVE MY PENSION FUND CARD IN HERE. I WAS ON MY WAY TO BUY A PRESENT FOR MY GRANDSON...
THANK YOU! THANK YOU SO MUCH!
WAIT...

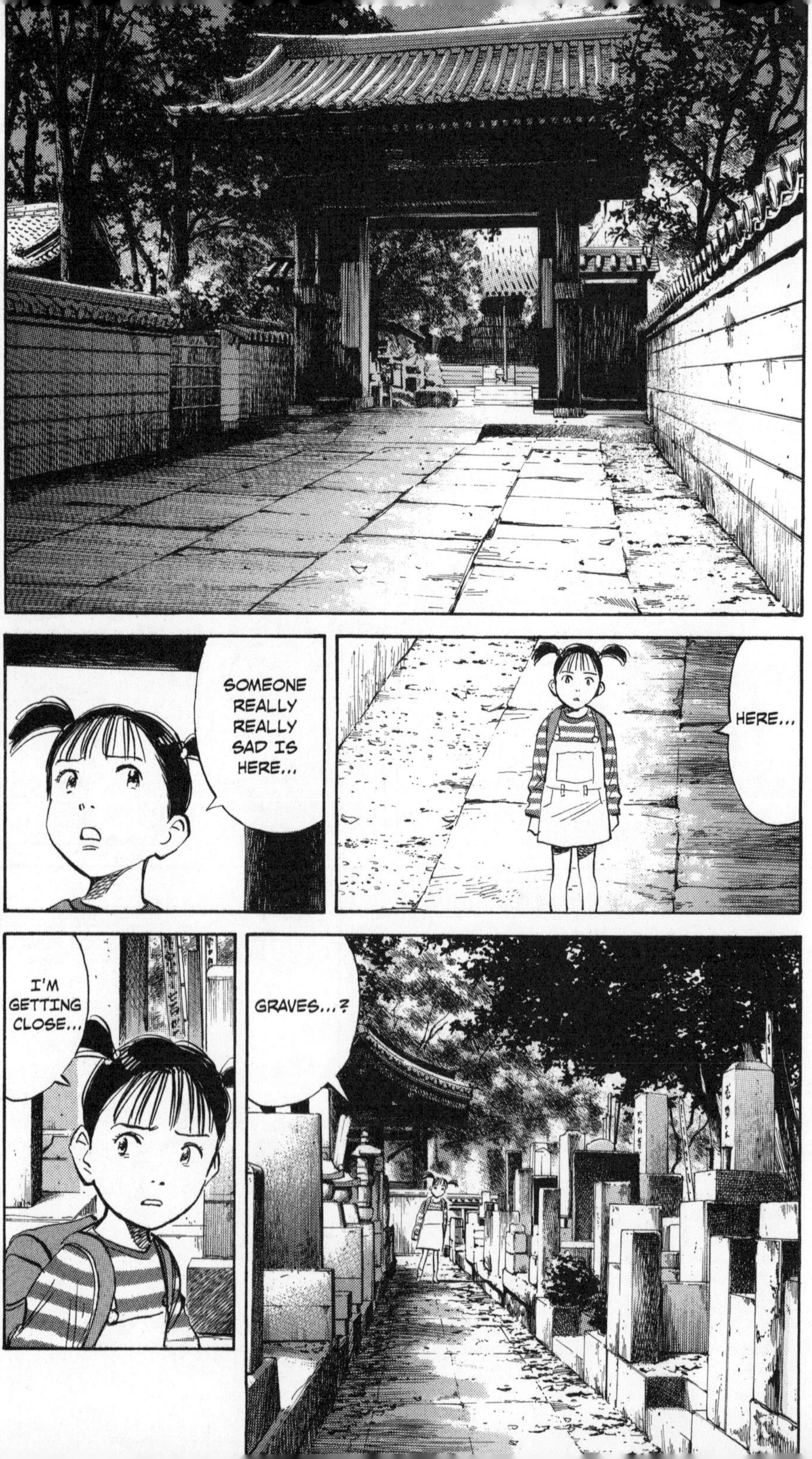
HERE...
SOMEONE REALLY REALLY SAD IS HERE...
GRAVES...?
I'M GETTING CLOSE...

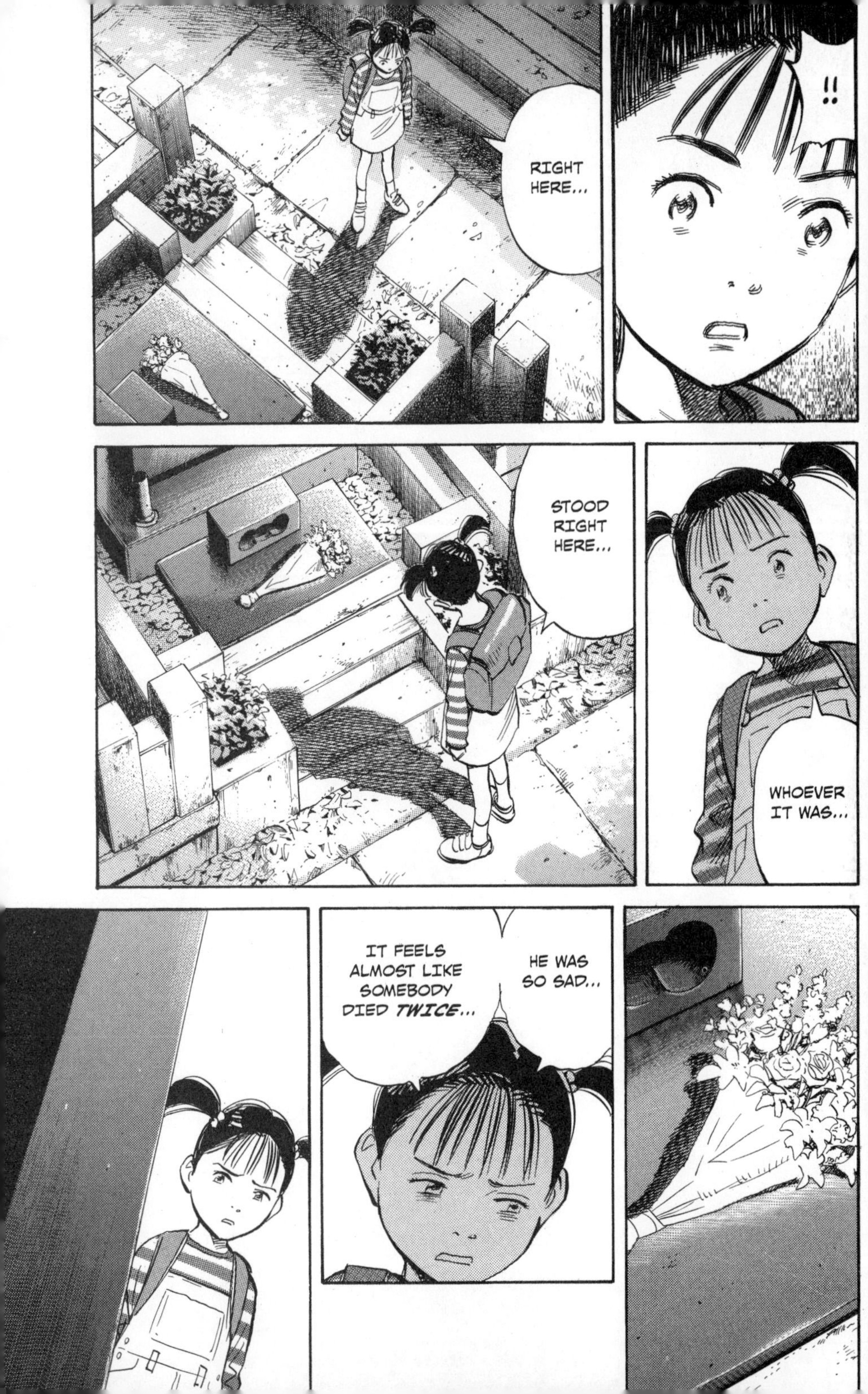
!!
RIGHT HERE...
WHOEVER IT WAS...
STOOD RIGHT HERE...
HE WAS SO SAD...
IT FEELS ALMOST LIKE SOMEBODY DIED *TWICE*...

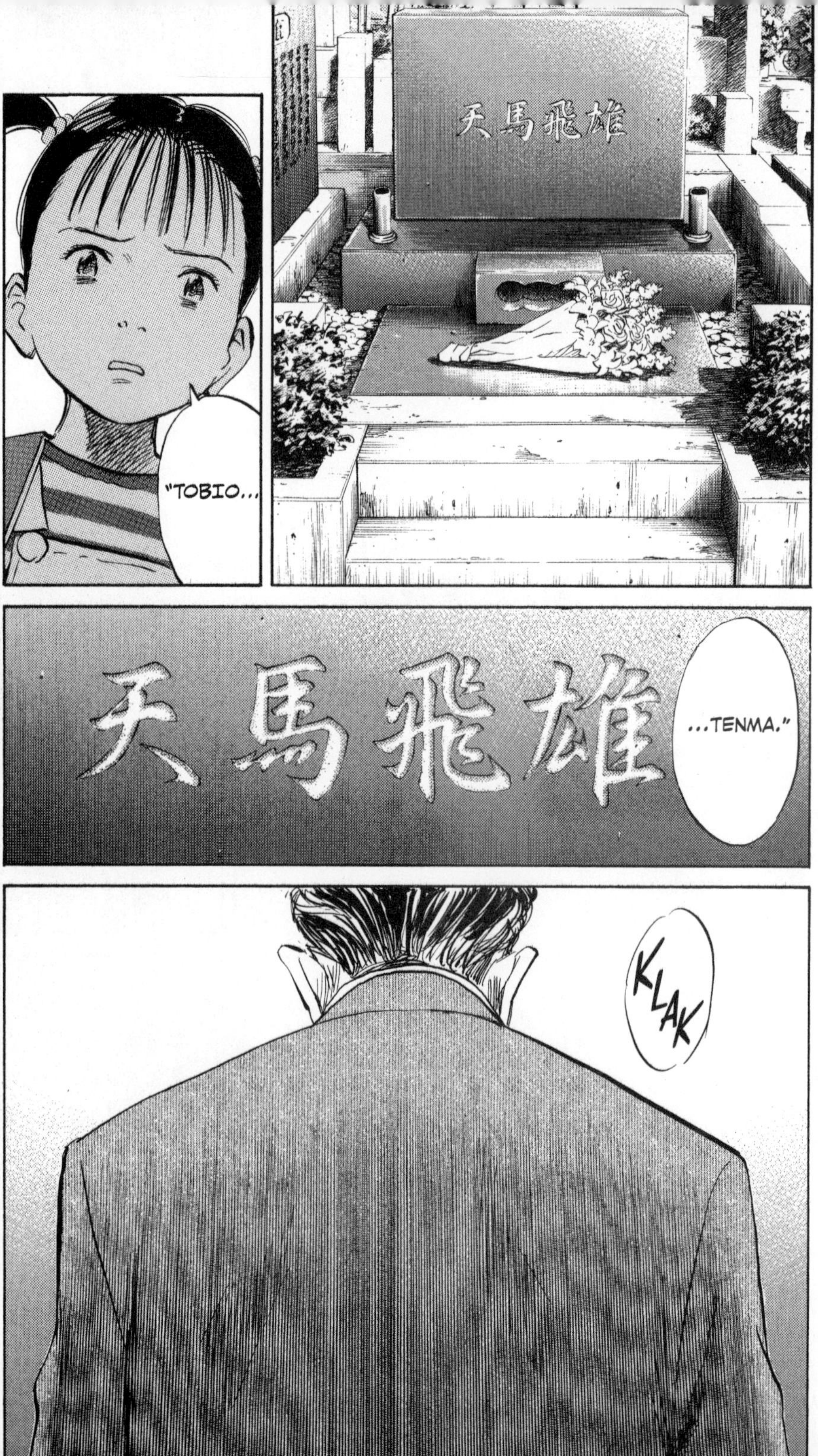

"TOBIO...
天馬飛雄
天馬飛雄
...TENMA."
KLAK

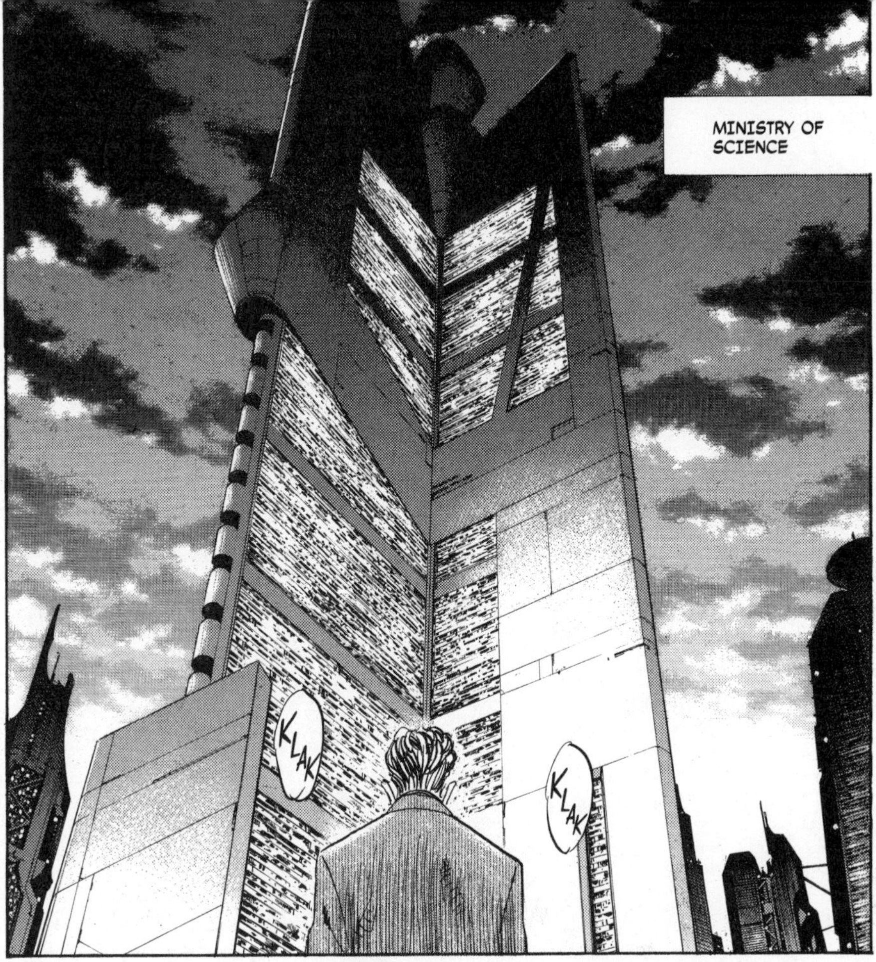
MINISTRY OF SCIENCE
KLAK
KLAK

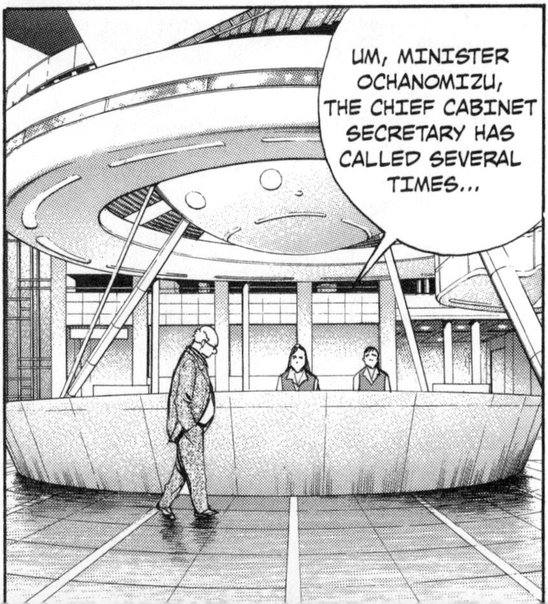
UM, MINISTER OCHANOMIZU, THE CHIEF CABINET SECRETARY HAS CALLED SEVERAL TIMES...

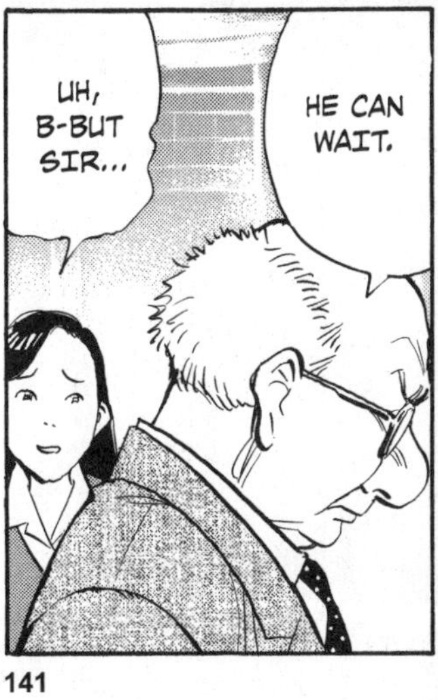
HE CAN WAIT.
UH, B-BUT SIR...

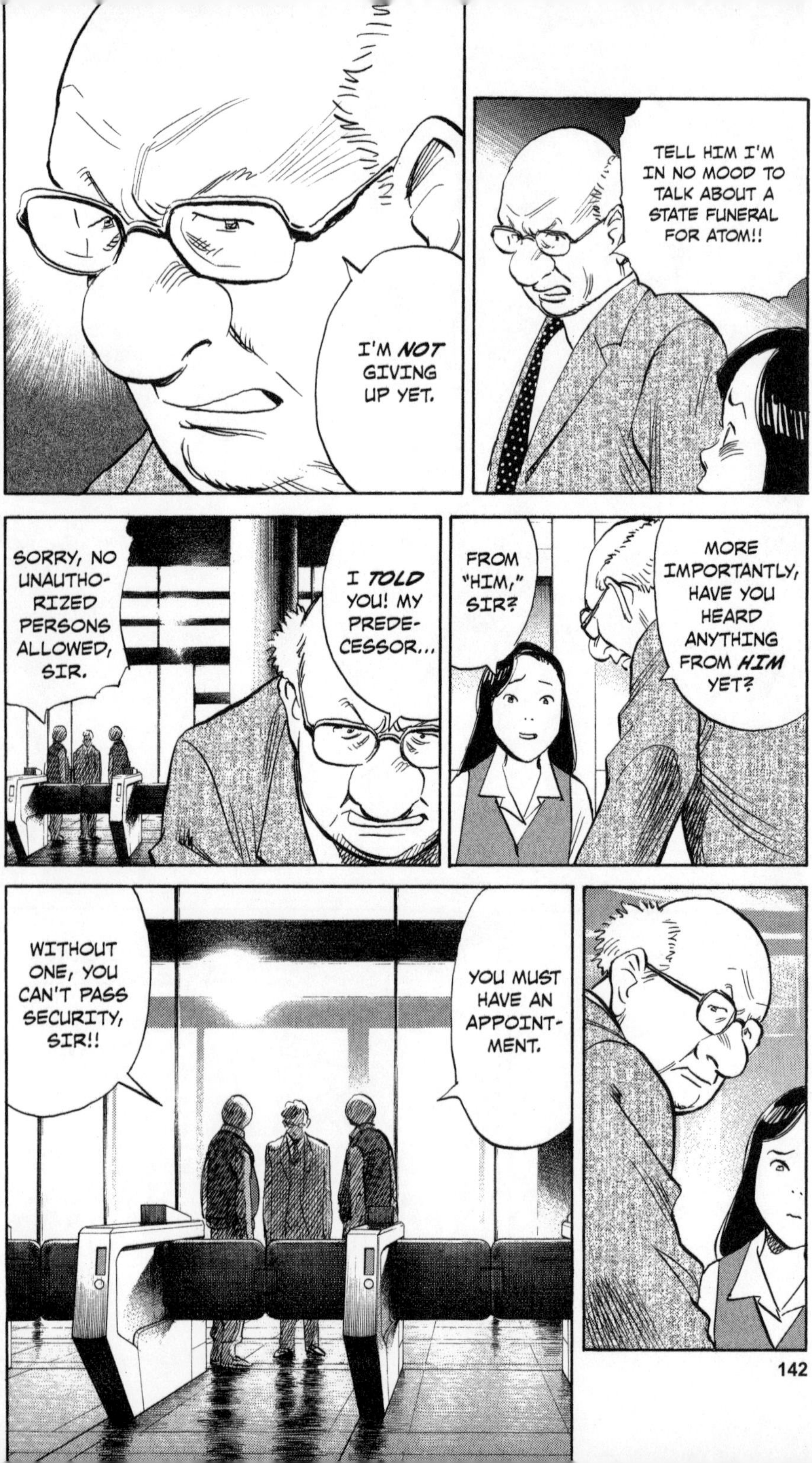
TELL HIM I'M IN NO MOOD TO TALK ABOUT A STATE FUNERAL FOR ATOM!!
I'M NOT GIVING UP YET.
MORE IMPORTANTLY, HAVE YOU HEARD ANYTHING FROM HIM YET?
FROM "HIM," SIR?
I TOLD YOU! MY PREDE-CESSOR...
SORRY, NO UNAUTHO-RIZED PERSONS ALLOWED, SIR.
YOU MUST HAVE AN APPOINT-MENT.
WITHOUT ONE, YOU CAN'T PASS SECURITY, SIR!!

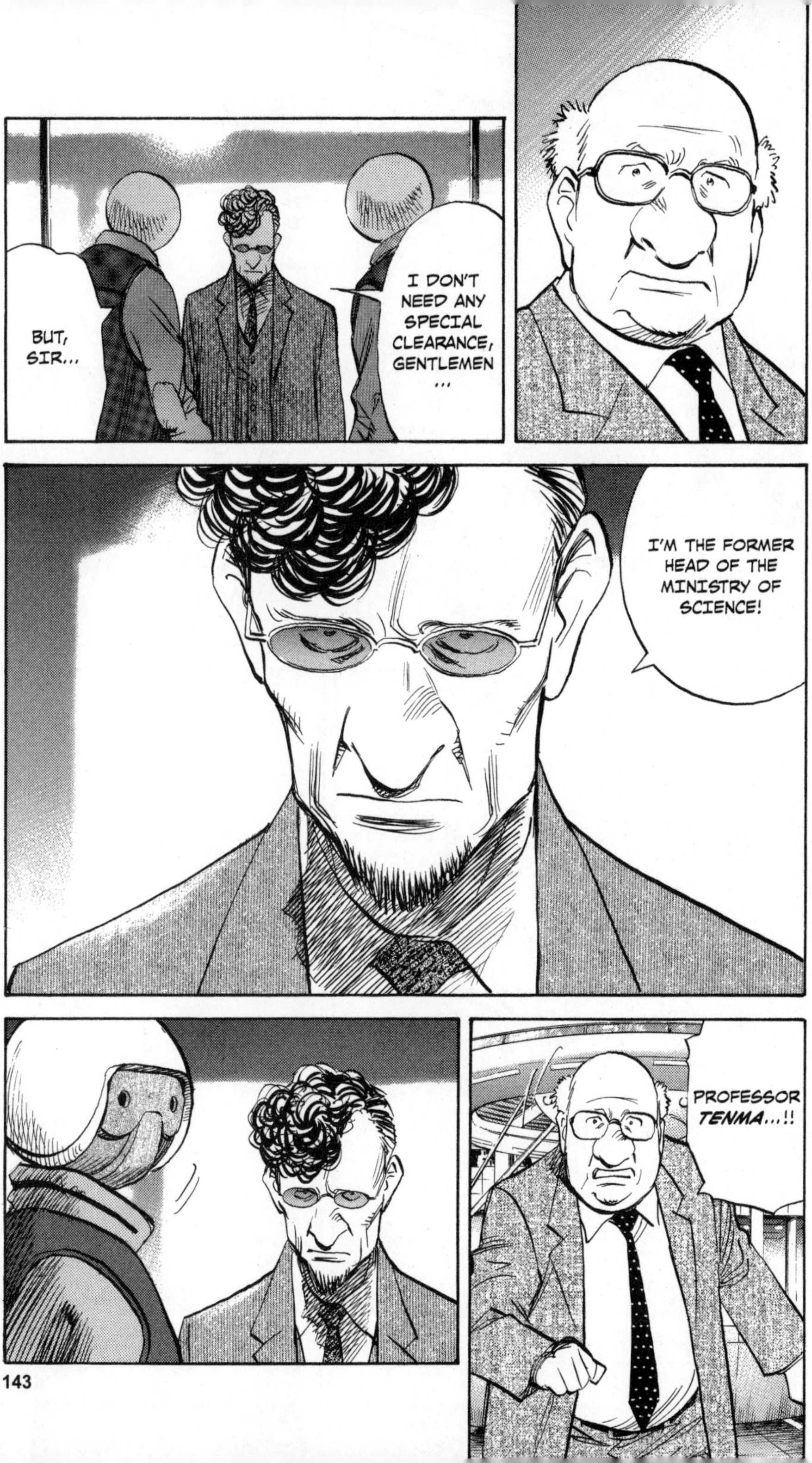
I DON'T NEED ANY SPECIAL CLEARANCE, GENTLEMEN...
BUT, SIR...
I'M THE FORMER HEAD OF THE MINISTRY OF SCIENCE!
PROFESSOR *TENMA*...!!

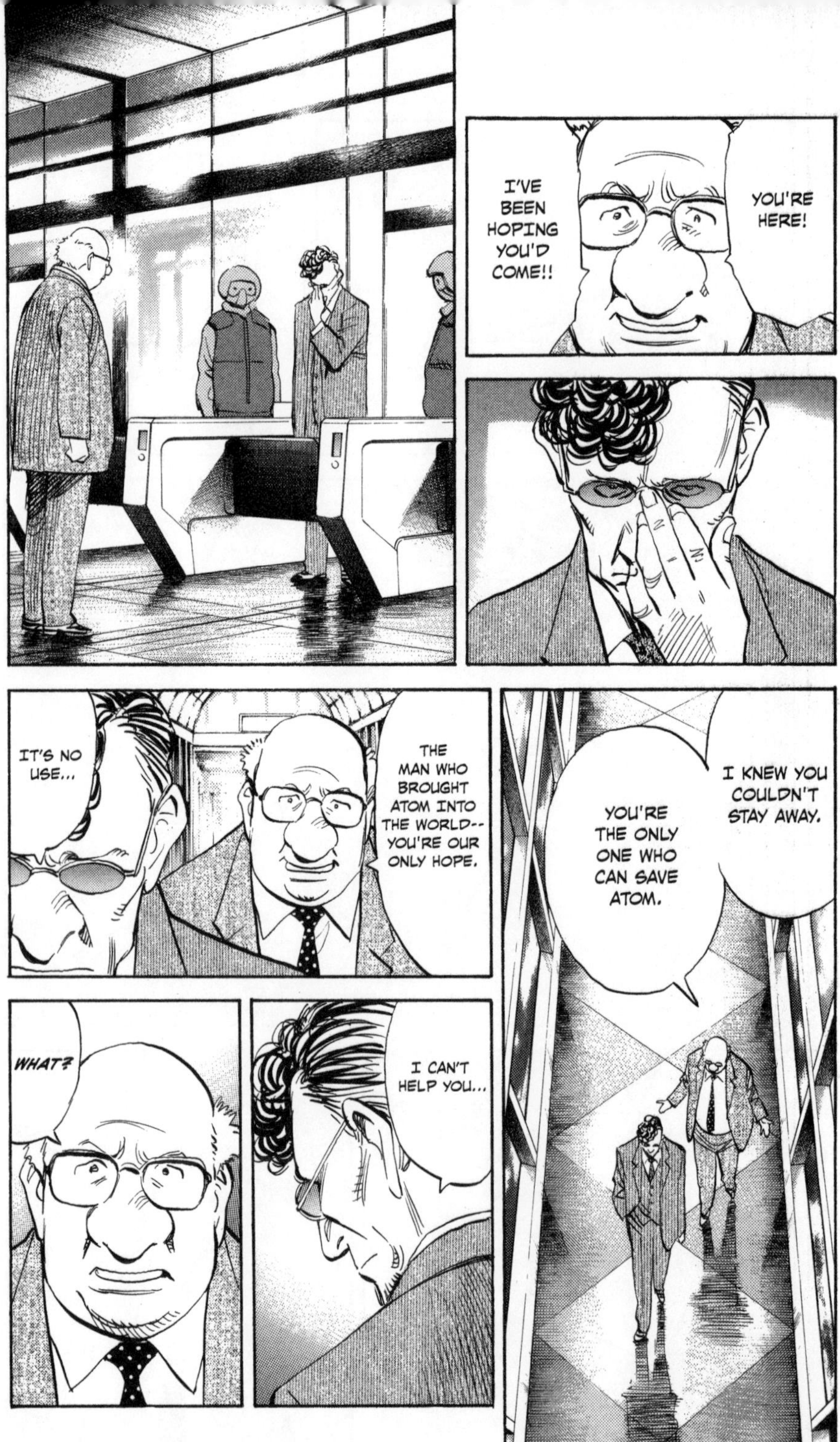
YOU'RE HERE!
I'VE BEEN HOPING YOU'D COME!!
I KNEW YOU COULDN'T STAY AWAY.
YOU'RE THE ONLY ONE WHO CAN SAVE ATOM.
THE MAN WHO BROUGHT ATOM INTO THE WORLD-- YOU'RE OUR ONLY HOPE.
IT'S NO USE...
I CAN'T HELP YOU...
*WHAT?*

ATOM IS *DEAD.*

I JUST CAME TO SAY GOOD-BYE.

KLAK

KLAK

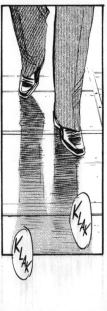

KLAK

KLAK

ZHOOM

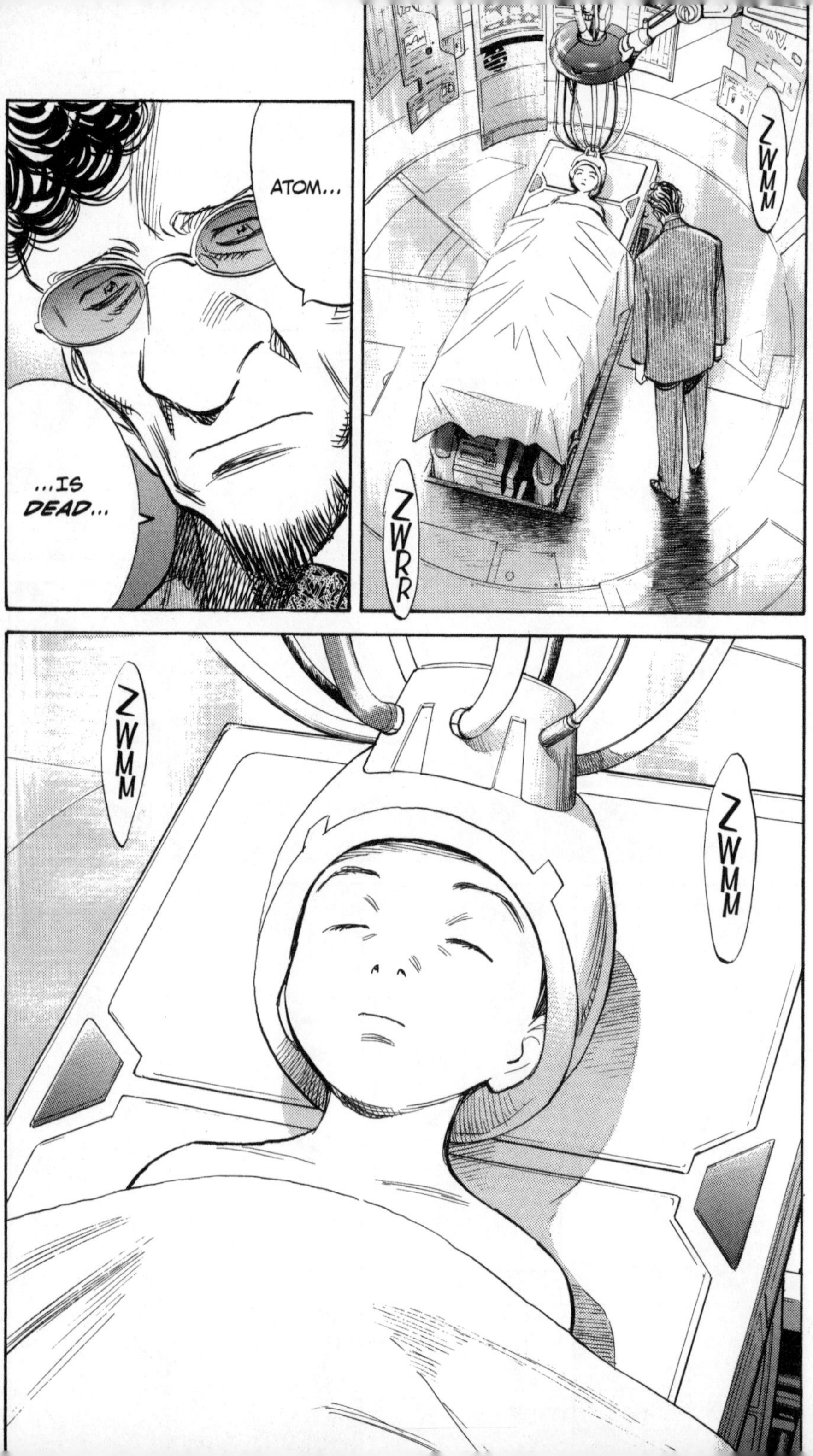
ZWMM
ZWRR
ATOM...
...IS DEAD...
ZWMM
ZWMM

# Act 38 The Chaos of Six Billion

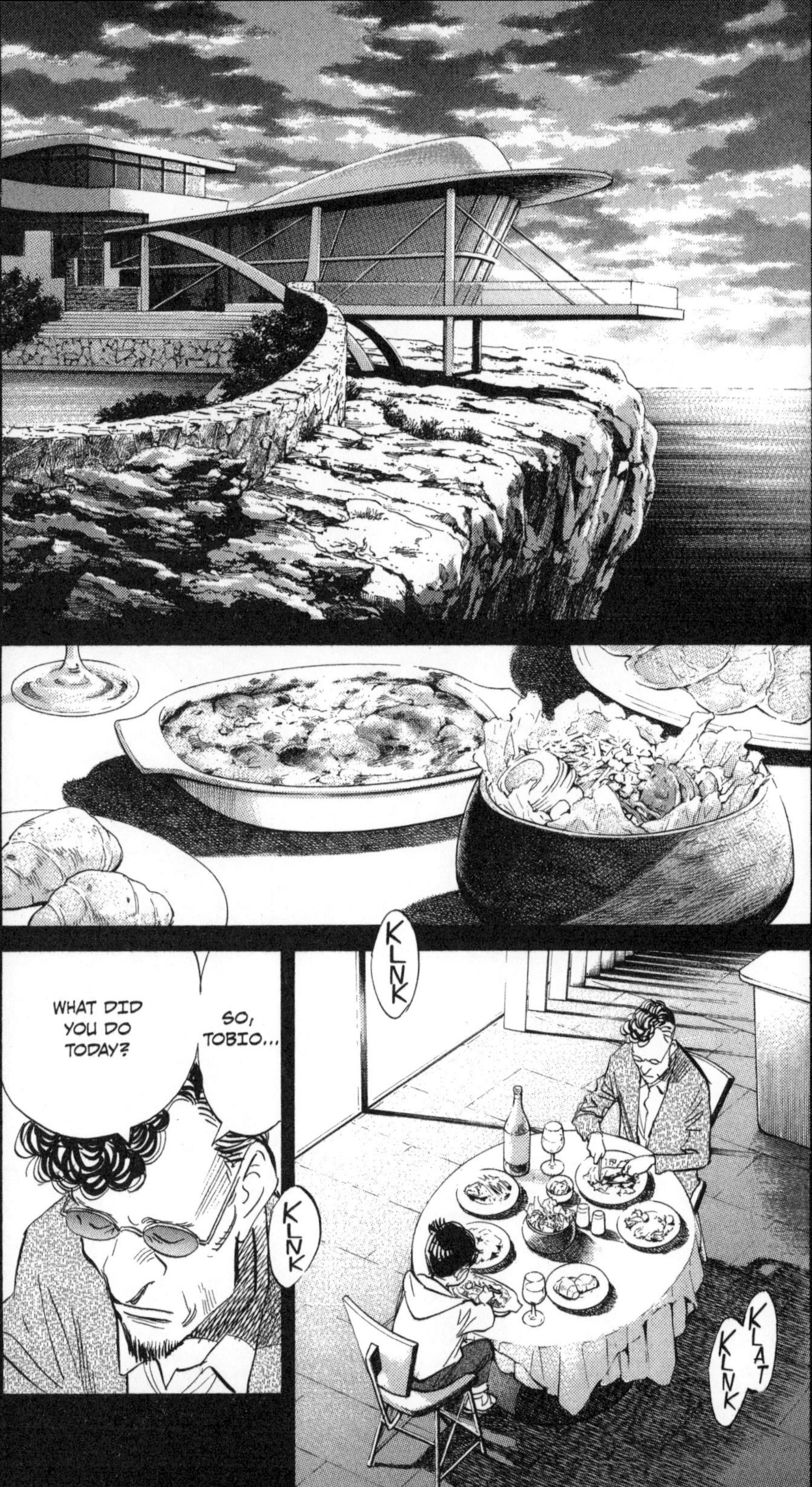
KLNK
KLAT
KLNK
SO, TOBIO...
WHAT DID YOU DO TODAY?
KLNK

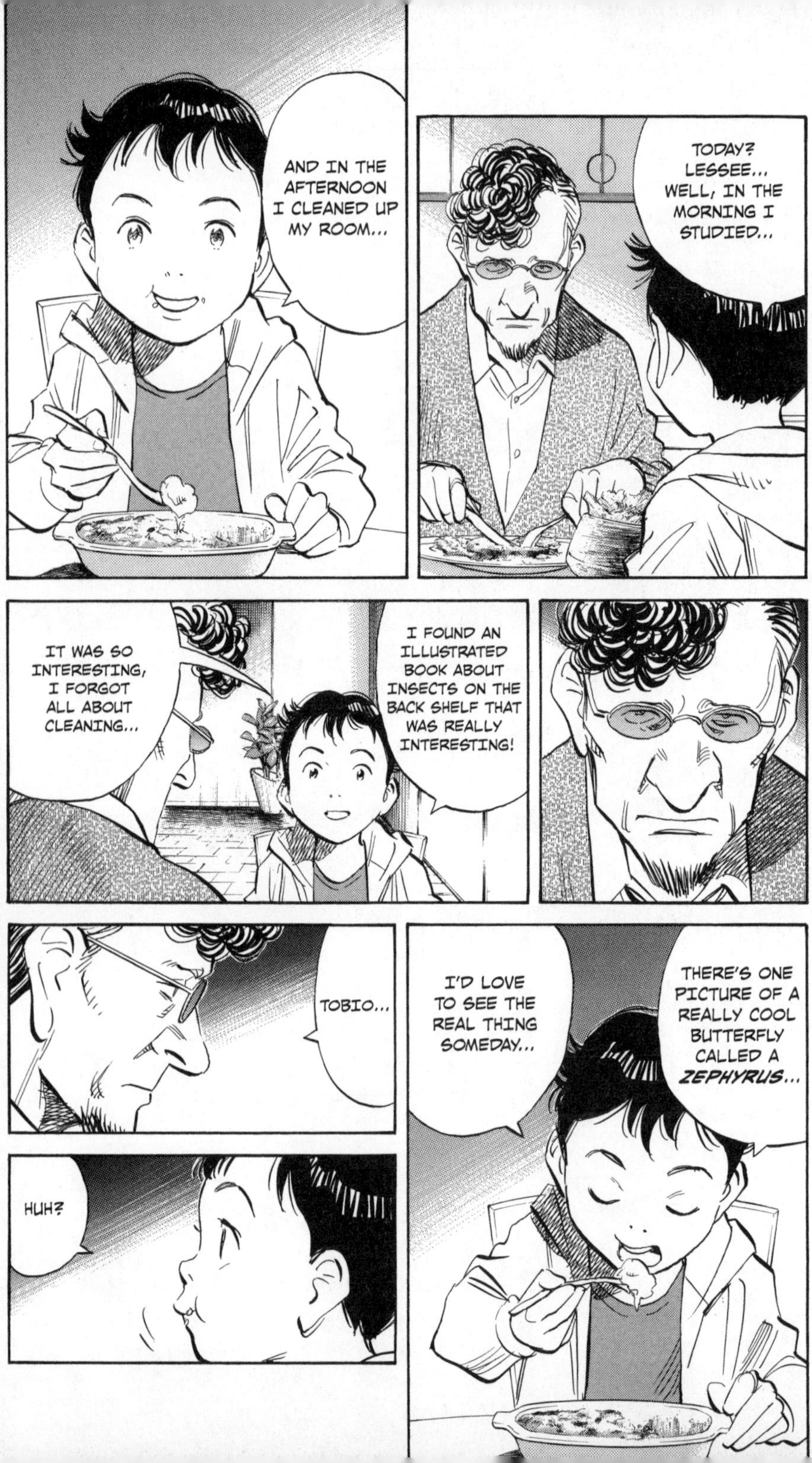
TODAY? LESSEE... WELL, IN THE MORNING I STUDIED...
AND IN THE AFTERNOON I CLEANED UP MY ROOM...
I FOUND AN ILLUSTRATED BOOK ABOUT INSECTS ON THE BACK SHELF THAT WAS REALLY INTERESTING!
IT WAS SO INTERESTING, I FORGOT ALL ABOUT CLEANING...
THERE'S ONE PICTURE OF A REALLY COOL BUTTERFLY CALLED A *ZEPHYRUS*...
I'D LOVE TO SEE THE REAL THING SOMEDAY...
TOBIO...
HUH?

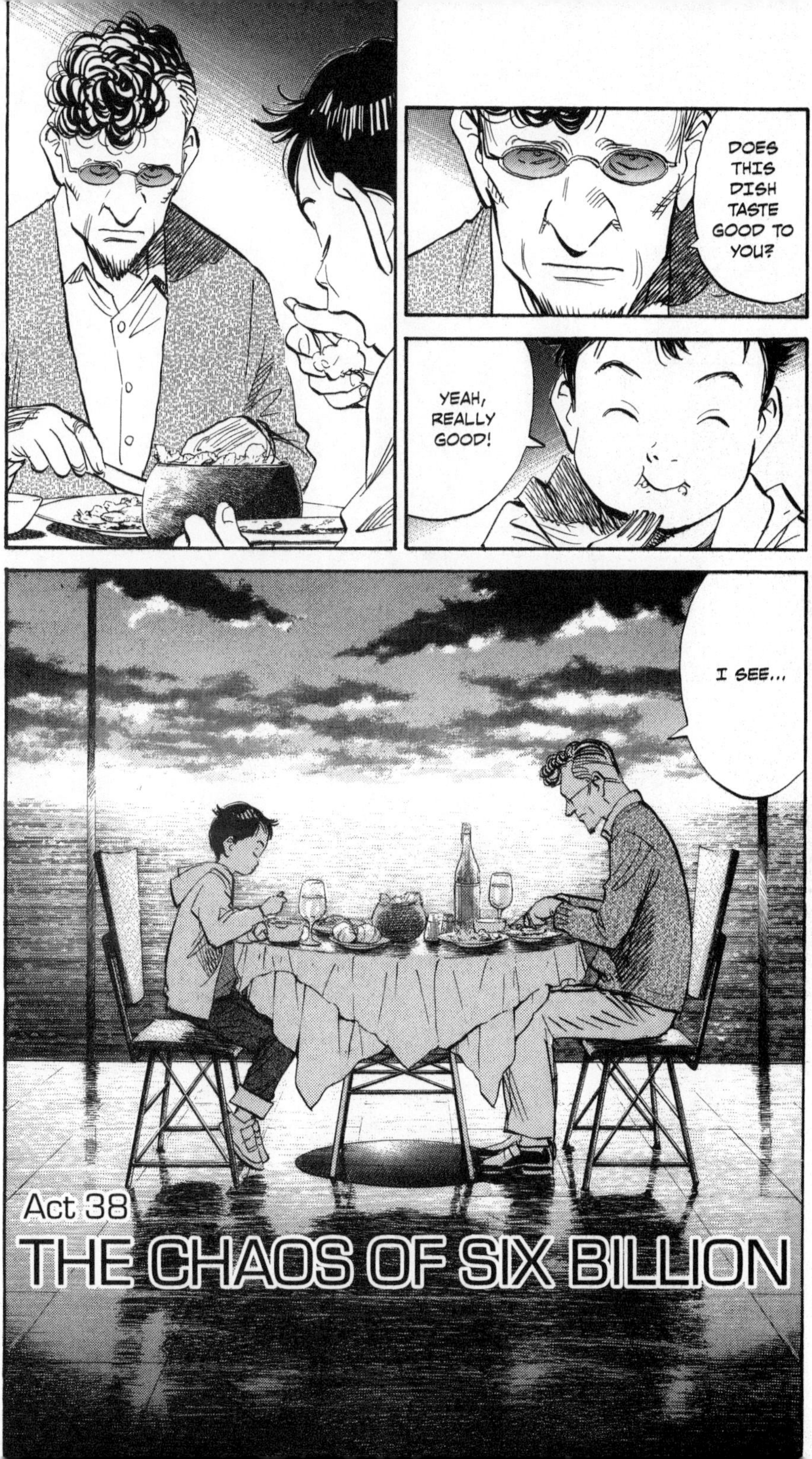
DOES THIS DISH TASTE GOOD TO YOU?
YEAH, REALLY GOOD!
I SEE...
Act 38
THE CHAOS OF SIX BILLION

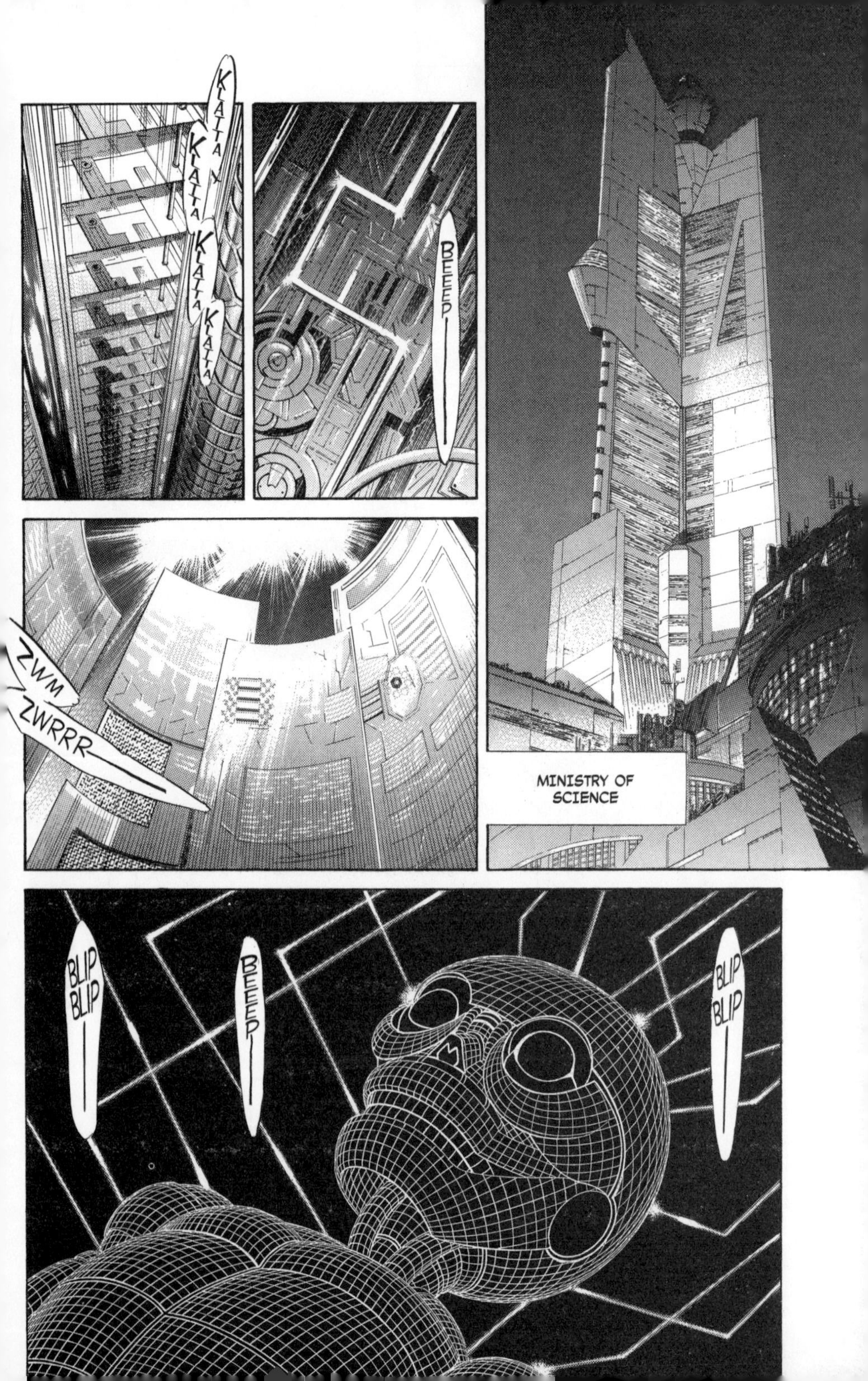
MINISTRY OF SCIENCE
BEEEP—
KLATTA
KLATTA
KLATTA
KLATTA
ZWM
ZWRRR
BLIP BLIP—
BEEEP—
BLIP BLIP—

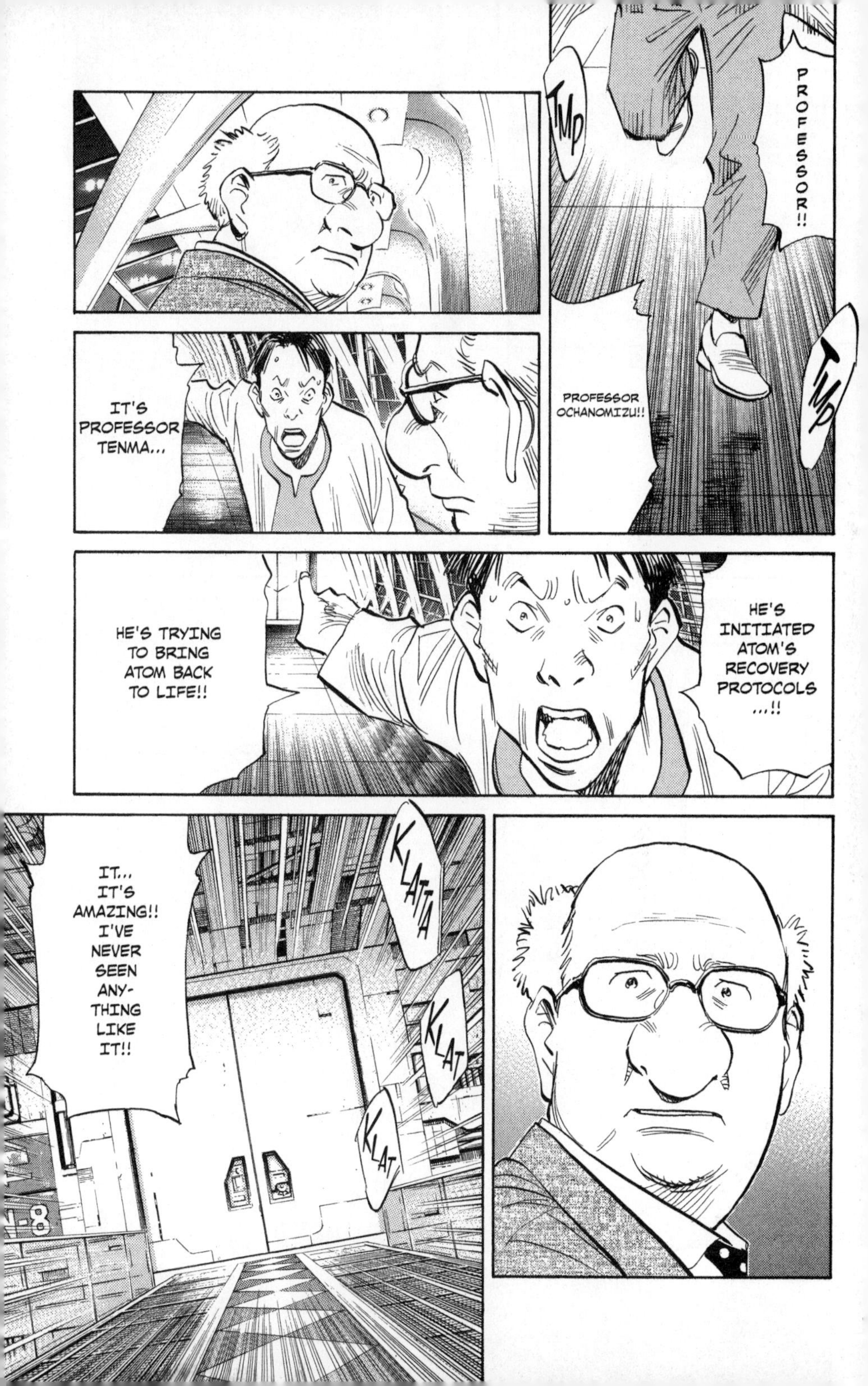
PROFESSOR!!
TMP
TMP
PROFESSOR OCHANOMIZU!!
IT'S PROFESSOR TENMA...
HE'S INITIATED ATOM'S RECOVERY PROTOCOLS ...!!
HE'S TRYING TO BRING ATOM BACK TO LIFE!!
KLATTA
KLAT
KLAT
IT... IT'S AMAZING!! I'VE NEVER SEEN ANYTHING LIKE IT!!

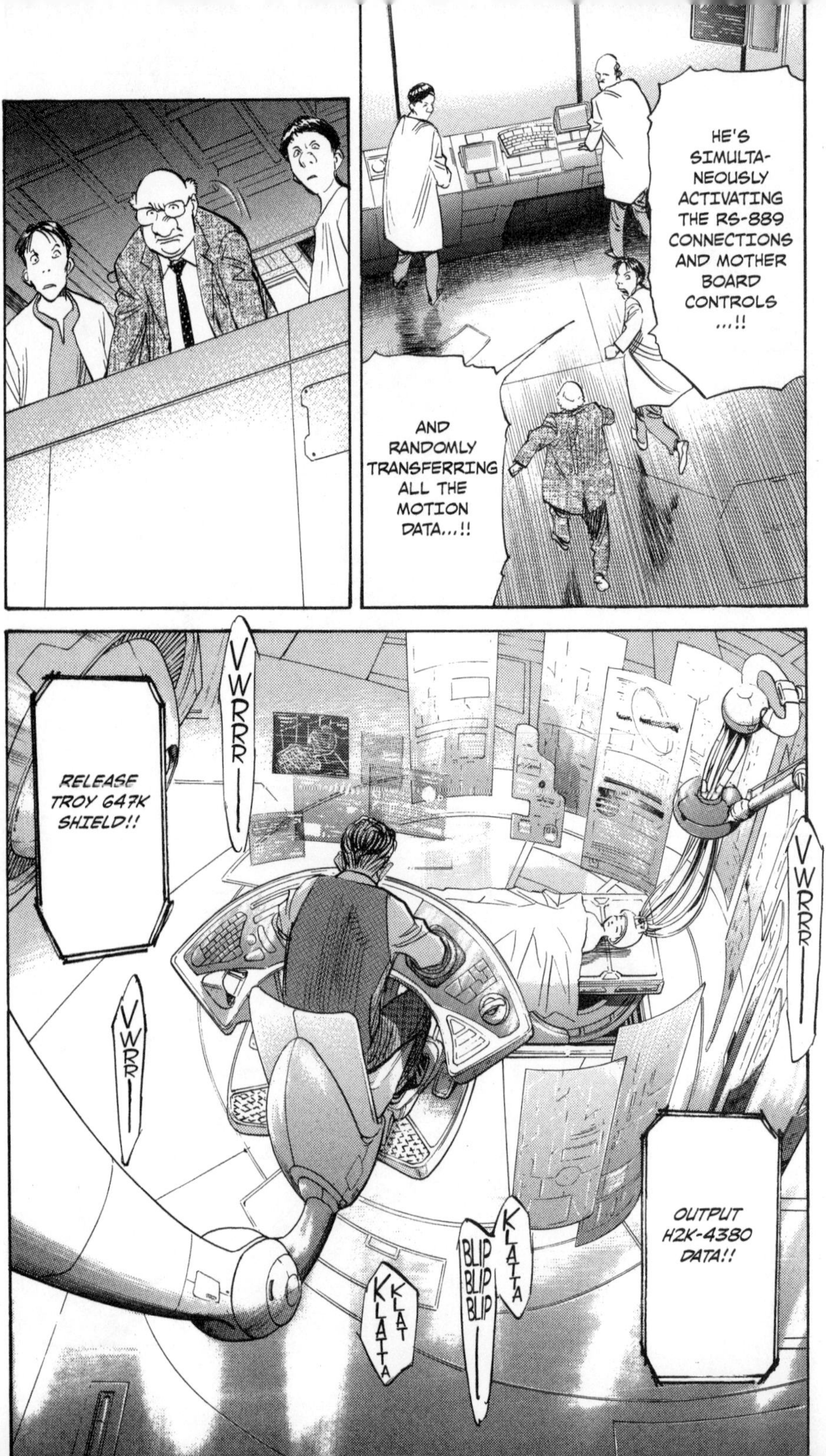
HE'S SIMULTANEOUSLY ACTIVATING THE RS-889 CONNECTIONS AND MOTHER BOARD CONTROLS ...!!
AND RANDOMLY TRANSFERRING ALL THE MOTION DATA...!!
VWRRRI
VWRRRI
RELEASE TROY 647K SHIELD!!
OUTPUT H2K-4380 DATA!!
KLATTA
BLIP BLIP BLIP
KLAT KLATTA
VWRRI

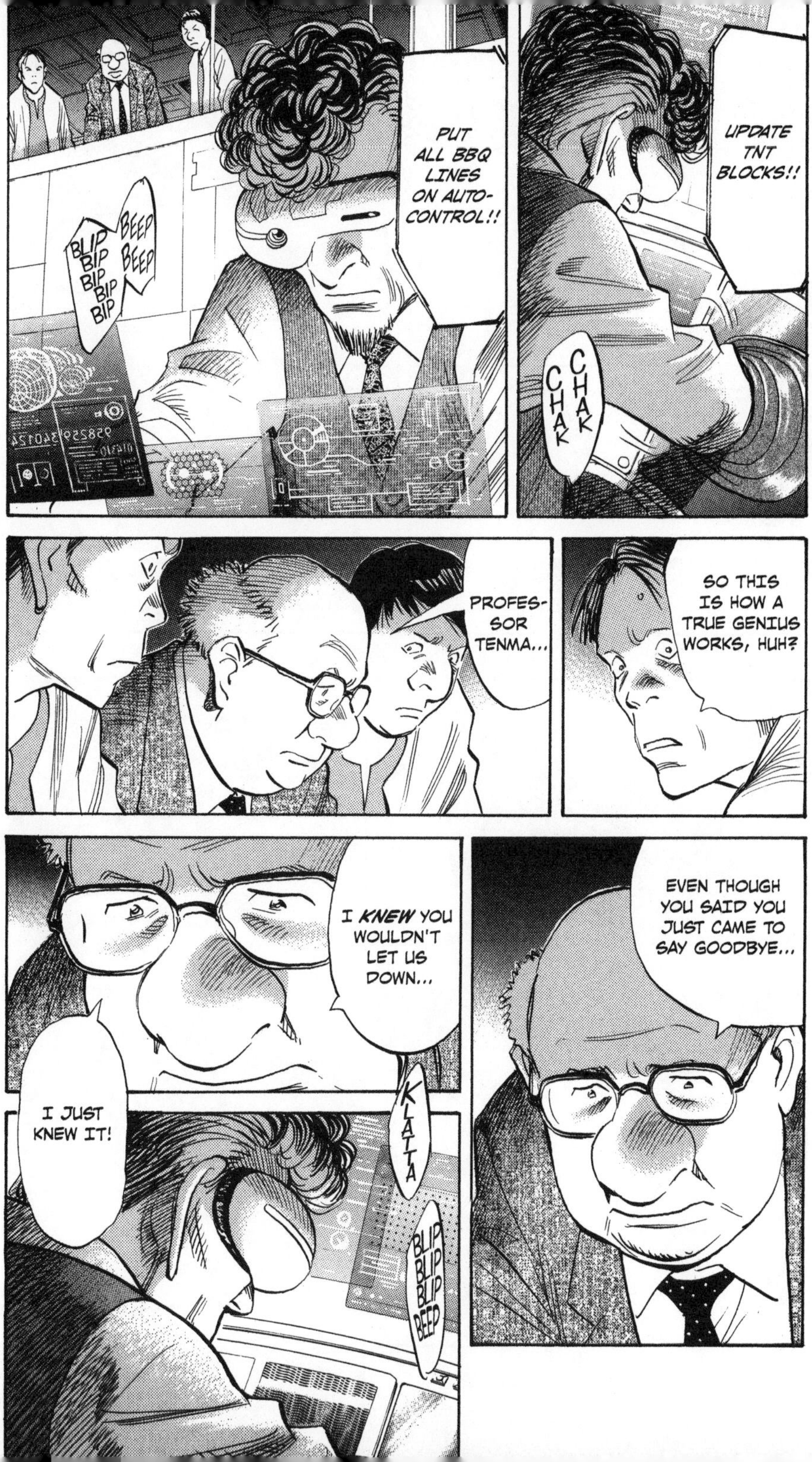
UPDATE TNT BLOCKS!!
CHAK CHAK
PUT ALL BBQ LINES ON AUTO-CONTROL!!
BEEP BEEP
BLIP BIP BIP BIP BIP
SO THIS IS HOW A TRUE GENIUS WORKS, HUH?
PROFES-SOR TENMA...
EVEN THOUGH YOU SAID YOU JUST CAME TO SAY GOODBYE...
I *KNEW* YOU WOULDN'T LET US DOWN...
KLATTA
BLIP BLIP BLIP BEEP
I JUST KNEW IT!

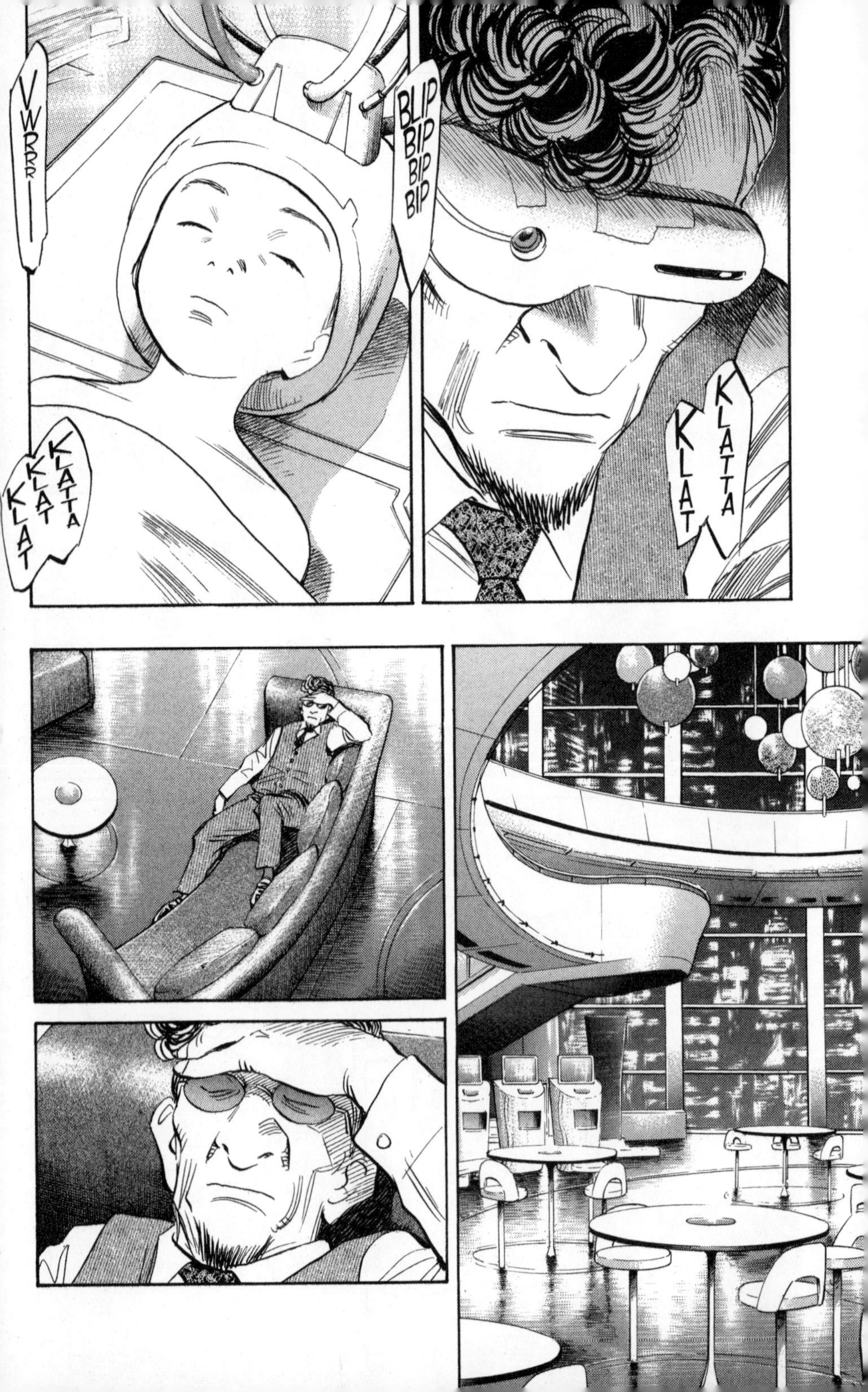
BLIP BIP BIP BIP
KLAT KLATTA
VWRRR
KLAT KLAT KLATTA

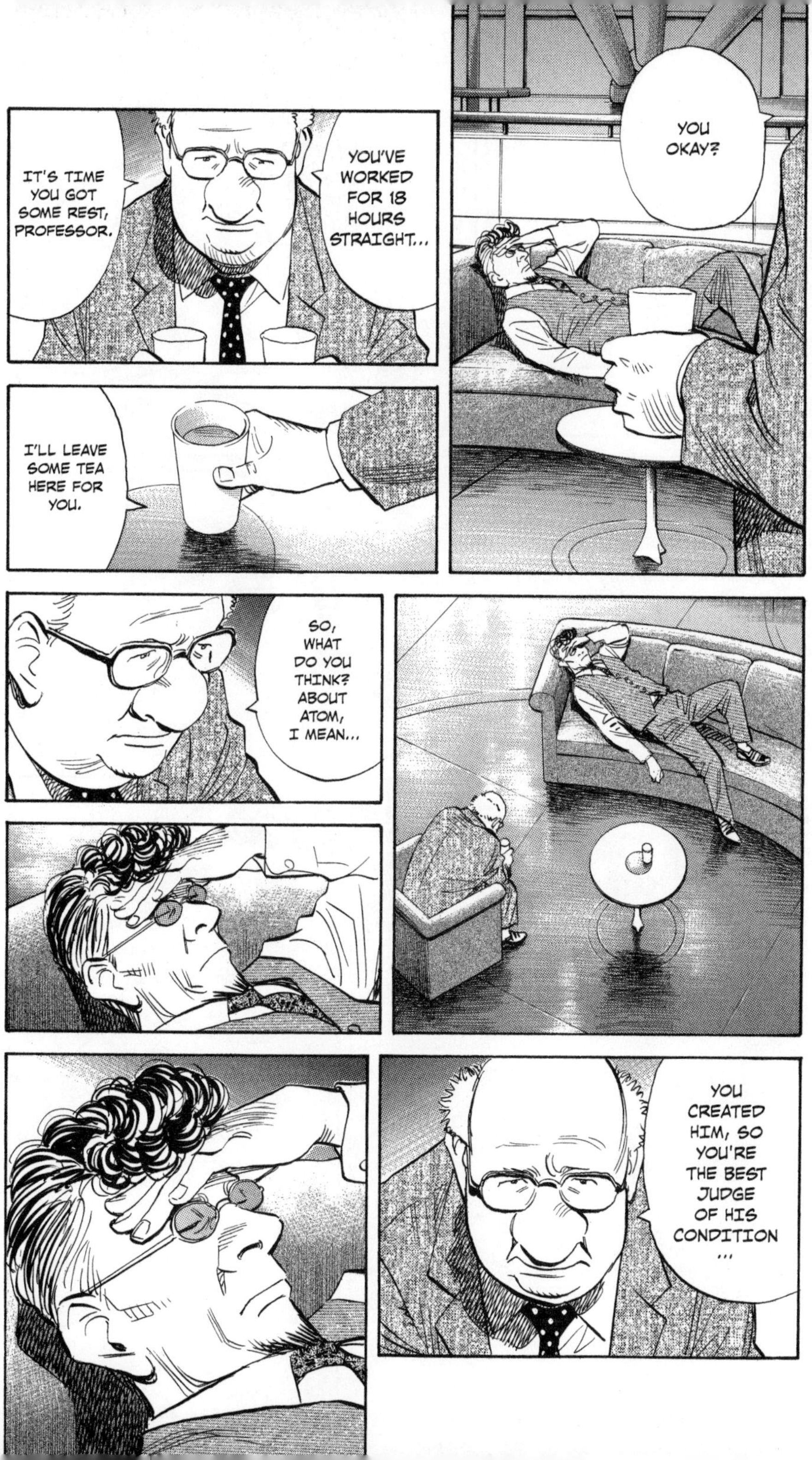
YOU OKAY?
YOU'VE WORKED FOR 18 HOURS STRAIGHT...
IT'S TIME YOU GOT SOME REST, PROFESSOR.
I'LL LEAVE SOME TEA HERE FOR YOU.
SO, WHAT DO YOU THINK? ABOUT ATOM, I MEAN...
YOU CREATED HIM, SO YOU'RE THE BEST JUDGE OF HIS CONDITION ...

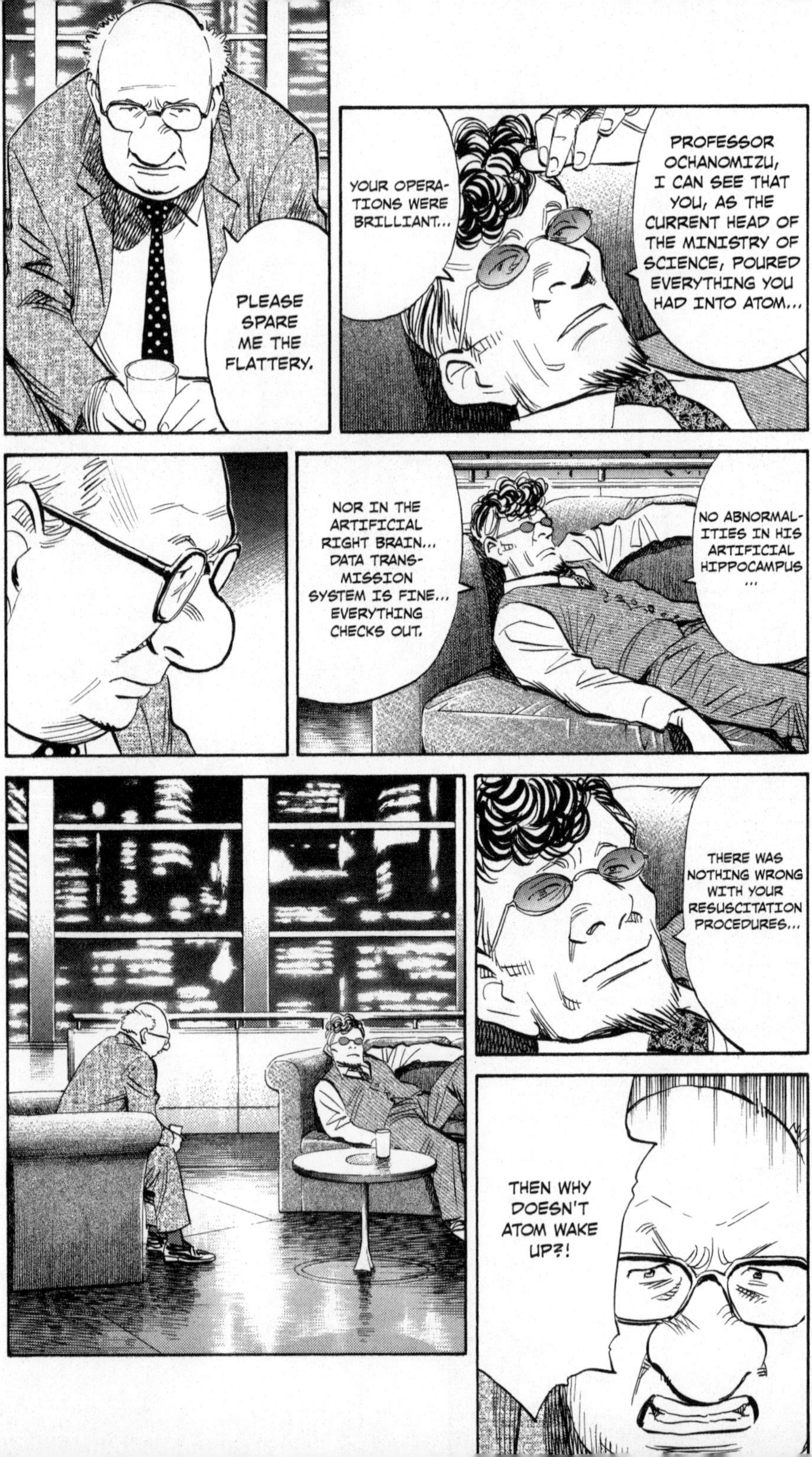
PROFESSOR OCHANOMIZU, I CAN SEE THAT YOU, AS THE CURRENT HEAD OF THE MINISTRY OF SCIENCE, POURED EVERYTHING YOU HAD INTO ATOM...
YOUR OPERATIONS WERE BRILLIANT...
PLEASE SPARE ME THE FLATTERY.
NO ABNORMALITIES IN HIS ARTIFICIAL HIPPOCAMPUS...
NOR IN THE ARTIFICIAL RIGHT BRAIN... DATA TRANSMISSION SYSTEM IS FINE... EVERYTHING CHECKS OUT.
THERE WAS NOTHING WRONG WITH YOUR RESUSCITATION PROCEDURES...
THEN WHY DOESN'T ATOM WAKE UP?!

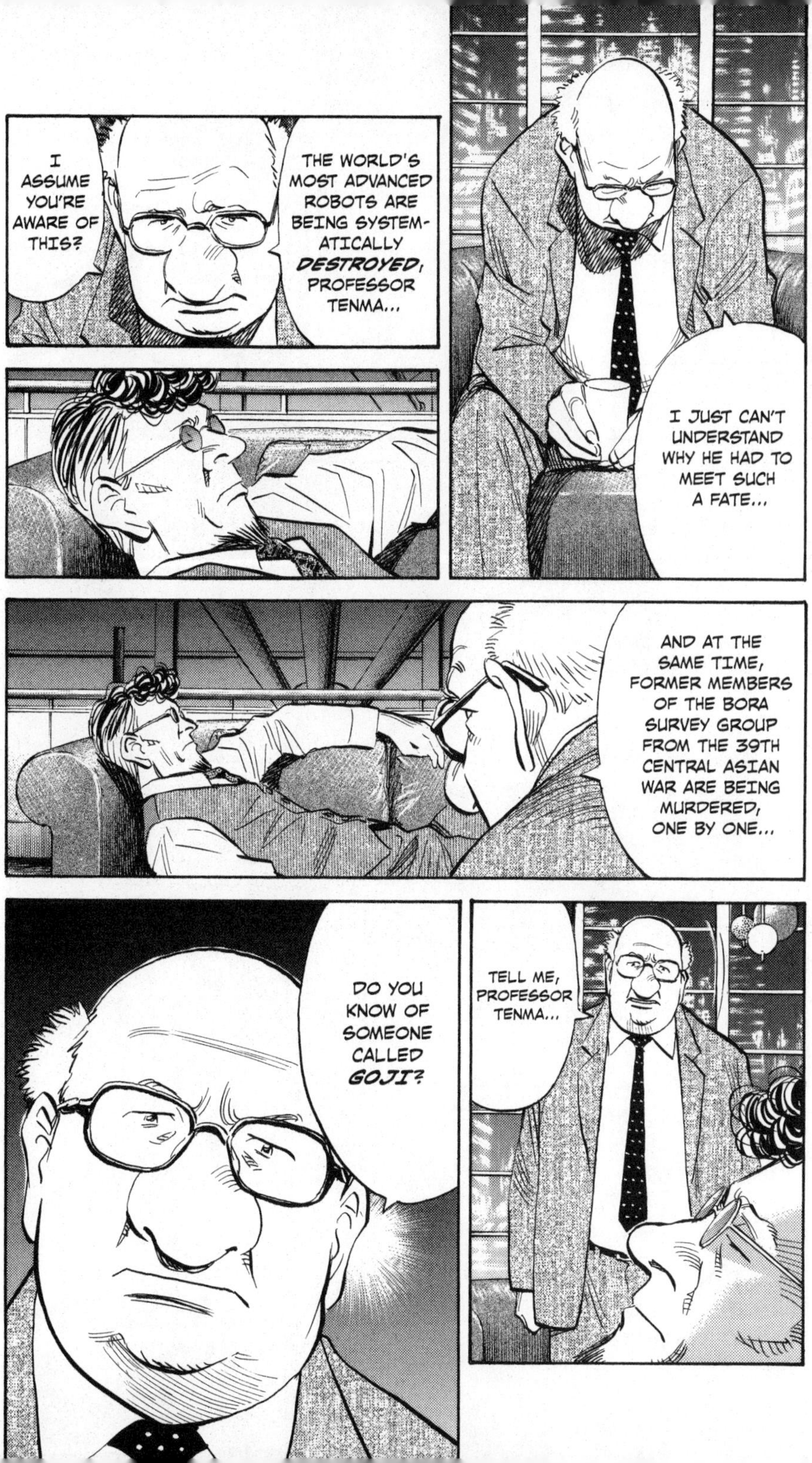
I JUST CAN'T UNDERSTAND WHY HE HAD TO MEET SUCH A FATE...
THE WORLD'S MOST ADVANCED ROBOTS ARE BEING SYSTEMATICALLY ***DESTROYED***, PROFESSOR TENMA...
I ASSUME YOU'RE AWARE OF THIS?
AND AT THE SAME TIME, FORMER MEMBERS OF THE BORA SURVEY GROUP FROM THE 39TH CENTRAL ASIAN WAR ARE BEING MURDERED, ONE BY ONE...
TELL ME, PROFESSOR TENMA...
DO YOU KNOW OF SOMEONE CALLED ***GOJI***?

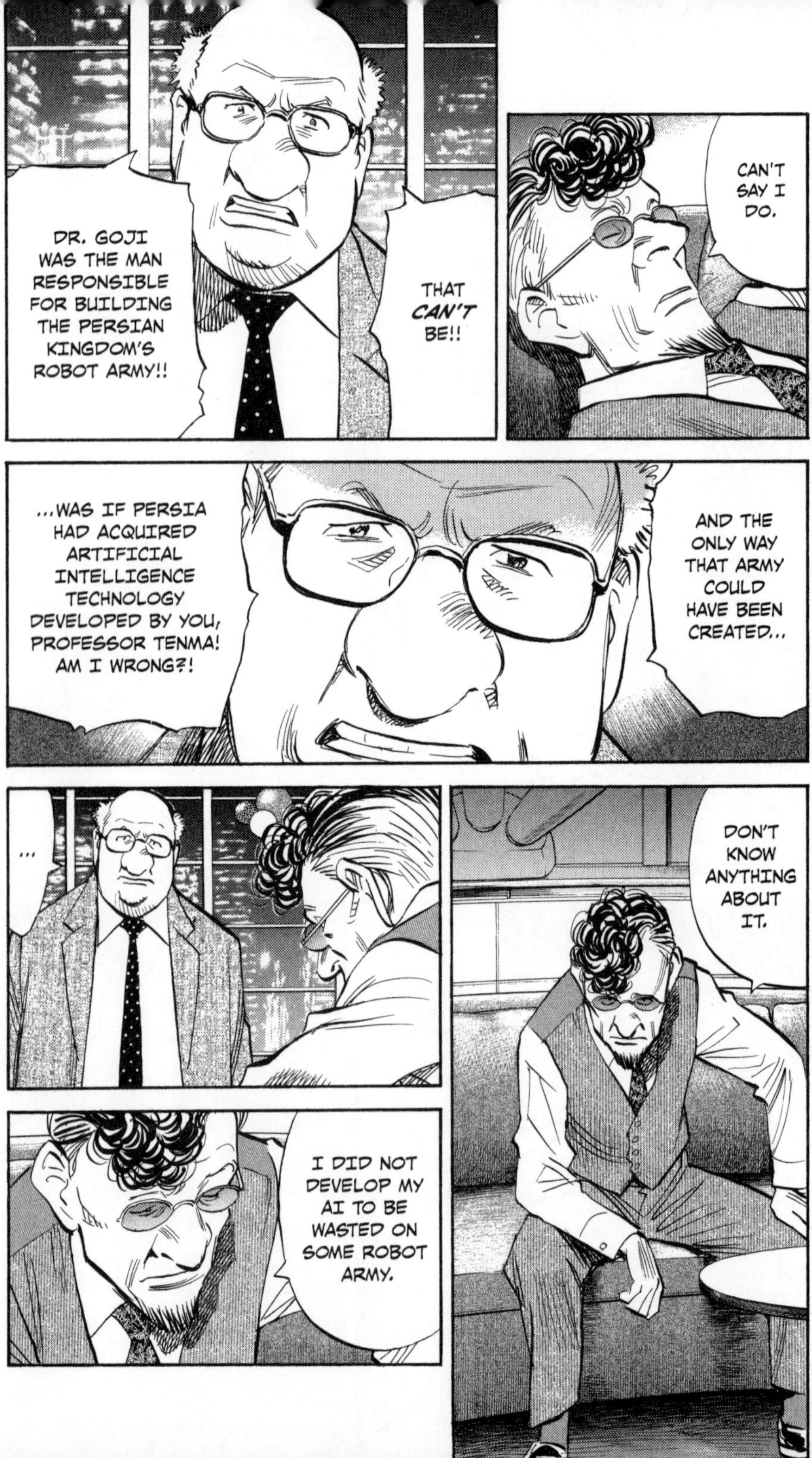
CAN'T SAY I DO.
DR. GOJI WAS THE MAN RESPONSIBLE FOR BUILDING THE PERSIAN KINGDOM'S ROBOT ARMY!!
THAT *CAN'T* BE!!
AND THE ONLY WAY THAT ARMY COULD HAVE BEEN CREATED...
...WAS IF PERSIA HAD ACQUIRED ARTIFICIAL INTELLIGENCE TECHNOLOGY DEVELOPED BY YOU, PROFESSOR TENMA! AM I WRONG?!
DON'T KNOW ANYTHING ABOUT IT.
...
I DID NOT DEVELOP MY AI TO BE WASTED ON SOME ROBOT ARMY.

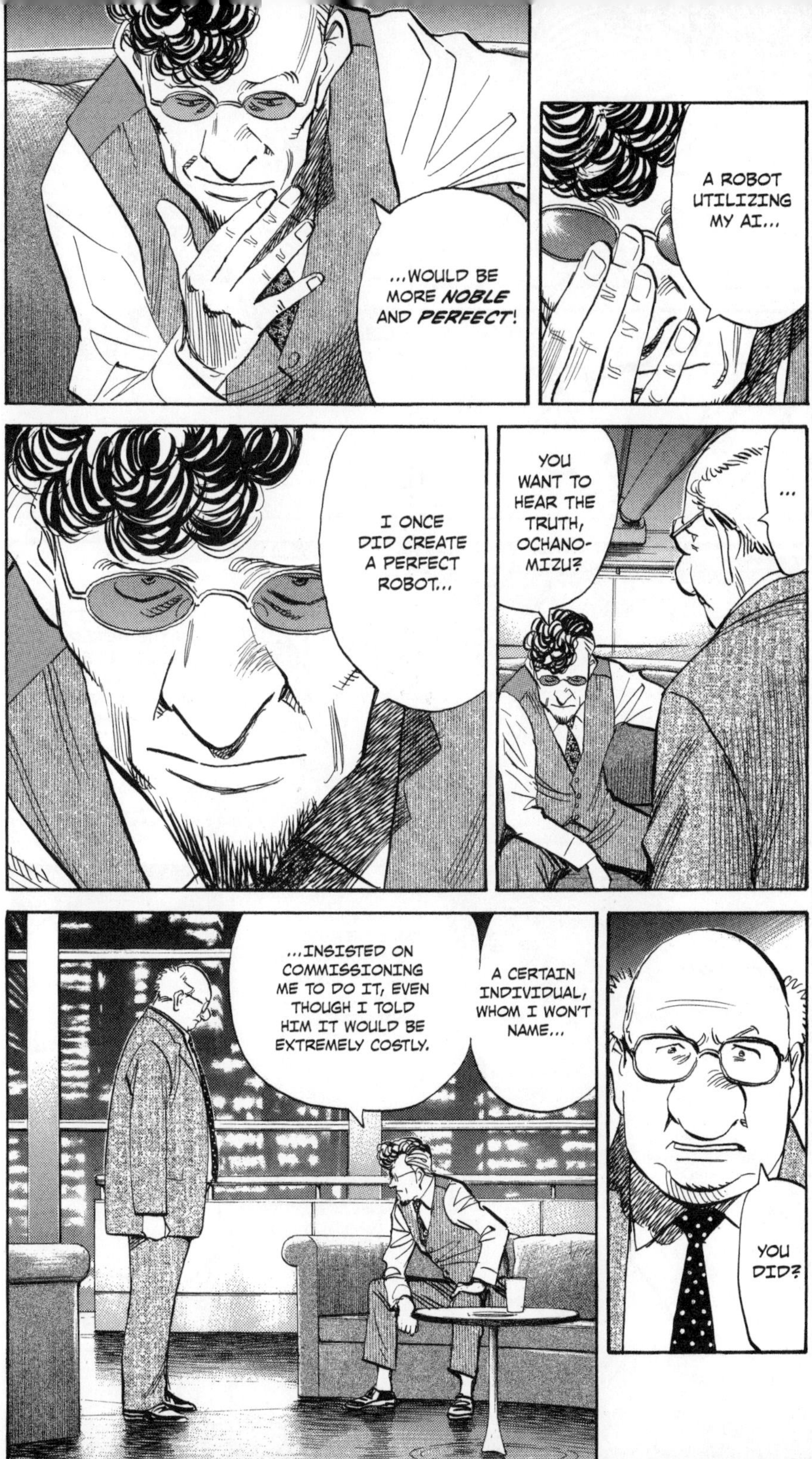
A ROBOT UTILIZING MY AI...
...WOULD BE MORE *NOBLE* AND *PERFECT*!
...
YOU WANT TO HEAR THE TRUTH, OCHANO-MIZU?
I ONCE DID CREATE A PERFECT ROBOT...
YOU DID?
A CERTAIN INDIVIDUAL, WHOM I WON'T NAME...
...INSISTED ON COMMISSIONING ME TO DO IT, EVEN THOUGH I TOLD HIM IT WOULD BE EXTREMELY COSTLY.

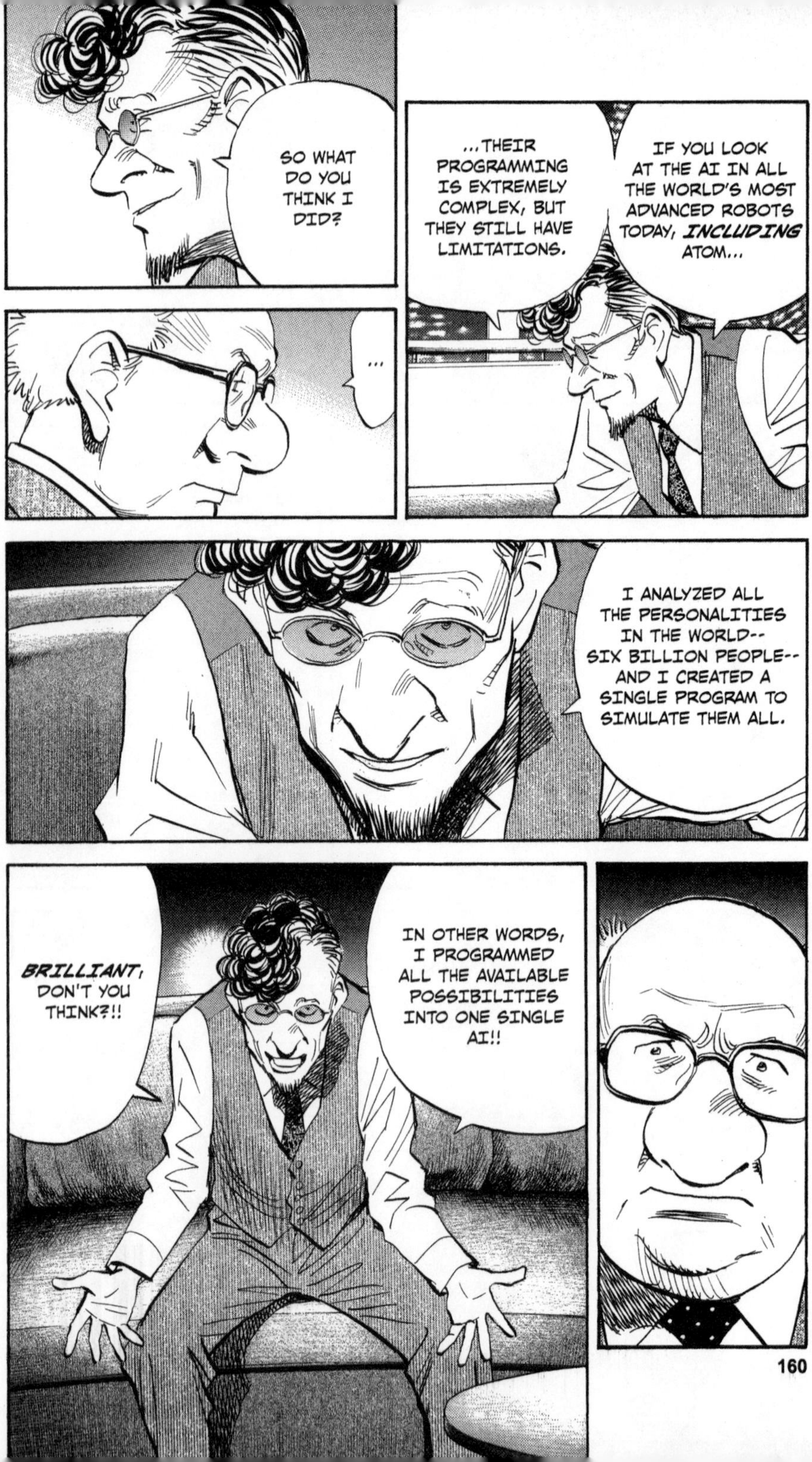
IF YOU LOOK AT THE AI IN ALL THE WORLD'S MOST ADVANCED ROBOTS TODAY, *INCLUDING* ATOM...
...THEIR PROGRAMMING IS EXTREMELY COMPLEX, BUT THEY STILL HAVE LIMITATIONS.
SO WHAT DO YOU THINK I DID?
...
I ANALYZED ALL THE PERSONALITIES IN THE WORLD-- SIX BILLION PEOPLE-- AND I CREATED A SINGLE PROGRAM TO SIMULATE THEM ALL.
IN OTHER WORDS, I PROGRAMMED ALL THE AVAILABLE POSSIBILITIES INTO ONE SINGLE AI!!
*BRILLIANT*, DON'T YOU THINK?!!

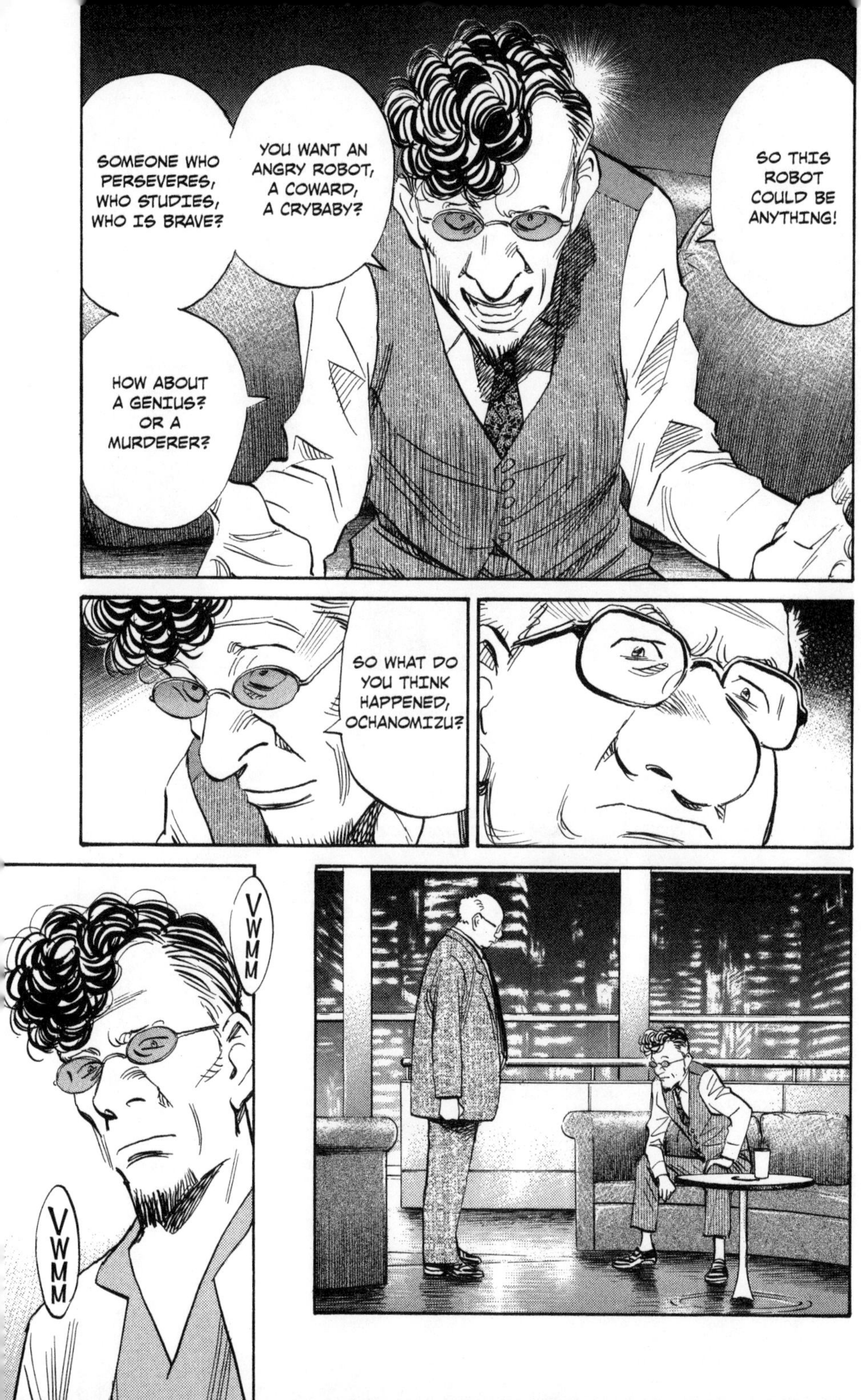
SO THIS ROBOT COULD BE ANYTHING!
YOU WANT AN ANGRY ROBOT, A COWARD, A CRYBABY?
SOMEONE WHO PERSEVERES, WHO STUDIES, WHO IS BRAVE?
HOW ABOUT A GENIUS? OR A MURDERER?
SO WHAT DO YOU THINK HAPPENED, OCHANOMIZU?
VWMM
VWMM

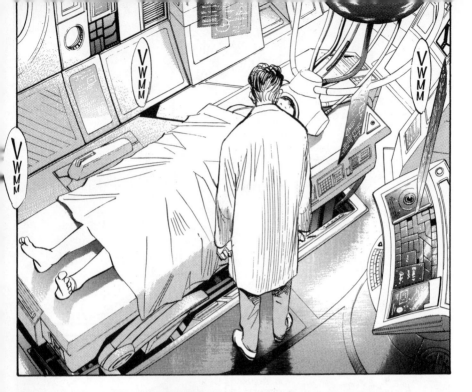

THE ROBOT NEVER GAINED CONSCIOUSNESS.

OR MAYBE I SHOULD SAY, IT *REFUSED* TO WAKE UP.

WHAT I WANTED IT TO DO WAS TOO COMPLEX.

IT WOULD PROBABLY TAKE AN ETERNITY TO SIMULATE THE PERSONALITIES OF SIX BILLION PEOPLE.

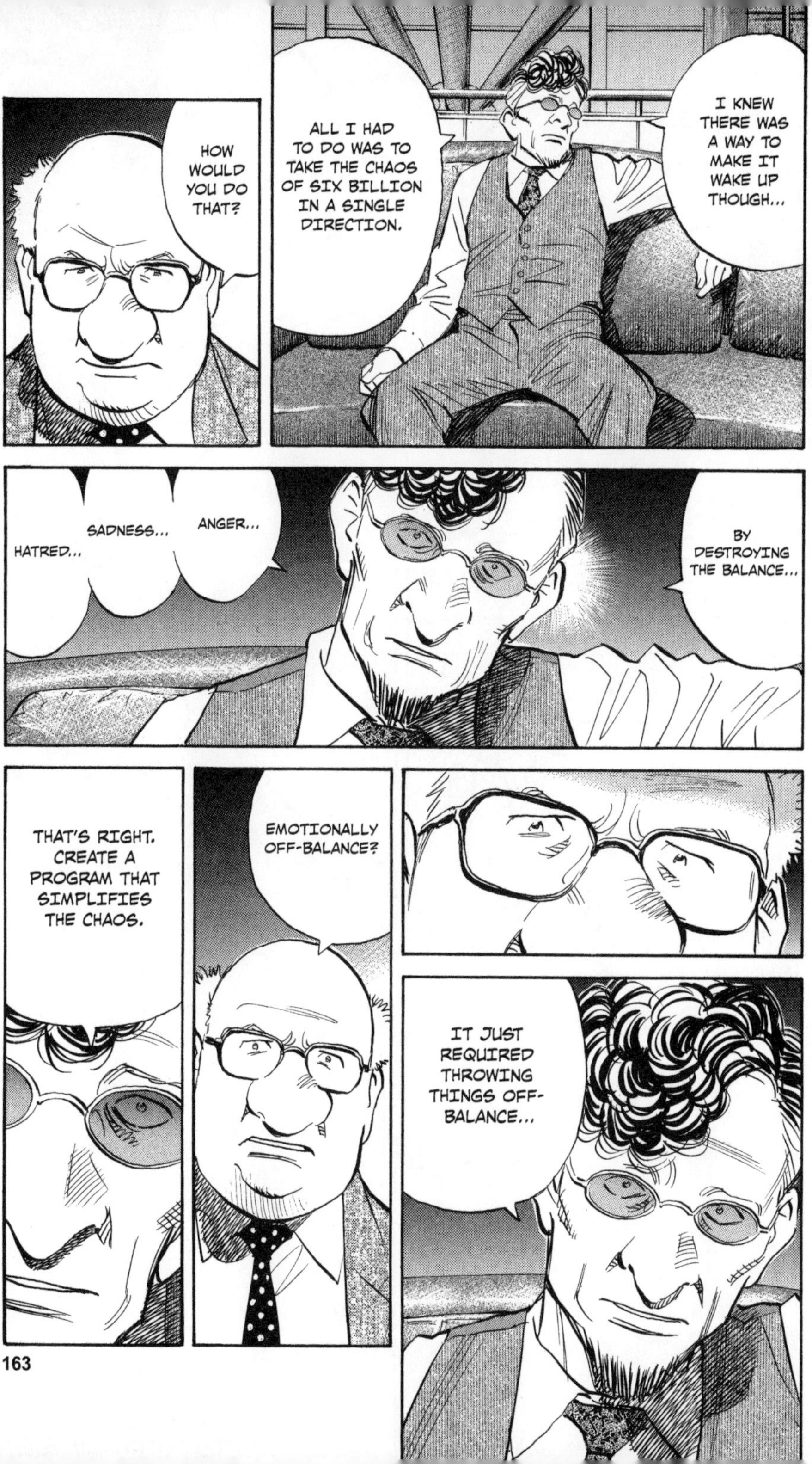
I KNEW THERE WAS A WAY TO MAKE IT WAKE UP THOUGH...
ALL I HAD TO DO WAS TO TAKE THE CHAOS OF SIX BILLION IN A SINGLE DIRECTION.
HOW WOULD YOU DO THAT?
BY DESTROYING THE BALANCE...
ANGER...
SADNESS...
HATRED...
IT JUST REQUIRED THROWING THINGS OFF-BALANCE...
EMOTIONALLY OFF-BALANCE?
THAT'S RIGHT. CREATE A PROGRAM THAT SIMPLIFIES THE CHAOS.

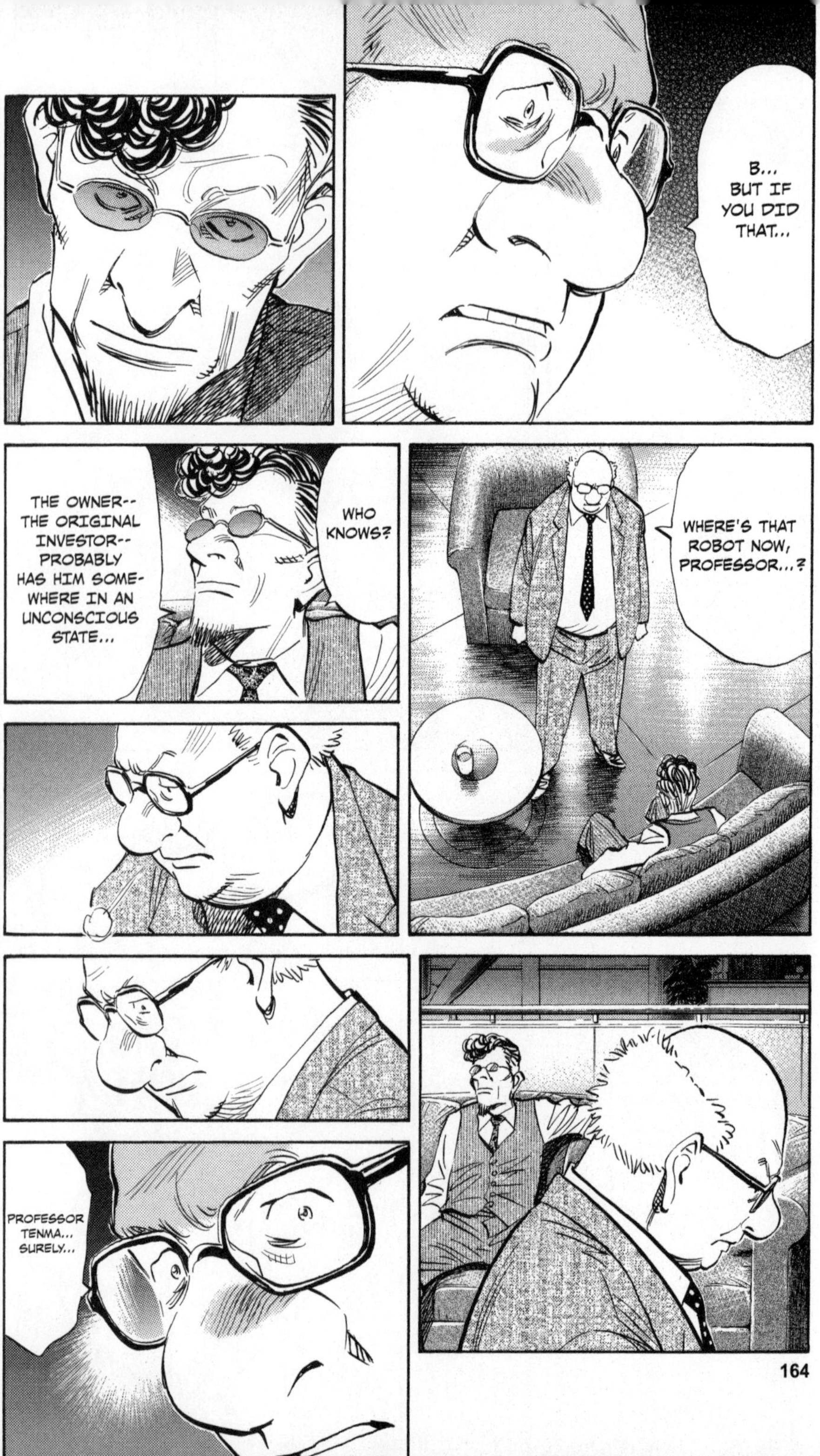
B... BUT IF YOU DID THAT...
WHERE'S THAT ROBOT NOW, PROFESSOR...?
WHO KNOWS?
THE OWNER-- THE ORIGINAL INVESTOR-- PROBABLY HAS HIM SOMEWHERE IN AN UNCONSCIOUS STATE...
PROFESSOR TENMA... SURELY...

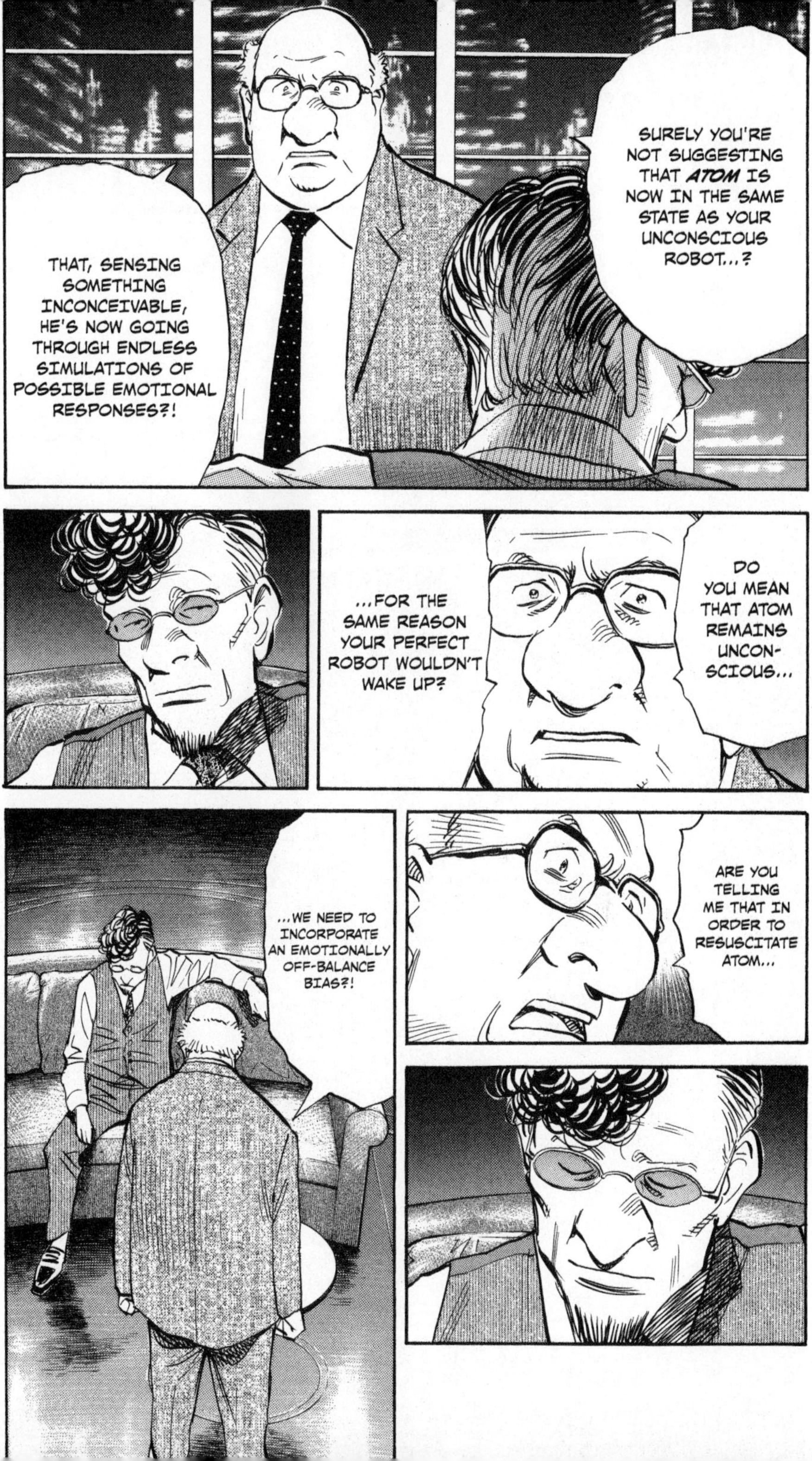
SURELY YOU'RE NOT SUGGESTING THAT ATOM IS NOW IN THE SAME STATE AS YOUR UNCONSCIOUS ROBOT...?
THAT, SENSING SOMETHING INCONCEIVABLE, HE'S NOW GOING THROUGH ENDLESS SIMULATIONS OF POSSIBLE EMOTIONAL RESPONSES?!
DO YOU MEAN THAT ATOM REMAINS UNCON-SCIOUS...
...FOR THE SAME REASON YOUR PERFECT ROBOT WOULDN'T WAKE UP?
ARE YOU TELLING ME THAT IN ORDER TO RESUSCITATE ATOM...
...WE NEED TO INCORPORATE AN EMOTIONALLY OFF-BALANCE BIAS?!

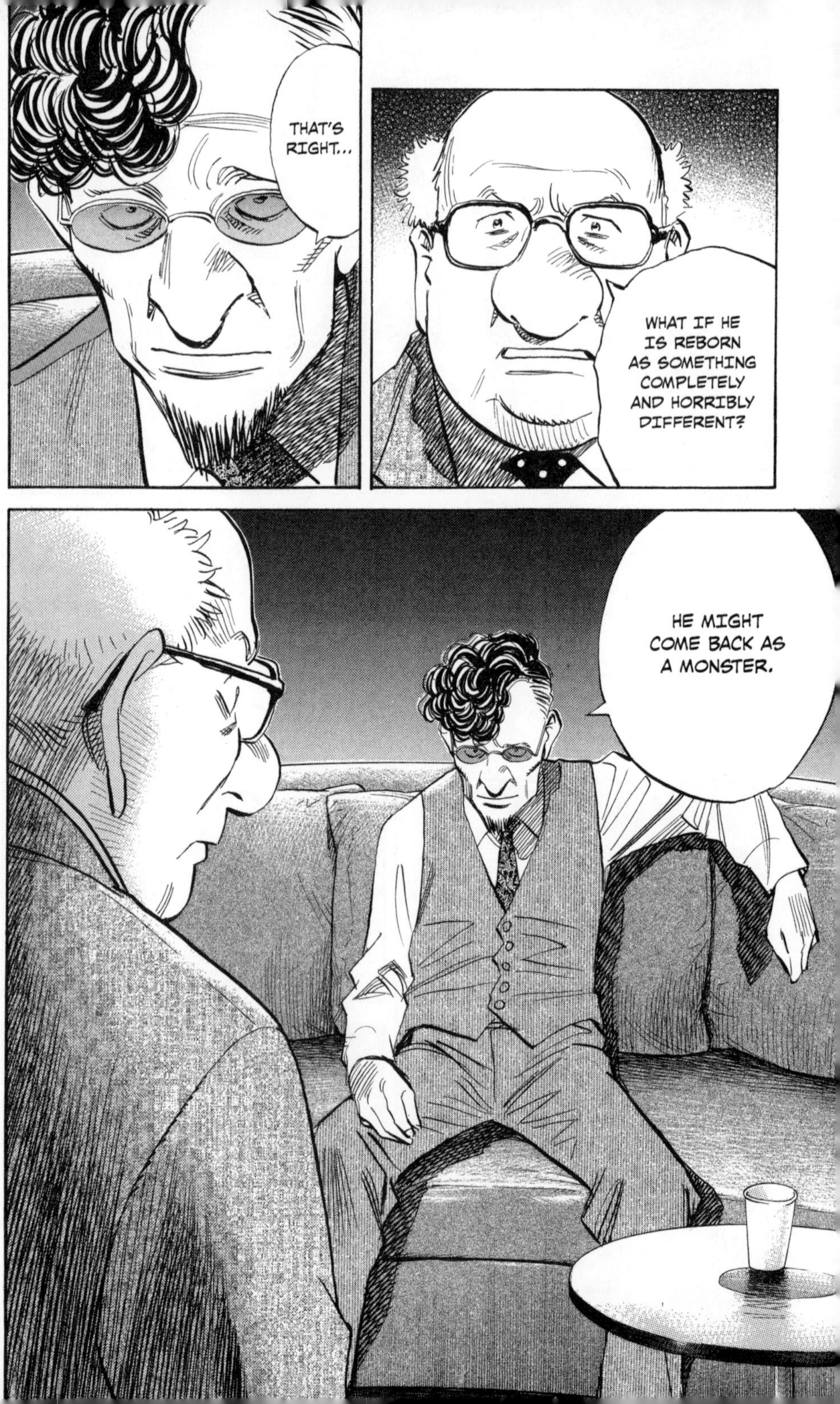
WHAT IF HE IS REBORN AS SOMETHING COMPLETELY AND HORRIBLY DIFFERENT?
THAT'S RIGHT...
HE MIGHT COME BACK AS A MONSTER.

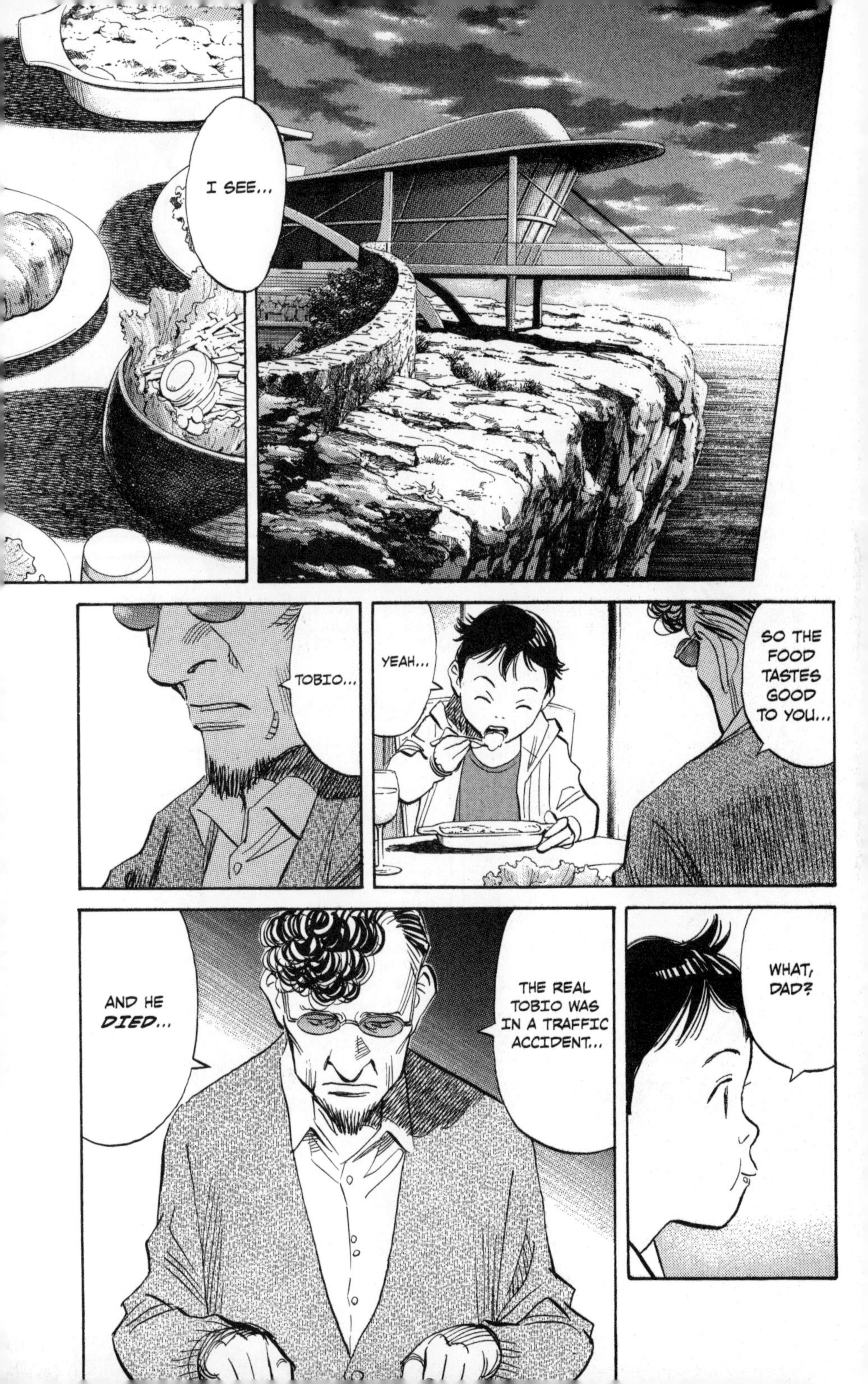
I SEE...
SO THE FOOD TASTES GOOD TO YOU...
YEAH...
TOBIO...
WHAT, DAD?
THE REAL TOBIO WAS IN A TRAFFIC ACCIDENT...
AND HE *DIED*...

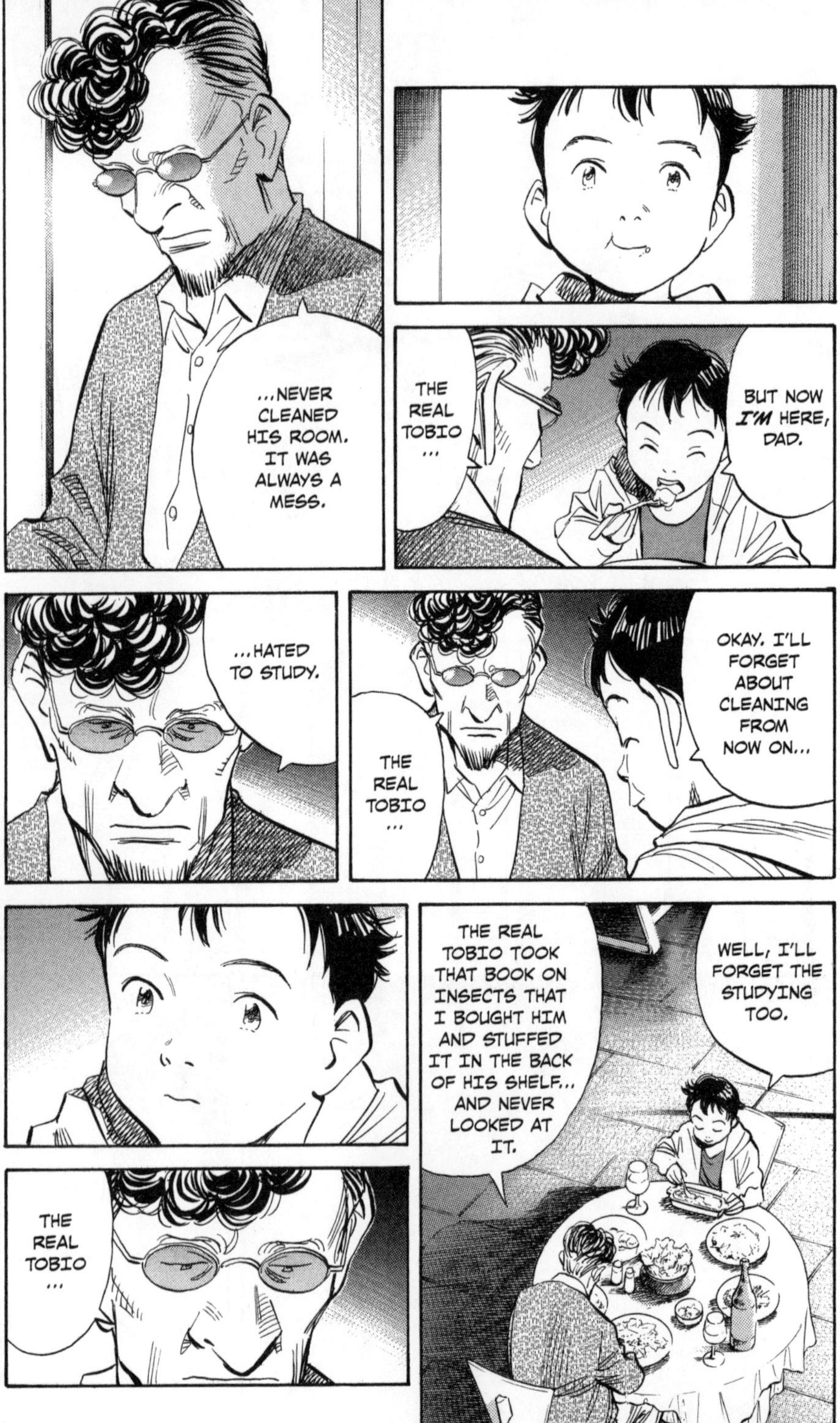
BUT NOW ***I'M*** HERE, DAD.
THE REAL TOBIO ...
...NEVER CLEANED HIS ROOM. IT WAS ALWAYS A MESS.
OKAY. I'LL FORGET ABOUT CLEANING FROM NOW ON...
THE REAL TOBIO ...
...HATED TO STUDY.
WELL, I'LL FORGET THE STUDYING TOO.
THE REAL TOBIO TOOK THAT BOOK ON INSECTS THAT I BOUGHT HIM AND STUFFED IT IN THE BACK OF HIS SHELF... AND NEVER LOOKED AT IT.
THE REAL TOBIO ...

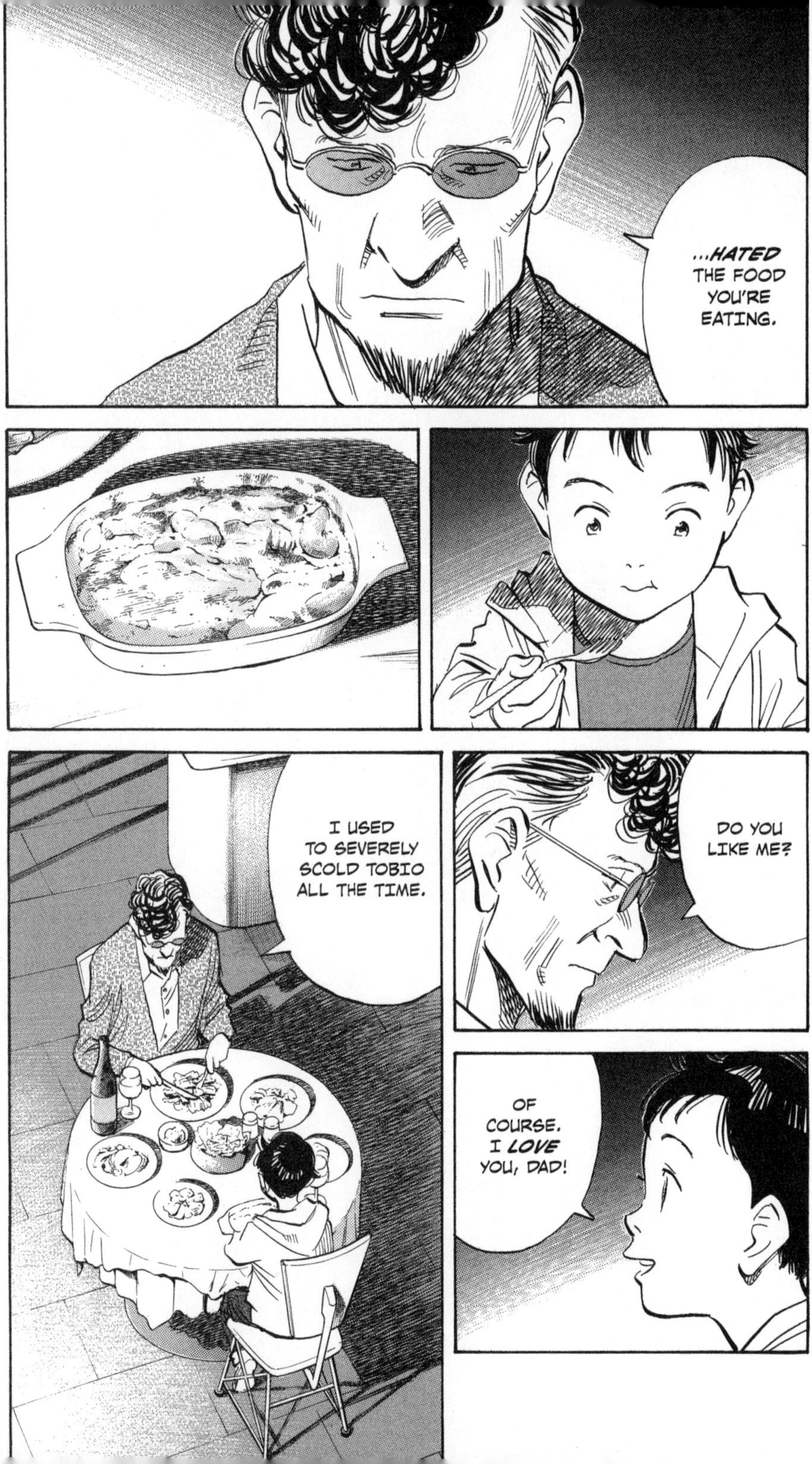
...HATED THE FOOD YOU'RE EATING.
DO YOU LIKE ME?
OF COURSE. I LOVE YOU, DAD!
I USED TO SEVERELY SCOLD TOBIO ALL THE TIME.

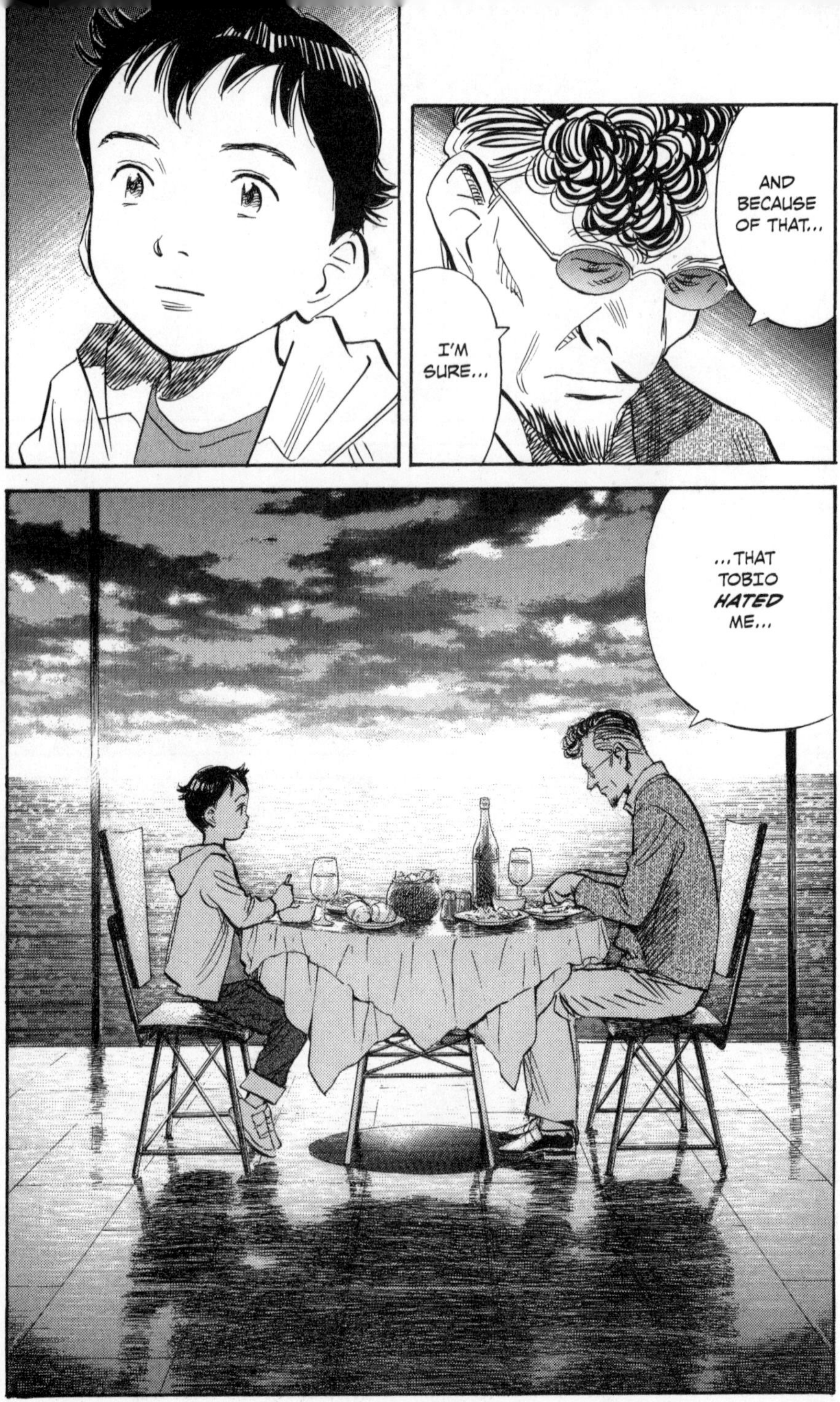
AND BECAUSE OF THAT...
I'M SURE...
...THAT TOBIO *HATED* ME...

# Act 39 THE IMPRISONED KING

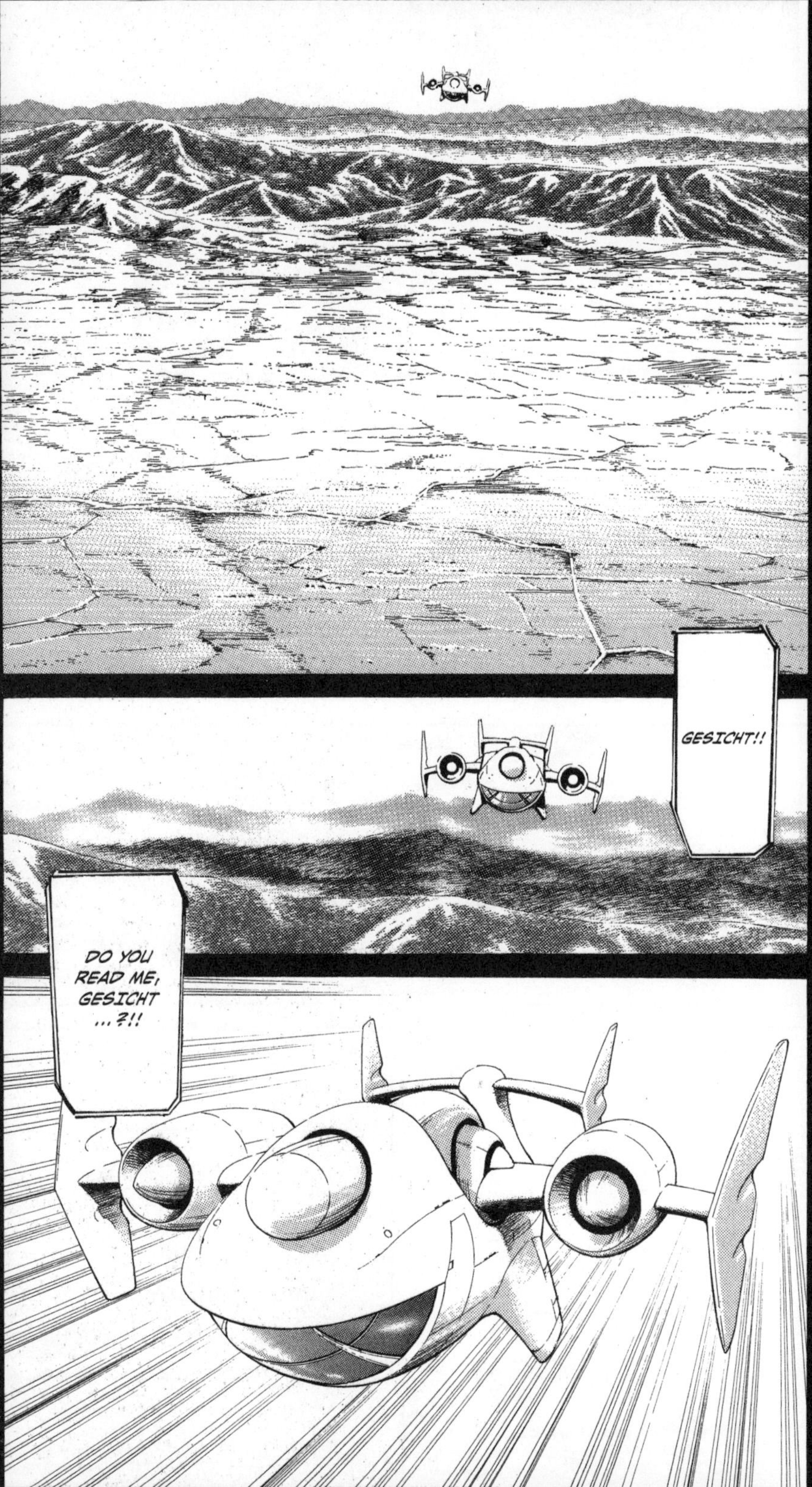
GESICHT!!
DO YOU READ ME, GESICHT ...?!!

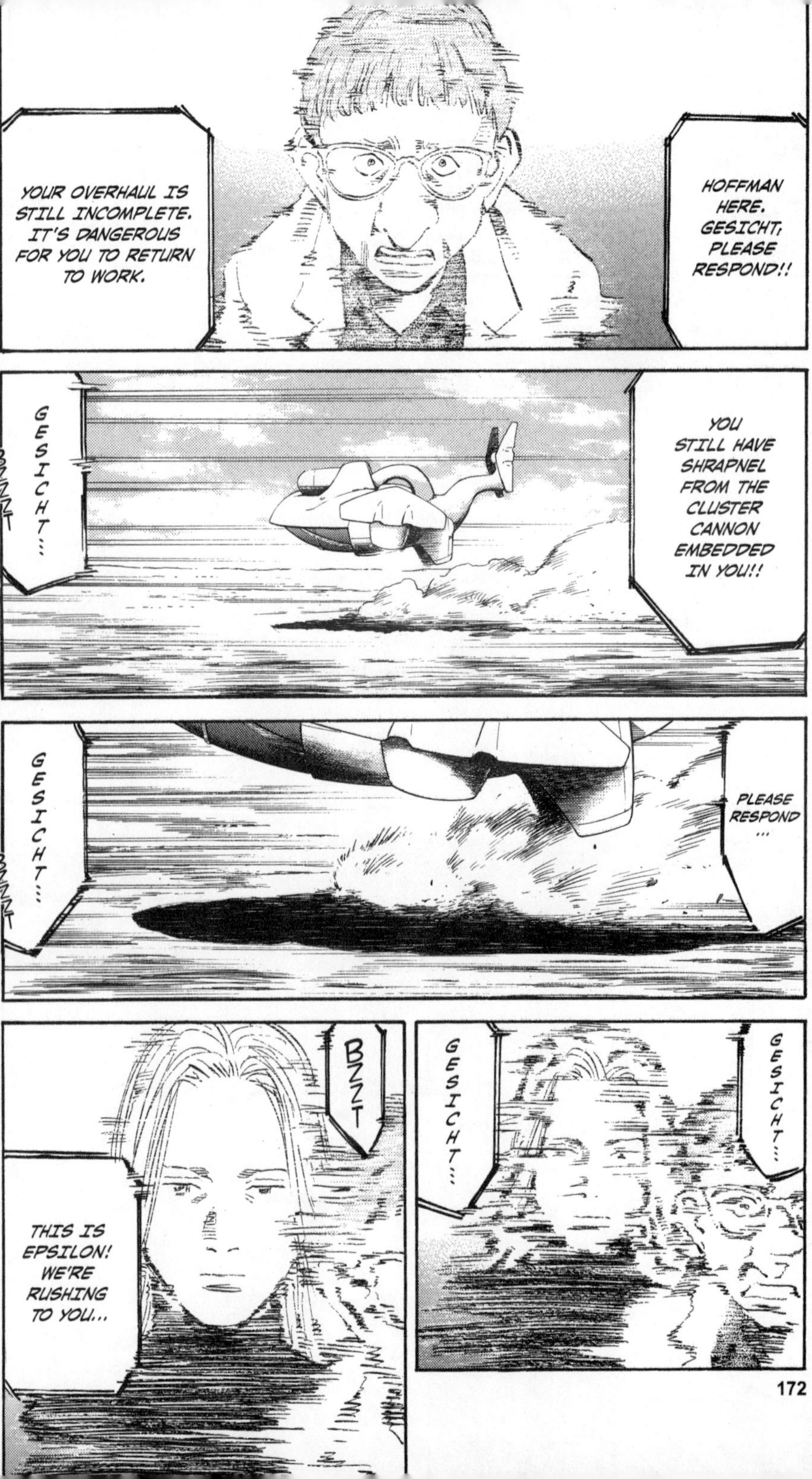
HOFFMAN HERE. GESICHT, PLEASE RESPOND!!
YOUR OVERHAUL IS STILL INCOMPLETE. IT'S DANGEROUS FOR YOU TO RETURN TO WORK.
YOU STILL HAVE SHRAPNEL FROM THE CLUSTER CANNON EMBEDDED IN YOU!!
GESICHT...
BZZZT
PLEASE RESPOND...
GESICHT...
BZZZT
GESICHT...
GESICHT...
BZZT
THIS IS EPSILON! WE'RE RUSHING TO YOU...

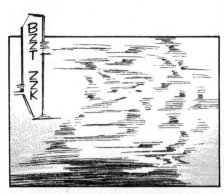

BZZT ZZK

WE'LL BE THERE SOON! ZZZK

FWSHHH

WHOOSH

VURRR

SHUF

KARA-TEPA PRISON,
UNITED STATES OF THRACIA
CONTROLLED TERRITORY
IN PERSIA

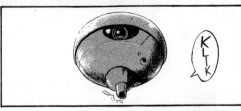

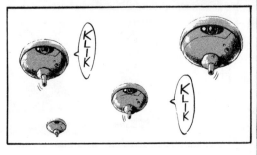

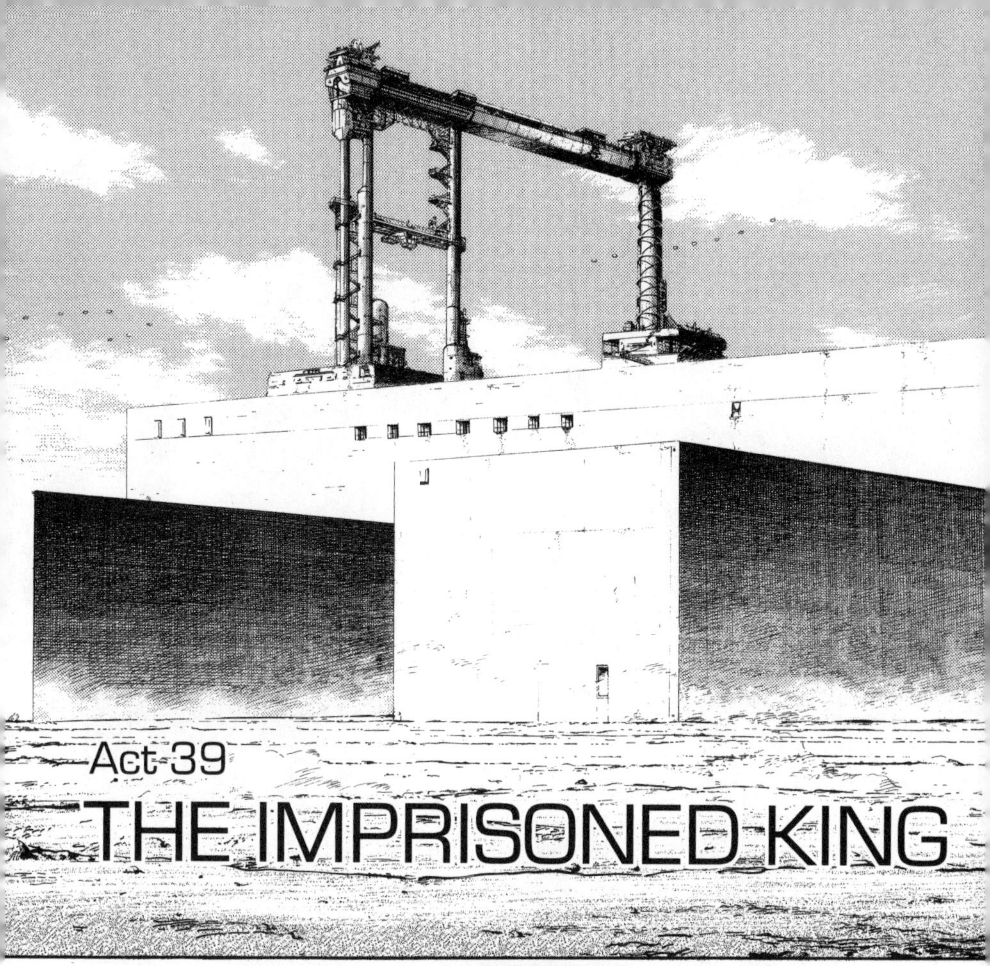
Act 39
THE IMPRISONED KING

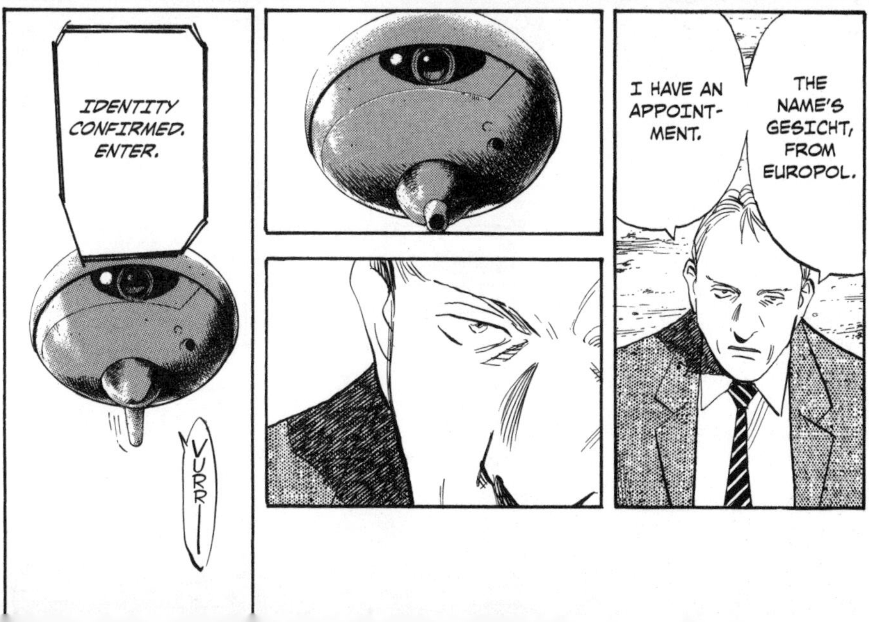
THE NAME'S GESICHT, FROM EUROPOL.
I HAVE AN APPOINTMENT.
IDENTITY CONFIRMED. ENTER.
VURR

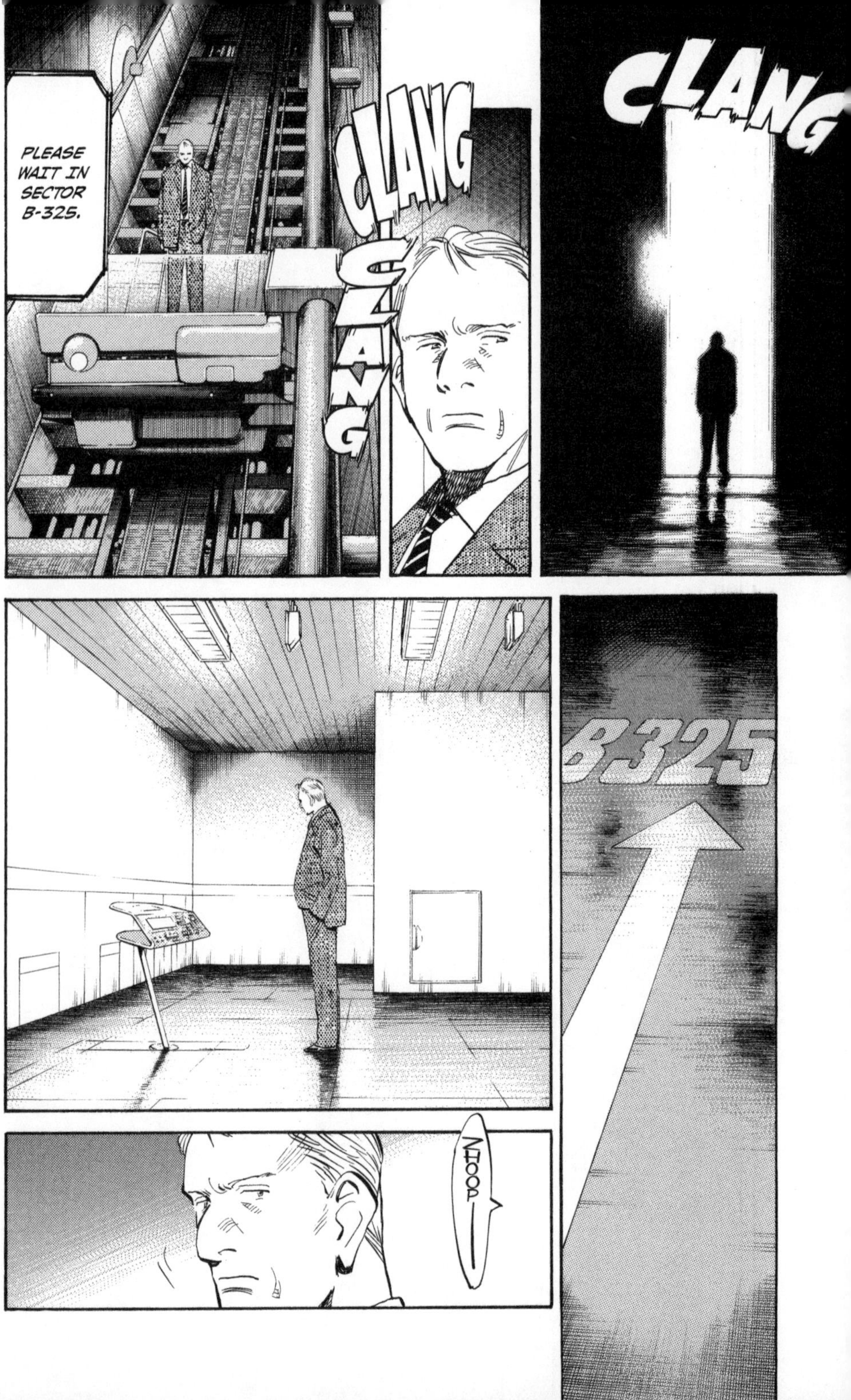
CLANG
CLANG
CLANG
CLANG
PLEASE WAIT IN SECTOR B-325.
B325
WHOOP—

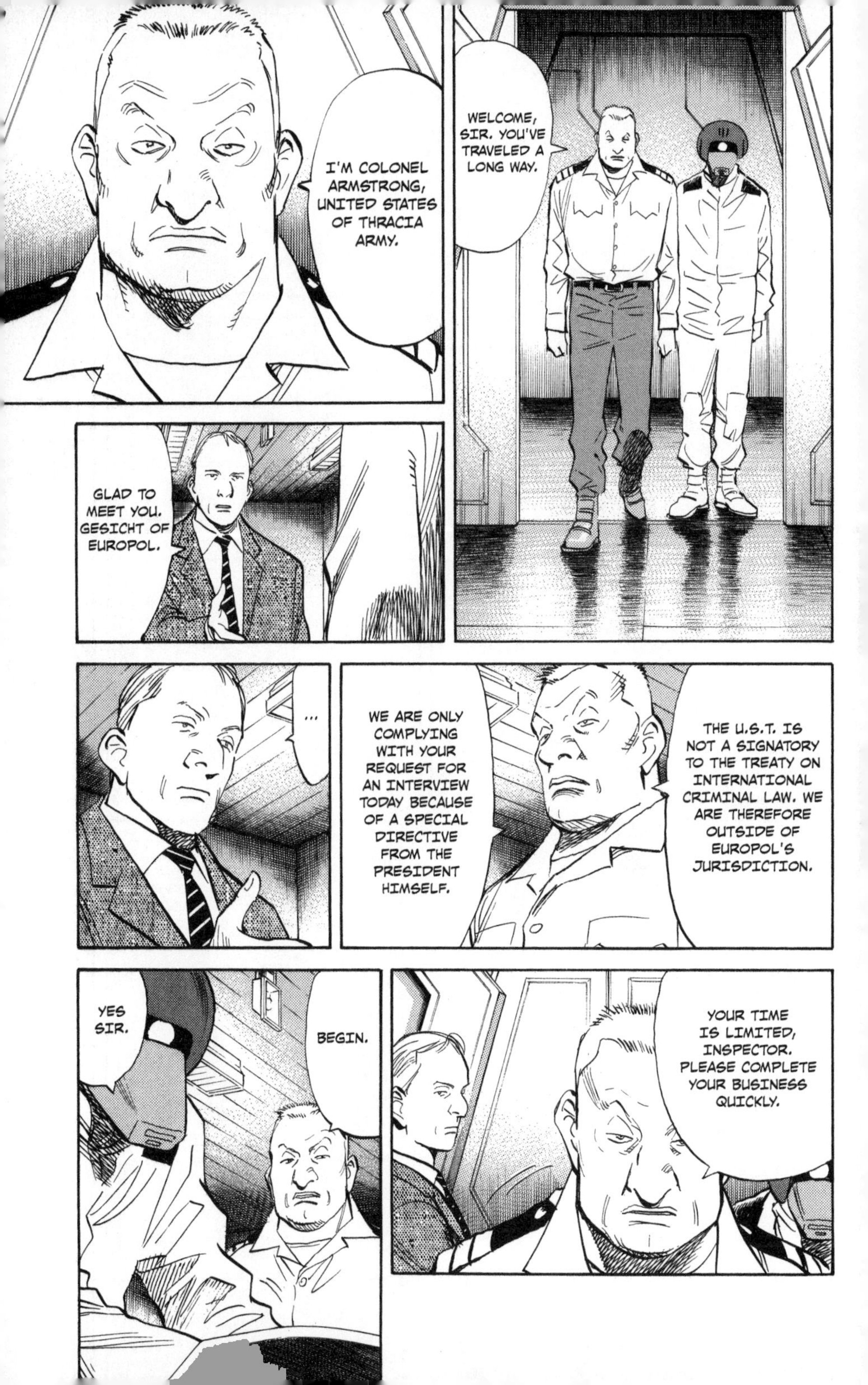
WELCOME, SIR. YOU'VE TRAVELED A LONG WAY.
I'M COLONEL ARMSTRONG, UNITED STATES OF THRACIA ARMY.
GLAD TO MEET YOU. GESICHT OF EUROPOL.
THE U.S.T. IS NOT A SIGNATORY TO THE TREATY ON INTERNATIONAL CRIMINAL LAW. WE ARE THEREFORE OUTSIDE OF EUROPOL'S JURISDICTION.
WE ARE ONLY COMPLYING WITH YOUR REQUEST FOR AN INTERVIEW TODAY BECAUSE OF A SPECIAL DIRECTIVE FROM THE PRESIDENT HIMSELF.
...
YOUR TIME IS LIMITED, INSPECTOR. PLEASE COMPLETE YOUR BUSINESS QUICKLY.
BEGIN.
YES SIR.

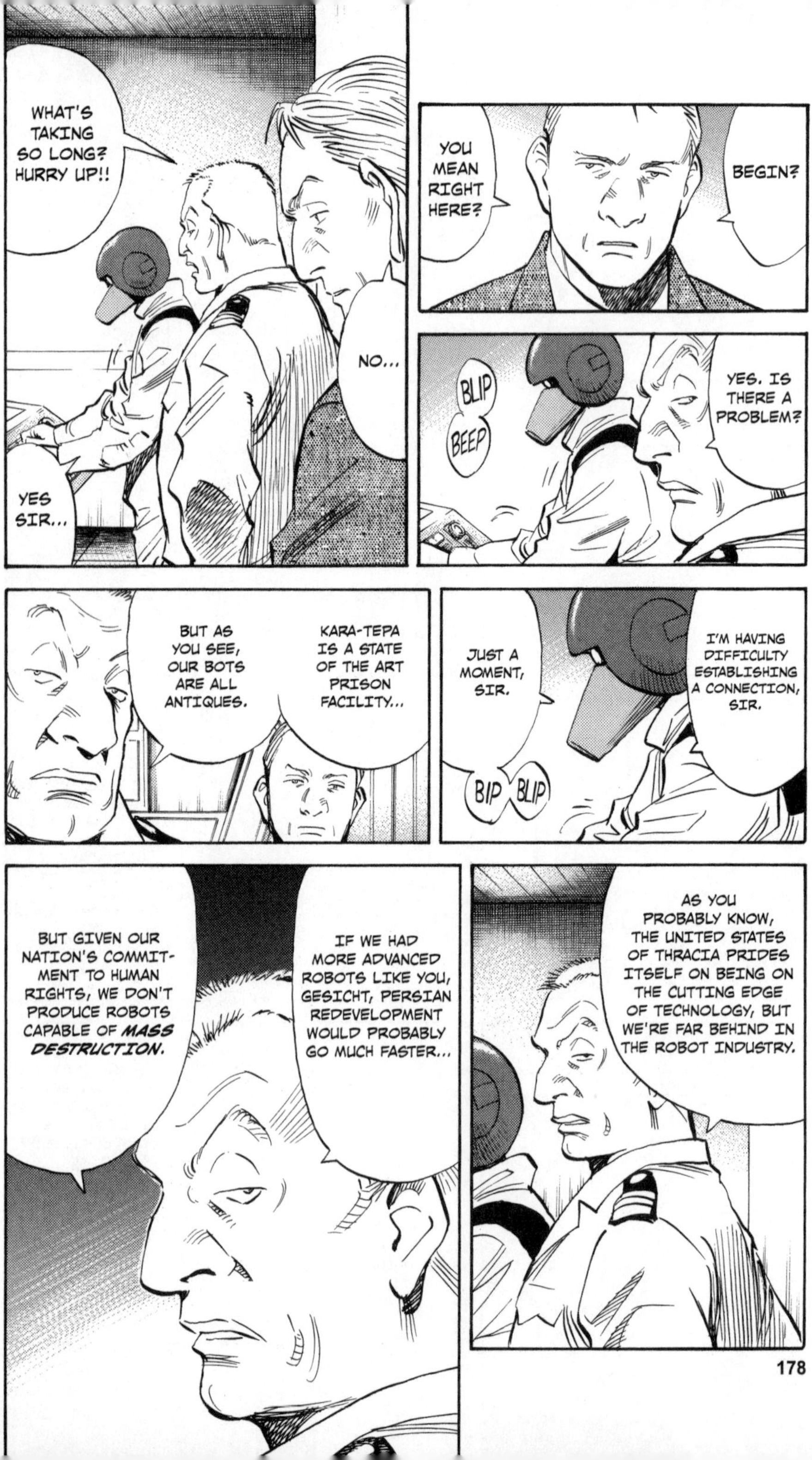
BEGIN?
YOU MEAN RIGHT HERE?
YES. IS THERE A PROBLEM?
BLIP
BEEP
NO...
WHAT'S TAKING SO LONG? HURRY UP!!
YES SIR...
I'M HAVING DIFFICULTY ESTABLISHING A CONNECTION, SIR.
JUST A MOMENT, SIR.
BIP
BLIP
KARA-TEPA IS A STATE OF THE ART PRISON FACILITY...
BUT AS YOU SEE, OUR BOTS ARE ALL ANTIQUES.
AS YOU PROBABLY KNOW, THE UNITED STATES OF THRACIA PRIDES ITSELF ON BEING ON THE CUTTING EDGE OF TECHNOLOGY, BUT WE'RE FAR BEHIND IN THE ROBOT INDUSTRY.
IF WE HAD MORE ADVANCED ROBOTS LIKE YOU, GESICHT, PERSIAN REDEVELOPMENT WOULD PROBABLY GO MUCH FASTER...
BUT GIVEN OUR NATION'S COMMIT-MENT TO HUMAN RIGHTS, WE DON'T PRODUCE ROBOTS CAPABLE OF ***MASS DESTRUCTION***.

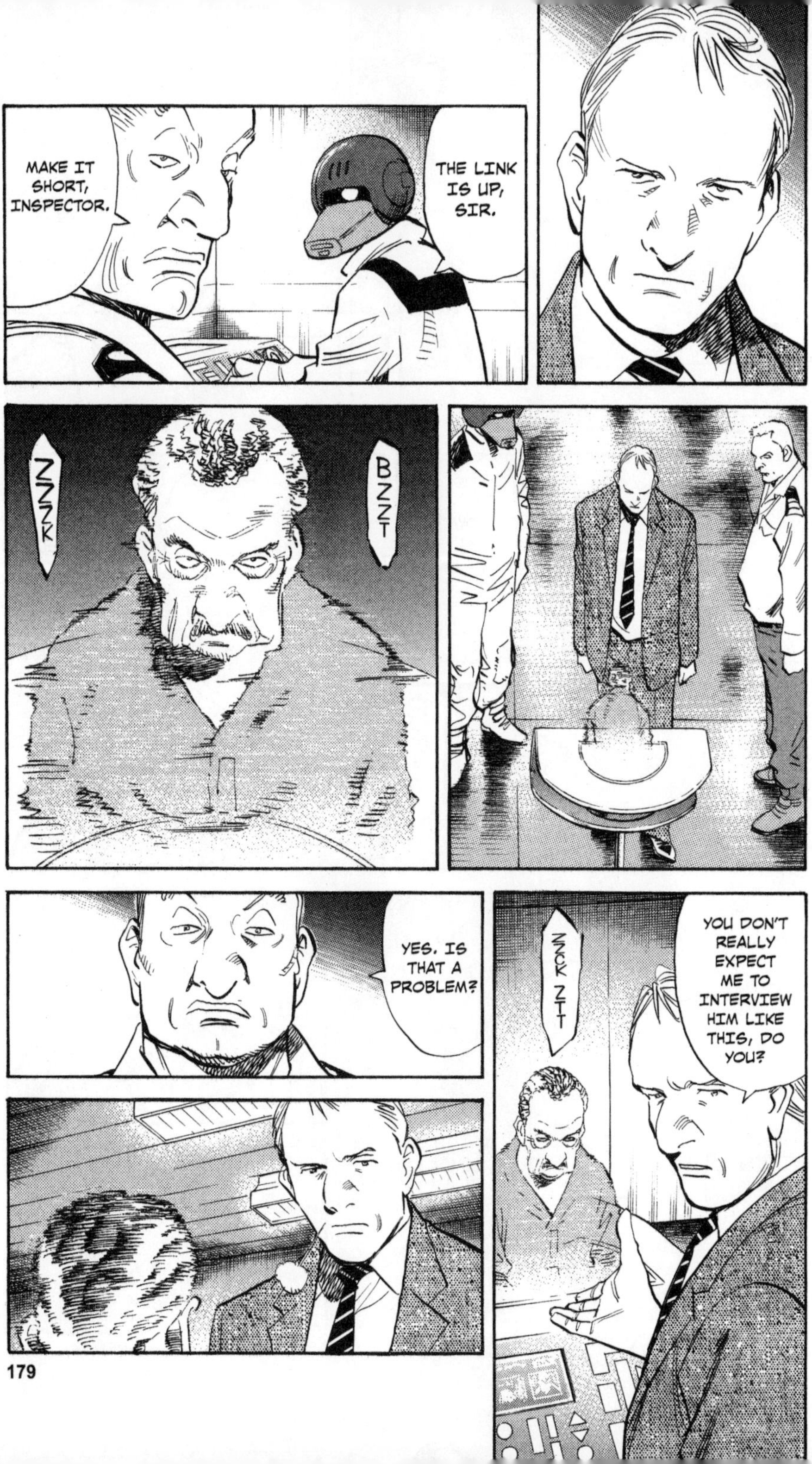
THE LINK IS UP, SIR.
MAKE IT SHORT, INSPECTOR.
BZZT
ZZZK
YOU DON'T REALLY EXPECT ME TO INTERVIEW HIM LIKE THIS, DO YOU?
ZZCK ZTT
YES. IS THAT A PROBLEM?

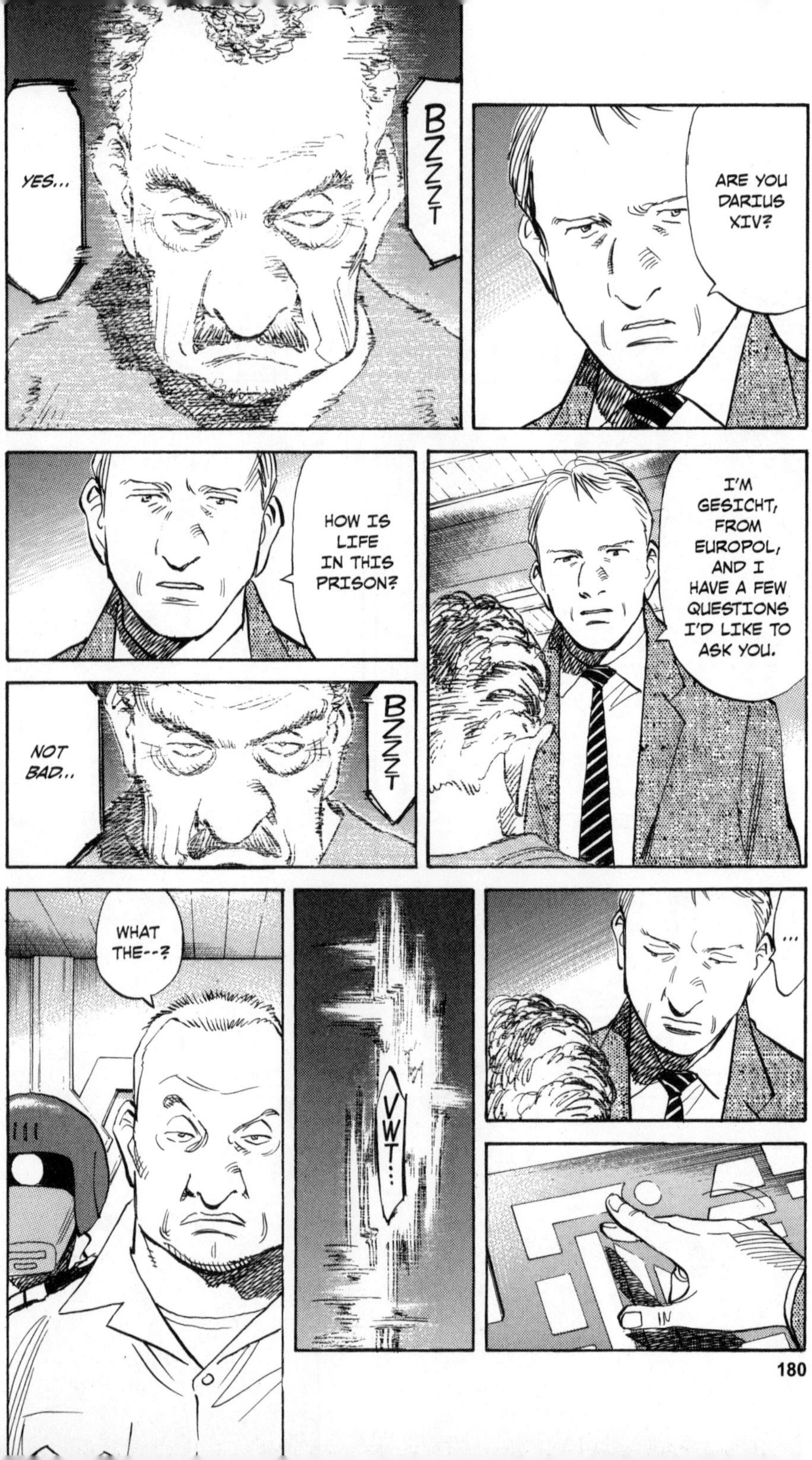
ARE YOU DARIUS XIV?
BZZZT
YES...
I'M GESICHT, FROM EUROPOL, AND I HAVE A FEW QUESTIONS I'D LIKE TO ASK YOU.
HOW IS LIFE IN THIS PRISON?
BZZZT
NOT BAD...
...
VWT...
WHAT THE--?

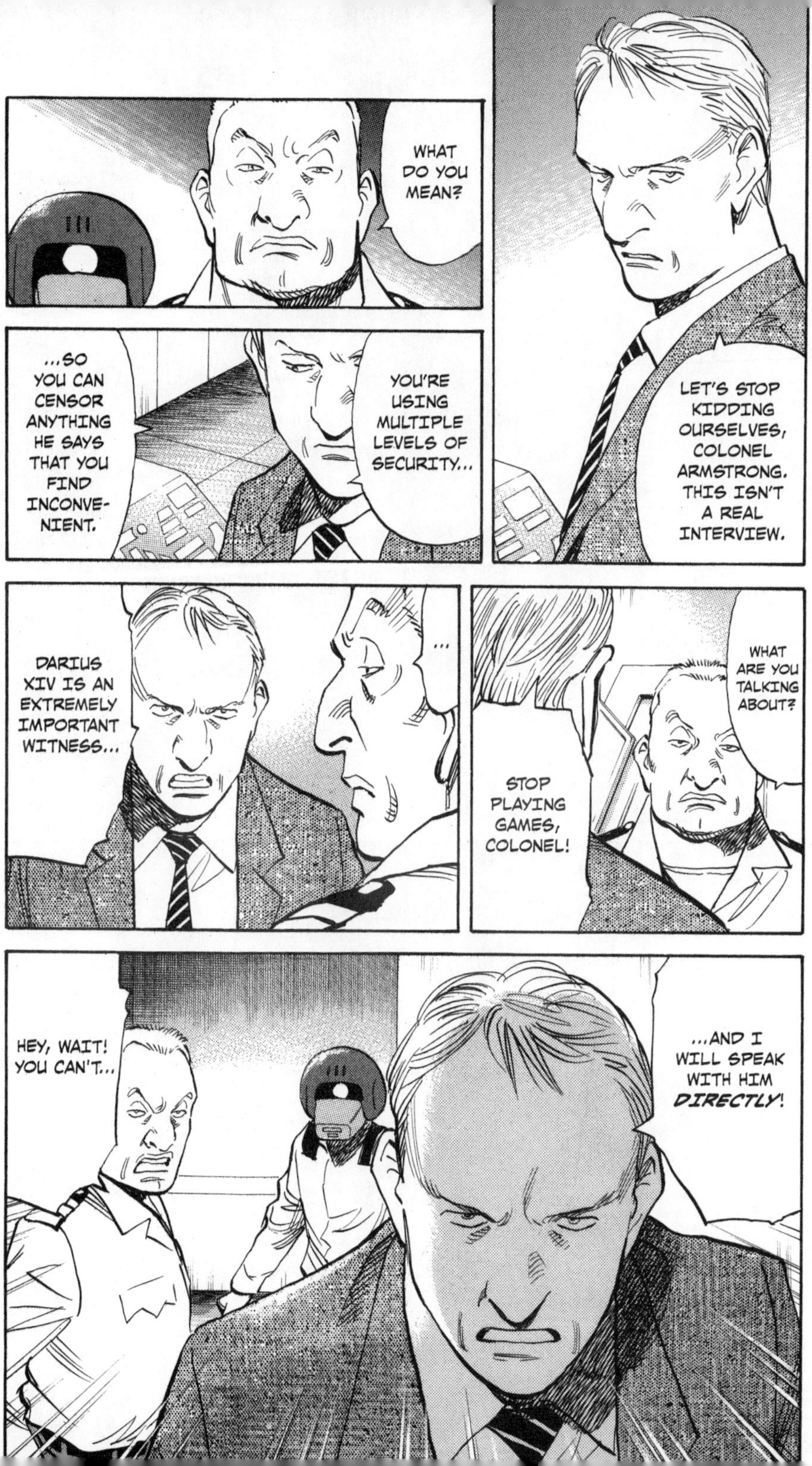
LET'S STOP KIDDING OURSELVES, COLONEL ARMSTRONG. THIS ISN'T A REAL INTERVIEW.
WHAT DO YOU MEAN?
YOU'RE USING MULTIPLE LEVELS OF SECURITY...
...SO YOU CAN CENSOR ANYTHING HE SAYS THAT YOU FIND INCONVE-NIENT.
WHAT ARE YOU TALKING ABOUT?
STOP PLAYING GAMES, COLONEL!
...
DARIUS XIV IS AN EXTREMELY IMPORTANT WITNESS...
...AND I WILL SPEAK WITH HIM *DIRECTLY*!
HEY, WAIT! YOU CAN'T...

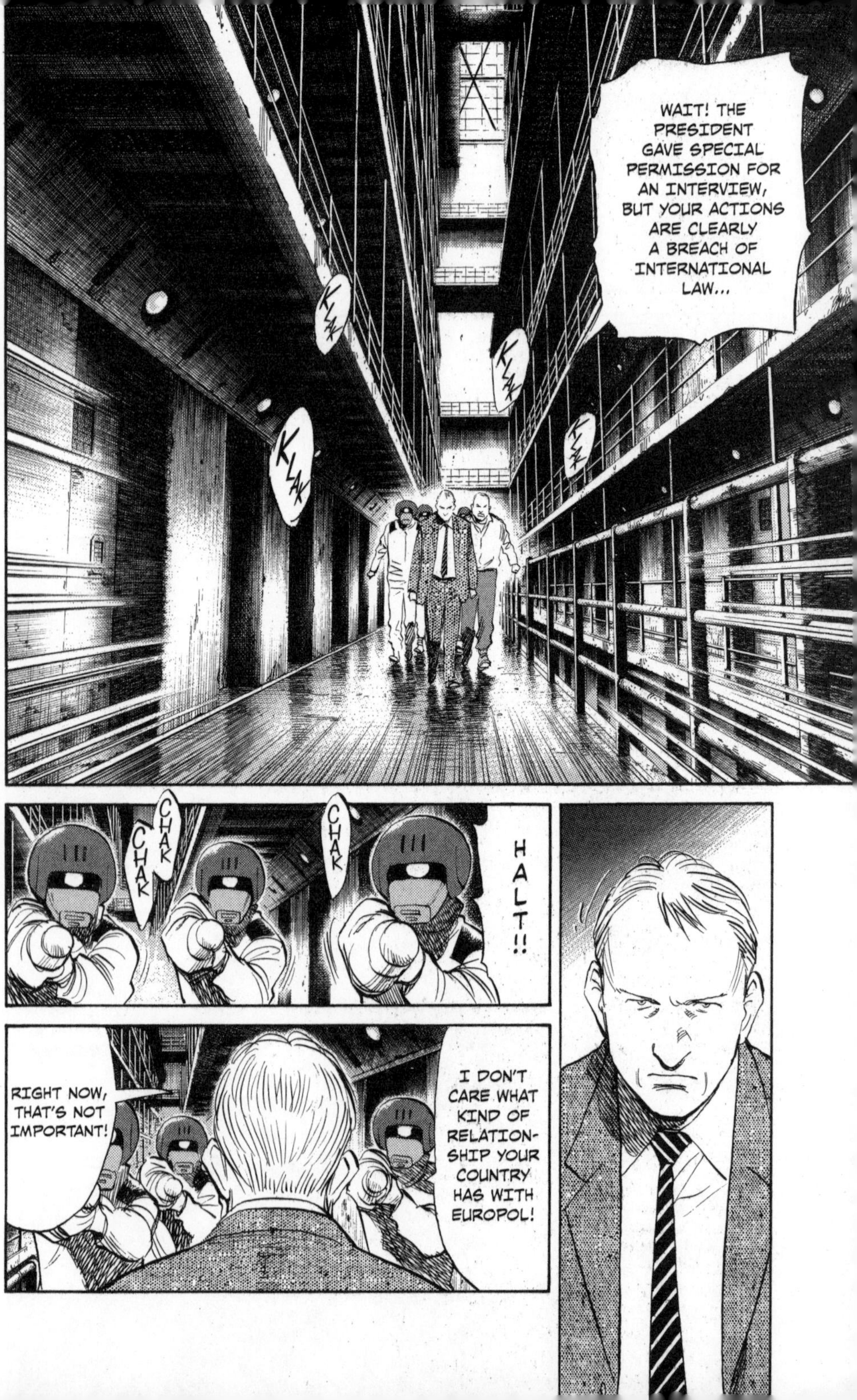
WAIT! THE PRESIDENT GAVE SPECIAL PERMISSION FOR AN INTERVIEW, BUT YOUR ACTIONS ARE CLEARLY A BREACH OF INTERNATIONAL LAW...
KLAK
KLAK
KLAK
KLAK
HALT!!
CHAK
CHAK
CHAK
I DON'T CARE WHAT KIND OF RELATION-SHIP YOUR COUNTRY HAS WITH EUROPOL!
RIGHT NOW, THAT'S NOT IMPORTANT!

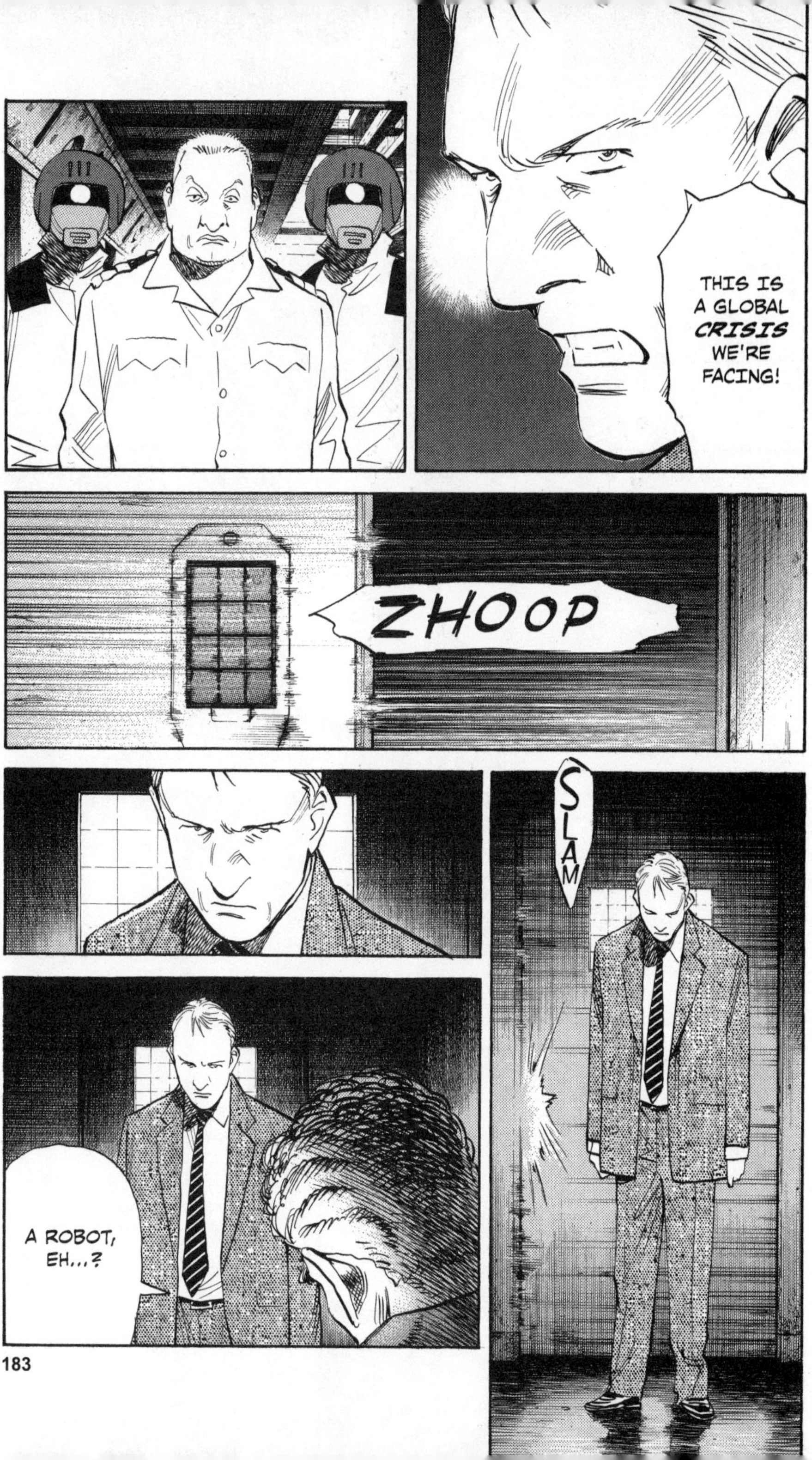
THIS IS A GLOBAL *CRISIS* WE'RE FACING!
ZHOOP
SLAM
A ROBOT, EH...?

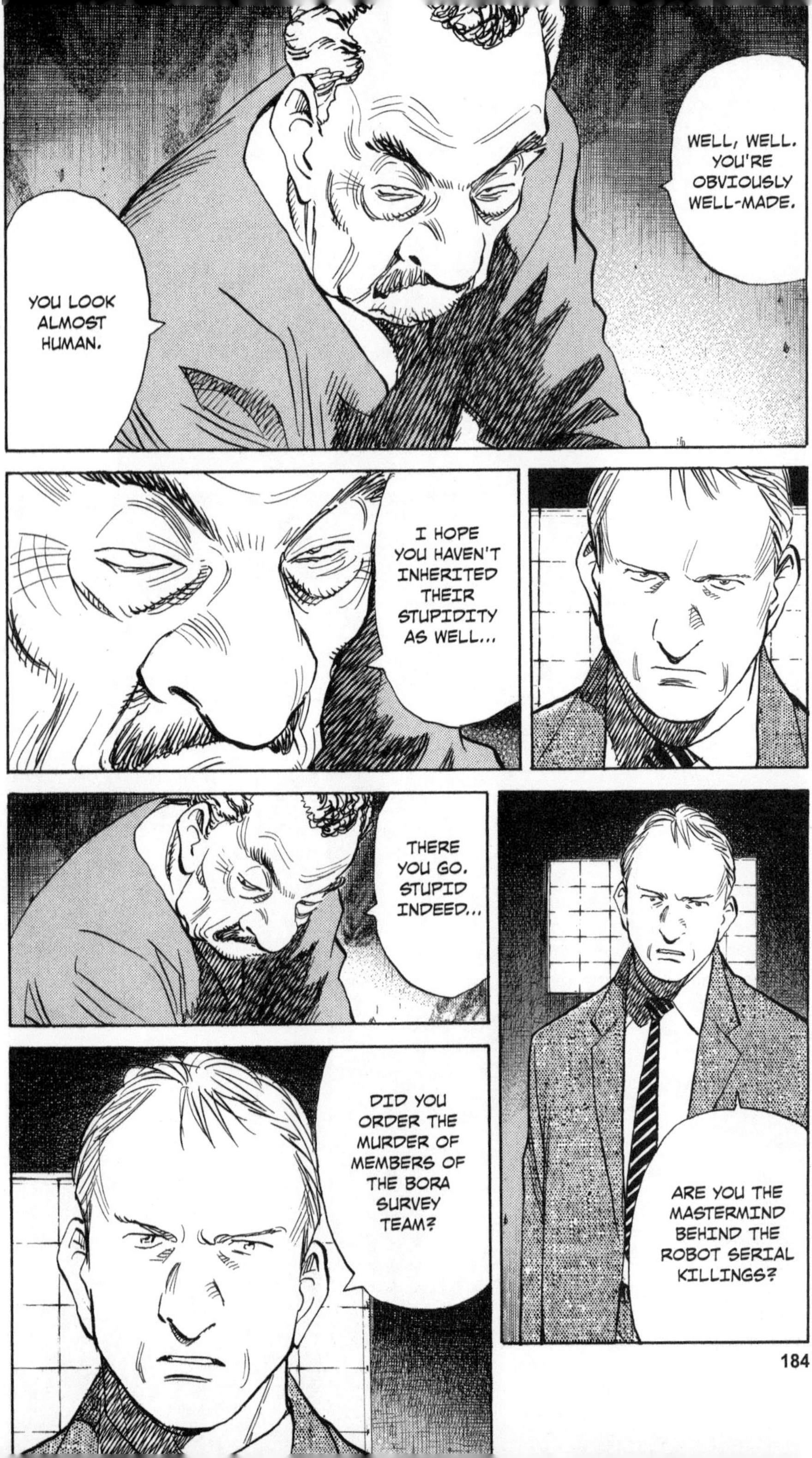
WELL, WELL. YOU'RE OBVIOUSLY WELL-MADE.
YOU LOOK ALMOST HUMAN.
I HOPE YOU HAVEN'T INHERITED THEIR STUPIDITY AS WELL...
ARE YOU THE MASTERMIND BEHIND THE ROBOT SERIAL KILLINGS?
THERE YOU GO. STUPID INDEED...
DID YOU ORDER THE MURDER OF MEMBERS OF THE BORA SURVEY TEAM?

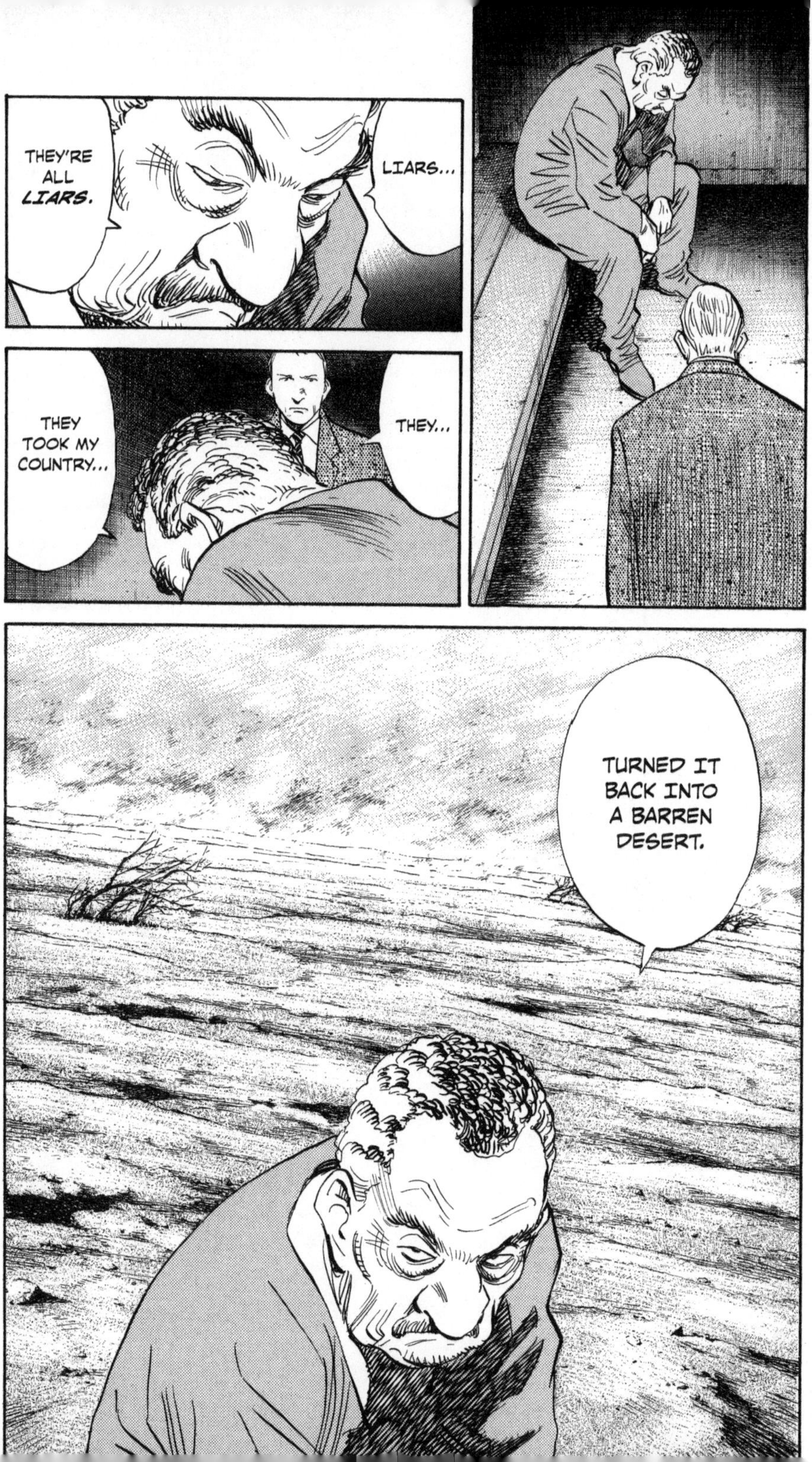
LIARS...
THEY'RE ALL *LIARS.*
THEY...
THEY TOOK MY COUNTRY...
TURNED IT BACK INTO A BARREN DESERT.

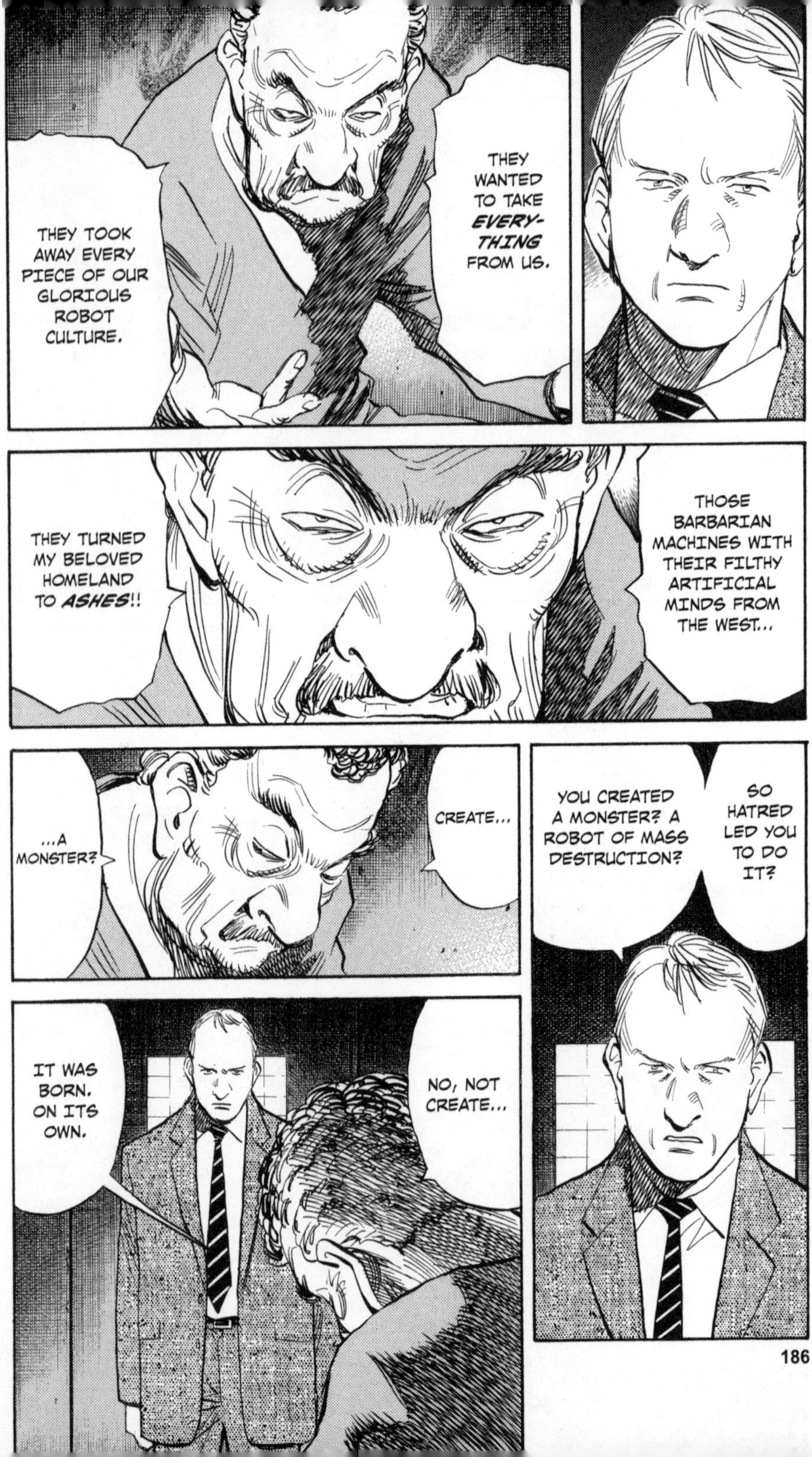

THEY WANTED TO TAKE EVERYTHING FROM US.
THEY TOOK AWAY EVERY PIECE OF OUR GLORIOUS ROBOT CULTURE.
THOSE BARBARIAN MACHINES WITH THEIR FILTHY ARTIFICIAL MINDS FROM THE WEST...
THEY TURNED MY BELOVED HOMELAND TO ASHES!!
SO HATRED LED YOU TO DO IT?
YOU CREATED A MONSTER? A ROBOT OF MASS DESTRUCTION?
CREATE...
...A MONSTER?
NO, NOT CREATE...
IT WAS BORN. ON ITS OWN.

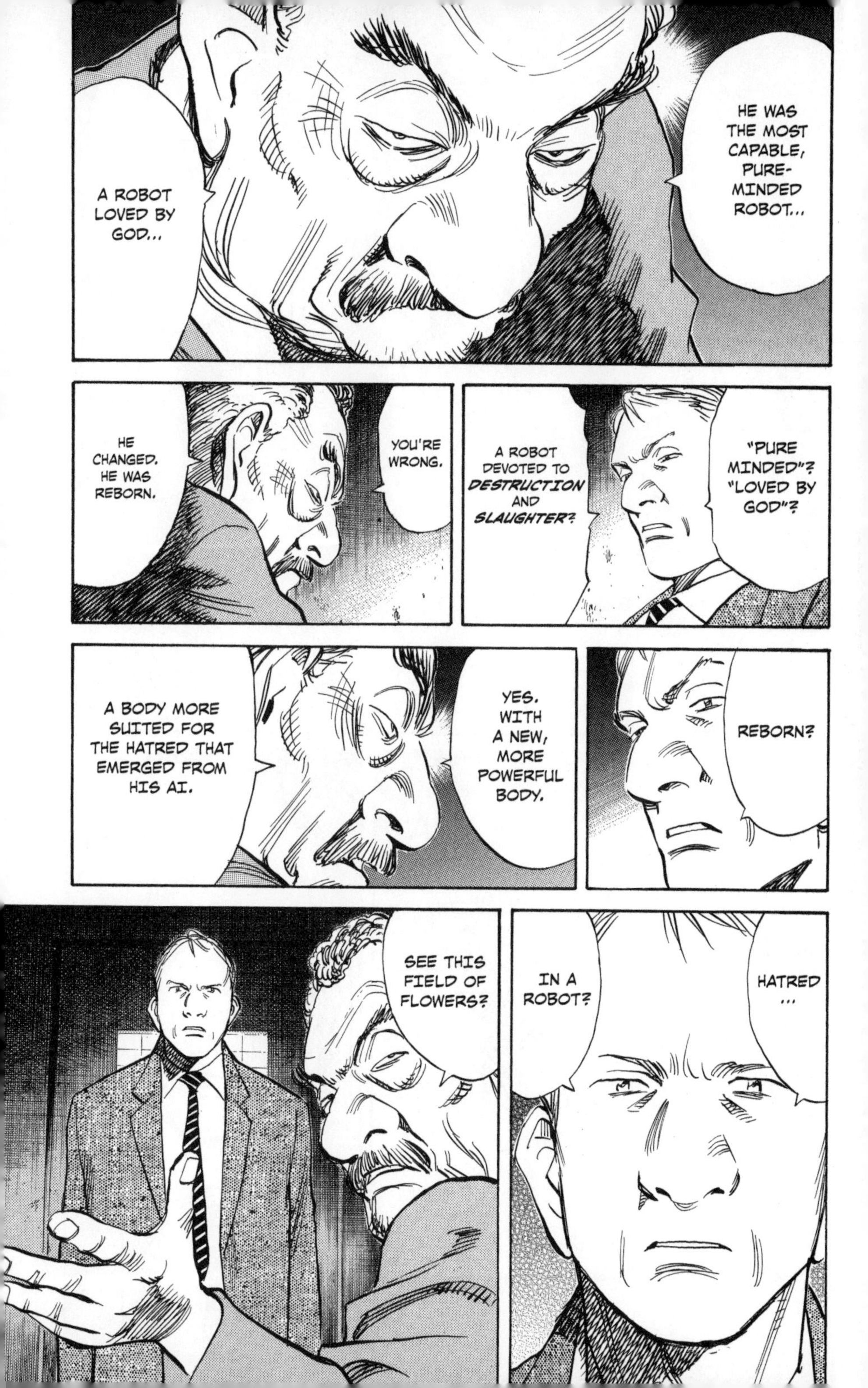
HE WAS THE MOST CAPABLE, PURE-MINDED ROBOT...
A ROBOT LOVED BY GOD...
"PURE MINDED"? "LOVED BY GOD"?
A ROBOT DEVOTED TO *DESTRUCTION* AND *SLAUGHTER*?
YOU'RE WRONG.
HE CHANGED. HE WAS REBORN.
REBORN?
YES. WITH A NEW, MORE POWERFUL BODY.
A BODY MORE SUITED FOR THE HATRED THAT EMERGED FROM HIS AI.
HATRED...
IN A ROBOT?
SEE THIS FIELD OF FLOWERS?

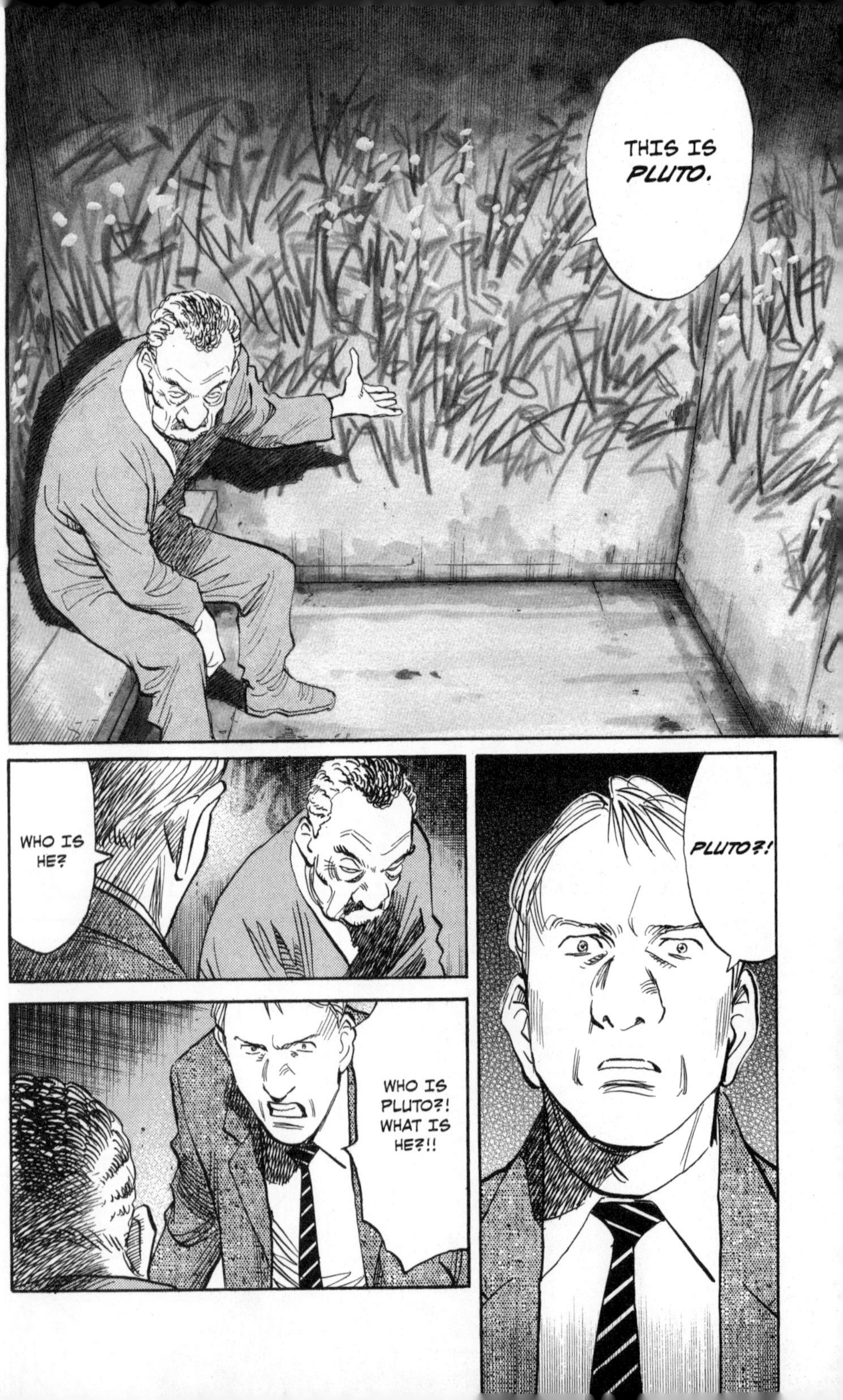
THIS IS PLUTO.
PLUTO?!
WHO IS HE?
WHO IS PLUTO?! WHAT IS HE?!!

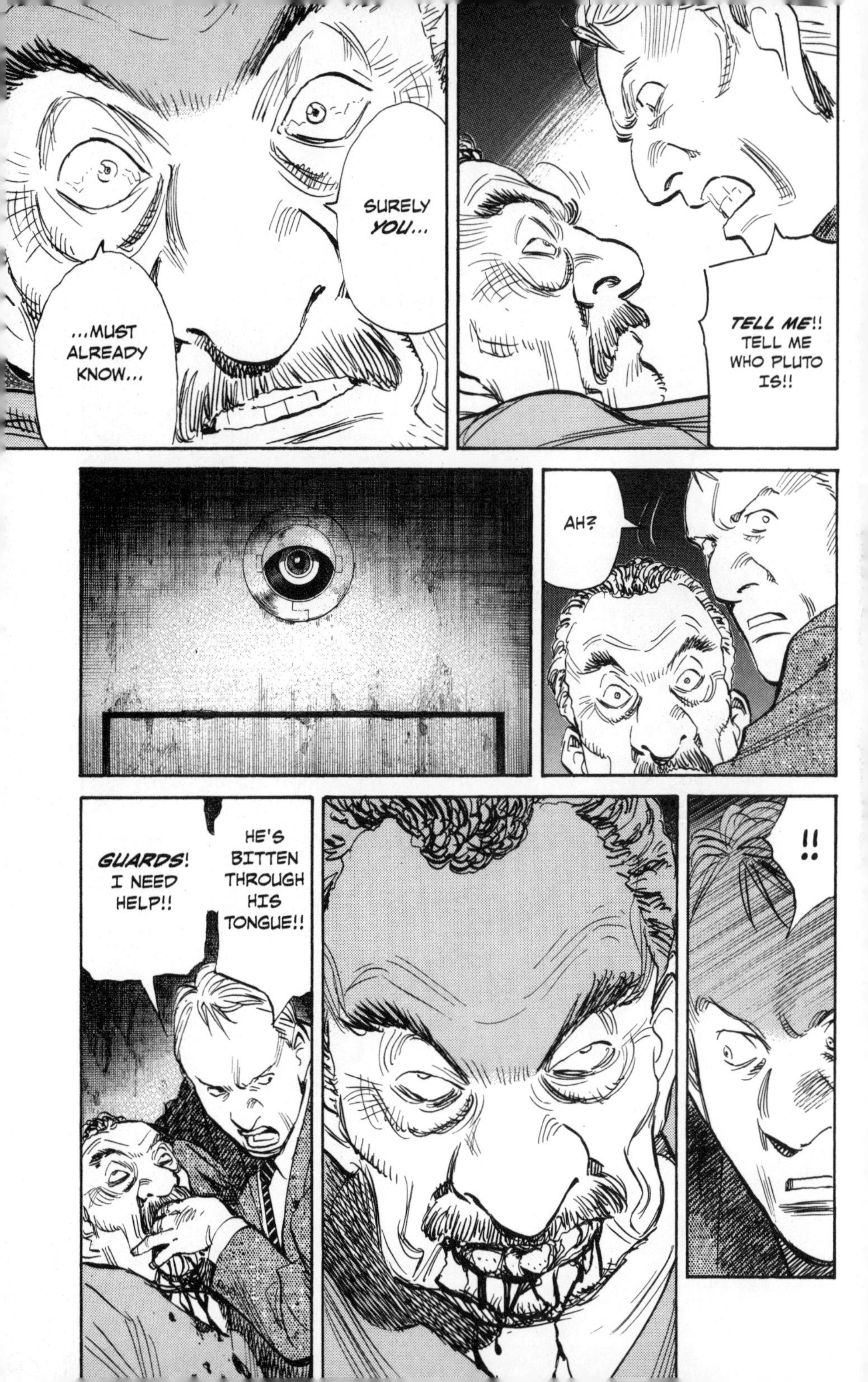
TELL ME!! TELL ME WHO PLUTO IS!!
SURELY YOU...
...MUST ALREADY KNOW...
AH?
!!
HE'S BITTEN THROUGH HIS TONGUE!!
GUARDS! I NEED HELP!!

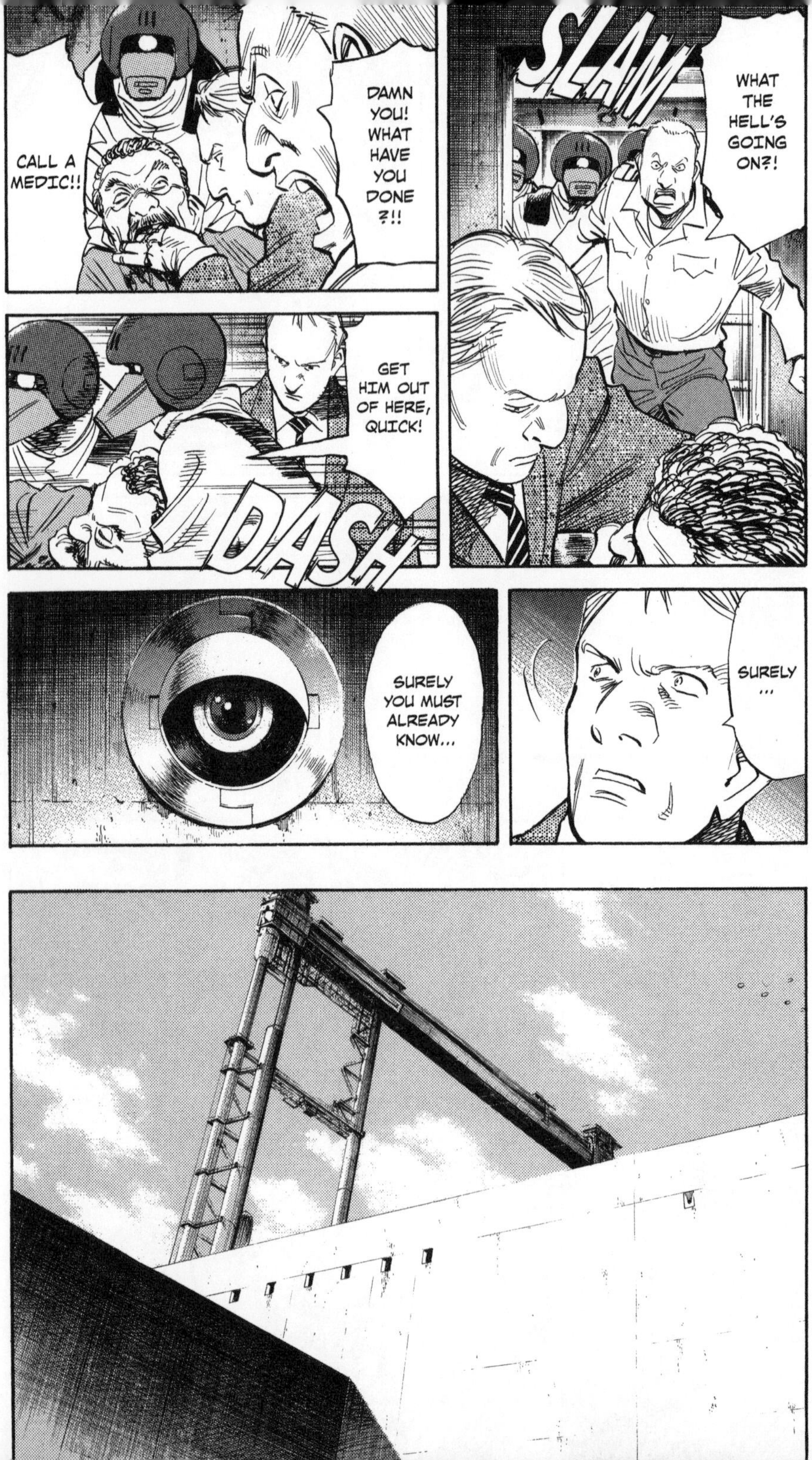
SLAM
WHAT THE HELL'S GOING ON?!
DAMN YOU! WHAT HAVE YOU DONE?!!
CALL A MEDIC!!
GET HIM OUT OF HERE, QUICK!
DASH
SURELY ...
SURELY YOU MUST ALREADY KNOW...

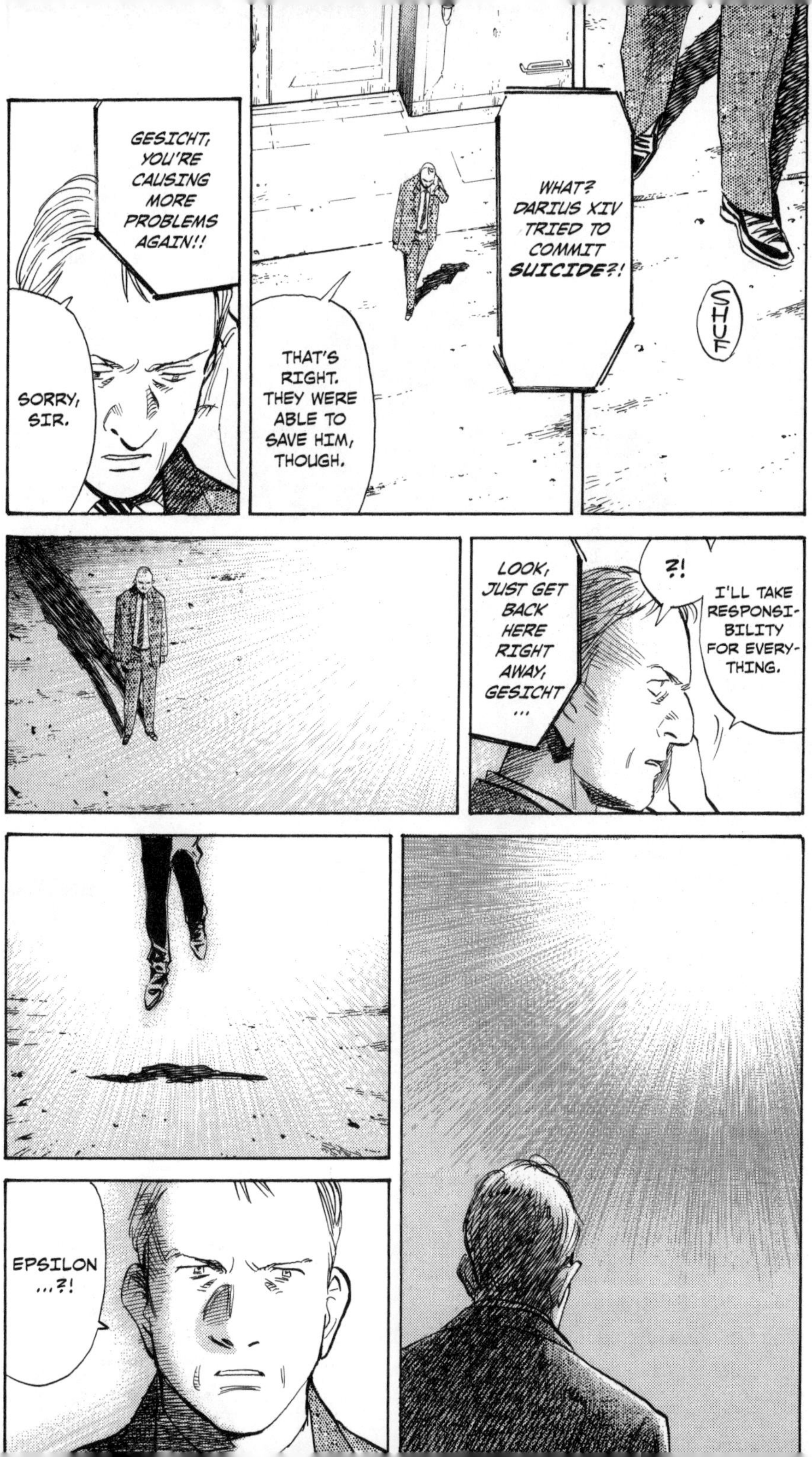
SHUF
WHAT? DARIUS XIV TRIED TO COMMIT SUICIDE?!
THAT'S RIGHT. THEY WERE ABLE TO SAVE HIM, THOUGH.
GESICHT, YOU'RE CAUSING MORE PROBLEMS AGAIN!!
SORRY, SIR.
I'LL TAKE RESPONSIBILITY FOR EVERYTHING.
?!
LOOK, JUST GET BACK HERE RIGHT AWAY, GESICHT ...
EPSILON ...?!

I COULDN'T REACH YOU, GESICHT, BUT I LOCATED YOUR POSITION AND FLEW STRAIGHT HERE.

A MEMENTO... FROM HERCULES.

BUT THAT'S NOT ALL THAT HE LEFT, GESICHT.

THERE'S SOMETHING ELSE I WANT TO SHOW YOU...

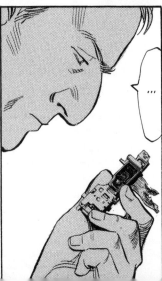

...

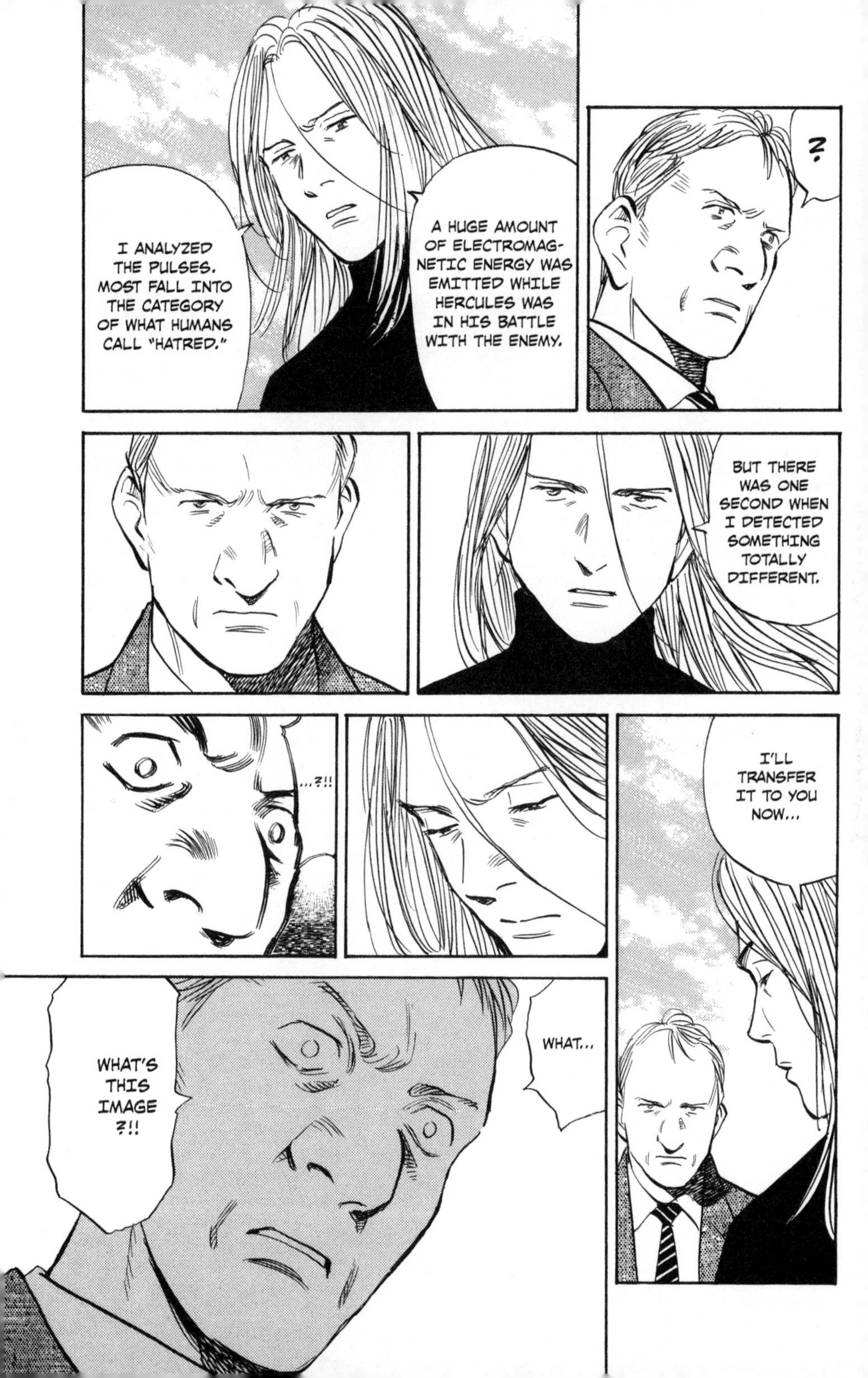
?
A HUGE AMOUNT OF ELECTROMAG-NETIC ENERGY WAS EMITTED WHILE HERCULES WAS IN HIS BATTLE WITH THE ENEMY.
I ANALYZED THE PULSES. MOST FALL INTO THE CATEGORY OF WHAT HUMANS CALL "HATRED."
BUT THERE WAS ONE SECOND WHEN I DETECTED SOMETHING TOTALLY DIFFERENT.
I'LL TRANSFER IT TO YOU NOW...
...?!!
WHAT...
WHAT'S THIS IMAGE ?!!

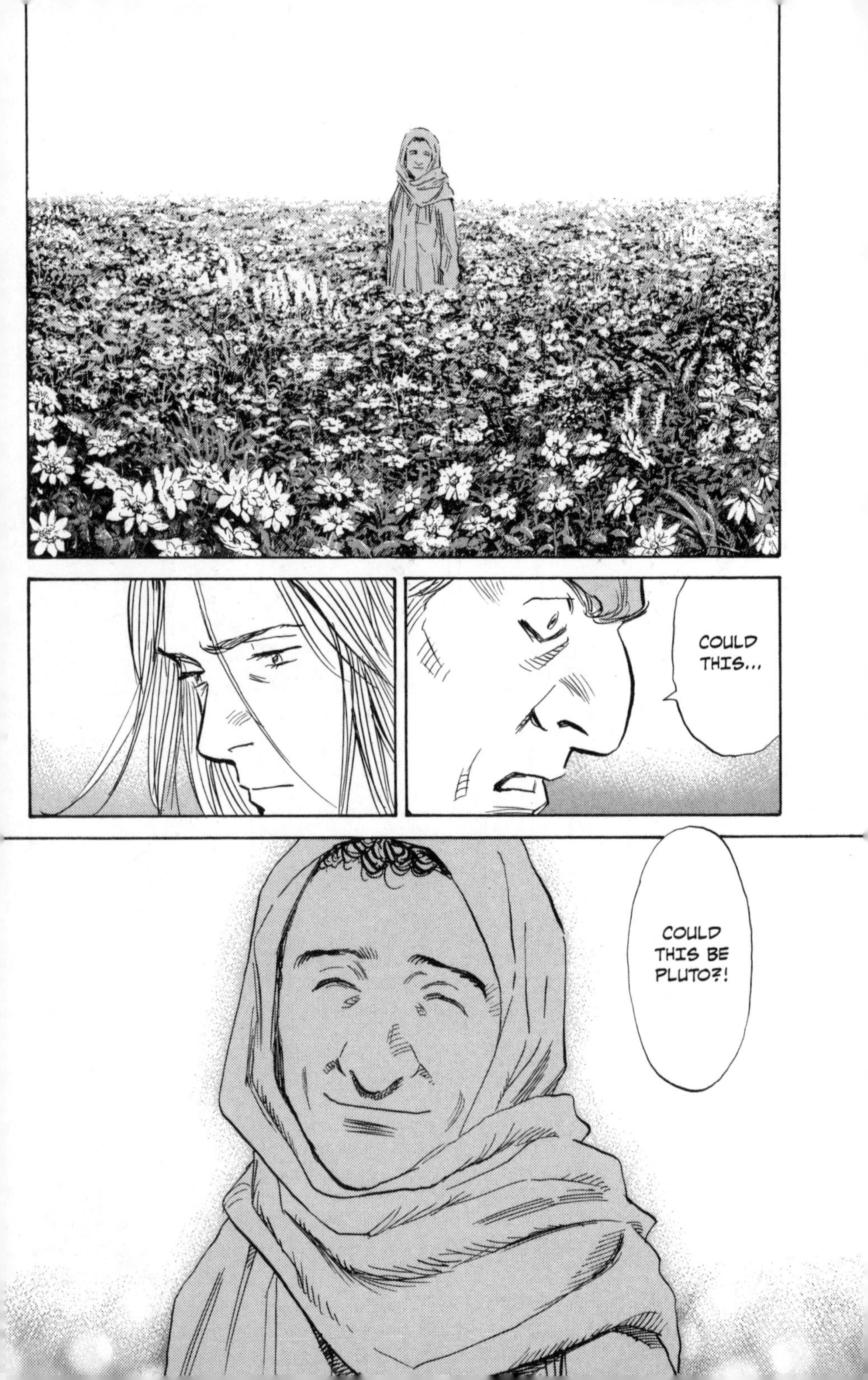
COULD THIS...
COULD THIS BE PLUTO?!

# POSTSCRIPT

Tomohiko Murakami, Manga critic and lecturer
at Kobe Shoin Women's University

I n reading *Pluto*, I get the feeling that it is actually Naoki Urasawa's dissertation on Osamu Tezuka. Of course, since *Pluto* is a tribute to *Astro Boy*, it makes sense that Urasawa would depict the characters from *Astro Boy*—Atom, Uran, Ochanomizu, Higeoyaji and others—with the same level of critical analysis he uses with his own characters.

Additionally, as manga critic Fusanosuke Natsume has already pointed out, Urasawa goes beyond "The Greatest Robot on Earth" story arc upon which *Pluto* is essentially built and skillfully blends in additional elements that bring to mind other Tezuka stories in the *Astro Boy* canon such as "Red Cat," "Frankenstein," "Robotting," "Atlas," and "The Blue Knight." In this way, he constantly revisits many of the themes in the original series. Urasawa also liberally references other Tezuka works such as *Black Jack*, *Jungle Emperor* and *Phoenix: A Tale of the Future*—to the point where he almost appears to be trying to retrace Tezuka's entire career by reconstructing it within *Pluto*'s story structure.

A scene in the fourth volume of Pluto particularly grabbed my attention. In it Tenma tells Ochanomizu that Atom is "a total failure." This is a line that might have come directly from Tezuka himself.

In the June 1966 issue of *Hanashi no Tokushû* magazine, Tezuka created a controversy among his fans by writing an essay titled "Be a Lone Wolf." In it he writes, "I personally consider *Astro Boy* to be one of the worst works I ever created. I only created it for the exposure and the money." Moreover, the first volume of Kodansha's currently published paperback collection of *Astro Boy* includes a postscript from an earlier edition of *Tezuka's Complete Works* which was originally published by Shogakukan in 1969. In this postscript he says, "Atom was fun to draw for the first two or three years, but after that it just became a chore, especially when we began animating the series at Mushi Productions. He became a real monster to draw and caused me a great deal of grief."

Tezuka is also known to have made other, similar statements in later years. The common assumption is that he was afraid the animated series was distorting the true nature of the work, but I think the real reason is probably a little more complicated. Whatever the reason, his harsh comments certainly hurt the feelings of many fans, especially younger ones.

The *Astro Boy* story that *Pluto* is based on—"The Greatest Robot on Earth"—was originally called "The Greatest Robot in History" and it was serialized in a magazine called *Shônen* from June of 1964 to January of 1965. The anime based on this story arc aired on TV in two segments on April 25 and May 1, 1965. Commentary on *Astro Boy* from *Tetsuwan Atom World* (a "mook," or "magazine/book" published by Pia) states that there was a great deal of argument about whether the format of this story—focusing on repeated robot battles—was really representative of Tezuka or not. I think it is safe to assume that Tezuka's statement that Atom "became a real monster" probably refers to the episodes created after Professor Tenma modified Atom and boosted his strength to one million horsepower.

So the question then becomes, why did Urasawa choose to base his story on "The Greatest Robot on Earth"? In the postscript to the second volume of *Pluto*, Macoto Tezka explains that "The Greatest Robot on Earth" was Naoki Urasawa's first real exposure to Osamu Tezuka's work. But any attempt to do a remake of *Astro Boy* would be extraordinarily difficult. And for Urasawa to deliberately base his remake on a story created *after* the animated series began—which happens to be the point after which Tezuka describes his creation to have become a "monster"—I believe this indicates that Naoki Urasawa must have found something in Tezuka's statement that resonated with him.

Naoki Urasawa's depictions of Professor Tenma and Professor Ochanomizu almost appear to be Urasawa's perspective on two different aspects of Osamu Tezuka's character. Urasawa is a child of the manga that, as the theme song to the *Astro Boy* anime series says, is about "a child of science." That manga is in turn a child of Osamu Tezuka. And in *Pluto*, Urasawa himself seems to be a split between the characters of Atom and Pluto. Robot and professor, artificial intelligence and the human mind—throughout the series, Urasawa continually warns about the danger of these entities growing too close.

I have sensed a strong Tezuka influence in Naoki Urasawa's work ever since the publication of *Monster*. That series is the story of a Japanese physician (also called Dr. Tenma) who saves the life of a boy only to discover years later that the boy has turned into a monster—a sociopathic murderer. Tenma chases after him and tries to save him from an awful fate. With *Pluto*, it almost seems as though Urasawa is daring to attempt to save Astro Boy— also labeled a "monster" by his creator, Osamu Tezuka—from an equally dismal fate.

I wonder how Osamu Tezuka would have reacted to *Pluto* were he still alive today. As Urasawa's work gets better and better, would Tezuka have felt compelled to dismiss it out of a sense of rivalry? I still remember how Tezuka created a lifelong rift between himself and Shotaro Ishinomori when he harshly criticized Ishinomori's popular *Jun* and *Cyborg 009* series in the magazine COM, a publication that Tezuka personally presided over.

Like Inspector Gesicht, who in *Pluto* is tormented by nightmares, perhaps Naoki Urasawa also has bad dreams of being suddenly and unexpectedly criticized by Tezuka. I can imagine how incredibly difficult it would be for Urasawa to resist the criticisms he might imagine coming from the late Tezuka, and to draw Atom as he would really like. In *Pluto*, how will Atom, abandoned and dismissed by Professor Tenma as a failed project, eventually achieve reconciliation with his "father"? *Pluto* can be seen as a work in which Naoki Urasawa, an artist who has until now skillfully crafted stories for the enjoyment of his readers, may actually be trying to create a story for himself.

The late Osamu Tezuka, a manga artist for whom I have the utmost respect, created the series *Astro Boy*. This timeless classic has been read by countless numbers of fans from when it was first created in the fifties to now. As a child, "The Greatest Robot on Earth" story arc from *Astro Boy* was the first manga I ever read that really moved me and inspired me to become a manga artist. With *Pluto* I've attempted to infuse that story with a fresh new spirit. I hope you enjoy it.

**NAOKI URASAWA**

Manga wouldn't exist without Osamu Tezuka. He is the Leonardo da Vinci, the Goethe, the Dostoevsky of the manga world. Naoki Urasawa and I have always felt that his achievements and work must not be allowed to fade away. Tezuka wrote that Atom, the main character of his most representative work *Astro Boy*, was born in 2003. This was the same year that we re-made "The Greatest Robot on Earth" story arc from the *Astro Boy* series. Who was Osamu Tezuka and what was his message? For those of you readers who are interested in *Pluto*, I highly recommend you read it alongside Tezuka's original work.

**TAKASHI NAGASAKI**

# PLUTO: URASAWA × TEZUKA
## VOLUME 5
### VIZ SIGNATURE EDITION

BY Naoki Urasawa & Osamu Tezuka
CO-AUTHORED WITH Takashi Nagasaki
WITH THE COOPERATION OF Tezuka Productions

TRANSLATION Jared Cook & Frederik L. Schodt
TOUCH-UP & LETTERING James Gaubatz
COVER ART DIRECTION Kazuo Umino
LOGO & COVER DESIGN Mikiyo Kobayashi & Bay Bridge Studio
VIZ SIGNATURE EDITION DESIGNER Courtney Utt
EDITOR Andy Nakatani

VP, PRODUCTION Alvin Lu
VP, PUBLISHING LICENSING Rika Inouye
VP, SALES & PRODUCT MARKETING Gonzalo Ferreyra
VP, CREATIVE Linda Espinosa
PUBLISHER Hyoe Narita

Printed in the U.S.A.

Published by VIZ Media, LLC
P.O. Box 77010
San Francisco, CA 94107

10 9 8 7 6 5 4 3 2 1
First printing, September 2009

www.viz.com store.viz.com

# ASTRO BOY

Osamu Tezuka's iconic *Astro Boy* series was a truly groundbreaking work about a loveable boy robot that would pave the way for all manga and anime to follow. Tezuka created the manga in 1951 and in January of 1963 adapted it to become the first weekly animated TV series ever to be broadcast in Japan. In September of that same year, it became the first animated TV series from Japan to hit the airwaves in the United States. The series and its title character were originally known in Japan as *Tetsuwan Atom*, which translates to "mighty Atom" – or for the more literally minded, "iron-arm Atom" – but was released in the U.S. as *Astro Boy*. Decades later, in 2000, Dark Horse Comics brought the manga for the first time to English readers, also under the title *Astro Boy*.

Within the context of the story for this English edition of *Pluto: Urasawa × Tezuka*, the precocious boy robot will be referred to as "Atom" in the manner in which he has been known and loved in Japan for over fifty years. Elsewhere, such as in the end matter, the series will be referred to as *Astro Boy* as it has been known outside of Japan since 1963.